W9-BZX-999

Mad About Scraps™

Annie's Attic®

Mad About Scraps™

Copyright © 2007 DRG, 306 East Parr Road, Berne, Indiana 46711

All rights reserved.
This publication may not be reproduced in part or in whole
without written permission from the publisher.

EDITOR	Brenda Stratton
ART DIRECTOR	Brad Snow
PUBLISHING SERVICES DIRECTOR	Brenda Gallmeyer
ASSOCIATE EDITOR	Kristine M. Frye
COPY SUPERVISOR	Michelle Beck
COPY EDITOR	Susanna Tobias
TECHNICAL EDITOR	Shirley Brown
GRAPHIC ARTS SUPERVISOR	Ronda Bechinski
GRAPHIC ARTISTS	Erin Augsburger, Pam Gregory
PRODUCTION ASSISTANTS	Marj Morgan, Judy Neuenschwander
TECHNICAL ARTIST	Nicole Gage
PHOTOGRAPHY	Tammy Christian, Don Clark, Matthew Owen, Jackie Schaffel
PHOTO STYLISTS	Tammy M. Smith, Tammy Steiner
CHIEF EXECUTIVE OFFICER	David J. McKee
BOOK MARKETING DIRECTOR	Dwight Seward

Printed in China
First Printing: 2007
Library of Congress Number: 2006937174
Hard Cover: ISBN-13: 978-1-59635-155-4
Soft Cover: ISBN-13: 978-1-59635-171-4

Every effort has been made to ensure the accuracy and completeness of the instructions in this book.
However, we cannot be responsible for human error or for the results when using materials other than
those specified in the instructions, or for variations in individual work.

DRGbooks.com

1 2 3 4 5 6 7 8 9

Introduction

Start sorting through your scraps!

One thing enthusiastic crocheters everywhere seem to have in common is that we have an ample supply of leftover bits of yarn and thread. Because it's nearly unthinkable to waste even the tiniest piece, we tend to save

it until our storage room—or lack thereof—that we clear out and use our treasured scraps to create something wonderful.

Many of our projects have special memories attached to them which often makes parting with the resulting remnants difficult. With fondness we remember that special dress for a precious toddler, a beautiful afghan to keep Mom warm and cozy or a special sweater made especially for Dad. Honor those memories by turning your scraps into yet another beautiful and useful item to enjoy.

We've selected a wide variety of projects in both yarn and thread to crochet for almost any occasion, whether you decide to keep the project for yourself, to give it

to someone for a special occasion or just to show someone how much you care. Choose your favorite gifts, children's items, toys, home decor, pet accessories, afghans, holiday decor, fashions and accessories.

Whatever you're in the mood to crochet, we're sure you'll find just the right project within these pages. So, get out your hook, dive into that overabundant stash of scrap yarn and thread and enjoy crocheting fantastic, colorful works of fiber art!

Contents

Artful Accessories

Chapter Contents

Reversible Tote Bag

DESIGN BY DARLA FANTON

Fill it with yarn, your pet or whatever you like—
you'll find as many uses for this tote as it has colors.
Crocheted with a double-ended hook, the reversible
design gives you the opportunity to practice your
technique while using up scraps!

SKILL LEVEL
INTERMEDIATE

FINISHED SIZE
14 x 15½ x 4 inches, excluding
Handles

MATERIALS
Medium (worsted)
   weight yarn:
      9 oz/450 yds/255g black
      5 oz/250 yds/142g total
         small amounts scraps in
         variety of colors
Size I/9/5.5mm flexible double-
   ended crochet hook or size
   needed to obtain gauge
Size I/9/5.5mm crochet hook
Tapestry needle
4-hole ⅞-inch assorted color
   buttons: 8

GAUGE
5 on double sts = 1 inch; 9 on
   double rows = 1 inch

PATTERN NOTES
Fasten off scrap colors at end of
each 2-row section.

Carry black along edge of work.

Read General Instructions
before beginning pattern.

GENERAL INSTRUCTIONS
To **pull up lp**, insert hook in
designated lp, bar or st, yo, pull
lp through, leaving lp on hook.

To **work lps off hook when
adding a new color**, with new
color, place slip knot on hook,

pull slip knot through first lp
on hook, [yo, pull through 2
lps on hook] across. Last lp rem
on hook at end of row is first
vertical bar of next row.

To **work lps off with a color already in use**, pick up color from row below, yo, pull through one lp on hook, [yo, pull through 2 lps on hook] across.

To **turn**, rotate hook 180 degrees and slide all lps to opposite end of hook. **Do not turn** unless otherwise stated.

You will always have 1 lp left on your hook at the end of each row, this will be the first st of the next row.

SPECIAL STITCH
Double decrease (double dec): Pull up lp under next 3 vertical bars at same time.

INSTRUCTIONS

TOTE
Front
Row 1: With double-ended hook and black, ch 202, working through **back lps** *(see Stitch Guide)* only *(see Stitch Guide)*, insert hook in 2nd ch from hook, yo, pull lp through, [insert hook in back lp of next ch, yo, pull lp through, leaving all lps on hook] across, slide all sts to opposite end of hook, turn. *(202 lps on hook)*

Row 2: Work lps off hook to add new color *(see General Instructions)*, do not turn.

Row 3: With same scrap color and working right to left, ch 1, sk first vertical bar, [pull up a lp under next vertical bar] 66 times, **double dec** *(see Special Stitch)*, [pull up lp under next vertical bar] 62 times, pull up

lp under next 3 vertical bars at same time, [pull up lp under next vertical bar] 67 times, slide all sts to opposite end of hook, turn. *(198 lps on hook)*

Row 4: Pick up black, yo, pull through 1 lp, [yo, pull through 2 lps *(1 lp of each color)*] across until 1 lp rem on hook, do not turn.

Row 5: With black and working right to left, ch 1, sk first vertical bar, [pull up lp under next vertical bar] 65 times, pull up lp under next 3 vertical bars at same time, [pull up lp under next vertical bar] 60 times, pull up lp under next 3 vertical bars at same time, [pull up lp under next vertical bar] 66 times, slide all sts to opposite end of hook, turn. *(194 lps on hook)*

Rows 6–65: Following established pattern, rep rows 2–5 noting that on each succeeding odd numbered row you will pick up 1 less st before the first double dec, 2 less sts before the 2nd double dec and 1 less st after the 2nd double dec.

Note: On row 65 there will be 0 sts picked up between the 2 double dec.

Row 66: Rep row 2. Leaving 16-inch length, fasten off black.

With tapestry needle and 16-inch length, working through **front lps** *(see Stitch Guide)* of the horizontal sts, join center seam.

Gusset

Row 1: With predominantly colored side facing and using black, working in starting ch on opposite side of row 1, pick up 202 sts, slide all sts to opposite end of hook, turn. *(202 lps on hook)*

Row 2: Rep row 2 of Front.

Row 3: With scrap color and working right to left, ch 1, sk first vertical bar, [pull up lp under next vertical bar] across, slide all sts to opposite end of hook, turn.

Row 4: Rep row 4 of Front.

Row 5: With black, rep row 3 of Gusset.

Rows 6–37: Rep rows 2–5 consecutively. At end of last row, fasten off.

Back

Rows 2–66: Working in rem lps of row 1 on Front, rep rows 2–66 of Front.

Top Band

Rnd 1: With predominantly black side facing and using crochet hook, join black with sc at top edge 3 inches in from right edge, evenly sp sc around, join with sl st in beg sc.

Rnd 2: Ch 1, sc in each st around, join with sl st in beg sc.

Rnds 3–7: Rep rnd 2.

Rnd 8: Ch 2 *(counts as first hdc)*, hdc in each st around, join with sl st in 2nd ch of beg ch-2.

Rnds 9–15: Rep rnd 2. At the end of last rnd, fasten off.

Fold Top Band in half toward colored side. With tapestry needle and black, sew top edge of Top Band to rnd 1 of Top Band, tucking in yarn ends to conceal them as work progresses.

Handle
Make 4.
Row 1: With black and crochet hook, ch 6, sc in 2nd ch from hook, sc in each ch across, turn. *(5 sc)*

Row 2: Ch 1, sc in each sc across, turn.

Next rows: Rep row 2 until Handle measures 28 inches or desired length. At end of last row, fasten off.

Finishing
Center the end of 1 Handle over Top Band of Back on predominantly black side where rnds of Top Band were joined. Center 2nd Handle over Top Band on opposite side to match and using tapestry needle and black, sew tog working through all 4 thicknesses.

Center 1 button over Handle on each side and attach with an X or cross-stitch.

Rep for rem ends of Handles on Back, centering them in 3 inches from left side.

With black yarn, continue to sew the 2 Handles between the Top Band.

Rep for rem 2 Handles and Front. ■

Stretchy Style

DESIGN BY BELINDA "BENDY" CARTER

With only a few yards of leftover elastic thread and some pretty beads, you can crochet this dazzling, dainty bracelet. It's quick to stitch and, with beads in her favorite colors, will make a perfect gift for your hard-to-buy-for teen!

SKILL LEVEL ◼◼◼◻
INTERMEDIATE

FINISHED SIZES
Instructions given fit sizes small and medium; changes for large and X-large are in [ ].

MATERIALS
Stretchrite nylon elastic sewing thread (30 yds per spool):
   1 spool white
Size B/1/2.25mm crochet hook or size needed to obtain gauge
Create-A-Craft rocaille beads:
   30g bag ice blue
   30g bag gold

GAUGE
2 beaded sts = 1 inch

PATTERN NOTE
Do not stretch elastic when crocheting with it.

INSTRUCTIONS

BRACELET
1. Thread 126 [144] beads onto thread, alternating 1 blue bead then 1 gold bead.

2. *Ch 1, pulling 6 beads through ch st, tighten ch so that beads do not go back through *(there are now 6 beads on lp on hook)*, place 3 beads on each side of hook, push 3 more beads up to last ch st, yo, pull thread only through lp on hook, sc in back strand of lp just made *(at the top of the lp just above*

the last 3 beads which were pushed forward), you have just completed a beaded st, rep from * until all beads are used, join with sl st in beg ch to form ring. Fasten off. *(14 [16] beaded sts)* ◼

Denim Blues

DESIGNS BY CINDY CARLSON

Roll stitches take this hat and scarf set from already done to do it some more! Stitch it in blues like we have, or pick another favorite color, to make a winter accessory that's cute, fun and functional.

SKILL LEVEL ■■■□ INTERMEDIATE

FINISHED SIZES
Hat: 9 x 21 inches
Scarf: 9 x 53 inches

MATERIALS
Red Heart Super Saver medium (worsted) weight yarn (7 oz/364 yds/198g per skein):
  2 skeins #311 white
Red Heart Classic medium (worsted) weight yarn (3 oz/167 yds/85g per skein):
  3 skeins #974 country blues
Size H/8/5mm crochet hook or size needed to obtain gauge
Tapestry needle

GAUGE
6 dc = 2 inches; 2 dc rows = 1 inch

SPECIAL STITCHES
Roll stitch (roll st): Yo 7 times, insert hook in indicated st or sp, yo, pull up lp, yo, pull through all lps on hook, ch 1 to secure.

Surface chain (surface ch): Holding yarn on WS of work, insert hook from RS to WS between any 2 sts on indicated row, yo, pull up lp to RS of work, [insert hook between next 2 sts, yo, pull up lp to RS of work and through lp on hook] across to end of row. Fasten off.

INSTRUCTIONS

HAT
Motif
Make 7.
Rnd 1 (RS): With country blues, ch 5, sl st in first ch to form ring, ch 3, 12 **roll sts** (see Special Stitches) in ring, join with sl st in top of first roll st. Fasten off. (12 roll sts)

Rnd 2: With RS facing, join white with sc in sp between any 2 roll sts, sc in same sp, 2 sc in sp between same roll st and next roll st, *(2 sc, ch 2, 2 sc) between same roll st and next roll st**, [2 sc between same roll st and next roll st] twice, rep from * around, ending last rep at **, join with sl st in beg sc. Fasten off. (32 sc, 4 ch-2 sps)

Crown
Row 1 (RS): With RS facing, join white with sc in any corner ch-2 sp of any Motif, *sc in each of next 8 sc, sc in next ch-2 sp**, sc in any ch-2 sp on next Motif,

rep from * across until 7 Motifs have been joined, ending last rep at **, turn. *(70 sc)*

Row 2: Ch 1, sc in each sc across, turn.

Row 3: Ch 3 *(counts as first dc)*, dc in each rem sc across, turn.

Row 4: Ch 3, dc in next dc, **bpdc** *(see Stitch Guide)* around each of next 2 dc, dc in each of next 2 dc, bpdc around each of next 2 dc, [dc in each of next 4 dc, bpdc around each of next 2 dc, dc in each of next 2 dc, bpdc around each of next 2 dc] across, ending with dc in each of last 2 dc, turn.

Row 5: Ch 3, dc in each dc, **fpdc** *(see Stitch Guide)* around each bpdc across, turn.

Row 6: Ch 3, dc in each dc and bpdc in each fpdc across, turn.

Rows 7 & 8: Rep rows 5 and 6.

Rows 9–13: Ch 1, sc in each st across, turn. At end of last row, leaving long end, fasten off

Surface Chain
With RS facing, work **surface ch** *(see Special Stitches)* with country blues over rows 2, 9, and 11.

Finishing
With tapestry needle, weave long end through sc sts of last row, pull tightly tog, sew tog down side of Hat and to top of Motifs. Fasten off.

Bottom Border
Rnd 1: With RS facing, join white with sc in ch-2 sp at bottom of Motif at back seam, sc in each sc and in each ch-2 sp around, join with sl st in beg sc. *(70 sc)*

Rnd 2: Ch 1, sc in each st around, join with sl st in beg sc. Fasten off.

Rnd 3: With RS facing, join country blues with sl st in first st, ch 1, sl st in each st around, join with sl st in beg sl st. Fasten off.

Tassel
With country blues, ch 1 *(center ch)*, (ch 16, {sl st, ch 10, sl st} in center ch) 5 times. Leaving long end for sewing, fasten off.

With tapestry needle and end, sew Tassel to top of Hat.

SCARF
Motif
Make 18.
Rnds 1 & 2: Rep rnds 1 and 2 of Motif for Hat.

First Half of Body
Row 1 (RS): Beg at lower edge,

with RS facing, join white with sc in any corner ch-2 sp of any Motif, *sc in each of next 8 sc, sc in next ch-2 sp**, sc in any ch-2 sp on next Motif, rep from * across until 3 Motifs have been joined, ending last rep at **, turn. *(30 sc)*

Row 2: Ch 3 *(counts as first dc)*, dc in each sc across, turn.

Row 3: Ch 3, dc in next dc, fpdc around each of next 2 dc, dc in each of next 2 dc, fpdc around each of next 2 dc, [dc in each of next 4 dc, fpdc around each of next 2 dc, dc in each of next 2 dc, fpdc around each of next 2 dc] twice, dc in each of last 2 dc, turn.

Row 4: Ch 3, dc in each dc and bpdc around each fpdc across, turn.

Row 5: Ch 3, dc in each dc and fpdc around each bpdc across, turn.

Row 6: Rep row 4.

Row 7: Working through both thicknesses of last row and any Motif at the same time, ch 1, sc in first st of last row and ch-2 sp on any Motif, *sc in each of next 8 sts on last row and in 8

sc of Motif, sc in next st on last row and in ch-2 sp of Motif**, sc in next st on last row and first ch-2 sp on next Motif, rep from * across until 3 Motifs have been joined, ending last rep at **. Fasten off.

Row 8: Working across opposite sides of Motifs just joined, rep row 1 of Crown across 3 Motifs. *(30 sc)*

Rows 9–15: Rep rows 2–8.

Rows 16–18: Rep rows 2–4.

Rows 19–27: Rep rows 5 and 6 alternately, ending with row 5.

Rows 28–30: Ch 1, sc in each st across, turn. At end of last row, fasten off.

2nd Half of Body
Rows 1–30: Rep rows 1–30 of First Half of Body.

Bottom Border
Row 1: With RS facing, join white with sc in first ch-2 sp of Motif at bottom of First Half of Body, rep row 1 of Crown across 3 Motifs. *(30 sc)*

Row 2: Ch 1, sc in each sc across. Fasten off.

Rep at bottom of 2nd Half of Body.

Fringe
With RS facing, join country blues with sl st in **front lp** *(see Stitch Guide)* only of first sc on row 2 of Bottom Border of First Half of Body; working in front lps only across, *ch 10, sl st in same st as last sl st made**, sl st in next st, rep from * across to last st, ending last rep at **, **turn**; working in rem lps across same row, sl st in first st, ◊ch 16, sl st in same st as last sl st made◊◊, sl st in next st, rep from ◊ across to last st, ending last rep at ◊◊. Fasten off.

Rep on Bottom Border of 2nd Half of Body.

Join First and 2nd Halves of Body
With WS tog, working through both thicknesses of First and 2nd Halves of Body at the same time, join country blues with sl st in first st of row 30, [ch 1, sl st in next st] across. Fasten off.

Finishing
With country blues, work surface ch across rows 1, 8, 15, 28 and 29 on First and 2nd Halves of Body. ■

Blooming Violets

DESIGN BY DONNA COLLINSWORTH

A simple strip of delicate thread flowers creates the dainty, feminine look for this fun fashion accessory that's sure to steal your heart. It's just the right touch for a sweet style that makes the wearer feel special!

SKILL LEVEL ◼◼◼◻
INTERMEDIATE

FINISHED SIZE
24 inches, excluding elastic

MATERIALS
South Maid size 10 crochet cotton (300 yds per ball):
    100 yds #26 shaded purples
Size 7/1.65mm steel crochet hook or size needed to obtain gauge
Embroidery needle
5 inches ¼-inch-wide elastic

GAUGE
Each Square = 1 inch

SPECIAL STITCH
Puff stitch (puff st): Pull up ½-inch lp, [yo, insert hook in same st, pull up ½-inch lp] 4 times, yo, pull through all lps on hook, ch 1 to secure.

INSTRUCTIONS

SQUARE
Make 10.
Rnd 1: Ch 4, sl st in first ch to form ring, ch 1, 8 sc in ring, join with sl st in beg sc. *(8 sc)*

Rnd 2: Puff st *(see Special Stitch)* in first sc, ch 2, puff st in next sc, ch 4, [puff st in next sc, ch 2, puff st in next sc, ch 4] around, join with sl st in first puff st.

Rnd 3: Sl st in ch-2 sp, ch 1, 4 sc in same ch-2 sp, (3 sc, ch 2, 3 sc) in next ch-4 sp, [4 sc in ch-2 sp, (3 sc, ch 2, 3 sc) in next ch-4 sp] around, join with sl st in beg sc. Fasten off.

Sew Squares tog in 1 long strip.

Elastic Casing
Row 1: Join with sl st in end Square in corner ch-2 sp, ch 1, sc in same ch sp, sc in each of next 10 sc, sc in next corner ch-2 sp, turn. *(12 sc)*

Row 2: Ch 1, sc in each of next 12 sc, turn.

Next rows: Rep row 2 until entire Headband measures 24 inches.

Holding last row of casing to opposite end of Headband and using care not to twist, sl st tog. Fasten off.

Finishing
Sew each end of elastic at junction of Elastic Casing. Fold casing in half and sew edges closed. ◼

30-minute Cloche

DESIGN BY KATHERINE ENG

Crochet this stylish cloche from start to finish in under an hour. Since it doesn't take much yarn, it's a great way to use up your leftovers, and is a great gift to stitch in multiples for family, friends and local charities.

SKILL LEVEL ●□□□
BEGINNER

FINISHED SIZE
One size fits most

MATERIALS

Lion Brand Homespun bulky (chunky) weight yarn (6 oz/185 yds/170g per skein):
    2½ oz/31 yds/71g
      #315 tudor
Size H/8/5mm crochet hook or size needed to obtain gauge
Tapestry needle

GAUGE
Rnds 1 and 2 = 2 inches

INSTRUCTIONS

CLOCHE
Rnd 1: Ch 4, sl st in first ch to form ring, ch 1, 8 sc in ring, join with sl st in beg sc. *(8 sc)*

Rnd 2: Ch 1, 2 sc in each st around, join with sl st in beg sc. *(16 sc)*

Rnds 3 & 4: Ch 1, sc in first st, ch 1, [sc in next st, ch 1] around, join with sl st in beg sc.

Rnd 5: Ch 1, 2 sc in first st, ch 1, [2 sc in next st, ch 1] around, join with sl st in beg sc. *(36 sc)*

Rnds 6 & 7: Ch 1, sc in each of first 2 sts, ch 1, [sc in each of next 2 sts, ch 1] around, join with sl st in beg sc.

Rnds 8 & 9: Ch 1, sc in each of first 2 sts, ch 2, [sc in each of next 2 sts, ch 2] around, join with sl st in beg sc.

Rnds 10–20: Ch 1, sc in each of first 2 sts, ch 3, [sc in each of next 2 sts, ch 3] around, join with sl st in beg sc.

Rnd 21: Ch 1, sc in each of first 2 sts, (sc, ch 3, sc) in next ch sp, [sc in each of next 2 sts, (sc, ch 3, sc) in next ch sp] around, join with sl st in beg sc. Fasten off. ■

Beaded Blue Jeans Bag

DESIGN BY LORI ZELLER

Are you a crocheter who sews? Make this sassy little beaded bag as a special treat for yourself or someone you care about! It's just two simple granny squares and a bit of denim fabric turned into the perfect bag to hold your keys, phone and wallet.

SKILL LEVEL ■■■□
INTERMEDIATE

FINISHED SIZE
5½ x 6 inches, excluding Strap

MATERIALS
Medium (worsted)
  weight yarn:
    1¼ oz/60 yds/35g each
    denim and navy
Size F/5/3.75mm crochet hook
  or size needed to obtain
  gauge
Tapestry needle
Sewing needle
Sewing thread
58 white 7mm pony beads

4 inches hook-and-loop tape
5¼ x 12 inch piece denim fabric

GAUGE
Rnds 1 and 2 = 2¼ inches across

SPECIAL STITCHES
Bead single crochet (bead sc):
Insert hook in indicated st, yo, pull lp through, pull up bead close to hook, yo, pull through all lps on hook.

Bead chain (bead ch): Pull up bead behind hook and ch over bead.

INSTRUCTIONS

BAG
Side
Make 2.
Rnd 1 (RS): With denim, ch 5, sl st in first ch to form ring, ch 3 *(counts as first dc)*, 2 dc in ring, ch 3, [3 dc in ring, ch 3] 3 times, join with sl st in 3rd ch of beg ch-3.

Rnd 2: Sl st in each of next 2 sts, sl st in next ch sp, ch 3, (2 dc, ch 3, 3 dc) in same ch sp, ch 1, *(3 dc, ch 3, 3 dc) in next ch sp, ch 1, rep from * around, join with sl st in 3rd ch of beg ch-3, **turn**. Fasten off.

Rnd 3 (WS): Thread 12 beads onto navy yarn, with WS facing, join with **bead sc** (see Special Stitches) in any ch-3 sp, ch 3, bead sc in same ch sp, ch 4, bead sc in next ch-1 sp, ch 4, *(bead sc, ch 3, bead sc) in next ch-3 sp, ch 4, bead sc in next ch-1 sp, ch 4, rep from * around, join with sl st in beg bead sc, **turn**. Fasten off.

Rnd 4: With RS facing, join denim with sl st in any ch-3 sp, ch 3, (2 dc, ch 3, 3 dc) in same ch sp, *[ch 1, 3 dc in next ch-4 sp] twice, ch 1**, (3 dc, ch 3, 3 dc) in next ch-3 sp, rep from * around, ending last rep at **, join with sl st in 3rd ch of beg ch-3.

Rnd 5: Sl st in each of next 2 dc, sl st in next ch-3 sp, ch 3, (2 dc, ch 3, 3 dc) in same ch sp, *[ch 1, 3 dc in next ch-1 sp] 3 times, ch 1**, (3 dc, ch 3, 3 dc) in next ch-3 sp, rep from * around, ending last rep at **, join with sl st in 3rd ch of beg ch-3. Fasten off.

Rnd 6: Thread 11 beads onto navy yarn, join with sc in any ch-3 sp, ch 2, sc in same ch sp, *[sc in each of next 3 dc, sc in next ch-1 sp] 4 times, sc in each of next 3 dc**, (sc, ch 2, sc) in next ch-3 sp, rep from * around, ending last rep at **, join with sl st in beg sc, **turn**.

Row 7: Now working in rows across top edge only, with WS facing, ch 1, sc in first ch-2 sp, bead sc in next sc, [sc in next sc, bead sc in next sc] 10 times, sc in last ch-2 sp, turn.

Row 8 (RS): Ch 1, sc in each st across. Fasten off.

Joining & Strap
Thread 12 beads onto navy yarn, holding Side pieces WS tog, working through both thicknesses down sides and across bottom edges, join with sc in first st at top of Side edge, sc in each st across, sc in ch-2 sp at corner, ch 1, **bead ch** (see Special Stitches), ch 1, sk next st, [sc in next sc, ch 1, bead ch, ch 1, sk next st] 11 times, sc in next ch-2 sp at corner, sc in each st across to top edge, for **Strap**, ch 200, sl st in first sc made on Joining, **turn**, sl st in each ch across Strap, sl st in last sc made on Joining. Fasten off.

Lining
Fold denim fabric in half with RS tog forming a folded piece that measures 6 x 5¼ inches. Leaving a ¼-inch seam allowance, sew sides to form a pocket. Fold down ¼ inch at top and sew for hem. Turn RS out.

Sew hook-and-loop tape to inside top edges.

Insert Lining into Bag and sew top edges of Bag and Lining tog. ■

Chocolate, Blueberry & Cranberry

DESIGNS BY KATHERINE ENG

For a great last-minute gift, stitch this quick and attractive scarf and hat set in yummy yarn colors. A medium-weight, wool-blend yarn makes it a warm and stylish accent for the cold winter months.

SKILL LEVEL ⬛⬛⬛▢
INTERMEDIATE

FINISHED SIZE
One size fits most

MATERIALS

Lion Brand Wool-Ease medium (worsted) weight yarn (3 oz/197 yds/85g per ball):
1 ball each of #138 cranberry, #126 chocolate brown and #170 peacock
Size G/6/4mm crochet hook or size needed to obtain gauge

GAUGE
Rnds 1–3 = 4 inches across

INSTRUCTIONS

SCARF
First Motif
Rnd 1: With cranberry, ch 4, sl st in first ch to form ring, ch 3 *(counts as first dc)*, dc in ring, ch 1, [2 dc in ring, ch 1] 7 times, join with sl st in 3rd ch of beg ch-3. Fasten off. *(16 dc)*

Rnd 2: Join chocolate brown with sc in any ch sp, *(3 dc, ch 2, 3 dc) in next ch sp**, sc in next ch sp, rep from * around ending last rep at **, join with sl st in beg sc. Fasten off.

Rnd 3: Join peacock with sc in any ch sp, ch 3, sc in same ch sp, *ch 1, sk next st, sc in next st, ch 1, sk next st, **fpdc** *(see Stitch Guide)* around next st, ch 1**, (sc, ch 3, sc) in next ch sp, rep from * around ending last rep at **, join with sl st in beg sc. Fasten off.

Rnd 4: Join cranberry with sc in any ch-3 sp, *3 dc in next ch sp, sc in next ch sp, 5 dc in next st, sc in next ch sp, 3 dc in next ch sp**, sc in next ch sp, rep from

* around ending last rep at **, join with sl st in beg sc.

Rnd 5: Ch 1, sc in first st, *ch 1, sk next st, (sc, ch 1, sc) in next st, ch 1, sk next st, sc in next st, ch 1, sk next st, (sc, ch 3, sc) in next st, (sc, ch 6, sc) in next st, (sc, ch 3, sc) in next st, ch 1, sk next st, sc in next st, ch 1, sk next st, (sc, ch 1, sc) in next st, ch 1, sk next st**, sc in next st, rep from * around, ending last rep at **, join with sl st in beg sc. Fasten off.

Next Motif
Rnds 1–4: Rep rnds 1–4 of First Motif.

Rnd 5: Ch 1, sc in first st, ch 1, sk next st, (sc, ch 1, sc) in next st, ch 1, sk next st, sc in next st, ch 1, sk next st, (sc, ch 3, sc) in next st, (sc, ch 3, drop lp from hook, insert hook in corresponding ch sp on last Motif, pull dropped lp through, ch 3, sc) in next st, work the following steps to complete rnd:

A. (Sc, ch 1, drop lp from hook, insert hook in corresponding ch sp on last Motif, pull dropped lp through, ch 1, sc) in next st,

B. *Ch 1, sk next st, sc in next st, ch 1, sk next st, (sc, drop lp from hook, insert hook in corresponding ch sp on last Motif, pull dropped lp through, sc) in next st, rep from * once,

C. Ch 1, sk next st, sc in next st, ch 1, sk next st, rep step A, (sc, ch 3, drop lp from hook,

insert hook in corresponding ch sp on last Motif, pull dropped lp through, ch 3, sc) in next st,

D. (Sc, ch 3, sc) in next st,

E. *Ch 1, sk next st, sc in next st, ch 1, sk next st, (sc, ch 1, sc) in next st**, rep from * once,

F. Ch 1, sk next st, rep step D, (sc, ch 6, sc) in next st,

G. Rep steps D, E, F and D (in that order),

H. Rep step E ending at **, ch 1, join with sl st in beg sc. Fasten off.

Work 8 more Next Motifs for a total of 10 Motifs for Scarf.

HAT *Done 01·21·10*
Rnds 1–3: Rep rnds 1–3 of First Motif.

Rnd 4: Join cranberry with sc in any ch-3 sp, *5 dc in next ch sp, sc in next ch sp, 5 dc in next st, sc in next ch sp, 5 dc in next ch sp**, sc in next ch sp, rep from * around ending last rep at **, join with sl st in beg sc. Fasten off.

Rnd 5: Join chocolate brown with sc in center dc of any 5-dc group, *5 dc in next sc**, sc in center dc on next 5-dc group, rep from * around ending last rep at **, join with sl st in beg sc.

Rnd 6: Ch 3, 4 dc in first sc, *sc in center dc of next dc group, 5

dc in next sc, rep from * around ending last rep at **, join with sl st in 3rd ch of beg ch-3. Fasten off.

Rnds 7 & 8: With peacock, rep rnds 5 and 6.

Rnds 9 & 10: Rep rnds 5 and 6.

Rnd 11: Join peacock with sc in first st, *[ch 1, sk next st, sc in next st] twice, ch 1, sk next st, dc around next sc, ch 1**, sc in next st, rep from * around, ending at **, join with sl st in beg sc. Fasten off.

Rnd 12: Join cranberry with sl st in any dc, ch 3, 4 dc in same st, sk next st, *sc in next st, sk next st**, 5 dc in next st, rep from * around ending last rep at **, join with sl st in 3rd ch of beg ch-3.

Rnd 13: Sl st in next st, ch 1, sc in next st, *5 dc in next sc**, sc in center st of next dc-group, rep from * around ending last rep at **, join with sl st in beg sc.

Rnd 14: Ch 3, 4 dc in first st, *sc in center st of next dc-group**, 5 dc in next sc, rep from * around ending last rep at **, join with sl st in 3rd ch of beg ch-3. Fasten off.

Rnd 15: Join peacock with sc in any sc, ch 2, sc in same st, *ch 3, (sc, ch 2, sc) in center dc on next dc-group, ch 3**, (sc, ch 2, sc) in next sc, rep from * around ending last rep at **, join with sl st in beg sc. Fasten off. ■

Cool Aquamarine

DESIGN BY MARY LAYFIELD

This artistically inspired necklace has an ethereal beauty, with shimmering beads winking out of furry yarn, and a fabulous pendant. It's an elegant way to use up your fur yarn scraps!

SKILL LEVEL ◖■□□
EASY

FINISHED SIZE
One size fits most

MATERIALS
Red Heart Foxy bulky
   (chunky) weight yarn
   (1¾ oz/89 yds/50g per ball):
      1 ball #9388 aquarium
Size E/4/3.5mm crochet hook
Sewing needle
Sewing thread
23-inch piece of silver-tone
   wire
Accessories from Blue Moon
   Bead Co.:
      2 packages 8mm #64600
         green/blue beads
         (18 beads)
      1 package 10x12mm
         #64676 baroque green/
         blue beads *(6 beads)*

1 package clear beads
  (26 beads)
1 pendant
Silver hook and eye

NECKLACE
1. Thread beads onto wire *(bend 1 end of wire to keep beads from sliding off)* in following order or as desired:

[1 clear, 8mm bead] 9 times, [1 clear, 1 oval] 3 times, 1 clear bead, pendant, 1 clear bead, [1 oval, 1 clear bead] 3 times, [8mm bead, 1 clear bead] 9 times, bend end of wire.

2. Attach hook and eye to bent ends of wire.

3. Working over wire between beads, join yarn with sc around wire, sc around wire, pull clear bead up close to last st, [2 sc around wire, ch 2, pull 8mm bead up close to last st, 2 sc around wire, pull clear bead up close to last st] 9 times, [2 sc around wire, ch 4, pull oval bead up close to last st, 2 sc around wire, pull clear bead up close to last st] 3 times, 2 sc around wire, pull pendant up close to last st, 2 sc around wire, pull clear bead up close to last st, [2 sc around wire, ch 4, pull oval bead up close to last st, 2 sc around wire, pull clear bead up close to last st] 3 times, [2 sc around wire, ch 2, pull 8mm bead up close to last st, 2 sc around wire, pull clear bead up close to last st] 9 times, 2 sc around wire. Fasten off. ■

Fancy Feet

DESIGNS BY JENNINE KOREJKO

Why wear boring, plain shoes when, with only a little time, novelty yarn and some beads or charms, you can whip up these fun, fanciful flip-flops! Use them as slippers or take them on a trip to the beach—they're a hit either way!

Pretty Purses

SKILL LEVEL ◼◼◻◻ EASY

MATERIALS
Eyelash bulky (chunky)
    weight yarn:
    1 oz/35 yds/50g white
Size G/6/4mm crochet hook
2 green wooden purse stickers
Craft glue
Pair flip-flops

INSTRUCTIONS

COVER
Holding flip-flop with heel toward you, join with sc around right strap near heel, 4 sc around strap, slide sts to very end of strap, continue to work sc around strap until completely covered, sk toe and sc around left strap until completely covered. Fasten off.

Rep on rem flip-flop.

Glue 1 purse sticker to center of each flip-flop.

Bangles & Bows

SKILL LEVEL ◼◼◻◻ EASY

MATERIALS
Patons Twister super
    bulky (super chunky) weight
    yarn (1¾ oz/47 yds/50g
    per ball):
    1 ball #05735 bongo blue
Size G/6/4mm crochet hook
Sewing needle
Sewing thread
2 charms
Pair flip-flops

INSTRUCTIONS

COVER
Holding flip-flop with heel toward you, join with sc around right strap near heel, 4 sc around strap, slide sts to very end of strap, continue to work sc around strap until completely covered, sk toe and sc around left strap until completely covered. Fasten off.

Cut 4 strands 6 inches in length. Hold 2 strands tog and tie into bow.

With sewing needle and sewing thread, sew 1 bow to center of flip-flop.

Rep on rem flip-flop.

Glue 1 charm to center of each bow.

Beaded Beauty

SKILL LEVEL
EASY

MATERIALS
Moda Dea Zing light (light worsted) weight yarn (1¾ oz/87 yds/50g per ball: 1 ball #1373 pink cosmo
Size G/6/4mm crochet hook

13 inches clear crystal drop beads on ribbon
Craft glue
Pair flip-flops

BEADS
Cut 2 pieces of beaded ribbon with 13 beads on each length. Place center of beaded ribbon on center of flip-flop strap, tack in place with small amount of glue. Place rem ends across top of strap and glue each end to secure (1 bead in center with 6 beads on each strap). Allow to dry.

COVER
Holding flip-flop with heel toward you, join with sc around right strap near heel, 4 sc around strap, slide sts to very end of strap, continue to sc around strap to first glued end, 5 sc around strap and glued end to next bead, [sk bead, 6 sc around strap and ribbon] 6 times, sk toe and center bead, [6 sc around strap and ribbon, sk bead] 6 times, 5 sc around strap and glued end, sc around rem of left strap until completely covered. Fasten off.

Rep on rem flip-flop. ■

Raspberry Sorbet & Blueberry Tassels

DESIGNS BY BELINDA "BENDY" CARTER

It isn't just for key chains and bracelets anymore! Turn your colorful plastic yarn and craft laces into snazzy fashion accessories for a look that's uniquely different. Start with a beaded belt and don't forget the tasseled purse!

Raspberry Sorbet

SKILL LEVEL ■■■☐
INTERMEDIATE

FINISHED SIZE
Instructions to fit all sizes, 1¼ inches wide

MATERIALS
Yummy Yarns Jelly Yarn fine (sport) weight plastic yarn (85 yds per ball): 1 ball raspberry sorbet
Size G/6/4mm crochet hook or size needed to obtain gauge
Silver ¾-inch D-rings: 2
1 package *(50 beads per package)* 9mm white carved rondelle #3791NB from Fire Mountain Gems & Beads

GAUGE
3 sc = 1¼ inches; 10 sc rows = 3 inches

SPECIAL STITCHES
Top stitch (top st): With yarn underneath, insert hook in center st on row, yo, pull lp through st and lp on hook.

Bead top chain stitch (bead top ch st): Pull bead up to work top st *(bead will appear on back side of work).*

Bead chain (bead ch): Pull bead up to hook, work ch around bead.

INSTRUCTIONS

BELT
Row 1 (RS): Join with sc around both D-rings, 2 sc around rings, turn. *(3 sc)*

Row 2: Ch 1, sc in each st across, turn.

Next rows: Rep row 2 until belt reaches desired length. At end of last row, fasten off.

Beading
Thread 1 bead on yarn for every 4 rows of Belt.

With WS facing, **top st** (see Special Stitches) in row 1, working top sts up center of Belt, top st in next row, [**bead**

top ch st (see Special Stitches) in next row, top st in each of next 3 rows] across Belt. Fasten off.

First String
With RS facing, join with sl st in center st of last row on Belt, ch 7, [**bead ch** (see Special Stitches),

ch 3] 6 times, bead ch, ch 1. Leaving 6-inch end, fasten off.

2nd String
With RS facing, join with sl st in first st of last row on Belt, ch 7, sl st in first bead ch on First String, [ch 3, sl st in next

bead ch of First String] 6 times, sl st in last ch on First String. Leaving 6-inch end, fasten off.

3rd String
With RS facing, join with sl st in last st of last row on Belt, ch 7, sl st in first bead ch on First String, [ch 3, sl st in next bead ch of First String] 6 times, sl st in last ch on First String. Leaving 6-inch end, fasten off.

Holding all 3 ends tog, tie in knot close to last ch. Trim ends.

Blueberry Tassles

SKILL LEVEL ■■■□ INTERMEDIATE

FINISHED SIZE
4 inches deep x 5 inches wide

MATERIALS
Toner Plastics Camp Hoochee Coochee Noodles CraftLace medium (worsted) weight plastic lace (50 yds per spool): 1 spool each main color (MC) and 3 contrasting colors (CC)
Size H/8/5mm crochet hook or size needed to obtain gauge
Tapestry needle
5-inch nickel purse frame
Silver 6mm jump rings: 2
Stitch marker

GAUGE
11 sts = 4 inches

INSTRUCTIONS

PURSE
Side
Make 2.
Row 1 (RS): With MC, ch 14, sc in 2nd ch from hook and in each ch across, turn. *(13 sc)*

Rows 2 & 3: Working in **front lps** *(see Stitch Guide)*, ch 1, sc in each st across, turn.

Row 4: Working in front lps, ch 1, sc in each of first 2 sts, place marker in **back lp** *(see Stitch Guide)* of last st made, sc in each st across, turn.

Row 5: Working in front lps, ch 1, sc in each st across, turn.

Row 6: Working in front lps, ch 1, sc in each of first 3 sts, place marker in back lp of last st made, sc in each st across, turn.

Rows 7 & 8: Rep rows 3 and 4.

Row 9: Working in front lps, ch 1, sc in first st, **sc dec** *(see Stitch Guide)* in next 2 sts, sc in each st across to last 3 sts, sc dec in next 2 sts, sc in last st, turn. *(11 sc)*

Row 10: Rep row 4.

Row 11: Rep row 9, **do not turn.** *(9 sc)*

Rnd 12: Now working in rnds, evenly sp sc down side, in starting ch on opposite side of row and up other side, working in back lps of sts, sc in each st across to last 2 sts, sc in next st, place marker in front lp of last st made, sc in last st, join with sl st in beg sc. Fasten off.

Knots
Cut strand of CC 10 inches long, place strand through first marked st so that strand is centered, holding ends of strand tog, make Knot close to st.

[Sk next st on same row, rep Knot in unused lp of next st] across row.

Work Knots on each marked row on Sides. Trim ends.

Frame
Cut strand of MC 55 inches long, using scissors, carefully cut down center length of strand *(use 1 side of strand for Front of Purse and the other side of strand for back of Purse)*, beg at row 7 on side, sew upper portions of Purse to purse frame.

Sew lower side edges of Sides tog.

Handle
Attach jump rings to purse frame. Cut 1 strand of each CC each 18 inches in length. Holding 3 strands tog, tie 1 end of strands to first jump ring, braid strands, tie other end to next jump ring. Trim ends. ■

Summer Tote

DESIGN BY MELISSA LEAPMAN

You've found the perfect beach bag! Enjoy your own little piece of paradise with this practical accessory. Stitch it in cotton scraps to make it washable between trips to the beach or pool, or line it with plastic and use it as a swim bag.

SKILL LEVEL
INTERMEDIATE

FINISHED SIZE
13 inches high

MATERIALS
Fine (sport) weight yarn
   3½ oz/315 yds/99g
      each fuchsia *(A)* and
      orange *(B)*
   1¾ oz/158 yds/50g each
      lemon yellow *(C)* and
      lime green *(D)*
Size E/4/3.5mm crochet hook or
   size needed to obtain gauge
Tapestry needle

GAUGE
9 dc = 2 inches; 5 dc rows =
2 inches

Motif = 3 inches square.

SPECIAL STITCH
Popcorn (pc): 4 dc in next st, drop lp from hook, insert hook in first st of 4-dc group, pull dropped lp through.

INSTRUCTIONS

TOTE
Bottom
Rnd 1: With A, ch 2, 7 sc in 2nd ch from hook, join with sl st in beg sc. *(7 sc)*

Rnd 2: Ch 1, 2 sc in each st around, join with sl st in beg sc. *(14 sc)*

Rnd 3: Ch 1, sc in first st, 2 sc in next st, [sc in next st, 2 sc in next st] around, join with sl st in beg sc. *(21 sc)*

Rnd 4: Ch 1, sc in each of first 2 sts, 2 sc in next st, [sc in each of next 2 sts, 2 sc in next st] around, join with sl st in beg sc. *(28 sc)*

Rnd 5: Ch 1, sc in each of first 3 sts, 2 sc in next st, [sc in each of next 3 sts, 2 sc in next st] around, join with sl st in beg sc. *(35 sc)*

Rnd 6: Ch 1, sc in each of first 4 sts, 2 sc in next st, [sc in each of next 4 sts, 2 sc in next st] around, join with sl st in beg sc. *(42 sc)*

Rnd 7: Ch 1, sc in each of first 5 sts, 2 sc in next st, [sc in each of next 5 sts, 2 sc in next st] around, join with sl st in beg sc. *(49 sc)*

Rnd 8: Ch 1, sc in each of first 6 sts, 2 sc in next st, [sc in each of next 6 sts, 2 sc in next st] around, join with sl st in beg sc. *(56 sc)*

Rnd 9: Ch 1, sc in each of first 7 sts, 2 sc in next st, [sc in each of next 7 sts, 2 sc in next st] around, join with sl st in beg sc. *(63 sc)*

Rnd 10: Ch 1, sc in each of first 8 sts, 2 sc in next st, [sc in each of next 8 sts, 2 sc in next st] around, join with sl st in beg sc. *(70 sc)*

Rnd 11: Ch 1, sc in each of first 9 sts, 2 sc in next st, [sc in each of next 9 sts, 2 sc in next st] around, join with sl st in beg sc. *(77 sc)*

Rnd 12: Ch 1, sc in each of first 10 sts, 2 sc in next st, [sc in each of next 10 sts, 2 sc in next st] around, join with sl st in beg sc. *(84 sc)*

Rnd 13: Ch 1, sc in each of first 11 sts, 2 sc in next st, [sc in each of next 11 sts, 2 sc in next st] around, join with sl st in beg sc. Fasten off. *(91 sc)*

MOTIF

Make 4 Motifs each using A/C/B, A/D/B and C/A/B.
Make 3 Motifs each using D/A/B, C/D/B and D/C/B.

Rnd 1: With first color, ch 5, sl st in first ch to form ring, ch 4 *(counts as first dc and ch-1)*, [dc in ring, ch 1] 15 times, join with sl st in 3rd ch of beg ch-4. *(16 dc, 16 ch sps)*

Rnd 2: (Sl st, ch 1, sc) in first ch sp, ch 3, **pc** *(see Special Stitch)* in next ch sp, ch 3, [sc in next ch sp, ch 3, pc in next ch sp, ch 3] around, join with sl st in beg sc. Fasten off.

Rnd 3: Join 2nd color with sl st in any sc between pc, ch 3 *(counts as first dc)*, 2 dc in same st, sc in next pc, 5 dc in next sc *(corner completed)*, sc in next pc, *3 dc in next sc, sc in next pc, 5 dc in next sc *(corner completed)*, sc in next pc, rep from * around, join with sl st in 3rd ch of beg ch-3. Fasten off. *(40 sts)*

Rnd 4: Join 3rd color with sc in any st, sc in each st around with 3 sc in each center corner st, join with sl st in beg sc. Fasten off. *(48 sc)*

Holding Motifs WS tog, matching sts, with B, sew tog through **back lps** *(see Stitch Guide)* in 3 rows of 7 Motifs each.

With B, sew 3 Motifs on each end tog through back lps to form circle. Easing to fit, with B, sew Bottom to 1 side of Motif circle through back lps.

TOP

Rnd 1: Working around top of Motif circle, join B with sl st in any st, ch 3, dc in each st and in each seam around, join with sl st in 3rd ch of beg ch-3. *(84 dc)*

Rnds 2–5: Ch 3, dc in each st around, join with sl st in 3rd ch of beg ch-3.

Rnd 6: Ch 4 *(counts as first dc and ch-1)*, sk next st, [dc in next st, ch 1, sk next st] around, join with sl st in 3rd ch of beg ch-4. *(42 dc, 42 ch sps)*

Rnd 7: Ch 3, dc in each st and in each ch sp around, join with sl st in 3rd ch of beg ch-3.

Rnds 8–11: Ch 3, dc in each st around, join with sl st in 3rd ch of beg ch-3.

Rnd 12: Ch 1, sc in first st, ch 3, sl st in 3rd ch from hook, sk next st, [sc in next st, ch 3, sl st in 3rd ch from hook, sk next st] around, join with sl st in beg sc. Fasten off.

Tie
Make 2.
With A, ch 130, sl st in 2nd ch from hook, sl st in each ch across. Fasten off.

Starting on 1 side of Top, weave 1 Tie through ch sps of rnd 6, knot ends.

Starting at other side of Top, weave other Tie through same ch sps in opposite direction, knot ends.

Pulling Ties will close top of Tote. ∎

Fabulous Fashions

Chapter Contents

Striped Ponchette

DESIGN BY DIANE POELLOT

This quick-to-make ponchette will keep your shoulders warm in a new American classic style! Stitch it using three of your favorite shades of complimentary colors for a flattering look to keep or share with a friend!

SKILL LEVEL ⬛⬛⬜⬜
EASY

FINISHED SIZE
12 inches long x 36 inches wide at neckline

MATERIALS
Medium (worsted)
weight yarn:
    3 oz/150 yds/85g each
    beige, cranberry and
    dark blue
Size K/10½/6.5mm afghan hook
    or size needed to obtain gauge
Tapestry needle

GAUGE
3 purl sts = 1 inch

SPECIAL STITCHES
Purl stitch (purl st): Bring yarn to front of work, working behind yarn, insert hook under next vertical bar and pull up lp on hook.

Purl increase (purl inc): Bring yarn to front of work, working behind yarn, insert hook under next horizontal bar and pull up lp on hook,

---
INSTRUCTIONS

PONCHETTE
Row 1: Starting at neckline with beige, ch 92, insert hook in 2nd ch from hook, pull up lp, pull up lp in each ch across. *(91 lps on hook)*, to work lps off hook, yo, pull through 1 lp on hook, [yo, pull through 2 lps on hook] across until 1 lp remains on hook.

Row 2: Sk first vertical bar, **purl st** *(see Special Stitches)* in each st across, work lps off hook until 1 lp remains.

Row 3: Sk first vertical bar, purl st in each st across, drop beige, join cranberry on left side of work, work lps off hook until 1 lp remains. Fasten off beige.

Row 4: Rep row 2.

Row 5: Sk first vertical bar, [purl st in each of next 9 sts, **purl inc** *(see Special Stitches)*] across. *(101 lps on hook)*, work lps off hook until 1 lp remains.

Row 6: Sk first vertical bar, purl st in each st across, drop cranberry, join dark blue, work lps off hook until 1 lp remains. Fasten off cranberry.

Row 7: Sk first vertical bar, purl st in each st, work lps off hook until 1 lp remains.

Row 8: Sk first vertical bar, [purl st in each of next 5 sts, purl inc] across, *(121 lps on hook)*, work lps off hook until 1 lp remains.

Row 9: Sk first vertical bar, purl st in each st across, drop dark blue, join beige, work lps off hook until 1 lp remains. Fasten off dark blue.

Row 10: Rep row 4.

Row 11: Sk first vertical bar, [purl st in each of next 10 sts, purl inc] across. *(133 lps on hook),* work lps off hook until 1 lp remains.

Rows 12 & 13: Rep rows 3 and 4.

Row 14: Sk first vertical bar, [purl st in each of next 6 sts, purl inc] across. *(155 lps on hook)* Work lps off hook until 1 lp remains.

Row 15: Rep row 6.

Rows 16 & 17: Rep row 2.

Row 18: Rep row 9.

Rows 19 & 20: Rep row 2.

Row 21: Rep row 3.

Rows 22 & 23: Rep row 2.

Row 24: Rep row 6.

Rows 25–27: Rep row 2.

Row 28: Sk first vertical bar, [bring yarn to front of work, working behind yarn, insert hook under next vertical bar, yo, pull through 2 lps on hook] across.

Fasten off.

Assembly
With matching colors, sew beg and end of each row tog. ■

Rosebuds 'n' Beads T-Shirt

DESIGNS BY NAZANIN S. FARD

Dress up any T-shirt with the sweet and dainty temptations of roses, rosebuds and leaves. Add a little extra charm with shiny beads and pearls and you have a darling top to wear on summer outings that's forever fresh!

SKILL LEVEL ◼◼◼◻
INTERMEDIATE

FINISHED SIZE
Rose: 1⅛ inches in diameter

MATERIALS
DMC Pearl Cotton size 5 (27 yds per skein):
1 skein each #3687 rose, #3689 pink and #320 green
Size 8 steel crochet hook or size needed to obtain gauge
Sewing needle
Sewing thread
T-shirt
⅛-inch gold beads (optional): 14

GAUGE
Rose = 1⅛ inches in diameter

INSTRUCTIONS

ROSE
Make 2 pink.
Make 1 rose.
Rnd 1: Ch 4, 9 dc in 4th ch from hook (first 3 chs count as first dc), join with sl st in 3rd ch of beg ch-4. (10 dc)

Rnd 2: Ch 3, [sk next dc, sl st in next dc, ch 3] around, ending with ch 3, sk last dc, join with sl st in 3rd ch of beg ch-3. (5 ch-3 sps)

Rnd 3: Ch 1, (sc, hdc, 4 dc, hdc, sc) in each ch-3 sp around, **do not join**. (5 petals)

Rnd 4: Sl st in first unworked dc of rnd 1, [ch 5, sl st in next unworked dc of rnd 1] around, ch 5, join with sl st in beg sl st. (5 ch-5 sps)

Rnd 5: Ch 1, (sc, hdc, 5 dc, hdc, sc) in first ch-5 sp and in each ch-5 sp around, join with sl st in beg sc. Fasten off.

ROSEBUD
Make 1 pink.
Make 4 rose.
Ch 11, 3 dc in 4th ch from hook and in each ch across. Fasten off.

Roll into Rosebud shape and tack securely at bottom.

LEAF
Make 7.
With green, ch 8, sc in 2nd ch

from hook, hdc in next ch, dc in each of next 3 chs, hdc in next ch, 3 sc in last ch, working on opposite side of ch, hdc in next ch, dc in each of next 3 chs, hdc in next ch, sc in last ch, join with sl st in beg sc. Fasten off.

FINISHING
Place Roses, Rosebuds, Leaves and beads on T-shirt as shown in photo and sew in place with sewing needle and thread. ▪

Purple Pizzazz

DESIGN BY SHELLE CAIN

Sink into strands of softness, stitched together into a cascading multitude of textured yarns. It's a fashionable and unique temptation that's deliciously sumptuous, especially when you use your softest scraps!

SKILL LEVEL ◼◼◼◻
INTERMEDIATE

FINISHED SIZE
45 x 45 inches

MATERIALS

7 oz each of 7 different yarns (depending on yarn):
   Lion Brand Homespun and Fun Fur
   Bernat Galaxy, Frenzy, Boa and Eyelash
   Jo Ann Fabric Sensations Angel Hair
Size N/15/10mm crochet hook *(or any large size hook)*

PATTERN NOTE
Other fun yarns to include are any novelty yarn desired. There are many to choose from, and some have metallic accents which add a festive flair to your Wrap.

Some of the thinner yarns could be used by holding 2 strands together. Pick a color theme and make it unique!

INSTRUCTIONS

WRAP
Row 1: With first yarn, ch 153, *(203 for extra long wrap)*, dc in 3rd ch from hook and in each ch across, turn. Leave a 12-inch end

for fringe if desired. Fasten off.

Row 2: Join next yarn with sl st in first st, ch 3 *(counts as first dc)*, dc in each st across, turn. Fasten off.

Next rows: Rep row 2 using all 7 yarns, then rep sequence twice.

Fringe
Cut 12-inch strands of any yarn and fold in half, pull fold through, pull ends through fold *(including any ends left)*, pull to tighten. Trim ends.

Attach Fringe in end of each row across both short ends of Wrap. ◼

Hollywood Halter

DESIGN BY DARLA SIMS

You'll be retro-chic in this bold and sassy halter! It's a striking, yet simple statement that creates a wonderful summer splash of style for anyone looking to command attention with curve-conscious flair.

SKILL LEVEL ■■■□
INTERMEDIATE

FINISHED SIZES
Instructions given fit 28–30-inch bust *(X-small)*; changes for 32–34-inch bust *(small)*, 36–38-inch bust *(medium)* and 40–42-inch bust *(large)* are in [ ].

FINISHED GARMENT MEASUREMENTS
Bust: 30 inches *(X-small)* [34 inches *(small)*, 38 inches *(medium)*, 42 inches *(large)*]

MATERIALS

TLC Cotton Plus medium (worsted) weight yarn (3½ oz/178 yds/100g per skein):
3 [4, 5, 6] skeins #3001 white
1 skein each #3643 kiwi and #3752 hot pink

Sizes E/4/3.5mm, F/5/3.75mm and G/6/4mm crochet hooks or size needed to obtain gauge
Tapestry needle
Sewing needle
Sewing thread
½-inch white ball button

GAUGE
Size G hook: Shell and 3 dc = 2 inches; 2 rows = 1 inch

Take time to check gauge.

PATTERN NOTE
This pattern stitch produces a stretchy fabric, which results in seemingly more stitches per inch as your work progresses. This is the result of the weight of the fabric. This pattern stitch is actually perfect for a garment meant to fit closely to the body and has lots of give for comfort.

SPECIAL STITCHES
Shell: (2 dc, ch 1, 2 dc) in indicated st.

Cluster (cl): Holding last lp of each st on hook, 3 dc in next st, yo, pull though all lps on hook.

INSTRUCTIONS

HALTER
Back
Row 1 (RS): With white and size G hook, ch 61 [69, 77, 85], dc in 3rd ch from hook *(first 2 chs do not count as first st)*, dc in each of next 2 chs, [sk next 2 chs, **shell** *(see Special Stitches)* in next ch, sk next 2 chs, dc in

each of next 3 chs] across, turn. *(7 [8, 9, 10] shells)*

Row 2: Ch 2 *(counts as first post st)*, **fpdc** *(see Stitch Guide)* around each of next 2 sts, *shell in ch sp of next shell**, fpdc around each of next 3 sts, rep from * across, ending last rep at **, fpdc around each of next 2 sts, hdc *(counts as last fpdc)* in last st, turn.

Row 3: Ch 2, **bpdc** *(see Stitch Guide)* around each of next 2 sts, *shell in ch sp of next shell**, bpdc around each of next 3 sts, rep from * across, ending last rep at **, bpdc around each of next 2 sts, hdc in last st, turn.

Next rows: Rep rows 2 and 3 alternately until piece measures 8 inches from beg, ending with RS row.

Next row: With size F hook, ch 1, evenly sp 53 [59, 65, 74] sc across, turn.

Ribbing
With size E hook, ch 5, sc in 2nd ch from hook and in each of next 3 chs, *sk next st, sl st in each of next 2 sts, **turn**, sk 2 sl sts, working in **back lps** *(see Stitch Guide)* only, sc in each of next 4 sts, ch 1, **turn**, sc in each st across, rep from * across, ending with sl st in last sl st. Fasten off.

Front
Row 1 (RS): With white and size G hook, ch 61 [69, 77, 85], dc in 3rd ch *(first 2 chs do not count as first st)* from hook, dc in each of next 2 chs, [sk next 2 chs, shell

in next ch, sk next 2 chs, dc in each of next 3 chs] across, turn. *(7 [8, 9, 10] shells)*

Row 2: Ch 2 *(counts as first post st)*, fpdc around each of next 2 sts, *shell in ch sp of next shell**, fpdc around each of next 3 sts, rep from * across, ending last rep at **, fpdc around each of next 2 sts, hdc *(counts as last fpdc)* in last st, turn.

Row 3: Ch 2, bpdc around each of next 2 sts *shell in ch sp of next shell**, bpdc around each of next 3 sts, rep from * across, ending last rep at **, bpdc around each of next 3 sts, hdc in last st, turn.

Next rows: Rep rows 2 and 3 alternately until piece is same length as Back to top of Back Ribbing, ending with RS row. At end of last row, fasten off.

First Neck Shaping
Row 1: Sk first 6 [8, 8, 9] sts or chs, join with sc in next st or ch, sc in each of next 22 [24, 28, 31] sts or chs, leaving rem sts and chs unworked, turn. *(23 [25, 29, 32] sc)*

Row 2: Ch 1, sc in each st across, turn.

Row 3: Ch 1, **sc dec** (see Stitch Guide) in first 2 sts, sc in each st across with sc dec in last 2 sts, turn. (21 [23, 27, 30] sc)

Row 4: Ch 1, sc in each st across, turn.

Row 5: Ch 1, sc dec in first 2 sts, sc in each st across with sc dec in last 2 sts, turn. (19 [21, 25, 28] sc)

Row 6: Ch 1, sc in each st across, turn.

Row 7: Ch 1, sc in each st across with sc dec in last 2 sts, turn. (18 [20, 24, 27] sc)

Next rows: Rep rows 6 and 7 alternately until there are 5 [5, 5, 6] sts rem.

Neck Strap
Next rows: Work even until piece measures 3½ inches on Strap.

Next row: Ch 1, sc in first 1 [1, 1, 2] sts, ch 2, sk next 2 sts (buttonhole), sc in each st across, turn.

Next row: Ch 1, sc in each st and ch across, turn.

Next row: Ch 1, sc dec in first 2 sts, sc in each st across with sc dec in last st, turn.

Last row: Ch 1, sc dec in 3 [3, 3, 4] sts. Fasten off.

2nd Neck Shaping
Row 1: Sk center st, join with sc in next st or ch on last row of Front, sc in each of next 22 [24, 28, 31] sts or chs, leaving rem sts and chs unworked, turn. (23 [25, 29, 32] sc)

Rows 2–6: Rep rows 2–6 of First Neck Shaping.

Row 7: Ch 1, sc dec in first 2 sts, sc in each st across, turn. (18 [20, 24, 27] sc)

Next rows: Rep rows 6 and 7 alternately until there are 5 [5, 5, 6] sts.

Neck Strap
Next rows: Work even until piece is the same length as Strap on First Shaping to last 2 rows.

Next row: Ch 1, sc dec in first 2 sts, sc in each st across with sc in dec in last 2 sts, turn.

Last row: Ch 1, sc dec in 3 [3, 3, 4] sts. Fasten off.

Sew button to Strap opposite buttonhole.

Sew side seams.

Front Edging
With white and size F hook, with RS facing, join with sl st in first sk st on Front, working across Front, evenly sp sc across to last sk st at opposite side, with sc dec in 3 sts at center front. Fasten off.

Bottom Edging
Rnd 1: With white and size F hook, join with sc at side seam, evenly sp 120 [138, 150, 168] sc around, join with sl st in beg sc.

Rnd 2: Ch 1, sc in first st, *sk next 2 sts, 5 dc in next st, sk next 2 sts**, sc in next st, rep from * around, ending last rep at ** adjusting sts if necessary, join with sl st in beg sc. Fasten off.

Rnd 3: Join kiwi with sl st in first st, ch 5 (counts as first tr and ch-1 sp), ({tr, ch 1} twice, tr) in same st, *sc in center dc of next dc group**, ({tr, ch 1} 3 times, tr) in next sc, rep from * around, ending last rep at **, join with sl st in 4th ch of beg ch-5. Fasten off.

Rnd 4: Join hot pink with sc in last sc made, *ch 4, [cl (see Special Stitches) in next ch-1 sp, ch 1] twice, cl in next ch-1 sp, ch 4**, sc in next sc, rep from * around, ending last rep at **, join with sl st in beg sc. Fasten off. ∎

Spring Squares

DESIGN BY GINNY ALVORD-CLARK

Demure and ladylike, this adorable top is stitched in a parade of spring's favorite hues. The colorful flower squares form the accents for this easy-to-wear sweater, crocheted in a sport weight yarn.

SKILL LEVEL ◼◼◼◻ INTERMEDIATE

FINISHED SIZES
Instructions given fit 30-32-inch bust *(small)*; changes for 38-40-inch bust *(large)* and 46-48-inch bust *(X-large)* are in [ ].

FINISHED GARMENT MEASUREMENTS
Bust: 37½ inches *(small)*
[45½ inches *(large)*,
53½ inches *(X-large)*]

MATERIALS
Fine (sport) weight yarn (4 oz/400 yds/113g per skein):
4 [5, 6] skeins white
1 skein each yellow, lilac, blue, pink and green

Size D/3/3.25mm crochet hook or hook size needed to obtain gauge
Tapestry needle

GAUGE

11 dc = 2 inches, 3 dc rows = 1 inch

Each Square on Body = 3¾ [4½, 5¼] inches across

Each Square on Sleeve = 3 inches across

Take time to check gauge.

SPECIAL STITCH

Picot: Ch 3, sl st in top of last st made.

INSTRUCTIONS

FRONT
Bottom Border
Square

Make 5.

Note: The border is formed with 5 squares. Each Square has a yellow center, white petals and a pastel background, then 2 rnds of either pink, blue, yellow, lilac or green. These colors are referred to as background color.

Rnd 1: With yellow, ch 3, sl st in first ch to form ring, ch 1, 8 sc in ring, join with sl st in beg sc. *(8 sc)*

Rnd 2: Ch 1, 2 sc in each st around, join with sl st in beg sc. Fasten off. *(16 sc)*

Rnd 3: Join white with sl st in any st, ch 2 *(counts as first hdc)*, (dc, tr, dc, hdc) in same st, ch 1, sk next st, *(hdc, dc, tr, dc, hdc) in next st, ch 1, sk next st, rep from * around, join with sl st in 2nd ch of beg ch-2, **turn.** Fasten off. *(8 petals)*

Rnd 4: Working behind petals, join 1 background color with sc in any sk st on rnd 2, ch 5, [sc in next sk st on rnd 2, ch 5] around, join with sl st in beg sc. *(8 ch sps)*

Rnd 5: Sl st in first ch sp, ch 3 *(counts as first dc)*, (3 dc, ch 3, 4 dc) in same ch sp, ch 1, 4 dc in next ch sp, ch 1, *(4 dc, ch 3, 4 dc) in next ch sp, ch 1, 4 dc in next ch sp, ch 1, rep from * around, join with sl st in 3rd ch of beg ch-3. *(12 ch sps)*

Rnds 6 [6 & 7, 6–8]: Sl st in each of next 3 sts, (sl st, ch 3, 3 dc, ch 3, 4 dc) in next corner ch-3 sp, ch 1, [4 dc in next ch sp, ch 1] across to next corner ch-3 sp, *(4 dc, ch 3, 4 dc) in corner ch sp, ch 1, [4 dc in next ch sp, ch 1] across to next corner ch-3 sp, rep from * around, join with sl st in 3rd ch of beg ch-3. At end of last rnd, turn. Fasten off. *(16 [20, 24] ch sps at end of in last rnd)*

Rnd 7 [8, 9]: Join white with sl st in any corner ch-3 sp, ch 3, (3 dc, ch 3, 4 dc) in same ch sp, ch 1, [4 dc in next ch sp, ch 1] across to next corner ch-3 sp, *(4 dc, ch 3, 4 dc) in corner ch sp, ch 1, [4 dc in next ch sp, ch 1] across to next corner ch-3 sp, rep from * around, join with sl st in 3rd ch of beg ch-3. Fasten off.

With white, sew Squares tog through **back lps** *(see Stitch Guide)* in desired color sequence forming a strip.

Body

Row 1: Working across 1 long edge of Bottom Border, join white with sc in first st, evenly sp 102 [124, 146] sc across, turn. *(103 [125, 147] sc)*

Row 2: Ch 4 *(counts as first dc and ch-1)*, sk next st, dc in next st, [ch 1, sk next st, dc in next st] across, turn.

Row 3: Ch 3, dc in each ch sp and in each st across, turn.

Rows 4–46 [4–48, 4–50]: Ch 3, dc in each st across, turn.

First Shoulder

Row 47 [49, 51]: Ch 3 , dc in each of next 23 [30, 40] sts, leaving rem sts unworked, turn. *(24 [31, 41] dc)*

Row 48 [50, 52]: Ch 3, dc in each st across, turn. Fasten off.

Neck Shaping

Row 47 [49, 51]: Sk next 55 [63, 65] sts on row 46 [48, 50], join white with sl st in next st, ch 3, dc in each st across, turn. *(24 [31, 41] dc)*

Row 48 [50, 52]: Ch 3, dc in each st across. Fasten off.

BACK
Work same as Front.

FINISHING
Hold Back and Front tog with RS facing, sew shoulder seams.

NECK EDGING
Rnd 1: Working in sts and ends of rows around neck opening, join white with sc in any st, evenly sp 125 [140, 143] sc around, join with sl st in beg sc. Fasten off. *(126 [141, 144] sc)*

Rnd 2: Join lilac with sc in any st, **picot** *(see Special Stitch)*, ch 2, sk next 2 sts, [sc in next st, picot, ch 2, sk next 2 sts] around, join with sl st in beg sc. Fasten off.

SLEEVE
Make 2.
Border
Square
Make 1 each yellow, blue, pink and lilac, these colors will be referred to as Background color.
Rnd 1: With yellow, ch 3, sl st in first ch to form ring, ch 1, 8 sc in ring, join with sl st in beg sc. *(8 sc)*

Rnd 2: Ch 1, 2 sc in each st around, join with sl st in beg sc. Fasten off. *(16 sc)*

Rnd 3: Join white with sl st in any st, ch 2, (dc, tr, dc, hdc) in same st, ch 1, sk next st, *(hdc, dc, tr, dc, hdc) in next st, ch 1, sk next st, rep from * around, join with sl st in 2nd ch of beg ch-2, **turn**. Fasten off. *(8 petals)*

Rnd 4: Working behind petals, join background color with sc in any sk st on rnd 2, ch 5, [sc in next sk st on rnd 2, ch 5] around, join with sl st in beg sc, turn. *(8 ch sps)*

Rnd 5: Sl st in first ch-3 sp, ch 3, (3 dc, ch 3, 4 dc) in same ch sp, ch 1, 4 dc in next ch sp, ch 1, *(4 dc, ch 3, 4 dc) in next ch sp, ch 1, 4 dc in next ch sp, ch 1, rep from * around, join with sl st in 3rd ch of beg ch-3, turn. Fasten off. *(12 ch sps)*

Rnd 6: Join white with sl st in any corner ch-3 sp, ch 3, (3 dc, ch 3, 4 dc) in same ch sp, ch 1, [4 dc in next ch sp, ch 1] across to next corner ch-3 sp, *(4 dc, ch 3, 4 dc) in next ch sp, ch 1, [4 dc in next ch sp, ch 1] across

to next corner ch-3 sp, rep from * around, join with sl st in 3rd ch of beg ch-3. Fasten off. *(16 dc and 3 ch-1 sps between each corner ch-3 sp)*

With white, sew Squares tog through back lps in desired color sequence forming strip.

Sleeve Body
Row 1: Working across 1 long edge of Border, join white with sc in first st, evenly sp 64 [66, 72] sc across, turn. *(65 [67, 73] sc)*

Row 2: Ch 4, sk next st, dc in next st, [ch 1, sk next st, dc in next st] across, turn.

Row 3: Ch 3, dc in each ch sp and in each st across, turn.

Rows 4–17 [4–19, 4–19]: Ch 3, dc in same st, dc in each st across with 2 dc in last st, turn. *(93 [99, 105] dc at end of in last row)*

Row 18 [20, 20]: Ch 3, dc in each st across. Fasten off.

Matching center of last row on Sleeve to shoulder seam, sew Sleeve to Body.

Sew Sleeve and side seams. ■

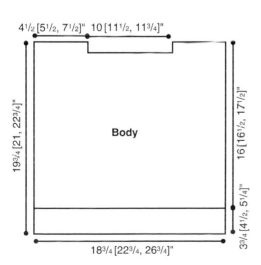

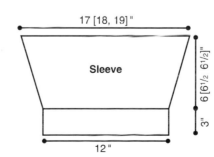

Colorful Carnival

DESIGN BY GINNY ALVORD-CLARK

Blocks bursting with vibrant color build this sensational scrap jacket. It's a colorful mosaic, perfectly engineered to craft those leftover materials into a creative asymmetrical design, whirling with a wild fusion of colors.

SKILL LEVEL ■■■■
EXPERIENCED

FINISHED SIZES
Instructions given fit 32–34-inch bust *(small)*; changes for 36–38-inch bust *(medium)* and 40–42-inch bust *(large)* are in [ ].

FINISHED GARMENT MEASUREMENTS
Bust: 38 inches *(small)* [43 inches *(medium)*, 48 inches *(large)*]

MATERIALS
Aunt Lydia's Classic Crochet size 10 crochet cotton (350 yds per ball):
700 [725, 750] yds #484 myrtle green
350 [375, 400] yds each #458 purple, #494 victory red, #493 French rose, #431 pumpkin and #421 goldenrod
Size F/5/3.75mm crochet hook or hook size needed to obtain gauge
Tapestry needle
Purple ½-inch flat buttons: 6
2 stitch markers

GAUGE
2 strands thread held tog:
4 sc and 3 ch-3 sps = 2 inches;
11 sc rows = 2 inches

Take time to check gauge.

PATTERN NOTES
Use 2 strands thread held together as 1 throughout.

Label Blocks and Triangles with number indicated as you are working them.

INSTRUCTIONS

BODY
Block No. 1
Row 1: With French rose, ch 32 [36, 40], sc in 2nd ch from hook, sc in each ch across, turn. *(31 [35, 39] sc)*

Row 2: Ch 1, sc in each of first 2 sts, ch 3, sk next 3 sts, [sc in next st, ch 3, sk next 3 sts] across to last 2 sts, sc in each of last 2 sts, turn. *(10 [11, 12] sc, 7 [8, 9] ch sps)*

Pattern is established in row 2.

Rows 3–9: Work in pattern across, turn. At end of last row, fasten off.

Row 10: Join pumpkin with sc in first st, work in pattern across, turn.

Row 11: Work in pattern across, turn. Fasten off.

Row 12: Join French rose with sc in first st, work in pattern across, turn.

Rows 13–15: Work in pattern across, turn. At end of last row, fasten off.

Row 16: Join victory red with sc in first st, work in pattern across, turn.

Row 17: Work in pattern across, turn. Fasten off.

Row 18: Join French rose with sc in first st, work in pattern across, turn.

Rows 19–25: Work in pattern across, turn.

Row 26: Ch 1, sc in first 2 sts, 3 sc in next ch sp and sc in each st across. Fasten off. *(31 sc)*

Block No. 2
Note: Work the following rows in the same manner as Block No. 1. For the sake of simplicity, only the number of rows and the color will be given. Fasten off at end of each color section.

Row 1: With goldenrod, rep row 1 of Block No. 1.
Work 4 more rows in goldenrod.
Work 2 rows in pumpkin.
Work 12 rows in goldenrod.
Work 2 rows in pumpkin.
Work 4 rows in goldenrod.

Row 26: Rep row 26 of Block No. 1.

Block No. 3
Row 1: With victory red, rep row 1 of Block No. 1.
Work 4 more rows in victory red.Work 2 rows in goldenrod.
Work 12 rows in victory red.
Work 2 rows in French rose.
Work 4 rows in victory red.

Row 26: Rep row 26 of Block No. 1.

Block No. 4
Row 1: With pumpkin, rep row 1 of Block No. 1.
Work 4 more rows in pumpkin.
Work 2 rows in goldenrod.
Work 12 rows in pumpkin.
Work 2 rows in victory red.
Work 4 rows in pumpkin.

Row 26: Rep row 26 of Block No. 1.

Block No. 5
Row 1: With victory red, rep row 1 of Block No. 1.
Work 8 more rows in victory red.
Work 2 rows in pumpkin.
Work 4 rows in victory red.
Work 2 rows in goldenrod.
Work 8 rows in victory red.

Row 26: Rep row 26 of Block No. 1.

Block No. 6
Row 1: With purple, rep row 1 of Block No. 1.
Work 14 more rows in purple.
Work 2 rows in goldenrod.
Work 2 rows in purple.
Work 2 rows in victory red.
Work 4 rows in purple.

Row 26: Rep row 26 of Block No. 1.

Block No. 7
Row 1: With myrtle green, rep row 1 of Block No. 1.
Work 6 more rows in myrtle green.
Work 5 rows in victory red.
Work 2 rows in purple.
Work 5 rows in victory red.
Work 6 rows in myrtle green.

Row 26: Rep row 26 of Block No. 1.

Block No. 8
Row 1: With pumpkin, rep row 1 of Block No. 1.
Work 8 more rows in pumpkin.
Work 2 rows in French rose.
Work 4 rows in pumpkin.
Work 2 rows in purple.
Work 8 rows in pumpkin.

Row 26: Rep row 26 of Block No. 1.

Block No. 9
Row 1: With victory red, rep row 1 of Block No. 1.
Work 14 more rows in victory red.
Work 2 rows in goldenrod.
Work 2 rows in victory red.
Work 2 rows in purple.
Work 4 rows in victory red.

Row 26: Rep row 26 of Block No. 1.

Block No. 10
Row 1: With pumpkin, rep row 1 of Block No. 1.
Work 4 more rows in pumpkin.
Work 2 rows in myrtle green.
Work 12 rows in pumpkin.
Work 2 rows in victory red.
Work 4 rows in pumpkin.

Block No. 11
Row 1: With French rose, rep row 1 of Block No. 1.
Work 4 more rows in French rose.
Work 2 rows in goldenrod.
Work 12 rows in French rose.
Work 2 rows in pumpkin.
Work 4 rows in French rose.

Row 26: Rep row 26 of Block No. 1.

Block No. 12
Row 1: With myrtle green, rep row 1 of Block No. 1.
Work 14 more rows in myrtle green.
Work 2 rows in victory red.
Work 2 rows in myrtle green.
Work 2 rows in purple.
Work 4 rows in myrtle green.

Row 26: Rep row 26 of Block No. 1.

Block No. 13
Row 1: With pumpkin, rep row 1 of Block No. 1.
Work 14 more rows in pumpkin.
Work 2 rows in French rose.
Work 2 rows in pumpkin.
Work 2 rows in victory red.
Work 4 rows in pumpkin.

Row 26: Rep row 26 of Block No. 1.

Block No. 14
Row 1: With goldenrod, rep row 1 of Block No. 1.
Work 14 more rows in goldenrod.
Work 2 rows in victory red.
Work 2 rows in goldenrod.

Work 2 rows in myrtle green.
Work 4 rows in goldenrod.

Row 26: Rep row 26 of Block No. 1.

Block No. 15
Row 1: With pumpkin, rep row 1 of Block No. 1.
Work 14 more rows in pumpkin.
Work 2 rows in goldenrod.
Work 2 rows in pumpkin.
Work 2 rows in French rose.
Work 4 rows in pumpkin.

Row 26: Rep row 26 of Block No. 1.

Block No. 16
Row 1: With purple, rep row 1 of Block No. 1.
Work 6 more rows in purpl
Work 5 rows in goldenrod.
Work 2 rows in myrtle green.
Work 5 rows in goldenrod.
Work 6 rows in purple.

Row 26: Rep row 26 of Block No. 1.

Block No. 17
Row 1: With purple, rep row 1 of Block No. 1.
Work 8 more rows in purple.
Work 2 rows in French rose.
Work 4 rows in purple.
Work 2 rows in pumpkin.
Work 8 rows in purple.

Row 26: Rep row 26 of Block No. 1.

Block No. 18
Row 1: With myrtle green, rep row 1 of Block No. 1.
Work 8 more rows in myrtle green.
Work 2 rows in victory red.

Work 4 rows in myrtle green.
Work 2 rows in French rose.
Work 8 rows in myrtle green.

Row 26: Rep row 26 of Block No. 1.

Block No. 19
Row 1: With victory red, rep row 1 of Block No. 1.
Work 14 more rows in victory red.
Work 2 rows in myrtle green.
Work 2 rows in victory red.
Work 2 rows in French rose.
Work 4 rows in victory red.

Row 26: Rep row 26 of Block No. 1.

Block No. 20
Row 1: With purple, rep row 1 of Block No. 1.
Work 4 more rows in purple.
Work 2 rows in French rose.
Work 12 rows in purple.
Work 2 rows in goldenrod.
Work 4 rows in purple.

Row 26: Rep row 26 of Block No. 1.

Block No. 21
Row 1: With French rose, rep row 1 of Block No. 1.
Work 6 more rows in French rose.
Work 5 rows in pumpkin.
Work 2 rows in goldenrod.
Work 5 rows in pumpkin.
Work 6 rows in French rose.

Row 26: Rep row 26 of Block No. 1.

Block No. 22
Row 1: With victory red, rep row 1 of Block No. 1.
Work 8 more rows in victory red.

Work 2 rows in purple.
Work 4 rows in victory red.
Work 2 rows in goldenrod.
Work 8 rows in victory red.

Row 26: Rep row 26 of Block No. 1.

Block No. 23
Row 1: With victory red, rep row 1 of Block No. 1.
Work 4 more rows in victory red.
Work 2 rows in pumpkin.
Work 12 rows in victory red.
Work 2 rows in goldenrod.
Work 4 rows in victory red.

Row 26: Rep row 26 of Block No. 1.

Block No. 24
Row 1: With French rose, rep row 1 of Block No. 1.
Work 14 more rows in French rose.
Work 2 rows in purple.
Work 2 rows in French rose.
Work 2 rows in victory red.
Work 4 rows in French rose.

Row 26: Rep row 26 of Block No. 1.

Block No. 25
Row 1: With pumpkin, row 1 of Block No. 1.
Work 6 more rows in pumpkin.
Work 5 rows in goldenrod.
Work 2 rows in purple.
Work 5 rows in goldenrod.
Work 6 rows in pumpkin.

Row 26: Rep row 26 of Block No. 1.

Block No. 26
Row 1: With myrtle green, rep row 1 of Block No. 1.
Work 4 more rows in myrtle green.

Work 2 rows in pumpkin.
Work 12 rows in myrtle green.
Work 2 rows in goldenrod.
Work 4 rows in myrtle green.

Row 26: Rep row 26 of Block No. 1.

Block No. 27
Row 1: With goldenrod, row 1 of Block No. 1.
Work 8 more rows in goldenrod.
Work 2 rows in victory red.
Work 4 rows in goldenrod.
Work 2 rows in purple.
Work 8 rows in goldenrod.

Row 26: Rep row 26 of Block No. 1.

Block No. 28
Row 1: With victory red, rep row 1 of Block No. 1.
Work 6 more rows in victory red.
Work 5 rows in goldenrod.
Work 2 rows in pumpkin.
Work 5 rows in goldenrod.
Work 6 rows in victory red.

Row 26: Rep row 26 of Block No. 1.

Block No. 29
Row 1: With pumpkin, rep row 1 of Block No. 1.
Work 8 more rows in pumpkin.
Work 2 rows in victory red.
Work 4 rows in pumpkin.
Work 2 rows in purple.
Work 8 rows in pumpkin.

Row 26: Rep row 26 of Block No. 1.

Block No. 30
Row 1: With goldenrod, rep row 1 of Block No. 1.
Work 6 more rows in goldenrod.

Work 5 rows in French rose.
Work 2 rows in pumpkin.
Work 5 rows in French rose.
Work 6 rows in goldenrod.

Row 26: Rep row 26 of Block No. 1.

Right Front Triangle
Row 1: With myrtle green, ch 32 [36, 40], sc in 2nd ch from hook, sc in each ch across, turn. *(31 [35, 39] sc)*

Row 2: Work in pattern across, turn.

Neck Shaping
Row 3: Ch 1, sl st in each of first 7 sts and chs, sc in each of next 2 chs, sc in next st, work in pattern across, turn. *(9 [10, 11] sc, 5 [6, 7] ch sps)*

Row 4: Work in pattern across, leaving last 2 sts unworked, turn. *(7 [8, 9] sc, 5 [6, 7] ch sps)*

Row 5: Ch 1, Sk first st, sl st in next ch, sc in each of next 2 chs, sc in next st, work in pattern across, turn. *(8 [9, 10] sc, 4 [5, 6] ch sps)*

Row 6: Work in pattern across, leaving last st unworked, turn. *(7 [8, 9] sc, 4 [5, 6] ch sps)*

Row 7: Ch 1, sk first st, sc in next st, work in pattern across, turn. *(6 [7, 8] sc, 4 [5, 6] ch sps)*

Row 8: Work in pattern across, turn.

Row 9: Ch 1, sl st in first st, ch 3, sk next ch sp, work in pattern across, turn. Fasten off. *(5 [6, 7] sc, 4 [5, 6] ch sps)*

Row 10: Join purple with sc in first st, work in pattern across to last ch sp, sc in each of next 2 chs, leaving rem ch unworked, turn. *(7 [8, 9] sc, 3 [4, 5] ch sps)*

Row 11: Ch 1, sk first st, sc in each of next 2 sts, work in pattern across, turn. Fasten off. *(6 [7, 8] sc, 3 [4, 5] ch sps)*

Row 12: Join myrtle green with sc in first st, work in pattern across, leaving last st unworked, turn. *(5 [6, 7] sc, 3 [4, 5] ch sps)*

Row 13: Ch 1, sk first st, sc in next ch, ch 2, sk next 2 chs, sc in next st, work in pattern across, turn.

Row 14: Work in pattern across to last ch sp, ch 2, sk next ch sp, sc in last st, turn.

Row 15: Ch 1, sl st in first st, ch 2, sk next ch sp, work in pattern across, turn. Fasten off. *(4 [5, 6] sc, 3 [4, 5] ch sps)*

Row 16: Join pumpkin with sc in first st, work in pattern across, leaving last ch-2 sp unworked, turn. *(4 [5, 6] sc, 3 [3, 4] ch sps)*

Row 17: Work in pattern across, turn. Fasten off.

Row 18: Join myrtle green with sc in first st, work in pattern across, turn.

Rows 19 & 20: Work in pattern across, turn.

Row 21: Ch 1, sc in first st, ch 2, sk next ch sp, work in pattern across, turn.

Row 22: Work in pattern across to last ch sp, ch 2, sk last ch sp, sc in last st, turn.

Row 23: Ch 1, sc in first st, ch 1, sk next ch sp, work in pattern across, turn.

Row 24: Work in pattern across to last ch-1 sp, sc in last ch, sc in last st, turn. *(5 [6, 7] sc, 1 [2, 3] ch sps)*

Rows 25 & 26: Work in pattern across, turn. At end of last row, fasten off.

Left Front Triangle

Row 1: With French rose, ch 32 [36, 40], sc in 2nd ch from hook, sc in each ch across, turn. *(31 [35, 39] sc)*

Row 2: Work in pattern across, turn.

Neck Shaping

Row 3: Work in pattern across to last 2 ch sps, sc in next 2 chs, leaving rem chs and sts unworked, turn. *(9 [10, 11] sc, 5 [6, 7] ch sps)*

Row 4: Ch 1, sl st in first 2 sts, sc in next st, work in pattern across, turn. *(7 [8, 9] sc, 5 [6, 7] ch sps)*

Row 5: Work in pattern across to last ch sp, sc in next 2 chs, leaving last ch and st unworked, turn. *(8 [9, 10] sc, 4 [5, 6] ch sps)*

Row 6: Ch 1, sl st in first st, sc in next st, work in pattern across, turn. *(7 [8, 9] sc, 4 [5, 6] ch sps)*

Row 7: Ch 1, work in pattern across, leaving last st unworked, turn. *(6 [7, 8] sc, 4 [5, 6] ch sps)*

Row 8: Work in pattern across, turn.

Row 9: Work in pattern across to last ch sp, ch 3, sk last ch sp, sl st in last st, turn. Fasten off. *(5 [6, 7] sc, 4 [5, 6] ch sps)*

Row 10: Join myrtle green with sc in 2nd ch of first ch sp, work in pattern across, turn. *(7 [8, 9] sc, 3 [4, 5] ch sps)*

Row 11: Work in pattern across, leaving last st unworked, turn. Fasten off. *(6 [7, 8] sc, 3 [4, 5] ch sps)*

Row 12: Join French rose with sc in 2nd st, work in pattern across, turn. *(5 [6, 7] sc, 3 [4, 5] ch sps)*

Row 13: Work in pattern across to last ch sp, ch 2, sc in 3rd ch of next ch sp, leaving last st unworked, turn.

Row 14: Ch 1, sc in first st, ch 2, sk next ch sp, work in pattern across, turn.

Row 15: Work in pattern across to last ch sp, ch 2, sk next ch sp, sl st in last st, turn. Fasten off. *(4 [5, 6] sc, 3 [4, 5] ch sps)*

Row 16: Sk first ch sp, join purple with sc in next st, work in pattern across, turn. *(4 [5, 6] sc, 3 [3, 4] ch sps)*

Row 17: Work in pattern across, turn. Fasten off.

Row 18: Join French rose with sc in first st, work in pattern across, turn.

Rows 19 & 20: Work in pattern across, turn.

Row 21: Work in pattern across to last ch sp, ch 2, sk last ch sp, sc in last st, turn.

Row 22: Ch 1, sc in first st, ch 2, sk next ch sp, work in pattern across, turn.

Row 23: Work in pattern across to last ch sp, ch 1, sk last ch sp, sc in last st, turn.

Row 24: Ch 1, sc in first st, sc in next ch, work in pattern across, turn. *(5 [6, 7] sc, 1 [2, 3] ch sps)*

Rows 25 & 26: Work in pattern across, turn. At end of last row, fasten off.

SLEEVE

Make 2.
Note: *Use same instructions when working Sleeves on both medium and large sizes.*

Row 1: With French rose, ch 60 [68], sc in 2nd ch from hook, sc in each ch across, turn. *(59 [67] sc)*

Row 2: Ch 1, sc in each of first 2 sts, ch 3, sk next 3 sts, [sc in next st, ch 3, sk next 3 sts] across to last 2 sts, sc in each of last 2 sts, turn. *(17 [19] sc, 14 [16] ch sps)*

Row 3: Ch 1, 2 sc in first st, sc in next st, work in pattern across to last st, 2 sc in last st, turn. *(19 [21] sc, 14 [16] ch sps)*

Rows 4–6: Ch 1, sc in each of first 3 sts, work in pattern across to last 3 sts, sc in each of last 3 sts, turn.

Row 7: Ch 1, 2 sc in first st, ch 1, sk next st, sc in next st, work in pattern across to last 3 sts, sc in next st, ch 1, sk next st, 2 sc in last st, turn. *(19 [21] sc, 16 [18] ch sps)*

Rows 8–10: Ch 1, sc in each of first 2 sts, ch 1, sk next ch sp, sc in next st, work in pattern across to last ch sp, ch 1, sk last ch sp, sc in each of last 2 sts, turn.

Row 11: Ch 1, 2 sc in first st, ch 2, sk next st and next ch sp, sc in next st, work in pattern across to last ch sp, ch 2, sk last ch sp and next st, 2 sc in last st, turn.

Rows 12–14: Ch 1, sc in first st, ch 3, sk next ch sp, work in pattern across to last st, sc in last st, turn. *(17 [19] sc, 16 [18] ch sps)*

Row 15: Ch 1, 2 sc in first st, work in pattern across to last st, 2 sc in last st, turn. *(19 [21] sc, 16 [18] ch sps)*

Rows 16–19: Work in pattern across, turn.

Note: *St and inc pattern is established in rows 3–19. Join new color with sc at beg of each color section. At end of each color section, fasten off.*

Rows 20–100: Working in st and inc pattern, work 3 more rows victory red, work 6 rows of myrtle green, 12 rows of goldenrod, 6 rows of myrtle green, 22 rows of French rose, 12 rows of pumpkin, 8 rows of goldenrod and 12 rows of victory red, ending with 29 sc and 26 ch sps in last row. At end of last row,

for **small size only**, fasten off, for **medium and large sizes, do not fasten off.**

**Medium & Large Sizes
Rows [101–104]:** Work in pattern across, turn. At end of last row, fasten off.

ASSEMBLY

1. With purple, using sc, assemble Left Front, Right Front and Back according to assembly diagrams.

2. With purple, sc top of Triangles on Fronts to corresponding sts of 2 inside Blocks on Back for shoulder seams.

3. Matching top center of Sleeves to shoulder seam, with purple, sc Sleeves in place, sc Sleeve and side seams tog.

OUTER EDGING

Rnd 1: Working in sts and in ends of rows around outer edge of Body, working in starting chs on opposite side of row 1 on Blocks across bottom edge, join purple with sc in first ch of Left Front, sc in same ch, sc in each ch across to last ch of last Block, 3 sc in last ch, sc in each row across to corner

before neck shaping, 3 sc in next row, evenly sp sts so piece lies flat, sc across neck to corner after neck shaping, 3 sc in next row, sc in each row across, sc in same st as first sc, join with sl st in first sc.

Rnd 2: Ch 1, 3 sc in first st, sc in each st around to center corner st before Right Front, 3 sc in corner st, sc in each of next 4 sts, for **buttonhole**, ch 2, sk next 2 sts, [sc in each of next 13 sts, for **buttonhole**, ch 2, sk next 2 sts] 5 times, sc in each st around with 3 sc in each center corner st, join. Fasten off. *(6 buttonholes)*

Sew buttons to Left Front Edging opposite buttonholes.

SLEEVE EDGING

Rnd 1: Working in starting ch on opposite side of row 1 on Sleeve, join purple with sc in first ch, sc in each ch around, join with sl st in beg sc.

Rnd 2: Ch 1, sc in each st around, join with sl st in beg sc. Fasten off.

Rep on other Sleeve. ■

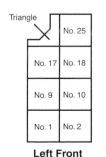

Left Front Assembly

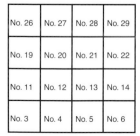

Back Assembly

Right Front Assembly

Kaleidoscope Colors

DESIGNS BY TAMMY HILDEBRAND

Savor the rainbow of color that makes scrap projects so appealing with this lovely jacket and scarf set. It coordinates with a multitude of wardrobe possibilities and works well for dressy or casual occasions.

SKILL LEVEL ■■■□ INTERMEDIATE

FINISHED SIZES
Jacket: Instructions given fit 32–34-inch bust *(small)*; 36–38-inch bust *(medium)*, 40–42-inch bust *(large)* and 44–46-inch bust *(X-large)* are in [ ].

Use specified hook size to achieve desired Jacket size.

Scarf: 4 inches wide x 56½ inches long

FINISHED GARMENT MEASUREMENTS
Bust: 31½ inches *(small)* [36 inches *(medium)*, 40½ inches *(large)*, 45 inches *(X-large)*]

MATERIALS
Jacket
Lion Brand Microspun light (DK) weight yarn (2½ oz/168 yds/70g per skein):
    2 [3, 4, 5] skeins #910-098 French vanilla *(MC)*
    5 yds desired color for each Motif *(CC)*
Sizes G/6/4mm [H/8/5mm, J/10/6mm and K/10½/6.5mm] crochet hooks or size needed to obtain gauge
Scarf
Lion Brand Microspun light (DK) weight yarn (2½ oz/168 yds/ 70g per skein):

1 skein #910-098 French vanilla *(MC)*
    5 yds desired color for each motif *(CC)*
Size G/6/4mm crochet hook or size needed to obtain gauge

GAUGE
Size G hook *(small)*: First Motif of Jacket = 3½ inches square

Size H hook *(medium)*: First Motif of Jacket = 4 inches square

Size J hook *(large)*: First Motif of Jacket = 4½ inches square

Size K hook *(X-large)*: First Motif of Jacket = 5 inches square

SPECIAL STITCHES
Open shell: ({Dc, ch 3} 3 times, dc) in indicated st or sp.

Joining open shell: (Dc, ch 3, dc, ch 1, remove lp from hook, insert hook in corresponding ch-3 sp of open shell on previous Motif, pick up dropped lp, pull through ch-3 sp, ch 1, dc, ch 3, dc) in indicated sp on working Motif.

Joining chain-5 space (joining ch-5 sp): Ch 2, remove lp from hook, insert hook in corresponding ch-5 sp on previous Motif, pick up dropped lp, draw through ch-5 sp, ch 2.

INSTRUCTIONS

SCARF
First Motif
Rnd 1 (RS): With CC, ch 4, sl st in first ch to form ring, ch 4 *(counts as first dc and ch-1)*, [dc in ring, ch 1] 11 times, join with sl st in 3rd ch of beg ch-4. *(12 dc, 12 ch-1 sps)*

Rnd 2: Sl st in first ch-1 sp, ch 1, (sc, ch 3, sc) in same ch sp and in each ch sp around, join with sl st in beg sc. Fasten off. *(12 ch-3 sps, 24 sc)*

Rnd 3: With RS facing, join MC with sc in any ch-3 sp, *ch 5, sc in next ch sp, **open shell** *(see Special Stitches)* in next ch sp**, sc in next ch sp, rep from * around, ending last rep at **, join with sl st in beg sc. Fasten off. *(4 ch-5 sps, 4 open shells)*

2nd Motif
Rnds 1 & 2: Rep rnds 1 and 2 of First Motif.

Rnd 3: With RS facing, join MC with sl st in any ch-3 sp, ch 1, sc in same ch sp, ch 5, sc in next

ch sp, **joining open shell** *(see Special Stitches)* in next ch sp, sc in next sp, **joining ch-5 sp** *(see Special Stitches)*, sc in next ch sp, joining open shell in next ch sp *(1 side joined)*, continue around as for rnd 3 of First Motif.

Remaining 14 Motifs
Rnds 1–3: Rep rnds 1–3 of 2nd Motif.

Border
With RS facing, join MC with sl st in center ch-5 sp at either narrow end of Scarf, ch 3 *(counts as first dc)*, 6 dc in same ch sp, *sc in next ch-3 sp, 3 sc in next ch sp, sc in next ch sp, 5 dc in next ch-5 sp, 5 sc in next ch-3 sp, [dc in joining st between working Motif and next Motif, 5 sc in first ch-3 sp on next Motif, 7 dc in next ch-5 sp, 5 sc in next ch-3 sp] across to last Motif, dc in joining st between next working Motif and last Motif, 5 sc in first ch-3 sp on last Motif, 5 dc in next ch-5 sp, sc in next ch-3 sp, 3 sc in next sp, sc in next ch-3 sp**, 7 dc in next ch-5 sp, rep from * around, ending last rep at **, join with sl st in 3rd ch of beg ch-3. Fasten off.

JACKET

Body
First Motif
Small Size Only
Rnd 1 (RS): With size G hook and CC, ch 4, sl st in first ch to form ring, ch 4 *(counts as first dc and ch-1)*, [dc in ring, ch 1] 11 times, join with sl st in 3rd ch of beg ch-4. *(12 dc, 12 ch-1 sps)*

Medium & Large Sizes Only
Rnd 1 (RS): With size H [J] hook

and CC, ch 4, sl st in first ch to form ring, ch 1, 12 sc in ring, join with sl st in beg sc. *(12 sc)*

Rnd 2: Ch 4 *(counts as first dc and ch-1)*, [dc in next sc, ch 1] around, join with sl st in 3rd ch of beg ch-4. *(12 dc, 12 ch-1 sps)*

X-Large Size Only
Rnd 1 (RS): With size K hook and CC, ch 4, sl st in first ch to form ring, ch 2 *(counts as first hdc)*, 11 hdc in ring, join with sl st in 2nd ch of beg ch-2. *(12 hdc)*

Rnd 2: Ch 4 *(counts as first dc and ch-1)*, [dc in next hdc, ch 1] around, join with sl st in 3rd ch of beg ch-4. *(12 dc, 12 ch-1 sps)*

All Sizes
Rnd 2 [3, 3, 3]: Rep rnd 2 of First Motif for Scarf.

Rnd 3 [4, 4, 4]: With RS facing, using size G [H, J, K] hook, rep rnd 3 of First Motif for Scarf.

2nd Motif
Rnds 1–2 [1–3, 1–3, 1–3]: Rep rnds 1–2 [1–3, 1–3, 1–3] of First Motif for Jacket.

Rnd 3 [4, 4, 4]: Rep rnd 3 of 2nd Motif for Scarf.

Remaining 52 Motifs
Rnds 1–3 [1–4, 1–4, 1–4]: Following Assembly Diagram, rep rnds 1–3 [1–4, 1–4, 1–4] of 2nd Motif, joining on as many sides as indicated on diagram.

Leave armhole openings as indicated on Assembly Diagram. When working 4 Motifs across top strip at shoulder edge, fold

2 Front pieces across Back and join Front to Back at shoulder edge on rnd 3 [4, 4, 4].

Body Edging

With RS facing, join MC with sl st in ch-5 sp at center of Back neck, ch 3, 6 dc in same ch sp, sc in next ch-3 sp, dc in joining between Motifs, sc in next ch-3 sp, 7 dc in next ch-5 sp, 5 sc in next ch-3 sp, *[dc in joining between Motifs, 5 sc in next ch-3 sp, 7 dc in next ch-5 sp, 5 sc in next ch-3 sp]* 4 times, **dc in joining between Motifs, 5 sc in next ch-3 sp, 5 dc in next ch-5 sp, sc in next ch-3 sp, 3 sc in next ch-3 sp, sc in next ch-3 sp, 5 dc in next ch-5 sp, 5 sc in next ch-3 sp**, work between * 7 times, work between ** once, work between * 4 times, dc in joining between Motifs, 5 sc in next ch-3 sp, 7 dc in next ch-5 sp, sc in next ch-3 sp, dc in joining between Motifs, sc in next ch-3 sp, join with sl st in 3rd ch of beg ch-3. Fasten off.

SLEEVE
Make 2.
First Motif
Rnds 1–3 [1–4, 1–4, 1–4]: Rep rnds 1–3 [1–4, 1–4, 1–4] of First Motif for Jacket Body.

2nd Motif
Rnds 1–3 [1–4, 1–4, 1–4]: Rep rnds 1–3 [1–4, 1– 4, 1–4] of 2nd Motif for Jacket Body.

Remaining 18 Motifs
Rnds 1-3 [4, 4, 4]: Following Assembly Diagram, rep rnds 1–3 [4, 4, 4] of 2nd Motif, joining as many sides as indicated and always joining last Motif on each strip to First Motif to form tube. Join each Motif on last strip at top of Sleeve to corresponding Motif at armhole opening of Jacket.

Sleeve Edging

With RS facing, join MC with sl st in joining between any 2 Motifs at bottom of either Sleeve, ch 3 *(counts as first dc)*, *5 sc in next ch-3 sp, 7 dc in next ch-5 sp, 5 sc in next ch-3 sp**, dc in joining between 2 Motifs, rep from * around, ending last rep at **, join with sl st in 3rd ch of beg ch-3. Fasten off.

Rep on rem Sleeve. ■

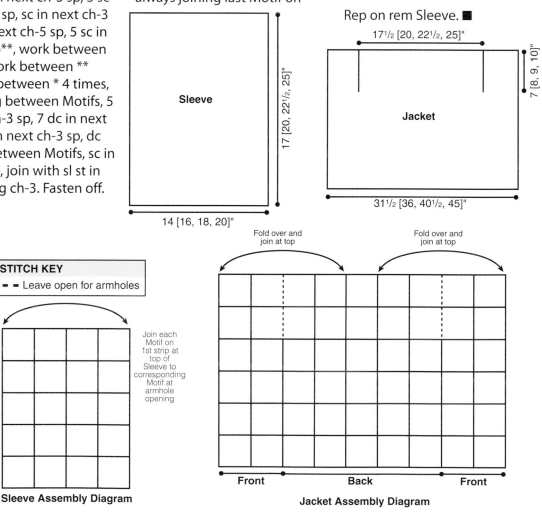

STITCH KEY
– – Leave open for armholes

Join last Motif on each strip to first Motif to form tube

Join each Motif on 1st strip at top of Sleeve to corresponding Motif at armhole opening

Sleeve Assembly Diagram

Fold over and join at top   Fold over and join at top

Front   Back   Front

Jacket Assembly Diagram

Sleeve
17 [20, 22½, 25]"
14 [16, 18, 20]"

17½ [20, 22½, 25]"
Jacket
7 [8, 9, 10]"
31½ [36, 40½, 45]"

Flower Garden Bolero

DESIGN BY SUE CHILDRESS

Have a spoonful of summer dished up in a vest of bright, lacy flowers on a bed of lime green. It's a wardrobe must that's light for the spring and summer months, and sized large enough to layer over turtlenecks for fall and winter.

SKILL LEVEL INTERMEDIATE

FINISHED SIZES
Instructions given fit size 30–32-inch bust *(small)*; changes for [34–36 inch bust *(medium)* and 38–49 inch bust *(large)* are in [ ].

FINISHED GARMENT MEASUREMENTS
Chest: 40 inches *(small)* [48 inches *(medium)*, 56 inches *(large)*]

Length: 24 inches *(small)* [28 inches *(medium)*, 32 inches *(large)*]

MATERIALS
Medium (worsted) weight yarn (2½ oz/121 yds/50g per skein):
    3 [4, 5] skeins MC
    1 [2, 2] skeins each of 6 assorted CCs

Size F/5/3./5mm crochet hook or size needed to obtain gauge
Sewing needle
Sewing thread
⅞-inch buttons: 4 [5, 5]

GAUGE
Motif = 3½ inches between opposite points

Take time to check gauge.

INSTRUCTIONS

MOTIF
Rnd 1 (RS): With any CC, ch 6, sl st in first ch to form ring, ch 1, 12 sc in ring, join with sl st in beg sc. *(12 sc)*

Rnd 2: Ch 1, sc in first sc, ch 6, [sk next sc, sc in next sc, ch 6] 5 times, sk last sc, join with sl st in beg sc. *(6 ch-6 sps)*

Rnd 3: Ch 1, sc in first st, 10 hdc in next ch-6 sp, [sc in next sc, 10 hdc in next ch-6 sp] 5 times, join with sl st in beg sc. Fasten off.

Make a total of 56 [80, 106] Motifs in desired CCs.

JOINING MOTIFS IN ROWS

Motif Row 1: With RS facing, using joining diagram as guide, join MC with sl st between 5th and 6th hdc on any petal of any Motif, working across top half of Motif, ch 1, 2 sc in same sp, *[ch 5, 2 sc in next sc on same Motif, ch 5, 2 sc between 5th and 6th hdc on next petal of same Motif] 3 times**, with RS facing, working across top half of next Motif, 2 sc between 5th and 6th hdc of any petal on next Motif, rep from * across until last Motif for size being worked has been joined, ending last rep at **, working across opposite half of each Motif on row, [ch 5, 2 sc in next sc on same Motif, ch 5, 2 sc between 5th and 6th hdc on next petal of same Motif] twice, ch 5, 2 sc in next sc on same Motif, ◊ch 5, 2 sc in joined sts between Motifs, ch 5, 2 sc in next sc on next Motif, [ch 5, 2 sc between 5th and 6th hdc on same Motif, ch 5, 2 sc in next sc on same Motif] twice, rep from ◊ across, ch 5, join with sl st in beg sc. Fasten off.

Motif Rows 2–6 [2–7, 2–8]: Rep Motif row 1, joining as many Motifs as is indicated on joining diagram for desired size.

Rows 5 & 6 [5 & 7, 6 & 8] will each have 3 separate sections to divide for right front, back and left front.

JOINING ROWS

Rows 1 & 2: With RS facing, beg at right-hand edge, join MC with sl st in ch-5 sp on first Motif of row 2 at point A indicated on Diagram A, ch 1, 2 sc in same ch

sp, ch 2, 2 sc in next ch-5 sp on first Motif of row 1 at point B indicated on Diagram A, continue across, following Diagram A, until all Motifs on row 2 have been joined to row 1. Fasten off.

Continuing in established pattern, join rem rows.

Shoulder Seams

Matching points indicated on joining diagram, join shoulder seams in established pattern for Joining Rows.

Vest Edging

With RS facing, join MC with sl st in any ch-5 sp at center back neck opening, ch 1, beg in same ch sp, 6 sc in same ch and in each ch-5 sp around with 2 sc in each ch-2 sp around entire outer edge of Vest, join with sl st in beg sc. Fasten off.

Armhole Edging

With RS facing, join MC with sl st in any ch-5 sp on either armhole, ch 1, beg in same ch sp, 6 sc in the same ch and in each ch-5 sp around with 2 sc in each ch-2 sp around, join with sl st in beg sc. Fasten off.

Rep on rem armhole.

Buttonhole Band

With RS facing, join MC with sl st in 3rd sc of 6-sc group over ch-5 sp at bottom of right front opening at point indicated on Diagram A, ch 1, sc in same st and in each of next 8 sc, [ch 5, sk next sc, sc in each of next 25 sc] 3 [4, 4] times, ch 5, sk next sc, sc in each of

next 12 sc, sl st in next st. Fasten off.

Finishing

Sew buttons on left front opening opposite buttonholes.

Using joining diagram as guide, fold 1 Motif at top corner of each front opening in half to WS, tack in place with sewing thread. ■

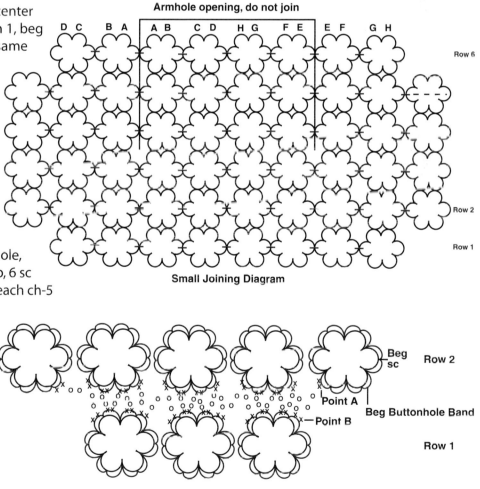

JOINING KEY
Folded motif (see Finishing instructions)
— Joining A–H (H) (L)
(see Shoulder Seam instructions)

Armhole opening, do not join

D C   B A   A B   C D   H G   F E   E F   G H

Row 6

Row 2

Row 1

Small Joining Diagram

Beg sc   Row 2

Point A
Beg Buttonhole Band
Point B

Row 1

Diagram A

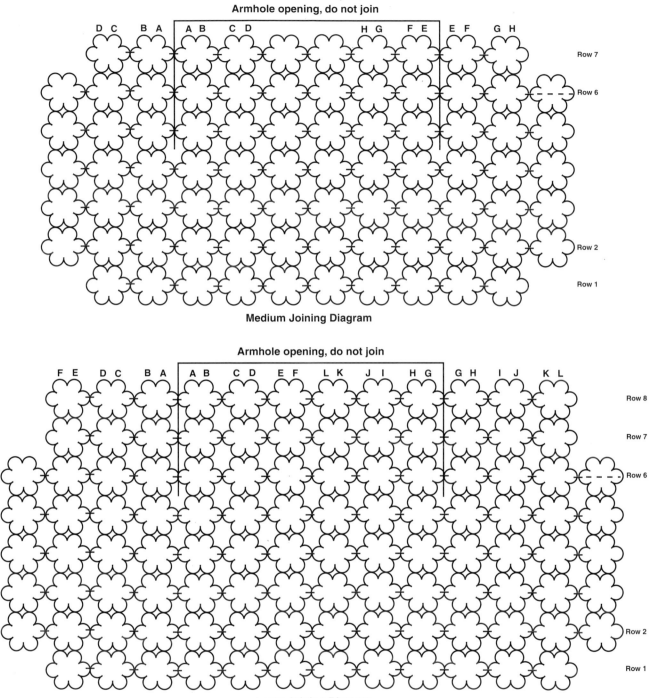

Armhole opening, do not join

D C   B A   A B   C D   H G   F E   E F   G H

Medium Joining Diagram

Armhole opening, do not join

F E   D C   B A   A B   C D   E F   L K   J I   H G   G H   I J   K L

Large Joining Diagram

Simple Stripes

DESIGN BY JENNINE KOREJKO

This comfy style is simply two rectangles that are crocheted together into one great accent. It uses only a few ounces of each color, making it a fantastic scrap solution that works up in a flash.

SKILL LEVEL ▰▰▱▱
EASY

FINISHED SIZE
One size fits most

MATERIALS
Medium (worsted) weight yarn:
    3 oz/150 yds/90g off white
    2 oz/100 yds/57g light yellow
    1 oz/50 yds/28g assorted scrap colors
Size J/10/6mm crochet hook or size needed to obtain gauge
Tapestry needle

GAUGE
7 sts = 2 inches

INSTRUCTIONS

PONCHO
Side
Make 2.
Row 1 (RS): With any scrap color, loosely ch 81, dc in 4th ch from hook (*first 3 chs count as first dc*) and in each ch across, turn. (*79 dc*)

Row 2: Ch 1, sc in first dc, [ch 2, sk next dc, sc in next dc] across, turn. Fasten off.

Row 3: With RS facing, join next scrap color with sl st in first sc, ch 3 (*counts as first dc*), dc in next ch-2 sp, 2 dc in each ch-2 sp across, dc in last sc, turn. (*79 dc*)

Row 4: Ch 1, sc in first dc, [ch 2, sk next dc, sc in next dc] across. Fasten off.

Rows 5 & 6: Rep rows 3 and 4.

Row 7: Rep row 3. At end of row, fasten off.

Row 8: With WS facing, join off white with sc in first dc, [dc in next dc, sc in next dc] across, turn.

Row 9: Ch 1, sc in first sc, [ch 1, sk next dc, sc in next sc] across, turn. Fasten off.

Row 10: With WS facing, join light yellow with sc in first sc, [ch 2, hdc in 2nd ch from hook, sc in next sc] across, turn. Fasten off.

Row 11: With RS facing, join off white with sc in first sc, [ch 1, sc in next sc] across, turn.

Row 12: Ch 1, sc in first sc, [dc in next ch-1 sp, sc in next sc] across, turn. Fasten off.

Row 13: With RS facing, join scrap color with sl st in first sc, ch 3, dc in same sc, dc in each ch-1 sp and in each sc, across, turn. *(79 dc)*

Row 14: Ch 1, sc in first dc, [ch 2, sk next dc, sc in next dc] across, turn. Fasten off.

Row 15: With RS facing, join next scrap color with sl st in first sc, ch 3, dc in next ch-2 sp, 2 dc in each ch-2 sp across, ending with dc in last sc, turn. *(79 dc)*

Rows 16 & 17: Rep rows 14 and 15. At end of last row, fasten off.

Row 18: With WS facing, join light yellow with sc in first dc,

[ch 2, sk next dc, sc in next dc] across, turn. Fasten off.

Row 19: With RS facing, join off white with sl st in first sc, ch 3, dc in next ch-2 sp, 2 dc in each ch-2 sp across, ending with dc in last sc, turn. Fasten off.

Row 20: Rep row 18.

Row 21: With RS facing, join scrap color with sl st in first sc, ch 3, dc in next ch-2 sp, 2 dc in each ch-2 sp across, ending with dc in last sc, turn.

Row 22: Ch 1, sc in first dc, [ch 2, sk next dc, sc in next dc] across, turn. Fasten off.

Rows 23–29: Rep rows 3–9.

Assembly

Hold Sides tog with WS facing, last row of bottom piece at top and last row of top piece to right. Carefully match ends of rows of top piece to ch-2 sps on bottom piece. Join off white with sl st in end of row 29 of top piece and in first sc of row 29 of bottom piece, ch 2, sl st in same row on top piece and in first ch-1 sp on bottom piece, working through rows on top piece and corresponding ch-1 sps on bottom piece at same time, ch 2, sl st in next row, [ch 2, sk next row, sl st in next row] twice, ch 2, sl st in next row, ch 2, sk next row, sl st in next row, [ch 2, sl st in next row] twice,

[ch 2, sk next row, sl st in next row] 3 times, [ch 2, sl st in next row] 3 times, [ch 2, sk next row, sl st in next row] 3 times, ch 2, sl st in next row, ch 2, sk next row, sl st in next row. Fasten off.

Rep to join opposites edges of Sides.

Neck Edging

Hold Poncho with RS facing, with light yellow make slip knot on hook and join with sc in ch-1 sp to right of joining, ch 2, sc in 2nd ch from hook, [sl st in next ch-1 sp, ch 2, sc in 2nd ch from hook] 18 times, sl st in next ch-1 sp, [sl st in next ch-1 sp, ch 2, sc in 2nd ch from hook] around to last ch-1 sp, sl st in last ch-1 sp, join with sl st in beg sl st. Fasten off.

Bottom Edging

Rnd 1 (RS): Hold Poncho with RS facing, join off white with sc in 1 seam joining, working in starting ch on opposite side of row 1 on next piece, *[ch 1, sk next ch, sc in next ch] across to last 2 chs, ch 1, sk next ch, (sc, ch 1, sc) in last ch (corner)*, working in end of rows, ch 1, sc in first row, [ch 1, sc in next row] 3 times, ch 1, sk next row, sc in next row, [ch 1, sc in next row] twice, [ch 1, sk next row, sc in next row] 3 times, ch 1, sc in next row, ch 1, sk next row, sc in next row, [ch 1, sc in next row] twice, [ch 1, sk next row, sc in next row] twice, [ch 1, sc in next row] 3 times, ch 1, sk next row,

sc in next row, ch 1, sc in next row, ch 1, sc in next joining, ch 1, working in starting ch on opposite side of row 1, sc in first ch, rep between *, working in end of rows, ch 1, sc in first row, [ch 1, sc in next row] 3 times, ch 1, sk next row, sc in next row, [ch 1, sc in next row] twice, [ch 1, sk next row, sc in next row] 3 times, ch 1, sc in next row, ch 1, sk next row, sc in next row, [ch 1, sc in next row] twice, [ch 1, sk next row, sc in next row] twice, [ch 1, sc in next row] 3 times, ch 1, sk next row, sc in next row, ch 1, sc in next row, ch 1, join with sl st in beg sc.

Rnd 2: Sl st in next ch-1 sp, sc in same ch sp, ch 2, *(sc, ch 2) in each ch-1 sp across** to corner ch sp, (sc, ch 2, sc) in corner ch sp, rep from * around, ending last rep at **, join with sl st in beg sc.

Rnd 3: Sl st in next ch-2 sp, ch 4 (counts as a dc and ch-1), *(dc, ch 1) in each ch-2 sp across** to corner ch sp, (dc, ch 1, dc) in corner ch sp, rep from * around, ending last rep at **, join with sl st in 3rd ch of beg ch-4. Fasten off.

Rnd 4: With WS facing, join light yellow with sl st in any ch-1 sp, ch 2, sc in 2nd ch from hook, *sl st in next ch-1 sp, ch 2, sc in 2nd ch from hook, rep from * around, join with sl st in joining sl st. Fasten off. ∎

Cherished Children

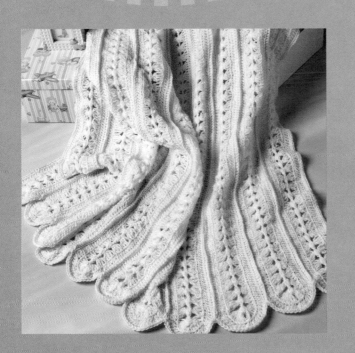

Chapter Contents

Choo-Choo Train Afghan

DESIGN BY BEVERLY MEWHORTER

Boys and girls alike will love this playful, kid-sized afghan, and crocheters will love the beginner skill level. Brightly colored train cars chugging across the lower edge make great "vehicles" for playing pretend or for learning about colors.

SKILL LEVEL ■□□□
BEGINNER

FINISHED SIZE
39 x 66 inches

MATERIALS

Medium (worsted) weight yarn:
    40 oz/2,000 yds/1,134g white
    2 oz/100 yds/57g each red, green, yellow, royal blue, orange and black
Sizes J/10/6mm and N/15/10mm crochet hooks or size needed to obtain gauge
Tapestry needle

GAUGE
2 strands of yarn held tog and size N hook: 2 dc = 1 inch

INSTRUCTIONS

AFGHAN
Row 1: With size N hook and 2 strands of white held tog, ch 106, sc in 2nd ch from hook and in each ch across, turn. *(105 sc)*

Rows 2–43: Ch 3 *(counts as first dc)*, dc in each st across, turn.

Row 44: Ch 1, sc in each st across, turn.

Row 45: Sl st in each st across. Fasten off.

Fringe
Cut 6 strands of white each 12 inches long. Fold strands in half, pull fold through st, pull ends through fold, pull to tighten.

Rep Fringe in end of each row on each short side of Afghan.

CABOOSE
Make 2.
Row 1: With size J hook and red, ch 23, sc in 2nd ch from hook and in each ch across, turn. *(22 sc)*

Rows 2–18: Ch 1, sc in each sc across, turn. At the end of last row, fasten off.

CAR
Make 2 each yellow, green and royal blue.
Row 1: With size J hook, ch 23, sc in 2nd ch from hook, sc in each ch across, turn. *(22 sc)*

Rows 2–12: Ch 1, sc in each sc across, turn. At the end of last row, fasten off.

ENGINE
Make 2.
Row 1: With size J hook and orange, ch 23, sc in 2nd ch from hook and in each ch across, turn. *(22 sc)*

Rows 2–12: Ch 1, sc in each sc across, turn.

Row 13: Ch 1, sc in each of next 12 sc, leaving rem sts unworked, turn. *(12 sc)*

Rows 14–20: Ch 1, sc in each sc across, turn. At the end of last row, fasten off.

Smoke Stack
Row 1: With size J hook, sk next

4 sts of row 12 of Engine, join green with sc in next st, sc in each of next 2 sts, turn. *(3 sc)*

Rows 2 & 3: Ch 1, sc in each sc across, turn.

Row 4: Ch 3, dc in same st, 2 dc in each st across, turn. *(6 dc)*

Row 5: Ch 1, 2 sc in first st, sc in each of next 4 sts, 2 sc in last st. Fasten off. *(8 sc)*

Wheel
Make 20.
With size J hook and black, ch 4, 13 dc in 4th ch from hook *(first 3 chs count as first dc)*, join with sl st in 4th of beg ch-4. Fasten off. *(14 dc)*

Wheel Bar
Make 10.
With size J hook and black, ch 15. Fasten off.

Window
Make 6.
Row 1: With size J hook and white, ch 7, sc in 2nd ch from hook, sc in

each ch across, turn. *(6 sc)*

Rows 2–4: Ch 1, sc in each sc across, turn.

Row 5: Sl st in each st across. Fasten off.

Assembly
1. Sew 1 Window to each Engine and 2 to each Caboose as shown in photo.

2. Arrange and sew 3 Cars centered 3 inches from bottom edge of Afghan, sew the Caboose and Engine curving upward from Cars toward each side as shown in photo.

3. Sew 2 Wheels to each Car, Engine and Caboose, sew Wheel Bars to Wheels.

Sew rem train on opposite end of Afghan in same manner. ■

Creature Comforts

DESIGNS BY KATHLEEN STUART

These adorable creatures, which are cleverly disguised hot water bottle covers, are ready to give quick, soothing comfort to a child. They work up easily in no time and also make cute pajama bags!

Lamb

SKILL LEVEL ◼◼◻◻
EASY

FINISHED SIZE
15 x 16 inches

MATERIALS
Lion Brand Jiffy bulky
(chunky) weight yarn (3
oz/135 yds/85g per skein):
2 skeins #099 fisherman
Medium (worsted)
weight yarn:
1 oz/50 yds/28g black
1 yd each light blue and
pale pink
Size J/10/6mm crochet hook or
size needed to obtain gauge
Tapestry needle
Sewing needle
Sewing thread

6 x 12-inch 2-quart rectangular hot water bottle

½-inch snap fastener

Stitch markers

GAUGE
3 sc = 1 inch

PATTERN NOTES
Do not join rounds unless otherwise stated.

Use a stitch marker to mark beginning of rounds.

INSTRUCTIONS

LAMB
Head
Rnd 1: With black, ch 2, 6 sc in 2nd ch from hook. *(6 sc)*

Rnd 2: [Sc in next st, 2 sc in next st] around. *(9 sc)*

Rnd 3: [Sc in each of next 2 sts, 2 sc in next st] around. *(12 sc)*

Rnd 4: Rep rnd 2. *(18 sc)*

Rnd 5: Rep rnd 3. *(24 sc)*

Rnd 6: [Sc in each of next 3 sts, 2 sc in next st] around. *(30 sc)*

Rnds 7 & 8: Sc in each st around. At the end of last rnd, pull up lp of fisherman, fasten off black.

Rnd 9: *[Sc in next st, tr in next st] twice, (sc, tr) in next st, rep from * around. *(36 sts)*

Rnd 10: [Tr in next st, sc in next st] around.

Rnd 11: [Sc in next st, tr in next st] around.

Rnd 12: Rep rnd 10.

Rnd 13: [Sc in next st, tr in next st, sc in next st, tr in next st, **sc dec** *(see Stitch Guide)* in next 2 sts] around. *(30 sts)*

Rnd 14: [Tr in next st, sc in next st, sc dec in next 2 sts] around. *(24 sts)*

Body
Rnd 15: Pull up lp, remove hook, using length of yarn from opposite end of skein, join fisherman with sl st in 13th st of rnd 14, ch 5, **fasten off**, pick up dropped lp, ch 6, sc in 2nd ch from hook, sc in each of next 4 chs, sc in each of next 12 sts on rnd 14, sc in next 4 chs, 3 sc in last ch, working on opposite side of ch, sc in each of next 4 chs, sc in same st as sl st on rnd 14, sc in each of next 11 sts on rnd 14, sc in each of next 4 chs, 2 sc in same ch as beg sc, **do not join**. *(46 sts)*

Rnd 16: [Sc in next st, tr in next st] around.

Rnd 17: [Tr in next st, sc in next st] around.

Rnds 18–37: Rep rnds 16 and 17 alternately.

Rnd 38: Working in **back lps** *(see Stitch Guide)* only, [sc in next st, tr in next st] around.

Rnd 39: [Tr in next st, sc in next st] around, join with sl st in beg tr. Fasten off.

Flap
Rnd 1: Working in unworked lps of rnd 37, join fisherman with sl st in 24th st, ch 24, join with sc in first st on rnd 37, tr in next st, [sc in next st, tr in next st] 10 times, working across ch, [sc in next ch, tr in next ch] 12 times. *(46 sts)*

Rnd 2: [Tr in next st, sc in next st] around.

Rnd 3: [Sc in next st, tr in next st] around.

Rnds 4 & 5: Rep rnds 2 and 3.

Rnd 6: Rep rnd 2.

Row 7: Now working in rows, flatten piece across, working through both thicknesses in top lps only, sl st in each st across. Fasten off.

With sewing needle and thread, sew snap fastener at center of Flap and Body opening.

Ear
Make 2.
Rnd 1: With fisherman, ch 2, 6 sc in 2nd ch from hook. *(6 sc)*

Rnd 2: 2 sc in each of next 3 sts, **change colors** *(see Stitch Guide)* to black in last st, 2 sc in each of next 3 sts, change to fisherman in last st. *(12 sc)*

Rnds 3–6: Sc in each of next 6 sts, change to black in last st, sc in each of next 6 sts, change to fisherman in last st. At the end of last rnd, leaving long end, fasten off.

With black section facing forward, flatten Ears and sew Ears to sides of Head between rnds 11 and 12.

Leg
Make 4.

Rnd 1: With black, ch 2, 6 sc in 2nd ch from hook. *(6 sc)*

Rnd 2: 2 sc in each sc around. *(12 sc)*

Rnd 3: [Sc in next sc, 2 sc in next sc] around. *(18 sc)*

Rnds 4–6: Sc in each sc around. At the end of last rnd, change to fisherman in last st. Fasten off black.

Rnd 7: [Sc in next st, tr in next st] around.

Rnd 8: [Tr in next st, sc in next st] around.

Rnds 9 & 10: Rep rnds 7 and 8.

Rnd 11: Rep rnd 7.

Rnd 12: [Tr in next st, sc dec in next 2 sts] around. Leaving long end, fasten off. *(12 sts)*

Flatten last rnd, sew Legs to Body as shown in photo.

Facial Features
With pale pink yarn, embroider nose using satin stitch *(see Fig. 1)* over upper side of rnds 1 and 2 as shown in photo, and embroider mouth with straight stitches *(see Fig. 2)* centered below nose.

**Satin Stitch
Fig. 1**

**Straight Stitch
Fig. 2**

With light blue, embroider eyes evenly spaced and centered above nose with satin stitch.

Bear

SKILL LEVEL ◼◼◻◻
EASY

FINISHED SIZE
13 x 13¼ inches

MATERIALS
Lion Brand Homespun bulky (chunky) weight yarn (6 oz/
185 yds/170g per skein):
1 skein #318 sierra
10 yds #309 deco
Medium (worsted) weight yarn :
1 yd black
Size J/10/6mm crochet hook or size needed to obtain gauge
Tapestry needle
Sewing needle
Sewing thread
5 x 8½-inch 1-quart hot water bottle
½-inch snap fastener
Stitch markers

GAUGE
3 sc = 1 inch

PATTERN NOTES
Do not join rounds unless otherwise stated.

Use a stitch marker to mark beginning of rounds.

INSTRUCTIONS

BEAR
Head
Rnd 1: Starting at snout with deco, ch 2, 6 sc in 2nd ch from hook. *(6 sc)*

Rnd 2: 2 sc in each st around. *(12 sc)*

Rnd 3: [Sc in next st, 2 sc in next st] around. *(18 sc)*

Rnd 4: Sc in each st around.

Rnd 5: Rep rnd 4, change color *(see Stitch Guide)* to sierra in last st.

Rnd 6: Working in back lps *(see Stitch Guide)* only, [sc in each of next 2 sts, 2 sc in next st] around. *(24 sc)*

Rnd 7: [Sc in each of next 3 sts, 2 sc in next st] around. *(30 sc)*

Rnds 8–11: Rep rnd 4.

Rnd 12: [Sc in each of next 2 sts, **sc dec** *(see Stitch Guide)* in next 2 sts] around. *(24 sc)*

Rnd 13: [Sc in each of next 2 sts, sc dec in next 2 sts] around. *(18 sc)*

Body
Rnd 14: Pull up lp, remove hook, working with length of yarn from opposite end of skein, join sierra with sl st in 10th st, ch 4, **fasten off**, pick up dropped lp, ch 5, sc in 2nd ch from hook, sc in each of next 3 chs, sc in each of next 9 sts on rnd 13, sc in each of next 3 chs, 3 sc in last ch, working on opposite side of ch, sc in each of next 3 chs, sc in same st as sl st on rnd 13, sc in each of next 8 sts on rnd 13, sc in each of next 3 chs, 2 sc in same ch as beg sc. *(36 sc)*

Rnds 15–34: Rep rnd 4.

Rnd 35: Working in back lps only, sc in each st around.

Rnd 36: Sc in each st around, join with sl st in next st. Fasten off.

Flap
Rnd 1: Working in unworked lps of rnd 34, join sierra with sl st in 18th st of rnd 34, ch 18, join with sc in first st of rnd 34, sc in each of next 18 sts, sc in each of next 18 chs. *(36 sc)*

Rnds 2–6: Sc in each st around.

Row 7: Now working in rows, flatten sides, working in top lps only through both thicknesses, sl st in each st across. Fasten off.

With sewing needle and thread, sew snap fastener at center of Flap and Body opening.

Ear
Make 2.
Rnd 1: With sierra, ch 2, 5 sc in 2nd ch from hook. *(5 sc)*

Rnd 2: 2 sc in each st around. *(10 sc)*

Rnd 3: [Sc in next st, 2 sc in next st] around. *(15 sc)*

Rnd 4: Sc in each st around.

Rnd 5: Rep rnd 4, join with sl st in beg st. Leaving long end, fasten off.

Flatten Ears and sew Ears to sides of Head between rnds 11 and 12.

Leg
Make 4.
Rnd 1: With sierra, ch 2, 5 sc in 2nd ch from hook. *(5 sc)*

Rnd 2: 2 sc in each st around. *(10 sc)*

Rnd 3: [Sc in next st, 2 sc in next st] around. *(15 sc)*

Rnds 4–12: Sc in each sc around.

Rnd 13: [Sc in next st, sc dec in next 2 sts] around, join with sl st in beg st. Leaving long end, fasten off. *(10 sc)*

Flatten rnd 13 of Leg and sew each Leg to Body as shown in photo.

Facial Features
With black, embroider nose and mouth in satin stitch *(see Fig. 1 on page 75)* over rnds 1 and 2 of snout as shown in photo. With black, embroider eyes on rnd 6 of Head centered above nose.

Turtle

SKILL LEVEL ▰▰▱▱
EASY

FINISHED SIZE
10 x 11½ inches

MATERIALS
Lion Brand Homespun bulky (chunky) weight yarn (6 oz/ 185 yds/170g per skein):
  1 skein #369 Florida Keys green
Lion Brand Boucle super bulky (super chunky) weight yarn (2½ oz/57 yds/70g per skein):
  1 skein #202 lime blue
Size J/10/6mm crochet hook or size needed to obtain gauge
Tapestry needle
Sewing needle
Sewing thread
½-inch snap fastener
6½ x 8½-inch round hot water bottle
Stitch markers

GAUGE
3 sc = 1 inch

PATTERN NOTES
Do not join rounds unless otherwise stated.

Use a stitch marker to mark beginning of rounds.

INSTRUCTIONS

TURTLE
Head
Rnd 1: With Florida Keys green, ch 2, 6 sc in 2nd ch from hook. *(6 sc)*

Rnd 2: 2 sc in each sc around. *(12 sc)*

Rnd 3: [Sc in next st, 2 sc in next st] around. *(18 sc)*

Rnd 4: [Sc in each of next 2 sts, 2 sc in next st] around. *(24 sc)*

Rnd 5: Sc in each sc around.

Rnds 6–9: Rep rnd 5.

Rnd 10: [Sc in each of next 2 sts, **sc dec** *(see Stitch Guide)* in next 2 sts] around. *(18 sc)*

Rnd 11: [Sc in next st, sc dec in next 2 sts] around. *(12 sc)*

Body
Rnd 12: Rep rnd 2. *(24 sc)*

Rnd 13: [Sc in each of next 3 sts, 2 sc in next st] around. *(30 sts)*

Rnd 14: [Sc in each of next 4 sts, 2 sc in next st] around. *(36 sts)*

Rnds 15 & 16: Rep rnd 5.

Rnd 17: Sc in each of first 8 sts, 2 sc in each of next 2 sts, sc in each of next 16 sts, 2 sc in each of next 2 sts, sc in each of last 8 sts. *(40 sc)*

Rnds 18–24: Sc in each st around.

Rnd 25: Sc in each of first 8 sts, [sc dec in next 2 sts] twice, sc in each of next 16 sts, [sc dec in next 2 sts] twice, sc in each of last 8 sts. *(36 sc)*

Rnd 26: [Sc in each of next 4 sts, sc dec in next 2 sts] around. *(30 sts)*

Rnd 27: Working in **back lps** *(see Stitch Guide)* only, [sc in each of next 3 sts, sc dec in next 2 sts] around. *(24 sc)*

Rnd 28: [Sc in each of next 2 sts, sc dec in next 2 sc] around. *(18 sc)*

Rnd 29: Sc in each st around, join with sl st in beg sc. Fasten off.

Flap
Rnd 1: Working in unworked lps of rnd 26, join Florida Keys green with sl st in 26th st on rnd 26, ch 15, join with sc in 10th st on rnd 26, sc in each of next 15 sts, working in chs, sc in each of next 15 chs. *(30 sc)*

Rnd 2: [Sc in each of next 3 sts, sc dec in next 2 sts] around. *(24 sts)*

Rnd 3: [Sc in each of next 2 sts, sc dec in next 2 sts] around. *(18 sts)*

Rnd 4: [Sc in next st, sc dec in next 2 sts] around. *(12 sc)*

Row 5: Now working in rows, flatten side, working in top lps, sl st in each st across. Fasten off.

With sewing needle and thread, sew snap fastener to center of Flap and Body opening.

Leg
Make 4.
Rnd 1: With Florida Keys green, ch 2, 6 sc in 2nd ch from hook. *(6 sc)*

Rnd 2: 2 sc in each st around. *(12 sc)*

Rnd 3: Sc in each st around.

Rnd 4: Rep rnd 3.

Rnd 5: [Sc dec in next 2 sts] 6 times. *(6 sc)*

Rnds 6 & 7: Rep rnd 3. At the end of last rnd, leaving long end, fasten off.

Flatten rnd 7 of each Leg and sew Legs to Body as shown in photo.

Tail
Rnd 1: With Florida Keys green, ch 2, 6 sc in 2nd ch from hook. *(6 sc)*

Rnd 2: [Sc in next st, 2 sc in next st] around. *(9 sc)*

Rnds 3 & 4: Sc in each st around. At the end of last rnd, leaving long end, fasten off.

Flatten rnd 4 and sew Tail to back end of Turtle.

Pentagon Shell Motif
Make 6.
With lime blue, ch 4, sl st in first ch to form ring, ch 3 *(counts as first dc)*, 2 dc in ring, [ch 2, 3 dc in ring] 4 times, ch 2, join with sl st in 3rd ch of beg ch-3. Fasten off. *(15 dc, 5 ch-2 sps)*

To form shell, crochet Pentagon Shell Motifs tog by placing 2 Motifs WS tog and working through both thicknesses, sc in top lps of Motifs. Crochet Motifs tog with 1 Motif at center and 5 around outer edge of the single center Motif. Shell will not lie flat. Sew shell to center top of Body.

Facial Features
With black yarn, embroider eyes in satin stitch *(see Fig. 1 on page 75)* st eyes between rnds 3 and 4 of Head as shown in photo. ■

Helicopter Booties

DESIGN BY LEANN WALTERS

Fly through this unique and completely adorable design to warm the toes of a special little one in your life. Stitch them for the child of a pilot or for a future flier, either way they're sure to delight anyone who sees them!

SKILL LEVEL ■■■□
INTERMEDIATE

FINISHED SIZES
4 inches *(small)* [4½ inches *(large)*], excluding tail

MATERIALS
Medium (worsted) weight yarn:
   1 oz/50 yds/28g each white and blue
Embroidery floss:
   Small amount each blue and maroon
Size F/5/3.75mm or G/6/4mm crochet hooks or size needed to obtain gauge
Tapestry needle

GAUGE
Size F hook *(small)*: 5 sc = 1 inch; 6 sc rnds = 1 inch

Size G hook *(large)*: 4 sc = 1 inch; 5 sc rnds = 1 inch

PATTERN NOTE
Use worsted yarn unless otherwise stated.

INSTRUCTIONS

BOOTIE
Body
Make 2.
Rnd 1: With white, ch 2, 6 sc in 2nd ch from hook, join with sl st in beg sc. *(6 sc)*

Rnd 2: Ch 1, 2 sc in each sc around, join with sl st in beg sc. *(12 sc)*

Rnd 3: Ch 1, sc in first st, 2 sc in next st, [sc in next sc, 2 sc in next sc] around, join with sl st in beg sc. *(18 sc)*

Rnd 4: Ch 1, sc in each of first 3 sts, 2 sc in next st, [sc in each of next 3 sc, 2 sc in next sc] 3 times, sc in each of last 2 sc, join with sl st in beg sc. *(22 sc)*

Rnd 5: Ch 1, sc in each sc around, join with sl st in beg sc.

Rnd 6: Ch 1, sc in each of first 3 sts, 2 sc in next st, [sc in each of next 3 sc, 2 sc in next sc] 4 times, sc in next sc, 2 sc in

last sc, join with sl st in beg sc. Fasten off *(28 sc)*

Rnd 7: Join blue with sc in first sc, ch 1, sk next sc, [sc in next sc, ch 1, sk next sc] around, join with sl st in beg sc. *(14 ch-1 sps)*

Rnd 8: Sl st in next ch-1 sp, ch 1, sc in same ch sp, ch 1, sc in next ch sp, **fpdc** *(see Stitch Guide)* around next sc, [sc in next ch-1 sp, ch 1] 9 times, sc in next ch-1 sp, fpdc around next sc, [sc in next ch-1 sp, ch 1] twice, join with sl st in beg sc.

Rnd 9: Sl st in next ch-1 sp, ch 1, sc in same ch sp, ch 1, fpdc around next dc, [ch 1, sc in next ch-1 sp] around to next dc, ch 1, fpdc around next dc, [ch 1, sc in next ch-1 sp] twice, ch 1, join with sl st in beg sc.

Rnd 10: Sl st in next ch-1 sp, ch 1, sc in same ch sp, fpdc around next dc, [sc in next ch sp, ch 1] 9 times, sc in next ch sp, fpdc around next dc, [sc in next ch sp, ch 1] 3 times, join with sl st in beg sc. Fasten off.

Note: *There are 9 ch-1 sps across top between the landing props (formed by dc sts).*

Row 11: Now working in rows, join blue with sc in 5th ch-1 sp of 9 ch-1 sps, [ch 1, sc in next ch-1 sp] 4 times, ch 1, fpdc around next dc, [ch 1, sc in next ch-1 sp] 3 times, ch 1, fpdc around next dc, [ch 1, sc in next ch-1 sp] 4 times, ch 1, sc in same ch-1 sp as beg sc, turn.

Row 12: Ch 2, sc in first ch-1 sp, [ch 1, sc in next ch-1 sp] 4 times, **bpdc** *(see Stitch Guide)* around next dc, [sc in next ch-1 sp, ch 1] 3 times, sc in next ch-1 sp, bpdc around next dc, [sc in next ch-1 sp, ch 1] 4 times, sc in next ch-2 sp, turn.

Row 13: Ch 2, [sc in next ch-1 sp, ch 1] 4 times, fpdc around next dc, [ch 1, sc in next ch-1 sp] 3 times, ch 1, fpdc around next dc, [ch 1, sc in next ch-1 sp] 4 times, ch 1, sc in next ch-2 sp, turn.

Rows 14–17: Rep rows 12 and 13 alternately.

Rows 18–20: Ch 2, [sc in next ch-1 sp, ch 1] across, sc in ch-2 sp, turn.

Row 21: Ch 2, [sc in next ch-1 sp, ch 1] 3 times, [insert hook in next ch-1 sp, yo, pull up lp] 7 times, yo, pull through all 8 lps on hook, [ch 1, sc in next ch-1 sp] 3 times, ch 1, sc in next ch-2 sp, turn.

Row 22: Ch 2, [sc in next ch-1 sp, ch 1] 7 times, sc in last ch-2 sp, turn.

Row 23: Ch 1, [insert hook in next ch-1 sp, yo, pull up lp] 7 times, insert hook in last ch-2 sp, yo, pull up lp, yo, pull through all 9 lps on hook, ch 1. Leaving long end, fasten off.

Sew tail seam to row 18.

Helicopter Blade
First Blade
Rnd 1: Beg at top of Bootie, join white with sc at back left of Bootie just left of seam, evenly sp [ch 2, sc] 12 times around top, join with sl st in beg sc. *(12 ch-2 sps)*

Row 2: Ch 3 *(counts as first dc)*, 2 dc in first ch-2 sp, 3 dc in each of next 2 ch-2 sps, leaving rem ch sps unworked, turn. *(9 dc)*

Row 3: Ch 3, dc in each of next 8 dc. Fasten off.

Next Blade
Row 1: Join white with sl st in next unworked ch-2 sp of rnd 1 of First Blade, ch 3, 2 dc in same ch-2 sp, 3 dc in each of next 2 ch-2 sps, turn. *(9 dc)*

Row 2: Rep row 3 of First Blade.

Remaining Blades
Make 2.
Rows 1 & 2: Rep rows 1 and 2 of Next Blade.

Tie
Make 2.
With white, ch 75. Fasten off.

Weave through ch-2 sps of rnd 1 of Helicopter Blades.

Tail Rotor
Make 2.
With white, ch 4, dc in 4th ch from hook, ch 2, sl st in same ch, [ch 3, dc in same ch, ch 2, sl st in same ch] 3 times. Fasten off.

Sew to back of Helicopter.

Landing Props
With top of Helicopter facing and nose pointing to the right, join white with sl st on edge of Landing Props, ch 4, dc in same sp, evenly sp (dc, ch 1, dc) 3 times across Landing Props. Fasten off.

With top of Helicopter facing and nose pointing to the left, rep instructions for Landing Props.

Finishing
With blue, sl st from top center of rnd 6 of Body to rnd 1.

Embroider face with blue and maroon embroidery floss as shown in photo. ■

Cotton Candy

DESIGN BY CAROL ALEXANDER

This is not your typical sweetly colored baby blanket! Babies will love the bright colors in this enchanting afghan, as well as the polka-dot texture from rows of cluster stitches. It's great for a little boy or girl!

SKILL LEVEL ▰▱▱▱
BEGINNER

FINISHED SIZE
41 x 55 inches

MATERIALS
Medium (worsted)
weight yarn:
27 oz/1,350 yds/765g white
8 oz/400 yds/227g
variegated,
3 oz/150 yds/85g each
lime, pink, periwinkle and
yellow
Size H/8/5mm crochet hook or
size needed to obtain gauge
Tapestry needle

GAUGE
4 shells = 2 inches; 4 shell rows
= 1½ inches

PATTERN NOTES
Alternate in order for cluster

rows: periwinkle, pink, lime
and yellow.

If adjusting Afghan size, beginning chain must be a multiple
of 2 plus 3.

When changing colors on
cluster rows, do not cut
dropped color, but carry along
top of stitches, working over
them with new color.

SPECIAL STITCHES
Shell: (Sc, dc) in indicated st.

Cluster (cl): Holding back last
lp of each st on hook, 4 dc as
indicated, yo, pull through all
lps on hook.

**Beginning corner half double
crochet shell (beg corner hdc
shell):** Ch 2 *(counts as first hdc)*,

(2 hdc, ch 2, 3 hdc) in corner
ch sp.

**Corner half double crochet
shell (corner hdc shell):** (3 hdc,
ch 2, 3 hdc) in corner sp.

**Half double crochet shell (hdc
shell):** (2 hdc, ch 1, 2 hdc) in
indicated st.

Beginning double crochet shell (beg dc shell): Ch 3 *(counts as first dc)*, (dc, ch 2, 2 dc) in same ch sp.

Double crochet shell (dc shell): (2 dc, ch 2, 2 dc) in same ch sp.

INSTRUCTIONS

AFGHAN

Row 1 (RS): Beg at bottom edge with variegated, ch 121, **shell** *(see Special Stitches)* in 3rd ch from hook, [sk next ch, shell in next ch] across, turn. *(60 shells)*

Row 2: Ch 2, shell in sc of each shell across, turn.

Row 3: Rep row 2, **change color** *(see Stitch Guide)* to white in last st at end of row, turn. Fasten off variegated.

Rows 4–6: Rep row 2.

Row 7: Ch 2, sc in first sc, change to color for cl, **cl** *(see Special Stitches)* in next st, change to white, ch 1, [sc in each of next 2 sts, change to color for cl, cl in next st, change to white, ch 1] across, ending with sc in turning ch, drop and fasten off cl color, turn. *(40 cls)*

Row 8: Ch 2, sk first sc, sc in ch 1 sp, [sc in each of next 2 sc, sc in ch-1 sp] across, ending with sc in last sc and in turning ch, turn.

Note: *Push all cls to RS of Afghan.*

Row 9: Ch 2, shell in 2nd sc, [sk next sc, shell in next sc] across, turn. *(18 shells)*

Rows 10 & 11: Rep row 2. At the end of last row, change to variegated.

Rows 12–14: Rep row 2. At the end of last row, change to white.

Rows 15–17: Rep row 2. At the end of last row, fasten off. Join white with sl st at the beg of last row.

Next rows: [Rep rows 7–17 consecutively] 11 times, then rep rows 7–14. At end of last row, fasten off.

Last cl row will be in periwinkle to correspond to first cl row.

BORDER

Note: *Work sts evenly spaced on this rnd to keep edges flat and keep number of sts between opposite sides.*

Rnd 1: Join white with sl st in any corner of Afghan, **beg dc shell** *(see Special Stitches)* in same place, *dc evenly across to next corner**, **dc shell** *(see Special Stitches)* in corner, rep from * 3 times, ending last rep at **, join with sl st in 3rd ch of beg ch-3.

Rnd 2: Sl st in next dc, sl st in corner ch-2 sp, beg dc shell in same ch sp, dc in each dc across to next corner**, dc shell in corner sp, rep from * around, ending last rep at **, join with sl st in 3rd ch of beg ch-3. Fasten off.

Note: *On the following rnd 3, adjust spacing of sts as needed when working between brackets to accommodate st sequence,* keeping number of shells between opposite sides equal.

Rnd 3: Join variegated with sl st in any corner ch-2 sp, **beg corner hdc shell** *(see Special Stitches)* in same ch sp, *sk next dc, sl st in next dc, [sk next dc, **hdc shell** *(see Special Stitches)* in next dc, sk next dc, sl st in next dc] across, ending in 2nd dc from next corner sp, sk last st before corner sp**, corner hdc shell in corner sp, rep from * around, ending last rep at **, join with sl st in 2nd ch of beg ch-2. Fasten off.

Rnd 4: Join white with sl st in any corner ch-2 sp, beg dc shell in same ch sp, *sk next hdc, dc in next hdc, 2 tr over next sl st, [2 dc in ch-1 sp of next hdc shell, 2 tr over next sl st] across to next corner hdc shell, sk first 2 hdc of corner hdc shell, dc in next hdc**, dc shell in corner sp, rep from * around, ending last rep at **, join with sl st in 3rd ch of beg ch-3.

Rnd 5: Rep rnd 2.

Rnd 6: Join periwinkle with sl st in any corner ch-2 sp, ch 3, 7 dc in same ch sp, *ch 1, sk next 2 dc, **fpsc** *(see Stitch Guide)* around top of next dc, [ch 1, sk next 2 dc, 5 dc in next dc, ch 1, sk next 2 dc, fpsc around top of next dc] across, ending with last fpsc worked around top of 3rd dc from next corner sp, ch 1, sk next 2 dc**, 8 dc in corner sp, rep from * around, ending last rep at **, join with sl st in 3rd ch of beg ch-3. Fasten off. ■

Baby Bunnies

DESIGNS BY TAMMY HILDEBRAND

This adorable winter set for baby features plain pink and blue motifs alternating with cute whiskered bunny faces for a whimsical ensemble that will keep your little one extra cozy on frosty days.

SKILL LEVEL ◼◼◼◻
INTERMEDIATE

FINISHED SIZE
9–12 months

MATERIALS
Medium (worsted)
  weight yarn:
    2 oz/100 yds/57g light pink
    1 oz/50 yds/28g each light
    blue and white
Size G/6/4mm crochet hook or
  size needed to obtain gauge
Tapestry needle
3 x 5-inch piece of cardboard

GAUGE
Each Motif = 3 inches square.

SPECIAL STITCH
Join: Ch 1, drop lp from hook, insert hook in center ch of corresponding ch-3 on previous Motif, pick up lp and pull through ch-1.

INSTRUCTIONS

SCARF
Motif A
Rnd 1: With light pink, ch 3, sl st in first ch to form ring, ch 3 *(counts as first dc)*, 15 dc in ring, join with sl st 3rd ch of beg ch-3. Fasten off. *(16 dc)*

Rnd 2: Join light blue with sl st in any st, ch 3, (2 dc, ch 2, 3 dc) in same st, sk next 3 sts, *(3 dc, ch 2, 3 dc) in next st, sk next 3 sts, rep from * around, join with sl st in 3rd ch of beg ch-3. Fasten off.

Rnd 3: Join light pink with sc in any ch sp, (ch 3, sc) 3 times in same ch sp, sk next st, sc in next st, sk next st, (sc, ch 3, sc) in sp before next st, sk next st, sc in next st, *(sc, {ch 3, sc} 3 times) in next ch sp, sk next st, sc in next st, sk next st, (sc, ch 3, sc) in sp

before next st, sk next st, sc in next st, rep from * around, join with sl st in beg sc. Fasten off.

Motif B
Rnd 1: With white, ch 3, sl st in first ch to form ring, ch 3 *(counts as first dc)*, 15 dc in ring, join with sl st in 3rd ch of beg ch-3. *(16 dc)*

Row 2: For **first ear**, ch 5, sc in 2nd ch from hook, sl st in each

of next 3 chs, sl st in same st as joining, sl st in each of next 2 sts, for **2nd ear,** ch 5, sc in 2nd ch from hook, sl st in each of next 3 chs, sl st in same st as ch-5 leaving rem sts unworked. Fasten off.

Rnd 3: Join light blue with sl st in first st before first ear, ch 3, (2 dc, ch 2, 3 dc) in same st, working behind ears, sk next 3 sts, *(3 dc, ch 2, 3 dc) in next st, sk next 3 sts, rep from * around, join with sl st in 3rd ch of beg ch-3. Fasten off.

Rnd 4: Join light pink with sc in ch-2 sp before first ear, (ch 3, sc, **join**–see Special Stitch, sc, join, sc) in same ch sp, sk next st, sc in next st, sk next st, (sc, join, sc) in sp before next st, sk next st, sc in next st, (sc, join, sc, join, sc, ch 3, sc) in next ch-2 sp, sk next st, sc in next st, sk next st, (sc, ch 3, sc) in sp before next st, sk next st, sc in next st, *(sc, ch 3) 3 times in next ch sp, sc in same ch sp, sk next st, sc in next st, sk next st, (sc, ch 3, sc) in sp before next st, sk next st, sc in next st, rep from *, join with sl st in beg sc. Fasten off.

Tack top of ears to rnd 4 as shown in photo.

Facial Embroidery
With light pink and tapestry needle, work French knot *(see Fig. 1)* for nose according to Face Diagram. Then, work 6 straight stitches *(see Fig. 2)* beneath the French knot for whiskers as shown on Diagram.

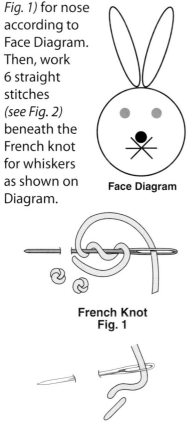

Face Diagram

French Knot
Fig. 1

Straight Stitch
Fig. 2

With light blue, work 2 French knots for eyes as shown on Diagram.

Motif C
Rnd 1: With light pink, ch 3, sl st in first ch to form ring, ch 3, 15 dc in ring, join with sl st in 3rd ch of beg ch-3. Fasten off. *(16 dc)*

Rnd 2: Join light blue with sl st in any st, ch 3, (2 dc, ch 2, 3 dc) in same st, sk next 3 sts, *(3 dc, ch 2, 3 dc) in next st, sk next 3 sts, rep from * around, join with sl st in 3rd ch of beg ch-3. Fasten off.

Rnd 3: Join light pink with sc in any ch-2 sp, ch 3, (sc, {join, sc} twice) in same ch sp, sk next st, sc in next st, sk next st, (sc, join, sc) in sp before next st, sk next st, sc in next st, (sc, {join, sc} twice, ch 3, sc) in next ch-2 sp, sk next st, sc in next st, sk next st, (sc, ch 3, sc) in sp before next st, sk next st, sc in next st, *(sc, {ch 3, sc} 3 times) in next ch sp, sk next st, sc in next st, sk next st, (sc, ch 3, sc) in sp before next st, sk next st, sc in next st, rep from *, join with sl st in first sc. Fasten off.

Alternating Motifs, work 4 each of Motif B and Motif C for total of 11 Motifs.

Edging
Join light pink with sc in any ch-3 sp, 2 sc in same ch sp, 3 sc in each ch-3 sp around with 2 sc in each joining, join with sl st in beg sc. Fasten off.

MITTENS
Motif A
Make 2.
Rnd 1: With light pink, ch 3, sl st in first ch to form ring, ch 3 *(counts as first dc)*, 15 dc in ring, join with sl st in 3rd ch of beg ch-3. Fasten off. *(16 dc)*

Rnd 2: Join light blue with sl st in any st, ch 3, (2 dc, ch 2, 3 dc) in same st, sk next 3 sts, *(3 dc, ch 2, 3 dc) in next st, sk next 3 sts, rep from * around, join with sl st in 3rd ch of beg ch-3. Fasten off.

Motif B
Make 2.
Rnd 1: With white, ch 3, sl st in first ch to form ring, ch 3, 15 dc in ring, join with sl st in 3rd ch of beg ch-3.

Row 2: For **first ear**, ch 5, sc in 2nd ch from hook, sl st in each of next 3 chs, sl st in same st as joining, sl st in each of next 2 sts, for **2nd ear**, ch 5, sc in 2nd ch from hook, sl st in each of next 3 chs, sl st in same st as ch-5, leaving rem sts unworked. Fasten off.

Rnd 3: Join light blue with sl st in first st before first ear, ch 3, (2 dc, ch 2, 3 dc) in same st, sk next 3 sts, *(3 dc, ch 2, 3 dc) in next st, sk next 3 sts, rep from * around, join with sl st in 3rd ch of beg ch-3. Fasten off.

Sew 1 Motif A and 1 Motif B WS tog through **back lps** *(see Stitch Guide)*. Rep with rem Motifs.

Facial Embroidery
Rep instructions given for Scarf.

Top
Rnd 1: Working around top edge of Motifs, join light pink with sc in any st, sc in each st and in each ch-2 sp around, join with sl st in beg sc. *(16 sc)*

Rnds 2 & 3: Ch 1, sc in each of first 2 sts, **sc dec** *(see Stitch Guide)* in next 2 sts, [sc in each of next 2 sts, sc dec in next 2 sts] around, join with sl st in beg sc. *(9 sc at end of last rnd)*

Rnd 4: Ch 1, sc in first st, sc dec in next 2 sts, [sc in next st, sc dec in next 2 sts] around, join with sl st in beg sc. Leaving long end, fasten off.

Weave long end through top of sts on last rnd, pull to close. Secure end.

Rep on other Motifs.

Tack top of ears to Top as shown in photo.

First Cuff
Rnd 1: Join light pink with sc in ch-2 sp on the bottom right-hand side of Motif B, sc in each st and in each ch sp around, join with sl st in beg sc.

Rnd 2: Ch 1, sc in each of first 7 sts, ch 2, sk next 2 sts, sc in each st around, join with sl st in beg sc.

Rnd 3: Ch 1, sc in each st and in each ch around, join with sl st in beg sc.

Rnds 4–6: Ch 1, sc in each st around, join with sl st in beg sc. At end of last rnd, fasten off.

2nd Cuff
Rnd 1: Join light pink with sc in ch-2 sp on right-hand side of Motif A, sc in each st and in each ch sp around, join with sl st in beg sc.

Rnd 2: Ch 1, sc in each of first 7 sts, ch 2, sk next 2 sts, sc in each st around, join with sl st in beg sc.

Rnd 3: Ch 1, sc in each st and in each ch around, join with sl st in beg sc.

Rnds 4–6: Ch 1, sc in each st around, join with sl st in beg sc. At end of last rnd, fasten off.

Thumb
Rnd 1: Join light pink with sc in first sk st on rnd 2 of Cuff, sc in next st, sc around next st on rnd 3, sc in bottom of next 2 chs, sc around next st on rnd 3, join with sl st in beg sc. *(6 sc)*

Rnds 2–6: Ch 1, sc in each st around, join with sl st in beg sc. At end of last rnd, leaving long end, fasten off.

Weave long end through sts on last rnd, pull to close. Secure end.

Rep on other Mitten.

Tie
Join light pink with sl st in center of Cuff on opposite side of Thumb, ch 100, sl st in center of Cuff on opposite side of Thumb on other Mitten. Fasten off.

HAT
Motif A
Rnd 1: With light pink, ch 3, sl st in first ch to form ring, ch 3, 15 dc in ring, join with sl st 3rd ch of beg ch-3. Fasten off. *(16 dc)*

Rnd 2: Join light blue with sl st in any st, ch 3, (2 dc, ch 2, 3 dc) in same st, sk next 3 sts, *(3 dc, ch 2, 3 dc) in next st, sk next 3 sts, rep from * around, join with sl st in 3rd ch of beg ch-3. Fasten off.

Rnd 3: Join light pink with sc in any ch sp, (ch 3, sc) 3 times in same ch sp, sk next st, sc in next st, sk next st, (sc, ch 3, sc) in sp before next st, sk next st, sc in next st, *(sc, {ch 3, sc} 3 times) in next ch sp, sk next st, sc in next st, sk next st, (sc, ch 3, sc) in sp before next st, sk next st, sc in next st, rep from * around, join with sl st in beg sc. Fasten off.

Motif B
Rnd 1: With white, ch 3, sl st in first ch to form ring, ch 3, 15 dc in ring, join with sl st in 3rd ch of beg ch-3.

Row 2: For **first ear**, ch 5, sc in 2nd ch from hook, sl st in each of next 3 chs, sl st in same st as joining, sl st in each of next 2 sts, for **2nd ear**, ch 5, sc in 2nd ch from hook, sl st in each of next 3 chs, sl st in same st as ch-5 leaving rem sts unworked. Fasten off.

Rnd 3: Join blue with sl st in first st before first ear, ch 3, (2 dc, ch 2, 3 dc) in same st, sk next 3 sts, *(3 dc, ch 2, 3 dc) in next st, sk next 3 sts, rep from * around, join with sl st in 3rd ch of beg ch-3. Fasten off.

Rnd 4: Join pink with sc in ch-2 sp before first ear, (ch 3, sc) 3 times in same ch sp, sk next st, sc in next st, sk next st, (sc, ch 3, sc) in sp before next st, sk next st, sc in next st, (sc, ch 3, {sc, **join}**–*see Special Stitches* twice, sc) in next ch sp, sk next st, sc in

next st, sk next st, (sc, join, sc) in sp before next st, sk next st, sc in next st, (sc, {join, sc} twice, ch 3, sc) in next ch-2 sp, sk next st, sc in next st, sk next st, (sc, ch 3, sc) in sp before next st, sk next st, sc in next st, (sc, {ch 3, sc} 3 times) in next ch sp, sk next st, sc in next st, sk next st, (sc, ch 3, sc) in sp before next st, sk next st, sc in next st, join with sl st in beg sc. Fasten off.

Facial Embroidery
Rep instructions given for Scarf on page 86.

Motif C
Rnd 1: With light pink, ch 3, sl st in first ch to form ring, ch 3, 15 dc in ring, join with sl st in 3rd ch of beg ch-3. Fasten off. *(16 dc)*

Rnd 2: Join light blue with sl st in any st, ch 3, (2 dc, ch 2, 3 dc) in same st, sk next 3 sts, *(3 dc, ch 2, 3 dc) in next st, sk next 3 sts, rep from * around, join with sl st in 3rd ch of beg ch-3. Fasten off.

Rnd 3: Join light pink with sc in any ch-2 sp, (ch 3, sc) 3 times in same ch sp, sk next st, sc in next st, sk next st, (sc, ch 3, sc) in sp before next st, sk next st, sc in next st, (sc, ch 3, {sc, join} twice, sc) in next ch sp, sk next st, sc in next st, sk next st, (sc, join, sc) in sp before next st, sk next st, sc in next st, (sc, {join, sc} twice, ch 3, sc) in next ch-2 sp, sk next st, sc in next st, sk next st, (sc, ch 3, sc) in sp before next st, sk next st, sc in next st, (sc, {ch 3, sc} 3 times) in next ch sp, sk next st,

sc in next st, sk next st, (sc, ch 3, sc) in sp before next st, sk next st, sc in next st, join with sl st in beg sc. Fasten off.

Work 1 more of each Motif B and Motif C.

Last Motif
Rnds 1–3: Rep rnds 1–3 of Motif B.

Rnd 4: Join light pink with sc in ch-2 sp before first ear, (ch 3, sc) in same ch sp, sk next st, sc in next st, sk next st, (sc, ch 3, sc) in sp before next st, sk next st, sc in next st, *(sc, ch 3, {sc, join} twice, sc) in next ch sp, sk next st, sc in next st, sk next st, (sc, join, sc) in sp before next st, sk next st, sc in next st*, (sc, {join, sc} twice, ch 3, sc) in next ch-2 sp, sk next st, sc in next st, sk next st, (sc, ch 3, sc) in sp before next st, sk next st, sc in next st, rep between *, (sc, join) twice in same ch sp as first sc, join with sl st in beg sc. Fasten off.

Top
Rnd 1: Working around top edge of Motifs, join light pink with sc in any ch-3 sp, 2 sc in same ch sp, 2 sc in center of each Motif joining around with 3 sc in each ch sp, join with sl st in beg sc. *(66 sc)*

Rnd 2: Ch 1, sc in each st around, join with sl st in beg sc.

Rnd 3: Ch 1, sc in each of first 9 sts, sc dec in next 2 sts, [sc in each of next 9 sts, sc dec in next 2 sts] around, join with sl st in beg sc. *(60 sc)*

Rnd 4: Ch 1, sc in each of first 3 sts, [sc dec in next 2 sts, sc in next st] around, join with sl st in beg sc. *(41 sc)*

Rnd 5: Ch 1, sc in first st, [sc dec in next 2 sts, sc in each of next 3 sts] around, join with sl st in beg sc. *(33 sc)*

Rnd 6: Ch 1, sc in each st around, join with sl st in beg sc. Leaving long end, fasten off.

Weave long end through top of sts on last rnd, pull to close. Secure end.

Pompom
Wrap 2 strands of light pink held tog around cardboard 20 times, slide lps off cardboard, tie separate 12-inch strand of light pink around center of all lps, cut lps. Trim ends. Sew to center of Top of Hat.

Tack ears to Top as shown in photo.

Cuff
Rnd 1: Join light pink with sc in any ch-3 sp on bottom edge, sc in same ch sp, 2 sc in each ch-3 sp around with sc in center of each Motif joining, join with sl st in beg sc.

Rnd 2: Working in **back lps** *(see Stitch Guide)*, ch 1, sc in each st around, join with sl st in beg sc.

Rnds 3–4: Working in both lps, ch 1, sc in each st around, join with sl st in beg sc. At end of last rnd, fasten off. ∎

Fairy Fluff

DESIGN BY NANCY NEHRING

Perfect to pack and go, this mile-a-minute afghan is the solution to long car trips or waiting for appointments. It uses a hairpin lace technique to give a soft and airy look to each strip, and it joins by working in the back loops.

SKILL LEVEL
INTERMEDIATE

FINISHED SIZE
44 x 46 inches

MATERIALS
TLC Baby light (light worsted) weight yarn (5 oz/360 yds/141g per skein):
1 skein each #5737 powder pink, #5881 powder blue, #5322 powder yellow and #5964 naptime multi
Red Heart Baby Teri medium (worsted) weight yarn (3 oz/192 yds/35g per skein):
2 skeins each #9137 pink, #9181 blue and #9121 yellow

Size H/8/5mm crochet hook
Hairpin lace loom
Stitch markers

GAUGE
4-lp bundle and ch-2 = 1 inch;
4 dc = 1 inch

Panel = 4 inches across

PATTERN NOTE
Set hairpin loom at 2 inches wide.

SPECIAL STITCH
Hairpin lace: Adjust loom (*see Pattern Note*), make slip knot, slide lp off hook and onto right-hand prong of loom (*see Fig. 1 # 1 on page 90*).

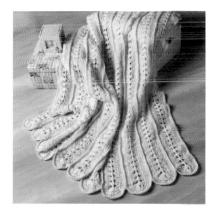

INSTRUCTIONS

PANEL
Make 4 each blue and pink. Make 3 yellow.
Row 1: For **first bundle** (*see Special Stitch*), wrap around 1 prong of hairpin loom and tie at center, wrap around other

prong ending at back, wrap 7 times around both prongs and end at back *(8 lps on each prong)*, insert crochet hook under all wraps, yo, pull to front; working loosely, [yo above wraps, insert hook under wraps, yo, pull to front] 3 times, yo, pull through all lps on hook, ch 2,

next bundle *(make 42)*, wrap yarn 4 times around both prongs and end at back *(4 lps on each prong)*, working loosely, [yo above wraps, insert hook in 2nd ch of ch-2 and under wraps, yo, pull through ch to front] 3 times, yo, pull through all loops on hook, ch 2,

last bundle, wrap yarn 8 times around both prongs and end at back *(8 lps on each prong)*, working loosely, [yo above wraps, insert hook in 2nd ch of ch-2 and under wraps, yo, pull through ch to front] 3 times, yo, pull through all lps on hook, ch 1. Fasten off.

Rnd 2: Now working in rnds, with matching color TLC Baby yarn, removing lps from prong as you go, join with sc in first lp, sc in each lp across 1 prong of hairpin lace loom, then across other prong, forming a long oval, join with sl st in beg sc. *(368 sc)*

Rnd 3: Working this rnd in **back lps** *(see Stitch Guide)*, ch 3, dc next st, 2 dc in next st, dc in each of next 2 sts, 2 dc in next st, dc in each of next 171 sts, [2 dc in next st, dc in each of next 2 sts] 5 times, dc in each of next 169 sts, [2 dc in next st, dc in each of next 2 sts] twice, 2 dc in last st, join with sl st in 3rd ch of beg ch-3. Fasten off. *(378 dc)*

ASSEMBLY

1. On each Panel, mark center 18 dc at each end, leaving 171 dc along each straight edge.

2. Lay Panels right side up in the following order: blue, pink, yellow, pink, blue, yellow, blue, pink, yellow, pink and blue.

3. For each seam, matching long straight edges, hold 2 Panels with WS tog, working in back lps of both layers as 1, join naptime multi with sc in next st past marked st, sc in each of next 169 sts. Fasten off.

4. Working around outer edge, join naptime multi with sc in any st, sk each seam, sc in each st around entire Afghan, join with sl st in beg sc. Fasten off. ■

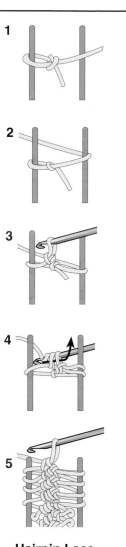

Hairpin Lace Fig. 1

Holding yarn in left hand, turn loom from right to left so the yarn passes behind both prongs and slip knot is on opposite prong *(see # 2)*.

Insert crochet hook under front and over back of slip knot, yo, pull lp through, yo, pull through lp on hook *(see # 3)*.

*Turn loom from right to left and sc in next new lp in same manner *(see # 4)*, rep from * number of times stated on each side.

Slide strip off loom, **do not fasten off**.

If loom becomes too full, slide all lps off, then thread last 3 or 4 lps back onto loom and continue working *(see # 5)*.

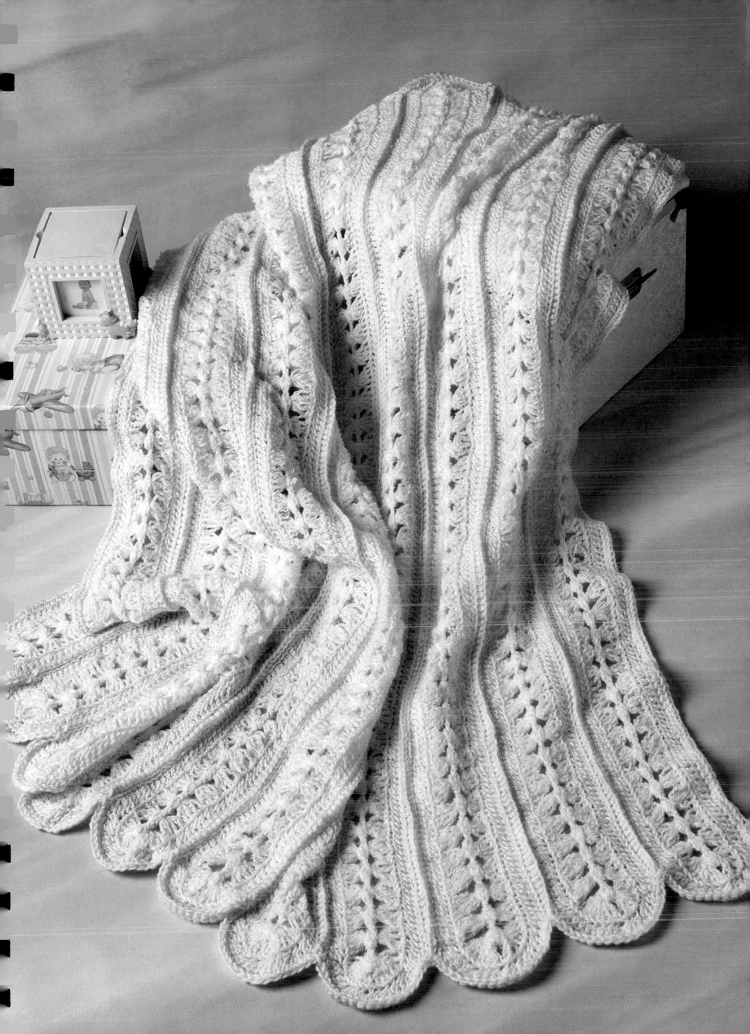

Baby Wrist Rattles

DESIGNS BY KATHLEEN STUART

Baby will be thoroughly enchanted with these entertaining little animal rattles designed to fit comfortably on the wrist—or strap them on an ankle and watch baby kick and squeal with joy.

SKILL LEVEL ◼◼☐☐
EASY

FINISHED SIZE
Animal heads: 2 inches in diameter

Strap opening: 1½ inches in diameter

MATERIALS
Fine (baby) weight yarn
  (1¾ oz/286 yds/50g per
  skein):
    1 skein each pink and
      yellow
    18 inches black
Embroidery floss (8¾ yds per
  skein):
    48 inches orange
Size G/6/4mm crochet hook or
  size needed to obtain gauge
Tapestry needle

9mm jingle bells: 4
Polyester fiberfill
Stitch markers

GAUGE
5 sc = 1 inch; 5 sc rnds = 1 inch

PATTERN NOTES
Do not join rounds unless otherwise stated.

Mark first stitch of each round.

INSTRUCTIONS

PIGGY
Snout
Rnd 1 (RS): With pink, ch 2, 6 sc in 2nd ch from hook, place st marker. *(6 sc)*

Rnd 2: Working in **back lps** *(see*

Stitch Guide) for this rnd only, sc in each st around.

Rnd 3: Sc in each sc around.

Head
Rnd 4: Working in back lps for this rnd only, 2 sc in each st around. *(12 sc)*

Rnd 5: [Sc in next sc, 2 sc in next sc] around. *(18 sc)*

Rnd 6: [Sc in each of next 2 sc, 2 sc in next sc] around. *(24 sc)*

Rnd 7: [Sc in each of next 3 sc, 2 sc in next sc] around. *(30 sc)*

Rnd 8: Sc in each of next 15 sc, working in **front lp** *(see Stitch Guide)* only of next st, (sc, hdc,

ch 3, sl st in first ch, hdc, sc) all in same st *(for first ear)*, sc in each of next 6 sc, working in front lp only of next st, (sc, hdc, ch 3, sl st in first ch, hdc, sc) all in same st *(for 2nd ear)*, sc in each of next 7 sc.

Rnd 9: Sc in each of next 15 sc, sc in back lp of rnd 7 directly behind ear, sk ear sts, sc in each of next 6 sc, sc in back lp of rnd 7 directly behind ear, sk ear sts, sc in each of next 7 sc. *(30 sc)*

Rnd 10: Rep rnd 3.

Rnd 11: [Sc in each of next 3 sc, **sc dec** *(see Stitch Guide)* in next 2 sc] 6 times. *(24 sc)*

Rnd 12: [Sc in each of next 2 sc, sc dec in next 2 sc] 6 times. *(18 sc)*

Rnd 13: [Sc in next sc, sc dec in next 2 sc] 6 times. *(12 sc)*

Rnd 14: [Sc in each of next 2 sc, sc dec in next 2 sc] 3 times. *(9 sc)*

Stuff lightly with fiberfill and insert 2 jingle bells into center area of fiberfill.

Wrist Strap
Rnds 15–44: Sc in each sc around. At the end of last rnd, join with sl st in next st. Leaving long end, fasten off.

Fold rnd 44 flat across and sew to end of rnd 14.

Eyes
With tapestry needle and black, embroider eyes over rnd 5 with straight stitches *(see Fig. 1)*.

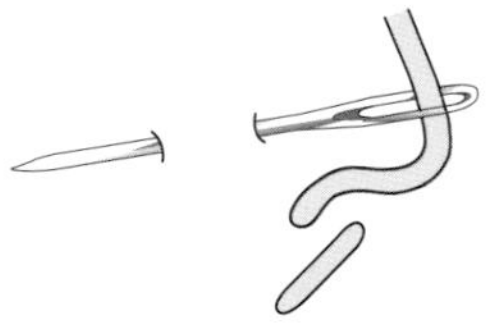

Straight Stitch
Fig. 1

DUCKIE
Rnd 1: With yellow, ch 2, 6 sc in 2nd ch from hook, place st marker. *(6 sc)*

Rnd 2: 2 sc in each sc around. *(12 sc)*

Rnd 3: [Sc in next sc, 2 sc in next sc] 6 times. *(18 sc)*

Rnd 4: [Sc in each of next 2 sc, 2 sc in next sc] 6 times. *(24 sc)*

Rnd 5: [Sc in each of next 3 sc, 2 sc in next sc] 6 times. *(30 sc)*

Rnds 6–8: Sc in each sc around.

Rnd 9: [Sc in each of next 3 sc, sc dec in next 2 sc] 6 times. *(24 sc)*

Rnd 10: [Sc in each of next 2 sc, sc dec in next 2 sc] 6 times. *(18 sc)*

Rnd 11: [Sc in next sc, sc dec in next 2 sc] 6 times. *(12 sc)*

Rnd 12: [Sc in each of next 2 sc, sc dec in next 2 sc] 3 times. *(9 sc)*

Stuff lightly with fiberfill and insert 2 jingle bells into center area of fiberfill.

Wrist Strap
Rnds 13–42: Sc in each sc around. At the end of last rnd, join with sl st in next st. Leaving long end, fasten off.

Fold rnd 42 flat across and sew to end of rnd 12.

Beak
With orange, ch 4, sc in 2nd ch from hook, (hdc, dc, hdc) in next ch, 2 sc in last ch, working on opposite side of ch, (hdc, dc, hdc) in next ch, sc in last ch, join with sl st in beg sc. Leaving 6-inch end, fasten off.

Sew Beak to center front of Head over rnd 1.

Eyes
With tapestry needle and black, embroider eyes over rnd 5 with straight stitches *(see Fig. 1)*. ■

Bubble Gum Baby

DESIGNS BY NAZANIN FARD

A variety of dimensional stitches gives interest and texture to this adorable child's jacket and blanket. Stitch the set for a lucky little one to keep out the chill of cold months ahead.

Popcorn Jacket

SKILL LEVEL ■■■□
INTERMEDIATE

FINISHED SIZES
Instructions given fit child's size 2; changes for size 4 and size 6 are in [ ].

FINISHED GARMENT MEASUREMENTS
Chest: 22 inches (size 2) [24 inches (size 4), 26 inches (size 6)]

Length: 12 inches (size 2) [14 inches (size 4), 16 inches (size 6)]

MATERIALS
Red Heart Econo Baby medium (worsted) weight yarn (7 oz/675 yds/198g per skein):
  1 skein #1722 light pink
1 skein #1680 pastel green
1 skein #1224 baby yellow
Size G/6/4mm crochet hook or size needed to obtain gauge
Tapestry needle
2 small buttons

GAUGE
4 dc = 1 inch; 2 dc and 1 sc rows = 1¼ inches

Take time to check gauge.

PATTERN NOTE
Sleeves are worked from top down and are attached to the body as they are worked; this way you can lengthen the sleeves as the child grows.

SPECIAL STITCH
Popcorn (pc): 5 dc in next st, drop lp from hook, insert hook

in top of first dc of group, pull dropped lp through, ch 1.

STITCH PATTERN
Row 1: Sc in 2nd ch from hook and in each ch across, turn.

Row 2: Ch 1, sc in each st across, turn.

Row 3: Ch 3 *(counts as first dc)*, dc in each of next 2 sts, [**pc** *(see Special Stitch)* in next st, dc in each of next 3 sts] across, ending with dc in each st across, turn.

Row 4: Ch 1, sc in each st across, turn.

Row 5: Ch 3, dc in each of next 4 sts, [pc in next st, dc in each of next 3 sts] across, ending with dc in each st across, turn.

Rep rows 2–5 for Pattern.

INSTRUCTIONS

JACKET
Right Front & Back
Rows 1–25 [1–29, 1–33]: With light pink, ch 23 [25, 27], work in Pattern until piece measures 9 [10½, 11½] inches from beg.

Row 26 [30, 34]: For **Front neckline**, work in Pattern across first 14 [16, 18] sts, leaving rem sts unworked, turn.

Rows 27–34 [31–38, 35–42]: Work in Pattern.

Row 35 [39, 43]: For **Back**, ch 10, dc in 4th ch from hook *(first 3 chs count as first dc)*, dc in next ch, pc in next ch, dc in each of next 3 chs, pc in next ch, work in Pattern across, turn.

Rows 36–67 [40–75, 44–83]: Work in Pattern.

Row 68 [76, 84]: Work row 2 of Pattern. Fasten off.

Left Front & Back
Row 1: With pastel green, ch 23 [25, 27], work row 1 of Pattern.

Row 2: Work row 2 of Pattern.

Row 3: Work row 5 of Pattern.

Rows 4–25 [4–29, 4–33]: Work in Pattern until piece measures 9 [10½, 11½] inches from beg.

Row 26 [30, 34]: For **Front neckline**, sl st in each of first 9 sts, work in Pattern across, turn.

Rows 27–34 [31–38, 35–42]: Work in Pattern.

Row 35 [39, 43]: For **Back**, work in Pattern across, ch 10, turn.

Row 36 [40, 44]: Sc in 2nd ch from hook and in each st across, turn.

Rows 37–67 [41–75, 45–83]: Work in Pattern.

Row 68 [76, 84]: Work row 2 of pattern. Fasten off.

Sew seam at center Back.

Sleeve
Row 1: Sk first 22 [26, 30] rows on body, join yellow with sc in next row, evenly sp 37 [41, 46] more sc across 23 rows, turn. *(38 [42, 45] sc)*

Row 2: Ch 1, **sc dec** *(see Stitch Guide)* in first 2 sts, sc in each st across to last 2 sts, sc dec in last 2 sts, turn. *(36 [40, 43] sc)*

Rows 3–20 [3–24, 3–29]: Work in Pattern, dec 1 st at both ends of row every 4th row 4 [5, 5] times. *(28 [30, 33] sts at end of last row)*

Rows 21–24 [25–28, 30–33]: Ch 1, sc in each st across, turn. At end of last row, fasten off.

Rep on other side of body for 2nd Sleeve.

Hood
Row 1: With RS facing, join yellow with sc in edge of right-hand side of neckline, evenly sp 27 sc across to center back seam, turn. *(28 sc)*

Row 2: Ch 3, dc in each st across, turn.

Row 3: Ch 1, sc in each st across, turn.

Rows 4–45 [4–47, 4–51]: Rep rows 2 and 3 alternately, ending with row 2. At end of last row, fasten off.

FINISHING
1. Sew back seam on Hood, sew last row to rem neck edge.

2. Sew Sleeve and side seams.

Hood Trim
Row 1: Working in ends of rows, join yellow with sc in first row of Hood, evenly sp sc across to last row of Hood, **do not turn**.

Row 2: Working from left to right, ch 1, **reverse sc** *(see Fig. 1)* in each st across. Fasten off.

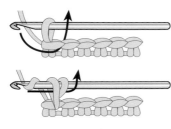

Fig. 1
Reverse Sc

Button Band
Row 1: With RS of Right Front facing, working in ends of rows, join light pink with sc in first row at bottom edge, [sc in each sc row and 2 sc in each dc row] across to neck edge, turn.

Rows 2–4: Ch 1, sc in each st across, turn. At end of last row, fasten off.

Buttonhole Band
Row 1: With RS of Left Front facing, working in ends of rows, join pastel green with sc in first row at neck edge, [sc in end of each sc row and 2 sc in end of each dc row] across to bottom edge, turn.

Row 2: Ch 1, sc in each st across, turn.

Row 3: Ch 1, sc in each of first 2 sts, ch 2, sk next 2 sts, sc in each of next 2 sts, ch 2, sk next 2 sts, sc in each st across, turn. *(2 buttonholes)*

Row 4: Ch 1, sc in each st and ch across. Fasten off.

Sew buttons to Button Band opposite buttonholes.

Slightly block Jacket to size.

Blocks Baby Afghan

SKILL LEVEL ◼◼◼◻
INTERMEDIATE

FINISHED SIZE
31 inches square

MATERIALS
Red Heart Econo Baby medium (worsted) weight yarn (7 oz/675 yds/198g per skein):
 1 skein #1722 light pink
 1 skein #1802 baby blue
 1 skein #1570 lavender
 1 skein #1680 pastel green
 1 skein #1001 white
 1 skein #1224 yellow
Size G/6/4mm crochet hook or size needed to obtain gauge

GAUGE
4 sts = 1 inch; each Block is 6¼ inches square without Edging

SPECIAL STITCH
Puff stitch (puff st): Yo, insert hook in next st, yo, pull lp though, [yo, insert hook in same st, yo, pull lp through] twice, yo, pull through all lps on hook.

INSTRUCTIONS

AFGHAN
Puff Block
Make 4.
Row 1 (RS): With light pink, ch 26, sc in 2nd ch from hook and in each ch across, turn. *(25 sc)*

Row 2 (WS): Ch 1, sc in each of first 2 sts, [**puff st** *(see Special Stitch)* in next st, sc in each of next 3 sts] 5 times, puff st in next st, sc in each of last 2 sts, turn.

Row 3: Ch 1, sc in each st across, turn.

Row 4: Ch 1, sc in each of first 4 sts, [puff st in next st, sc in each of next 3 sts] 5 times, sc in last st, turn.

Row 5: Ch 1, sc in each st across, turn.

Next rows: Rep rows 2–5 consecutively for pattern until piece measures 6¼ inches square. At end of last row, fasten off.

Diamond Block
Make 4.
Row 1: With baby blue, ch 25, sc in 2nd ch from hook and in each ch across, turn. *(24 sc)*

Rows 2 & 3: Ch 1, sc in each st across, turn.

Row 4: Ch 1, sc in each of first 2 sts, ***fptr** (see Stitch Guide)* around 2nd st 3 rows below, sk next 4 sts 3 rows below, fptr around next st 3 rows below, sk next 2 sts on this row**, sc in each of next 4 sts, rep from * across, ending last rep at **, sc in each of last 2 sts, turn.

Rows 5–7: Ch 1, sc in each st across, turn.

Row 8: Ch 1, [fptr around st above post st below, sk next st on this row, sc in each of next 4 sts, fptr above next post st below, sk next st on this row] across, sc in last st, turn.

Rows 9–11: Ch 1, sc in each st across, turn.

Next rows: Rep rows 4–11 consecutively for pattern until piece measures 6¼ inches square, ending with row 9. At end of last row, fasten off.

Pole Block
Make 4.

Row 1: With lavender, ch 26, sc in 2nd ch from hook and in each ch across, turn. *(25 sc)*

Rows 2 & 3: Ch 1, sc in each st across, turn.

Row 4: Ch 1, sc in each of first 2 sts, [**fpdc** *(see Stitch Guide)* around next st 3 rows below, sk next st on this row, sc in next st] across, sc in last st, turn.

Row 5: Ch 1, sc in each st across, turn.

Row 6: Ch 1, sc in first st, [fpdc around next st 3 rows below, sk next st on this row, sc in next st] across, turn.

Next rows: Rep rows 3–6 consecutively for pattern until piece measures 6¼ inches square. At end of last row, fasten off.

Stripe Block
Make 4.

Row 1: With pastel green, ch 26, sc in 2nd ch from hook and in each ch across, turn. *(25 sc)*

Rows 2–4: Ch 1, sc in each st across, turn. At end of last row, **do not turn**.

Row 5: Working in **front lps** *(see Stitch Guide)*, from left to right, **reverse sc** *(see Fig. 1 on page 98)* in each st across, do not turn.

Row 6: Working in **back lps** *(see Stitch Guide)* of row 4, ch 1, sc in each st across, turn.

Next rows: Rep rows 2–6 consecutively for pattern until pieces measures 6¼ inches square. At end of last row, fasten off.

BLOCK EDGING

Rnd 1: Working around outer edges in ends of rows and sts, join white with sc in first st, sc in each st across to last st, 3 sc in last st, evenly sp 25 sc in ends of rows down side, working in starting ch on opposite side of row 1, 3 sc in first ch, sc in each ch across with 3 sc in last ch, evenly sp 25 sc in ends of rows up side, 2 sc in first st worked in, join with sl st in beg sc.

Rnd 2: Ch 3 *(counts as first dc)*, dc in each st around with 3 dc in each center corner st, join with sl st in 3rd ch of beg ch-3. Fasten off.

Work Block Edging around each Block.

JOINING
Working in back lps, alternating Blocks, holding 2 Blocks WS tog, working through both thicknesses, with yellow, sc Blocks tog, continue until 4 Blocks are joined. Fasten off.

Rep in same manner to join another row of Blocks. When all Blocks are joined, rep in same manner across other edges until all edges are joined.

BORDER

Rnd 1: Working around entire outer edge, with RS facing, join yellow with sc in corner, sc in each st around with 3 sc in each center corner st, join with sl st in beg sc.

Rnd 2: Working from left to right, reverse sc in each st around, join with sl st in beg reverse sc. Fasten off. ■

Sailing Away

DESIGN BY ANN SMITH

Sailing, sailing, over the ocean blue… Stitch this adorable, colorful, delightfully designed cardigan that any little boy would love to wear! The bold colors and basic shapes are perfect for a toddler.

SKILL LEVEL ■■■□
INTERMEDIATE

FINISHED SIZES
Instructions given fit child's size 2; changes for size 4 and size 6 are in [ ].

FINISHED GARMENT MEASUREMENTS
Chest: 27 inches *(size 2)* [29 inches *(size 4)*, 31 inches *(size 6)*]

Length: 12½ inches *(size 2)* [14 inches *(size 4)*, 15½ inches *(size 6)*]

MATERIALS
Light (light worsted) weight yarn:
    7 [9, 10] oz/609 [783, 870] yds/198 [255, 284]g bright blue
    1 oz/87 yds/28g each yellow, white and red

Size F/5/3.75mm crochet hook or size needed to obtain gauge
Tapestry needle
⅝-inch anchor buttons: 5
Yarn bobbins
Stitch markers

GAUGE
16 sts = 4 inches; 18 rows = 4 inches

Take time to check gauge.

PATTERN NOTES
The sailboats are worked in single crochet following chart, reading from right to left on right side rows and left to right on wrong side rows.

The circles on chart are treble stitches that are worked on wrong side row of the Sweater.

Yellow waves are crocheted on the Sweater after the pieces are joined.

Use yarn bobbins for each separate color section to keep yarns from tangling.

BODY PATTERN
Row 1 (RS): Ch 1, sc in each st across, turn.

Row 2: Ch 1, sc in first sc, [tr in next sc, sc in each of next 3 sc] across, ending with tr in next sc, sc in last sc, turn.

Rows 3–5: Rep row 1.

Row 6: Ch 1, sc in each of first 3 sc, [tr in next sc, sc in each of next 3 sc] across, ending with tr in next sc, sc in each of last 3 sc, turn.

Rows 7–9: Rep row 1.

Rep rows 2–9 for Body Pattern.

SWEATER
Back
Foundation row (RS): Beg at lower edge with bright blue, ch 52 [56, 60], sc in 2nd ch from hook and in each ch across, turn. *(51 [55, 59] sc)*

Rows 2–4: Rep row 1 of Body Pattern.

Next rows: Beg Body Pattern with row 1, then rep rows 2–9 for Body Pattern until back measures 11½ [13, 14½] inches from beg. At end of last row, fasten off.

Right Front
Foundation row (RS): Beg at lower edge, with bright blue, ch 25 [27, 29], sc in 2nd ch from hook, sc in each ch across, turn. *(24 [26, 28] sc)*

Rows 2–4: Rep row 1 of Body Pattern.

Next rows: Beg right front chart with row 5, which is a RS row, work as chart indicates until Front measures 7½ inches from beg, ending on a WS row.

Next rows: [**Sc dec** *(see Stitch Guide)* at neck edge every row] 3 times. *(21 [23, 25] sts)*

Next rows: [Sc dec in next 2 sts at neck edge every other row] 5 times. *(16 [18, 20] sts)*

Next rows: When chart is completed, continue to sc in each st until Front measures the same as Back. At end of last row, fasten off.

Left Front

Work as for Right Front following Left Front chart and reversing neck shaping.

Sew Fronts and Back tog at shoulders.

From shoulder seam, place a marker 6 inches down on each Front and Back armhole edge.

Sleeve

Foundation row: With RS facing, join bright blue with sc at marker, work 47 [51, 55] sc evenly spaced between markers. *(48 [52, 56] sc)*

Row 1 (WS): Ch 1, sc in each of first 4 sts, [tr in next st, sc in each of next 3 sts] across, ending with tr in next st, sc in each of last 4 sts, turn.

Row 2: Ch 1, sc dec in first 2 sts, sc in each st across to last 2 sts, sc dec in last 2 sts, turn. *(45 [49, 53] sts)*

Row 3: Ch 1, sc in each st across, turn.

Row 4: Rep row 2. *(43 [47, 51] sts)*

Row 5: Ch 1, sc in first st, [tr in next st, sc in each of next 3 sts] across, ending with tr in next sc, sc in last sc, turn.

Next rows: Rep rows 2–5 until 23 sts rem. Adjust beg and ending of row 5 as work progresses so that the tr of working row ends up centered between tr of previous tr row.

Next rows: Work even in pattern until Sleeve measures from beg 6½ [7½, 9] inches, ending with row 5 on WS.

Cuff

Rnd 1 (RS): Ch 1, sc in each st around, join with sl st in beg sc, **do not turn.** *(23 sts)*

Rnd 2: Ch 1, sc in each sc around, join with sl st in beg sc.

Next rnds: Rep rnd 2 until Sleeve measures from beg 10½ [11½, 13] inches. At the end of last rnd, **turn.**

Last rnd: [Ch 1, sl st in next sc] around, ending with last sl st in joining. Fasten off.

Rep on rem armhole.

Sew Sleeve and side seams.

Waves

With RS facing, using chart as a guide, join yellow under a boat as indicated with an X on chart, [ch 3, sl st in indicated st 2 rows above, ch 3, sl st in indicated st below] across as indicated. Fasten off.

Rep Waves under each boat. Work Wave pattern around entire bottom edge of Sweater under the lower boats.

Body Band

Rnd 1 (RS): Join bright blue with sc at center back neck, work 12 sc across to shoulder seam, evenly sp 19 [25, 31] sc to neck edge, 3 sc in corner, evenly sp 25 [29, 35] sc down Front to corner, 3 sc in corner, sc across opposite side of foundation ch across bottom of Sweater, 3 sc in corner, evenly sp 25 [29, 35] sc up opposite Front, 3 sc in corner neckline, evenly sp 19 [25, 31] sc to shoulder seam, 11 sc along rem back neck, join with sl st in beg sc.

Rnd 2: Ch 2 *(counts as first hdc)*, **fphdc** *(see Stitch Guide)* around next sc, [sc in next sc, fphdc around next sc] around, join with sl st in 2nd ch of beg ch-2.

Rnd 3: Ch 2, *fphdc around next fphdc**, sc in next sc, rep from * to corner, [fphdc around fphdc, ch 1, sk next st, fphdc around next fphdc *(buttonhole)*, work in pattern across next 3 sts] 5 times, continue in pattern around, ending last rep at **, join with sl st in 2nd ch of beg ch-2.

Note: *Buttonholes do not extend all the way down the front opening of Sweater. If you desire buttonholes down front to bottom, make adjustment in number of sts between buttonholes.*

Rnd 4: Ch 1, sl st in each st around, working [ch 1, sl st in next st] 4 times at each lower corner, join with sl st in beg sl st.

Rnd 5: Working over last sl st rnd *(not in sl sts)*, [ch 1, sl st in next sp] around, ending with ch 1, join with sl st in first ch-1. Fasten off.

Rnd 6: With RS facing, join bright blue with sl st over fphdc of rnd 3 near side seam, sl st over each st of rnd 3, ending with sl st in same st as beg st. Fasten off.

Sew buttons opposite button-holes. ■

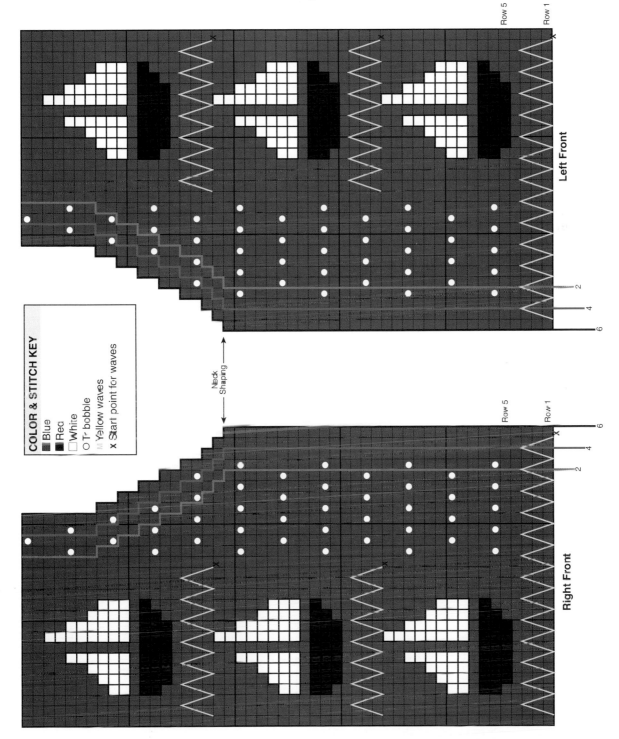

COLOR & STITCH KEY
- ■ Blue
- ■ Red
- ☐ White
- ○ Tr bobble
- M Yellow waves
- x Start point for waves

Neck Shaping

Left Front

Right Front

Row 5 Row 1

Tempting Toys

Chapter Contents

Charlie Chimp

DESIGN BY BARBARA ANDERSON

Crochet this cutie and let your favorite little ones "monkey" around with Charlie Chimp, a loveable addition to your children's toy box. He comes with his own banana and is always ready to play!

SKILL LEVEL ■■■□ INTERMEDIATE

FINISHED SIZE
9 inches tall, sitting

MATERIALS
Medium (worsted) weight yarn:
    4 oz/200 yds/113g brown
    1 oz/50 yds/28g each peach, turquoise and yellow
    ½ oz/25 yds/14g off-white
F/5/3.75mm crochet hook or size needed to obtain gauge
Tapestry needle
Sewing needle
Sewing thread
Black embroidery floss
12mm black animal eyes with washers: 2
12-inch chenille stem
½ x 1 inch strip hook-and-loop tape

Polyester fiberfill
Stitch marker

GAUGE
9 sc = 2 inches; 9 sc rows = 2 inches

PATTERN NOTES
Do not join rounds unless otherwise stated.

Mark first stitch of each round.

When changing colors, always change in last stitch made and drop yarn to wrong side of work.

Use separate skein or ball of yarn for each color section.

Do not carry yarn across from 1 section to another. Fasten off colors at end of each color section.

SPECIAL STITCH
Cluster (cl): Holding back last lp of each st on hook, 3 dc in next st, yo, pull through all lps on hook.

INSTRUCTIONS

CHIMP
Head
Rnd 1: Starting at muzzle, with peach, ch 4, 2 sc in 2nd ch from hook, 2 sc in next ch, 4 sc in end ch, working on opposite side of ch, for center bottom, 2 sc in each of last 2 chs, **do not join** (see Pattern Notes). (12 sc)

Rnd 2: [2 sc in next st, sc in next st] around. (18 sc)

Note: *To move first st, sc or sl st in first st.*

Rnd 3: Sc in each of first 14 sts leaving rem sts unworked, move marker *(first st has been moved)*.

Rnd 4: Sc in each of first 4 sts, 2 sc in each of next 10 sts, sc in each of last 4 sts, join with sl st in beg sc. Fasten off. *(28 sc)*

Rnd 5: Join brown with sl st in first st, ch 2 *(counts as first hdc)*, hdc in each of next 10 sts **changing colors** *(see Stitch Guide)* to peach in last st made *(see Pattern Notes)*, 2 hdc in each of next 6 sts changing to brown, hdc in each of last 11 sts, join with sl st in 2nd ch of beg ch-2. *(34 hdc)*

Rnd 6: Ch 2, hdc in each of next 4 sts, 2 hdc in each of next 5 sts, 2 hdc in next st changing to peach, hdc in each of next 4 sts, hdc in next st changing to brown, hdc in each of next 2 sts changing to peach, hdc in each of next 4 sts, hdc in next st changing to brown, 2 hdc in each of next 6 sts, hdc in each of last 5 sts, join with sl st in 2nd ch of beg ch-2. Fasten off peach. *(46 hdc)*

Rnd 7: Ch 2, hdc in each of next 17 sts, [2 hdc in next st, hdc in next st] 5 times, 2 hdc in next st, hdc in each of last 17 sts, join with sl st in 2nd ch of beg ch-2. *(52 hdc)*

Rnd 8: Ch 2, hdc in each st around, join with sl st in 2nd ch of beg ch-2, sl st in next st.

Rnd 9: Ch 2, [**hdc dec** *(see Stitch Guide)* in next 2 sts] 4 times, hdc in each of next 35 sts, [hdc dec in next 2 sts] 4 times, join with sl st in 2nd ch of beg ch-2. *(44 hdc)*

Attach eyes with washers 1¾ inches apart over rnd 6.

Rnd 10: Ch 2, hdc in each st around, join with sl st in 2nd ch of beg ch-2. Sl st in next st.

Rnd 11: Ch 2, hdc in each st around, join with sl st in 2nd ch of beg ch-2.

Rnd 12: Ch 2, hdc in each st around, join with sl st in 2nd ch of beg ch-2. Sl st in next st.

Rnd 13: Ch 2, hdc in each of next 3 sts, hdc dec in next 2 sts, [hdc in each of next 4 sts, hdc dec in next 2 sts] 5 times, hdc in each of next 6 sts, hdc dec in

last 2 sts, join with sl st in 2nd ch of beg ch-2. *(37 hdc)*

Rnd 14: Ch 2, hdc in each st around, join with sl st in 2nd ch of beg ch-2. Sl st in next st. Stuff.

Rnd 15: Ch 2, [hdc dec in next 2 sts, hdc in next st] around, join with sl st in 2nd ch of beg ch-2. *(25 hdc)*

Rnd 16: Ch 2, hdc in each st around, join with sl st in 2nd ch of beg ch-2. Sl st in next st.

Rnd 17: Ch 2, [hdc dec in next 2 sts] 12 times, join with sl st in 2nd ch of beg ch-2. Stuff. *(13 hdc)*

Rnd 18: Ch 2, [hdc dec in next 2 sts] 6 times, join with sl st in 2nd ch of beg ch-2. Leaving long end for sewing, fasten off.

Sew opening closed.

Nose & Mouth
With black floss, embroider 2 lazy daisy stitches *(see Fig. 1)* on rnd 2 for nostrils and embroi-der mouth line in outline stitch *(see Fig. 2)* between rnds 2 and 3 stitching over rnd 3 on edges as shown in photo.

**Lazy Daisy Stitch
Fig. 1**

**Outline Stitch
Fig. 2**

Brow
With 2 strands peach held tog, ch 20 leaving long end for sewing, fasten off.

Position ch around each eye section. Sew **back lps** *(see Stitch Guide)* of ch to Head, sew **front lps** *(see Stitch Guide)* between eyes to Head. Sew front lps of 3 chs to inside under each eye.

Ear
Make 2.
Row 1: With 2 strands peach held tog, ch 3 *(first 2 chs count as first hdc)*, 6 hdc in 3rd ch from hook, turn. *(7 hdc)*

Row 2: Ch 1, 2 sc in each st across. Fasten off. *(14 sc)*

Sew ears to rnd 8 on Head 3½ inches apart across top of Head.

Body
Rnd 1: Starting at neck, with brown, ch 24, sl st in first ch to form ring, ch 1, sc in each ch around, join with sl st in first sc. *(24 sc)*

Rnd 2: Ch 2, hdc in each st around, join with sl st in 2nd ch of beg ch-2.

Rnd 3: Ch 2, hdc in each st around, join with sl st in 2nd ch of beg ch-2. Sl st in next st.

Rnds 4–6: Rep rnds 2 and 3 alternately, ending with rnd 2.

Rnd 7: Ch 2, hdc in each of next 6 sts, [2 hdc in next st, hdc in next st] 5 times, 2 hdc in next st, hdc in each of last 6 sts, join with sl st in 2nd ch of beg ch-2. *(30 hdc)*

Rnds 8 & 9: Rep rnds 3 and 2.

Rnd 10: Ch 2, [2 hdc in next st, hdc in next st] twice, 2 hdc in next st, hdc in each of next 19 sts, [2 hdc in next st, hdc in next st] twice, 2 hdc in last st, join with sl st in 2nd ch of beg ch-2. Sl st in next st. *(36 hdc)*

Rnds 11–16: Rep rnds 2 and 3 alternately.

Rnd 17: Ch 2, hdc in next st, hdc dec in next 2 sts, [hdc in each of next 2 sts, hdc dec in next 2 sts] around, join with sl st in 2nd ch of beg ch-2. *(27 hdc)*

Rnd 18: Ch 2, hdc dec in next 2 sts, [hdc in next st, hdc dec in next 2 sts] around, join with sl st in 2nd ch of beg ch-2. *(18 hdc)*

Rnd 19: Ch 2, [hdc dec in next 2 sts] 8 times, hdc in last st, join with sl st in top of beg ch-2. Leaving long end for sewing, fasten off. Stuff. Sew opening closed.

Sew bottom of rnds 8–13 of Head to rnd 1 on Body.

Leg
Make 2.
Rnd 1: Starting at hip, with brown, ch 2, 8 sc in 2nd ch from hook, join with sl st in first sc. *(8 sc)*

Rnd 2: Ch 2, hdc in same st, 2 hdc in each st around, join with sl st in 2nd ch of beg ch-2. *(16 hdc)*

Rnd 3: Ch 2, [2 hdc in next st, hdc in each of next 2 sts] around, join with sl st in 2nd ch of beg ch-2. *(21 hdc)*

Rnd 4: Ch 2, hdc in each st around, join with sl st in 2nd ch of beg ch-2. Sl st in next st.

Rnd 5: Ch 2, hdc in each st around, join with sl st in 2nd ch of beg ch-2.

Rnds 6 & 7: Rep rnds 4 and 5.

Rnd 8: Ch 2, hdc dec in next 2 sts, hdc in each of next 16 sts, hdc dec in last 2 sts, join with sl st in 2nd ch of beg ch-2. *(19 hdc)*

Rnd 9: Ch 2, hdc in each st around, join with sl st in 2nd ch of beg ch-2. Sl st in next st.

Rnd 10: Ch 2, [hdc dec in next 2 sts] twice, hdc in each of next 4 sts, 2 hdc in each of next 2 sts, hdc in each of next 4 sts, [hdc dec in next 2 sts] twice, join with sl st in 2nd ch of beg ch-2. Stuff lightly. *(17 hdc)*

Rnd 11: Ch 2, hdc dec in next 2 sts, hdc in each of next 5 sts, 2 hdc in each of next 2 sts, hdc in each of next 5 sts, hdc dec in last 2 sts, join with sl st in 2nd ch of beg ch-2. Sl st in next st. *(17 hdc)*

Rnd 12: Ch 2, hdc dec in next 2 sts, hdc in each of next 5 sts, 2 hdc in each of next 2 sts, hdc in each of next 5 sts, hdc dec in last 2 sts, join with sl st in 2nd ch of beg ch-2.

Rnd 13: Ch 2, hdc in each st around, join with sl st in 2nd ch of beg ch-2. Sl st in next st.

Rnd 14: Ch 2, hdc in same st, 2 hdc in next st, hdc in each of next 4 sts, [hdc dec in next 2 sts] 3 times, hdc in each of next 4 sts, 2 hdc in last st, join with sl st in 2nd ch of beg ch-2.

Rnds 15 & 16: Rep rnds 4 and 5. At end of last rnd, fasten off.

Foot
Rnd 17: Sk first st, join peach with sc in next st, sc in each st around, **do not join**. *(17 sc)*

Rnd 18: Sc in each of first 6 sts, 2 sc in each of next 5 sts, sc in each of last 6 sts. *(22 sc)*

Rnd 19: Sc in each of first 8 sts, 2 sc in each of next 6 sts, sc in each of last 8 sts. Sc in first st. *(28 sc)*

Rnd 20: Sc in each st around. Sc in first st.

Rnd 21: Sc in each of first 10 sts, [**cl** *(see Special Stitch)*, ch 1, sc in next st] 4 times, sc in each of last 10 sts.

Rnd 22: [**Sc dec** *(see Stitch Guide)* in next 2 sts] twice, sc in each of next 6 sts, [sc in next ch, sc in next st] 4 times, sc in each of next 6 sts, [sc dec in next 2 sts] twice. *(24 sc)*

Rnd 23: [Sc dec in next 2 sts] around. *(12 sc)*

Rnd 24: Sc in each st around, join with sl st in beg sc. Leaving long end for sewing, fasten off. Stuff. Sew opening closed lengthwise.

Sew rnds 1–8 of Legs to sides of Body 1 inch apart across back over rnds 11–16.

Large Toe
Make 2.
Rnd 1: With peach, ch 4, sc in 2nd ch from hook, sc in next ch, 2 sc in end ch, working on opposite side of ch, sc in each of last 2 chs. *(6 sc)*

Rnd 2: Sc in each of first 3 sts, ch 3 leaving last 3 sts unworked, join with sl st in first sc. *(3 sc, 3 chs)*

Rnd 3: Ch 1, sc in each st and in each ch around. *(6 sc)*

Rnd 4: Sc in each of first 4 sts, sc dec in last 2 sts. *(5 sc)*

Rnd 5: Sc in each st around. Fasten off. Stuff.

Sew opening closed.

Sew unworked sts of rnd 2 to inside of foot over rnds 20 and 21.

Arm
Make 2.
Rnd 1: Starting at shoulder, with brown, ch 2, 6 sc in 2nd ch from hook, join with sl st in beg sc. *(6 sc)*

Rnd 2: Ch 2, hdc in same st as beg ch-2, 2 hdc in each st around, join with sl st in 2nd ch of beg ch-2. *(12 hdc)*

Rnd 3: Ch 2, hdc in same st, hdc in next st, [2 hdc in next st, hdc in next st] around, join with sl st in 2nd ch of beg ch-2. *(18 hdc)*

Rnd 4: Ch 2, hdc in each st around, join with sl st in 2nd ch of beg ch-2. Sl st in next st.

Rnd 5: Ch 2, hdc in each st around, join with sl st in 2nd ch of beg ch-2.

Rnds 6 & 7: Rep rnds 4 and 5.

Rnd 8: Ch 2, hdc dec in next 2 sts, hdc in each of next 13 sts, hdc dec in last 2 sts, join with sl st in 2nd ch of beg ch-2. *(16 hdc)*

Rnd 9: Ch 2, hdc dec in next 2 sts, hdc in each of last 13 sts, join with sl st in 2nd ch of beg ch-2. Sl st in next st. *(15 hdc)*

Rnds 10 & 11: Ch 2, hdc dec in next 2 sts, hdc in each of next 4 sts, 2 hdc in each of next 2 sts, hdc in each of next 4 sts, hdc dec in last 2 sts, join with sl st in 2nd ch of beg ch-2. At end of last rnd, sl st in next st. **Do not stuff**. *(15 hdc)*

Rnds 12 & 13: Rep rnds 10 and 11.

Rnd 14: Ch 2, hdc in each st around, join with sl st in 2nd ch of beg ch-2. Fasten off.

Rnd 15: For hand, join peach with sc in first st, sc in each st around. *(15 sc)*

Rnd 16: Sc in each st around. Sc in first st.

Rnd 17: Sc in each st around.

Rnds 18 & 19: Rep rnds 16 and 17.

Rnd 20: Sc in each st around. For left arm only, join with sl st in first sc. Fasten off.

Cut chenille stem in half. Fold 1 end under ½ inch, insert in Arm with folded end even with rnd 20, stuff around stem.

Row 21: Working in rows, through both thicknesses, for **right arm**, [cl in next st, sc in next st] 4 times. Leaving long end for sewing, fasten off.

Row 21: Working in rows, through both thicknesses, for **left arm**, join peach with sl st in 7th st on rnd 20, [cl in next st, sc in next st] 4 times. Leaving long end for sewing, fasten off.

Sew chs on ends of cl and sc to sts on rnd 20.

Thumb
Make 2.
Rnds 1–5: Rep rnds 1–5 of Large Toe.

Sew unworked sts of rnd 2 to inside of Arm over rnds 13–15.

Flatten rnds 1–3 of Arm, sew slightly cupped over rnds 2–4 on sides of Body 1¾ inches apart across back.

SHIRT
Row 1: Starting at neckline, with turquoise, ch 35, sc in 2nd ch from hook and in each ch across, turn. *(34 sc)*

Row 2: Working this row in front lps only, ch 3 *(counts as first dc)*, dc in each of next 4 sts, 2 dc in each of next 6 sts, dc in each of next 12 sts, 2 dc in each of next 6 sts, dc in each of last 5 sts, turn. *(46 dc)*

Row 3: Ch 3, dc in same st, dc in each of next 4 sts, [for **armhole**, ch 10, sk next 12 sts], dc in each of next 12 sts, rep between [ ], dc in each of next 4 sts, 2 dc in last st, turn. *(24 sts, 20 chs)*

Row 4: Ch 3, dc in each st and in each ch across, turn. *(44 dc)*

Row 5: Ch 3, dc in each of next 12 sts, [2 dc in next st, dc in next st] 9 times, dc in each of last 13 sts, turn. *(53 dc)*

Row 6: Ch 3, dc in each st across, turn. Fasten off.

Row 7: Join turquoise with sc in end of row 1, 2 sc in end of each of next 5 rows, working in back lps, 2 sc in first st on row 6, sc in each of next 51 sts, 2 sc in last st, 2 sc in end of each of next 5 rows, sc in end of row 1. Fasten off.

Sleeves
Rnd 1: Join turquoise with sl st in 5th ch on row 3, ch 3, dc in each of next 5 chs, 2 dc in end of row 3, dc in each of next 12 sts, 2 dc in end of row 3, dc in each of last 4 chs, join with sl st in 3rd ch of beg ch-3. *(26 dc)*

Rnd 2: Ch 3, dc in each st around, join with sl st in 3rd ch of beg ch-3.

Rnd 3: Working this rnd in back lps only, ch 1, sc in each st around, join with sl st in beg sc. Fasten off.

Rep in other armhole.

CONTINUED ON PAGE 134

Baby's Bowling Set

DESIGNS BY DONNA COLLINSWORTH

As babies learn hand-eye coordination, they love to watch you roll a ball back and forth, and then want to try it themselves. Add some soft bowling pins and you'll have an avid bowler in no time!

SKILL LEVEL ■□□□
BEGINNER

FINISHED SIZE
Ball: 5 inches in diameter

Bowling Pin: 7 inches tall

MATERIALS
Bulky (chunky)
   weight yarn:
      3 oz/90 yds/85g each
         yellow, blue, lavender,
         pink and aqua
Size J/10/6mm crochet hook or
   size needed to obtain gauge
Tapestry needle
Small jingle bells: 3
Several buttons and beads
Small amount sand
Small empty pill bottles: 4
Craft glue
Fiberfill

GAUGE
2 sc = 1 inch; 3 sc rows =
1½ inches

PATTERN NOTE
Experiment with placing different objects in pill bottles for different sounds.

INSTRUCTIONS

BOWLING PIN
Make 1 each blue, aqua and lavender, working each with a yellow stripe.
Rnd 1: With bowling pin color, ch 4, sl st in first ch to form ring, ch 1, 8 sc in ring, join with sl st in beg sc, **turn**. *(8 sc)*

Rnd 2: Ch 1, 2 sc in first sc, sc in next sc, [2 sc in next sc, sc in next sc] around, join with sl st in beg sc, turn. *(12 sc)*

Rnd 3: Ch 1, sc in each sc around, join with sl st in beg sc, turn.

Rnd 4: Rep rnd 3. Fasten off.

Rnd 5: Join yellow with sl st in first sc, **sc dec** *(see Stitch Guide)*

in first 2 sc, sc in next sc, [sc dec in next 2 sc, sc in next sc] around, join with sl st in beg sc, turn. *(8 sc)*

Rnd 6: Rep rnd 3. Fasten off.

Rnd 7: Join Bowling Pin color with sc in first sc, sc in same sc, sc in next sc, [2 sc in next sc, sc in next sc] around, join with sl st in beg sc, turn. *(12 sc)*

Rnd 8: Rep rnd 2. *(18 sc)*

Rnd 9: Ch 1, 2 sc in first sc, sc in each of next 2 sc, [2 sc in next sc, sc in each of next 2 sc] around, join with sl st in beg sc, turn. *(24 sc)*

Rnds 10–13: Rep rnd 3.

Rnd 14: Ch 1, sc dec in first 2 sc, sc in each of next 4 sc, [sc dec in next 2 sc, sc in each of next 4 sc] around, join with sl st in beg sc, turn. *(20 sc)*

Rnd 15: Rep rnd 3.

Rnd 16: Ch 1, sc dec in first 2 sc, sc in each of next 2 sc, [sc dec in next 2 sc, sc in each of next 2 sc] around, join with sl st in beg sc, turn. *(15 sc)*

Rnd 17: Ch 1, sc dec in first 2 sc,

sc in next sc, [sc dec in next 2 sc, sc in next sc] around, join with sl st in beg sc. Fasten off. *(10 sc)*

Base
With yellow, ch 4, sl st in first ch to form ring, ch 1, 10 sc in ring, join with sl st in beg sc. Fasten off. *(10 sc)*

Place beads, buttons or sand in pill bottle. Apply glue to lid and place on bottle.

Stuff Bowling Pin with fiberfill, inserting pill bottle at center, with care to place at center and stuff with fiberfill around bottle. Sew Base to Pin.

Ball
Rnd 1: With pink, ch 4, sl st in first ch to form ring, ch 1, 8 sc in ring, join with sl st in beg sc, turn. *(8 sc)*

Rnds 2–4: Ch 1, 2 sc in first sc, sc in next sc, [2 sc in next sc, sc in next sc] around, join with sl st in beg sc, turn. *(27 sc)*

Rnd 5: Ch 1, sc in each sc around, join with sl st in beg sc, turn.

Rnd 6: Rep rnd 5, fasten off.

Rnd 7: Join aqua with sc in first sc, rep rnd 5. Fasten off.

Rnd 8: Join yellow with sc in first sc, rep rnd 5. Fasten off.

Rnd 9: Join blue with sc in first sc, rep rnd 5. Fasten off.

Rnd 10: Join lavender with sc in first sc, rep rnd 5. Fasten off.

Rnd 11: Join pink with sc in first sc, rep rnd 5.

Rnds 12 & 13: Rep rnd 5.

Place jingle bells in pill bottle. Apply glue to lid and place on bottle.

Stuff Ball with fiberfill, inserting pill bottle at center of Ball, using care to place bottle at center and stuff with fiberfill around bottle.

Rnds 14–16: Ch 1, sc dec in first 2 sc, sc in next sc, [sc dec in next 2 sc, sc in next sc] around, join with sl st in beg sc, turn. *(8 sc)*

Insert stuffing to fill opening.

Rnd 17: Ch 1, sc dec in first 2 sc, [sc dec in next 2 sc] around, join with sl st in beg sc. Fasten off. *(4 sc)* ■

2-in-1 Games

DESIGNS BY ROSANNE KROPP

Traveling will be twice as fun with this cute-as-a-bug game tote; it features checkers on one side and tic-tac-toe on the other. It's easy to pack for trips to Grandma's house, since all the pieces store inside.

SKILL LEVEL ■■□□
EASY

FINISHED SIZE
14 inches square

MATERIALS
Red Heart Classic medium (worsted) weight yarn (3½ oz/190 yds/99g per skein):
2 skeins #848 skipper blue
1 skein each #261 maize, #676 emerald green and #230 yellow
1 oz/54 yds/28g each #902 jockey red, #245 orange and #12 black
Size G/6/4mm crochet hook or size needed to obtain gauge
Tapestry needle
Sewing needle
Black sewing thread
Fiberfill
10mm sew-on wiggly eyes: 11 pairs
¾-inch plastic ring: 24

3mm black chenille stem: 2 inches
¼-inch red pompoms: 2
Hot-glue gun
Stitch markers

GAUGE
7 sc = 2 inches; 7 sc rows = 2 inches

SPECIAL STITCH
Surface stitch (surface st):
Holding yarn at back of work, insert hook in sp between sts, yo, pull lp through sp and lp on hook.

INSTRUCTIONS

**TIC-TAC-TOE
GAME PIECES**
Head
Make 5 with jockey red heads and yellow bodies.
Make 5 with orange heads and emerald green bodies.

Rnd 1 (RS): With head color, ch 2, 6 sc in 2nd ch from hook, join with in beg sc. *(6 sc)*

Rnd 2: Ch 1, 2 sc in each sc around, join with sl st in beg sc. *(12 sc)*

Rnd 3: Ch 1, [sc in next sc, 2 sc in next sc] 6 times, join with sl st in beg sc. *(18 sc)*

Rnd 4: Working in **front lps** *(see Stitch Guide)* only, [4 sc in next sc, sl st in next sc] twice. Fasten off.

Body Top
Note: *Work in **back lps** (see Stitch Guide) only throughout Body Top.*

Row 1: Now working in rows, sk next 9 sc after last sl st of rnd 4, join body color with sc in next st, sc in each of next 13 sts, leaving last 4 sc unworked, turn. *(14 sc)*

Row 2: Ch 1, sc in each st across, turn.

Rows 3–8: Rep row 2.

Row 9: Ch 1, sc in first st, [**sc dec** *(see Stitch Guide)* in next 2 sts, sc in next st] 4 times, sc in last st, turn. *(10 sc)*

Row 10: Ch 1, sc in each st across, turn.

Row 11: Ch 1, [sc dec in next 2 sts] 5 times. Fasten off. *(5 sc)*

Body Bottom & Legs

Working tightly, with body color, ch 9, 4 dc in 4th ch from hook, *ch 3, sc in 2nd ch from hook, sc in next ch, sl st in top of last dc *(leg completed)*, [2 dc in each of next 2 chs, ch 3, sc in 2nd ch from hook, sc in next ch, sl st in top of last dc] twice*, 5 dc in last ch, working on opposite side of ch, rep between * once, join with sl st in 9th ch of beg ch-9. Leaving long end, fasten off. *(26 dc, 6 legs)*

Assembly

Line up Body Bottom and Body sts with first 4 dc of Body Bottom to rem 4 sts of rnd 3 of Head and opposite end 5 dc to end 5 sc of row 11 of Body Top. Holding Legs forward *(do not sew Legs)*, sew Body Bottom to Body Top, stuffing lightly with fiberfill before closing.

With sewing needle and black thread, sew eyes to upper portion of Head over rnd 2.

CHECKERS

Make 12 each jockey red and black checkers.
Join yarn to plastic ring, ch 1, 12 sc in ring, join with sl st in beg sc. Fasten off. *(12 sc)*

Caterpillar Head

Note: *Do not join rnds. Mark first st of each rnd.*

Rnd 1: With yellow, ch 2, 6 sc in 2nd ch from hook. *(6 sc)*

Rnd 2: 2 sc in each sc around. *(12 sc)*

Rnd 3: [Sc in next sc, 2 sc in next sc] 6 times. *(18 sc)*

Rnds 4 & 5: Sc in each sc around.

Rnd 6: [Sc dec in next 2 sc, sc in next sc] 6 times. *(12 sc)*

Rnd 7: [Sc dec in next 2 sc] 6

times, join with sl st in beg sc. **Do not fasten off.** Stuff Head with fiberfill. *(6 sc)*

Tail

Row 8: Now working in rows, ch 37, sl st in 2nd ch from hook, sl st in each ch across. Leaving long end, fasten off. *(36 sl sts)*

Weave long end through sts of rnd 7, pull tightly, knot to secure.

Alternating colors, string Checkers onto tail. Tie end of Tail in a soft knot.

Finishing

With sewing needle and black sewing thread, sew eyes to rnd 2 of Head.

Sk center 2 sc at top of Head, insert chenille stem at right, under next 2 sc and out again. Bend each end of stem to form antennae.

Glue base of each antenna to Head as shown in photo. Glue 1 red pompom to top of each antenna.

TOTE BAG
Tic-Tac-Toe Board
Row 1: With skipper blue, ch 49, sc in 2nd ch from hook, sc in each ch across, turn. *(48 sc)*

Rows 2–48: Ch 1, sc in each sc across, turn. At end of last row, fasten off.

Make 2 lines of **surface sts** *(see Special Stitch)* across, spaced 16 rows apart, 1 each of orange and yellow.

Make 2 lines of surface sts down, spaced 16 sc apart, 1 each red and emerald green.

Border
Join black with sc to outer edge of Board, evenly sp sc around outer edge, working 3 sc in each corner st, join with sl st in beg sc. Fasten off.

Checkerboard
Row 1: With skipper blue, ch 49, sc in 2nd ch from hook, sc in each of next 5 chs, **changing colors** *(see Stitch Guide)* to maize in last st made, sc in each of next 6 chs, [changing to skipper blue in last st, sc in each of next 6 chs, changing to maize in last st, sc in each of next 6 chs] 3 times, turn. *(8 blocks, 48 sc)*

Row 2: Ch 1, [with maize, sc in each of next 6 sc, changing to skipper blue in last st, sc in each of next 6 sc] 4 times, turn.

Row 3: Ch 1, [with skipper blue, sc in each of next 6 sc, changing to maize in last st, sc in each of next 6 sc] 4 times, turn.

Row 4: Rep row 2.

Row 5: Rep row 3.

Row 6: Rep row 2.

Rows 7–12: Rep rows 2 and 3 alternately in that order to reverse block colors. At the end of last row, change to skipper blue in last st, turn.

Rows 13–18: Rep rows 3 and 2 alternately in that order to reverse block colors. At the end of last row, change to maize in last st, turn.

Rows 19–48: Rep rows 7–18. At the end of last row, fasten off. Board has a total of 64 blocks, 8 x 8.

Border
Join black with sc to outer edge of Board, evenly sp sc around outer edge, working 3 sc in each corner st, join with sl st in beg sc. Fasten off.

Joining Boards
Row 1: With WS of Boards tog, join black with sc in any center corner sc and, working through both thicknesses, evenly sp sc across to next center corner sc, [2 sc in center corner sc, evenly sp sc across to next center corner sc] twice, ending with 1 sc in next center corner sc, **do not turn**.

Rnd 2: Now working in rnds, ch 1, working around top opening of Tote, evenly sp sc around entire edge, join with sl st in beg sc. Fasten off.

Handle
Make 2.
Row 1: With jockey red, ch 37, sc in 2nd ch from hook, sc in each ch across, turn. *(36 sc)*

Rows 2–4: Ch 1, sc in each sc across, turn. At the end of last row, fasten off.

With black sewing thread and needle, allowing 3½-inch sp between each end of Handle, sew ends of Handle to inside of top opening. ∎

Harvey the Bunny

DESIGN BY SHEILA LESLIE

This adorable bunny brings huggable happiness to baby's playtime. He's the perfect size for a good nap-time cuddle and doesn't mind being tugged around by the ears, as long as he gets plenty of hugs!

SKILL LEVEL ■■■□
INTERMEDIATE

FINISHED SIZE
6 inches tall, excluding Ears

MATERIALS
Fine (sport) weight yarn:
  ½ oz/45 yds/14g
    yellow
  ¼ oz/23 yds/7g each pink
    and black
Size F/5/3.75mm crochet hook
  or size needed to obtain
  gauge
Tapestry needle
Polyester fiberfill
Stitch marker

GAUGE
5 sc = 1 inch

PATTERN NOTES
Work in continuous rounds.

Do not join unless specified.

Mark beginning of rounds.

════ INSTRUCTIONS ════

BUNNY
Head & Body
Rnd 1: With yellow, starting at

top of Head, ch 2, 6 sc in 2nd ch from hook. *(6 sc)*

Rnd 2: 2 sc in each sc around. *(12 sc)*

Rnd 3: [Sc in next sc, 2 sc in next sc] around. *(18 sc)*

Rnd 4: [Sc in each of next 2 sc, 2 sc in next sc] around. *(24 sc)*

Rnd 5: [2 sc in next sc, sc in each of next 3 sc] around. *(30 sc)*

Rnds 6–13: Sc in each sc around.

Rnd 14: [Sc in each of next 3 sc, **sc dec** *(see Stitch Guide)* in next 2 sc] around. *(24 sc)*

Stuff Head with fiberfill.

Rnd 15: [Sc in next sc, sc dec in next 2 sc] around. *(16 sc)*

Rnd 16: Rep rnd 6.

Rnd 17: [Sc in next sc, 2 sc in next sc] around. *(24 sc)*

Rnd 18: [Sc in each of next 3 sc, 2 sc in next sc] around. *(30 sc)*

Rnds 19 & 20: Rep rnd 6.

Rnd 21: [Sc in each of next 4 sc, 2 sc in next sc] around. *(36 sc)*

Rnds 22–30: Rep rnd 6.

Rnd 31: [Sc in each of next 4 sc, sc dec in next 2 sc] around. *(30 sc)*

Stuff Body with fiberfill

Rnd 32: [Sc in each of next 3 sc, sc dec in next 2 sc] 6 times. *(24 sc)*

Rnd 33: [Sc in each of next 2 sc, sc dec in next 2 sc] around. *(18 sc)*

Rnd 34: [Sc in next sc, sc dec in next 2 sc] around. *(12 sc)*

Rnd 35: [Sc dec in next 2 sc] around, join with sl st in beg sc.

Fasten off.

Leg
Make 2.
Rnd 1 (RS): With yellow, ch 5, 3 sc in 2nd ch from hook, sc in next ch, hdc in each of next 2 chs, working on opposite side of ch, 3 hdc in next ch, hdc in each of next 2 chs, sc in last ch. *(12 sts)*

Rnd 2: 2 sc in each of next 3 sts, sc in each of next 3 sts, 2 hdc in each of next 3 sts, sc in each of last 3 sts. *(18 sts)*

Rnd 3: [Sc in next st, 2 sc in next st] 3 times, sc in each of next 3 sts, [hdc in next st, 2 hdc in next st] 3 times, sc in each of last 3 sts. *(24 sts)*

Rnd 4: Sc in each of first 12 sts, [sc in next st, sc dec in next 2 sts] 3 times, sc in each of last 3 sts. *(21 sts)*

Rnd 5: Sc in each of first 12 sts, [sc dec in next 2 sts] 3 times, sc in each of last 3 sts. *(18 sts)*

Rnds 6–8: Sc in each sc around.

Rnd 9: Sc in each sc around, join with sl st in beg sc. Fasten off.

Arm
Make 2.
Rnd 1: With yellow, ch 2, 6 sc in 2nd ch from hook.

CONTINUED ON PAGE 135

Baby Chicks

DESIGN BY DONNA COLLINSWORTH

Make these colorful cuties for a springtime picnic with friends and family. With these little chicks to decorate the tables, even the youngest of your guests is sure to be entertained!

SKILL LEVEL ◨◼☐☐
EASY

FINISHED SIZE
3 inches tall and 3½ inches long

MATERIALS
Bulky (chunky) novelty
  eyelash yarn:
    1¾ oz/61 yds/50g each
      blue, green and white
Size F/5/3.75mm crochet hook or
  size needed to obtain gauge
Tapestry needle
Metallic chenille stems
5mm black pompom: 6
Small piece of orange felt
Fiberfill
Tacky craft glue

GAUGE
Gauge not important for this project

INSTRUCTIONS

CHICK
Body
Rnd 1: Ch 4, sl st in first ch to form ring, ch 1, 10 hdc in ring, join with sl st in first hdc, **turn**. *(10 hdc)*

Rnd 2: Ch 1, 2 hdc in first hdc, hdc in next hdc, [2 hdc in next hdc, hdc in next hdc] 4 times, join with sl st in first hdc, turn. *(15 hdc)*

Rnd 3: Ch 1, hdc in first hdc, [2 hdc in next hdc, hdc in next hdc] 7 times, join with sl st in first hdc, turn. *(22 hdc)*

Rnd 4: Ch 1, hdc in each hdc, join with sl st in first hdc, turn.

Rnd 5: Rep rnd 4.

Rnd 6: Ch 1, hdc in first hdc, *hdc dec (see Stitch Guide)* in

next 2 hdc, hdc in each of next 5 hdc, rep from * twice, join with sl st in first hdc, turn. *(19 hdc)*

Rnd 7: Ch 1, hdc in first hdc, [hdc dec in next 2 hdc] 9 times, join with sl st in first hdc, turn. *(10 hdc)*

Rnd 8: Ch 1, hdc in first hdc, [hdc dec in next 2 sts, hdc in next hdc] 3 times, join with sl st in first hdc, turn. *(7 hdc)*

Rnd 9: Rep rnd 4.

Rnd 10: Ch 1, 2 hdc in each hdc, join with sl st in first hdc, turn. *(14 hdc)*

Rnd 11: Rep rnd 4.

Stuff piece with fiberfill.

Rnd 12: Ch 1, hdc dec in first 2 hdc, hdc in each of next 2 hdc,

[hdc dec in next 2 hdc, hdc in each of next 2 hdc] twice, hdc in each of next 2 hdc, turn. *(11 hdc)*

Rnd 13: Ch 1, hdc in first hdc, [hdc dec in next 2 hdc] 5 times, join with sl st in first hdc, turn. *(6 hdc)*

Stuff with fiberfill.

Rnd 14: Ch 1, [hdc dec in next 2 hdc] 3 times, join with sl st in first hdc. Fasten off. *(3 hdc)*

Wing
Make 2.
Row 1: Ch 3, hdc in 2nd ch from hook and in next ch, turn. *(2 hdc)*

Row 2: Ch 1, 2 hdc in each hdc across, turn. *(4 hdc)*

Row 3: Ch 1, hdc dec in first 2 hdc, hdc in each of next 2 hdc, turn. *(3 hdc)*

Row 4: Ch 1, hdc dec in first 2 hdc, hdc in next hdc, turn. *(2 hdc)*

Row 5: Ch 1, hdc dec in 2 hdc, turn. *(1 hdc)*

Row 6: Ch 1, hdc in hdc. Fasten off.

Finishing
1. Glue Wings to Chick as shown in photo. Glue 2 black pompoms on face for eyes.

2. From felt, cut small square. Fold point to point to form beak. Glue beak to face as shown in photo.

3. Cut chenille stem into 3 pieces: 1 piece 4-inches in length and 2 pieces each 1½-inches in length. Working from 1 end, bend 4-inch piece at 1½ inches then again at 1 inch, forming U-shape. Bend each end over ½ inch at each leg to beg the feet. Fold 1½-inch pieces in half and wrap 1 around each ½-inch bend of legs. Spread 3 pieces out to form toes. ∎

Bodacious Beanbag

DESIGN BY LORI ZELLER

Whether watching television or reading a favorite book, kids will love relaxing in this fun, colorful chair, stitched in a rainbow of bright medium-weight yarns. It's easy to make and brings a splash of color to the play room!

SKILL LEVEL ●■□□
EASY

FINISHED SIZE
16 inches tall loosely stuffed

MATERIALS
Medium (worsted)
  weight yarn:
  7 oz/350 yds/198g each
    deep violet, blue, green,
    gold, orange, burgundy
    and black
Size G/6/4mm steel crochet
  hook or size needed to
  obtain gauge
Tapestry needle
Stitch markers
Stuffing: beans, pellets or
  foam pieces

GAUGE
8 sc = 2 inches; 7 sc rows =
1½ inches

INSTRUCTIONS

BEANBAG CHAIR
Beanbag Panel
Make 1 each deep violet,
blue, green, gold, orange
and burgundy.
Row 1: Ch 3, sc in 2nd ch from
hook, sc in next ch, turn. *(2 sc)*

Row 2: Ch 1, 2 sc in each sc
across, turn. *(4 sc)*

Row 3: Ch 1, sc in each sc
across, turn.

Row 4: Ch 1, 2 sc in first sc, sc in

each sc across to last sc, 2 sc in
last sc, turn. *(6 sc)*

Rows 5–38: [Rep rows 3 and 4
alternately] 17 times. *(40 sc)*

Rows 39–113: Rep row 3.

Row 114: Ch 1, **sc dec** *(see
Stitch Guide)* in first 2 sc, sc in
each sc across to last 2 sc, sc
dec in last 2 sc, turn. *(38 sc)*

Row 115: Ch 1, sc in each sc across, turn.

Rows 116–147: [Rep rows 114 and 115 alternately] 16 times. *(6 sc)*

Row 148: Ch 1, sc dec in first 2 sc, sc in each of next 2 sc, sc dec in last 2 sc, turn. *(4 sc)*

Row 149: Ch 1, [sc dec in next 2 sc] twice, turn. *(2 sc)*

Row 150: Ch 1, sc in each of next 2 sc. *(2 sc)*

Rnd 151: Now working in rnds around entire Panel, ch 1, work 2 sc in end of last row, sc in end of each row across to first row at bottom of Panel, 2 sc in end of first row, place st marker in last sc made, working in starting ch on opposite side of row 1, sc in each of next 2 chs at bottom of Panel,

2 sc in end of first row, place st marker in first sc of 2-sc group, sc in end of each row across to last row at top of Panel, 2 sc in end of last row, place st marker in last sc made, sc in each of next 2 sc of row 150, join with sl st in beg sc. Fasten off.

Rnd 152: Join black with sc in marked sc of rnd 151, sc in same st, [sc in each sc around to next marked sc, 2 sc in marked sc] 3 times, sc in each of last 2 sc, join with sl st in beg sc. Leaving long end, fasten off.

End Circle
Make 2.
Rnd 1: With black, ch 2, 8 sc in 2nd ch from hook, join with sl st in beg sc. *(8 sc)*

Rnd 2: Ch 1, 2 sc in each sc around, join with sl st in beg sc. *(16 sc)*

Rnd 3: Ch 1, sc in first sc, 2 sc in next st, [sc in next sc, 2 sc in next sc] around, join with sl st in beg sc. *(24 sc)*

Rnd 4: Ch 1, sc in each of first 3 sts, 2 sc in next st, [sc in each of next 3 sc, 2 sc in next sc] around, join with sl st in beg sc. Leaving long end, fasten off. *(30 sc)*

Assembly
With panels in rainbow order *(deep violet, blue, green, gold, orange and burgundy)*, sew end sts of each Panel to an end circle.

Sew sides of Panels tog and fill Beanbag as desired with beans, pellets or foam pieces.

To close opening, sew opposite ends of Panels to rem end circle. ∎

Little Critters

DESIGNS BY LORI ZELLER

Stitch this set of six darling finger puppets to have for rainy days when there's "nothing to do." Kids will love creating and staging a puppet show for Mom and Dad with these diverse little creatures!

SKILL LEVEL ■□□□
BEGINNER

FINISHED SIZE
2–3 inches tall

MATERIALS
Fine (baby) pompadour
    yarn:
        small amount each white,
            yellow, peach, blue,
            green, pink, pastel print
Size 10 crochet cotton:
    5 yds red/silver metallic
Size C/2/2.75mm crochet hook or
    size needed to obtain gauge
Tapestry needle
Dimensional fabric paint:
    black, red, pink
Fiberfill
Stitch markers

GAUGE
8 sc = 1 inch; 8 sc rnds = 1 inch

PATTERN NOTES
Do not join rounds unless
otherwise stated.

Mark first stitch of each round.

INSTRUCTIONS

BASIC PUPPET
Rnd 1: Ch 2, 7 sc in 2nd ch from
hook. *(7 sc)*

Rnd 2: 2 sc in each sc around.
(14 sc)

Rnd 3: Sc in each sc around.

Rnds 4–6: Rep rnd 3.

Rnd 7: [**Sc dec** *(see Stitch Guide)*
in next 2 sc] around. *(7 sc)*

Rnd 8: Rep rnd 3.

Rnd 9: Rep rnd 2. *(14 sc)*

Rnd 10: Rep rnd 3.

Rnd 11: Sc in each of next 4
sc, *ch 5, hdc in 2nd ch from
hook, hdc in each of next 2 chs,
sc in next ch * *(first arm)*, sc in
each of next 7 sc of rnd 10, rep
between * *(2nd arm)*, sc in each
of last 3 sc of rnd 10.

Rnd 12: Sc in each of first 4 sc,
push arm to front and sk arm
sts, sc in each of next 7 sc, push
arm to front and sk arm sts, sc
in each of last 3 sc.

Rnds 13–18: Rep rnd 3. At the
end of last rnd, join with sl st in
beg sc. Fasten off.

SNOWMAN
Rnds 1–18: With white, work rnds 1–18 of Basic Puppet.

Hat
Rnd 1: With red/silver metallic crochet cotton, ch 2, 7 sc in 2nd ch from hook. *(7 sc)*

Rnd 2: 2 sc in each sc around. *(14 sc)*

Rnd 3: Working this rnd in **back lps** *(see Stitch Guide)* only, sc in each st around.

Rnds 4–6: Sc in each sc around.

Rnd 7: Working in **front lps** *(see Stitch Guide)* only, [sc in next st, 2 sc in next st] around, join with sl st in beg sc. Leaving long end, fasten off.

Finishing
Sew Hat to top of head.

Paint 2 black dots on face for eyes and 3 black dots on body for buttons.

Paint a small red mouth below eyes.

DUCK
Rnds 1–18: With yellow, work rnds 1–18 of Basic Puppet.

Beak
Rnd 1: With peach, ch 2, 6 sc in 2nd ch from hook. *(6 sc)*

Rnd 2: Sc in each sc around, join with sl st in beg sc. Leaving long end, fasten off.

Finishing
Stuff Beak lightly and sew to face. For eyes, paint 2 black dots above Beak.

ELEPHANT
Rnds 1–18: With blue, work rnds 1–18 of Basic Puppet.

Trunk
Rnd 1: With blue, ch 2, 4 sc in 2nd ch from hook. *(4 sc)*

Rnd 2: Sc in each sc around.

Rnd 3: Sc in each of next 3 sc, 2 sc in next sc. *(5 sc)*

Rnd 4: Sc in each of next 4 sc, 2 sc in next sc. *(6 sc)*

Rnd 5: Rep rnd 2.

Rnd 6: [Sc in next sc, 2 sc in next sc] 3 times. *(9 sc)*

Rnd 7: Rep rnd 2, join with sl st in beg sc. Leaving long end, fasten off.

Ear
Make 2.
With blue, ch 4, 6 dc in 4th ch from hook. Leaving long end, fasten off.

Finishing
Stuff Trunk with fiberfill and sew to face.

Sew Ears to sides of head.

For eyes, paint 2 black dots above Trunk.

RABBIT
Rnds 1–18: With pastels print, work rnds 1–18 of Basic Puppet.

Ear
Make 2.
With pastel print, ch 7, sc in 2nd ch from hook, sc in each ch across, ch 2, sl st in last sc, working on opposite side of ch, sc in each ch across. Leaving long end, fasten off.

PIG
Rnds 1–18: With pink, work rnds 1–18 of Basic Puppet.

Snout
Rnd 1: With pink, ch 2, 5 sc in 2nd ch from hook, join with sl st in beg sc. *(5 sc)*

Rnd 2: Working in back lps only this rnd, ch 1, sc in each sc around, join with sl st in beg sc. Leaving long end, fasten off.

Ear
Make 2.
With pink, ch 2, sc in 2nd ch from hook. Leaving long end, fasten off.

Finishing
Sew Snout to front of face and Ears to top of head.

For eyes, paint 2 black dots above Snout. ■

Finishing
Sew Ears to top of head.

For eyes, paint 2 black dots on face.

For nose, paint a pink dot between eyes.

OCTOPUS
Rnds 1–6: With green, work rnds 1–6 of Basic Puppet. *(14 sc)*

Rnds 7 & 8: Sc in each sc around.

Rnd 9: Sc in each of next 2 sc, [ch 10, 2 sc in 2nd ch from hook, 2 sc in each of next 8 chs, sc in next sc of rnd 8] 4 times, sc in each of next 2 sc, [ch 10, 2 sc in 2nd ch from hook, 2 sc in each of next 8 chs, sc in next sc of rnd 8] 4 times, sc in each of next 2 sc on rnd 8. *(8 legs)*

Rnd 10: Holding legs to front of work and leaving leg sts unworked, sc in each sc around. *(14 sc)*

Rnds 11 & 12: Sc in each sc around. At the end of last rnd, join with sl st in beg sc. Fasten off.

Finishing
For eyes, paint 2 black dots on face.

For mouth, paint a small red mouth below eyes.

Buddy the Butterfly

DESIGN BY DEBBIE TABOR

Cute as a bug and cuddly as can be, this whimsical little fellow is the perfect companion for playtime fun or naptime dreams! His quirky smile and bright eyes will cheer your little one.

SKILL LEVEL ■■■□
INTERMEDIATE

FINISHED SIZE
14 inches tall

MATERIALS
Red Heart Classic medium (worsted) weight yarn (3½ oz/190 yds/90g per skein):
    1 skein each #253 tangerine, #245 orange and #12 black
    1 oz/54 yds/28g each #339 mid brown and #1 white, 2 yds #513 parakeet
Size J/10/6mm double-ended crochet hook or size needed to obtain gauge
Size H/8/5mm crochet hook
Tapestry needle

⅛-inch-wide orange ribbon: 24 inches
Fiberfill
Stitch marker

GAUGE
4 sts = 1 inch; 6 rows = 1 inch

PATTERN NOTES
Do not join rounds unless otherwise stated.

Mark first stitch of each round.

GENERAL INSTRUCTIONS
To **pull up lp**, insert hook in designated lp, bar or st, yo, pull through, leaving lp on hook.

To **work lps off hook** when adding a new color, with new color, place slip knot on hook, pull slip knot through first lp on hook, [yo, pull through 2 lps on hook] across. Last lp rem on hook at end of row is first vertical bar of next row.

To **work lps off with a color already in use**, pick up color from row below, yo, pull through 1 lp on hook, [yo, pull through 2 lps on hook] across.

To **turn**, rotate hook 180 degrees and slide all lps to opposite end of hook. Do not turn unless otherwise stated.

You will always have 1 lp left on your hook at the end of each row, this will be the first st of the next row.

INSTRUCTIONS

BUTTERFLY
Wing
Make 2.

Row 1: With size J hook and tangerine, ch 62, **pull up lp** (see General Instructions) in 2nd ch from hook (see General Instructions), pull up lp in each ch across, turn. (62 lps on hook)

Row 2: With orange, make slip knot on hook, yo, pull through first lp on hook, [yo, pull through 2 lps on hook] across, **do not turn**.

Row 3: Ch 1, pull up lp in top strand of first horizontal bar, pull up lp in each top strand of each horizontal bar across, turn.

Row 4: With tangerine, yo, pull through first lp on hook, [yo, pull through 2 lps on hook] across, do not turn

Row 5: Rep row 3.

Row 6: With orange, rep row 4.

Rows 7–26: [Rep rows 3–6 consecutively] 5 times.

Row 27: Rep row 3.

Row 28: With black, rep row 2, fasten off black and beg following row with orange.

Rows 29–56: [Rep rows 3–6 consecutively] 7 times.

Row 57: Pull up lp in top strand of first horizontal bar, pull up lp and pull through st on hook, [insert hook in next horizontal bar, pull up lp and pull through st on hook] across. Fasten off.

Body
Row 1: With size J hook and black, ch 29, pull up lp in 2nd ch from hook, pull up lp in each ch across, turn. (29 lps on hook)

Row 2: With brown, rep row 2 of Wing.

Row 3: Rep row 3 of Wing.

Row 4: With black, rep row 4 of Wing.

Row 5: Rep row 3 of Wing.

Row 6: With brown, rep row 6 of Wing.

Rows 7–74: [Rep rows 3–6 consecutively] 17 times.

Rows 75 & 76: Rep rows 3 and 4.

Row 77: Rep row 57 of Wing.

Antenna
Make 2.
With size H hook and black, ch 20, sl st in 5th ch from hook, working in ring, 2 sc in each ch around (10 sc), sc in each ch of Antenna. Leaving long end, fasten off.

Foot & Leg
Make 2.
Rnd 1: With size H hook and white, ch 4, sl st in first ch to form ring, ch 1, 8 sc in ring. (8 sc)

Rnd 2: 2 sc in each sc around. (16 sc)

Rnd 3: Sc in each sc around.

Rnds 4–7: Rep rnd 3.

Rnd 8: Sc in next sc, [sk next sc, sc in each of next 2 sc] 5 times. (11 sc)

Rnd 9: Rep rnd 3.

Rnd 10: Sc in each of next 2 sc, [sk next sc, sc in each of next 2 sc] 3 times, join with sl st in next st. Fasten off. (8 sc)

Stuff Foot lightly with fiberfill.

Rnd 11: Join black with sc in first sc, sc in each sc around. (8 sc)

Rnds 12–28: Rep rnd 3.

Row 29: Now working in rows, with Foot facing forward, fold Leg flat horizontally, working through both thicknesses, 4 sc across. Leaving long end, fasten off.

Cut orange ribbon in half, weave ribbon through rnd 3 of Foot, cross ribbon ends and weave through rnd 6, tie ends in a bow, double knot to secure ribbon ends. Trim as desired.

With length of white yarn, tack Foot to Leg just above ribbon, knot. Fasten off.

Hand & Arm
Make 2.
Rnd 1: With size H hook and white, ch 4, sl st in first ch to form ring, 8 sc in ring. (8 sc)

Rnds 2–5: Sc in each sc around.

Rnd 6: (Sc, dc, tr, dc, sc) in first st for **thumb**, sc in each sc around.

Row 7: Now working in rows, with thumb pointing to the side, fold piece flat horizontally and working through both thicknesses, ch 1, 3 sc across. Fasten off.

Row 8: Join black with sc in first sc, 2 sc in next sc, sc in last sc, turn. *(4 sc)*

Rows 9–21: Ch 1, sc in each of next 4 sc, turn. At the end of last rnd, leaving long end, fasten off.

Assembly
Fold Wing in half so stripes are horizontal, with black, working in the center black row, weave running stitch and gather slightly or as desired.

With WS facing out, with orange, weave running stitch to close off the outer corners of Wing approximately 1 inch from outer edge diagonally across to 1 inch from opposite outer edge.

Turn RS out and with size H hook, join black and working through both thicknesses, sc across top of Wing including corner, down along folded edge of Wing and along bottom of Wing including corner, ch 3, turn, dc in each sc back around Wing, working 2 dc in corner edges as needed. Fasten off.

Stuff fiberfill loosely in both sections of Wing, shaping and flattening as work progresses.

With orange, weave running stitch to gather and close inner edge of Wing. Rep for 2nd Wing.

Fold row 1 of Body to row 77 and, with black, sew edge closed to form a tube, knot to secure, weave through sts at end of tube, pull to close opening and secure. Loosely stuff Body with fiberfill.

Weave another strand through opposite end of tube, pull opening closed, knot to secure.

To form Head, weave strand of black about 10 sts down from top to form neck, gather slightly and knot to secure.

With black, beg just below neck, whipstitch Wing to side of Body. Rep with 2nd Wing on opposite side of Body.

Sew Legs to bottom of Body. With thumb pointing upward, sew Arms to Body, centered between neck and black center-gathered stripe of Wing.

Sew Antennae to center top of Head. Tie a soft overhand knot in each Antenna close to the base to help Antenna stand up.

Facial Features
With parakeet, embroider eyes according to diagram. With white, backstitch *(see Fig. 1)* around each eye according to diagram. With white, embroider mouth with backstitch. ■

Backstitch
Fig. 1

Facial Features
Diagram

Harry the Horned Lizard

DESIGN BY BEVERLY MEWHORTER

Despite being known for a tough hide and sharp horns, this little lizard is really just an old softie made with fluffy medium-weight yarn and fiberfill. Harry is sure to delight the hearts of all little boys and girls!

SKILL LEVEL ■□□□
BEGINNER

FINISHED SIZE
11 inches long

MATERIALS
Bulky (chunky) weight yarn:
    6 oz/210 yds/170g variegated
Size K/10½/6.5mm crochet hook or size needed to obtain gauge
Tapestry needle
9mm animal eyes: 2
Fiberfill
Hot-glue gun

GAUGE
3 sc = 1 inch

INSTRUCTIONS

LIZARD
Body
Top
Rnd 1: Ch 2, 10 sc in 2nd ch from hook, join with sl st in beg sc. *(10 sc)*

Rnd 2: Ch 1, 2 sc in each sc around, join with sl st in beg sc. *(20 sc)*

Rnd 3: Ch 1, sc in each sc around, join with sl st in beg sc.

Rnd 4: Ch 1, sc in first sc, 2 sc in next sc, [sc in next sc, 2 sc in next st] around, join with sl st in beg sc. *(30 sc)*

Rnd 5: Rep rnd 3.

Rnd 6: Ch 1, sc in each of first 5 sc, *[sc in next sc, ch 2, sl st in last sc, sc in same sc] 10 times*, sc in each of next 5 sc, rep between *, join with sl st in beg sc. Fasten off.

Bottom
Rnds 1–5: Rep rnds 1–5 of Top. At the end of last rnd, leaving long end, fasten off.

Sew rnd 5 of Bottom to rnd 5 of Top, stuffing with fiberfill before closing.

Tail
Rnd 1: Ch 2, 3 sc in 2nd ch from hook, join with sl st in beg sc. *(3 sc)*

Rnd 2: Ch 1, 2 sc in each sc around, join with sl st in beg sc. *(6 sc)*

Rnd 3: Ch 1, sc in each sc around, join with sl st in beg sc.

Rnds 4–6: Rep rnd 3.

Rnd 7: Ch 1, sc in first sc, 2 sc in next sc, [sc in next sc, 2 sc in next sc] around, join with sl st in beg sc. *(9 sc)*

Rnd 8: Rep rnd 3.

Rnd 9: Rep rnd 7. Fasten off. *(13 sc)*

Stuff Tail and sew to Body across 5 sc of rnd 6.

Back Ridge

Ch 25, sc in 2nd ch from hook and in each ch across. Leaving long end, fasten off.

Sew Back Ridge down center of Top of Body to tip of Tail.

Head

Rnd 1: Ch 2, 4 sc in 2nd ch from hook, join with sl st in beg sc. *(4 sc)*

Rnd 2: Ch 1, sc in each sc around, join with sl st in beg sc.

Rnd 3: Ch 1, 2 sc in each sc around, join with sl st in beg sc. *(8 sc)*

Rnd 4: Rep rnd 2.

Rnd 5: Ch 1, sc in each of first 2 sc, [2 sc in next sc, sc in each of next 2 sc] twice, join with sl st in beg sc. *(10 sc)*

Rnds 6 & 7: Rep rnd 2, stuff Head with fiberfill.

Rnd 8: Ch 1, [**sc dec** *(see Stitch Guide)* in next 2 sc] around, join with sl st in beg sc. Leaving long end, fasten off. *(5 sc)*

Sew Head to end of Body opposite Tail across 5 sc of rnd 6.

Head Crown

Ch 9, sc in 2nd ch from hook, ch 3, sl st in top of next sc, [sc in next ch, ch 3, sl st in top of sc] rep across, ending with sc in last sc, leaving long end, fasten off.

Sew Crown to top of Head over rnd 6.

Eyebrow
Make 2.
Ch 3, sl st in 2nd ch from hook, sl st in next ch. Leaving long end, fasten off.

Sew in front of Crown at slight angle as shown in photo. Glue eyes below Eyebrows.

Mouth Ridge
Make 2.
Ch 10. Leaving long end, fasten off. Sew to each side of face.

Leg
Make 4.
Rnd 1: Ch 2, 7 sc in 2nd ch from hook, join with sl st in beg sc. *(7 sc)*

Rnds 2–6: Ch 1, sc in each sc around, join with sl st in beg sc.

Rnd 7: Ch 1, sc in each of next 2 sc, [sl st in next sc, ch 3, sl st in 2nd ch from hook, sl st in next ch, sl st in same sc] 3 times *(toes)*, sc in each of next 2 sc, join with sl st in beg sc. Leaving long end, fasten off.

Stuff lightly and sew opening closed.

Sew 2 Legs to each side of Body to rnd 5 of Bottom Body. ■

Charlie Chimp CONTINUED FROM PAGE 110

Sew hook-and-loop tape to back of Shirt.

BANANA
Rnd 1: With off-white, ch 2, 6 sc in 2nd ch from hook. *(6 sc)*

Rnd 2: 2 sc in each st around. *(12 sc)*

Rnds 3–10: Sc in each st around. Stuff.

Rnd 11: Sc in first st, 2 sc in each of next 3 sts, sc in each of next 2 sts, [sc dec in next 2 sts] 3 times. *(12 sc)*

Rnds 12–21: Sc in each st around.

Rnd 22: [Sc dec in next 2 sts] around, join with sl st in first sc. Leaving long end for sewing, fasten off. Stuff.

Sew opening closed.

Peel
Rnd 1: With yellow, ch 2, 6 sc in 2nd ch from hook. *(6 sc)*

Rnd 2: Working this rnd in back lps only, sc in each st around.

Rnd 3: 2 sc in each st around. *(12 sc)*

Rnd 4: For **sections**, [sl st in next st, ch 23, sc in 2nd ch from hook, hdc in next ch, dc in next ch, tr in each of next 19 chs, sk next st on rnd 3] 6 times, sl st in last st. Fasten off.

Sew tog ends of rows on 2 Peel sections forming 1 piece, rep with rem sections for a total of 3 pieces.

Sew long edges of Peel pieces tog halfway up as shown in photo.

Place Banana inside Peel. ■

Harvey the Bunny CONTINUED FROM PAGE 119

Rnd 2: 2 sc in each sc around. *(12 sc)*

Rnd 3: [Sc in each of next 3 sc, 2 sc in next sc] around. *(15 sc)*

Rnds 4–9: Sc in each sc around.

Rnd 10: Sc in each sc around, join with sl st in beg sc. Fasten off.

Cheek
Make 2.
Rnd 1: With yellow, ch 2, 6 sc in 2nd ch from hook. *(6 sc)*

Rnd 2: 2 sc in each sc around. *(12 sc)*

Rnd 3: [Sc in each of next 3 sc, 2 sc in next sc] around. *(15 sc)*

Rnd 4: Sc in each sc around, join with sl st in beg sc. Fasten off.

Nose
Rnd 1: With pink, ch 2, 5 sc in 2nd ch. *(5 sc)*

Rnd 2: Sc in each sc around, join with sl st in beg sc. Fasten off.

Ear
Make 2.
Inner Ear
Rnd 1 (RS): With pink, ch 10, sc in 2nd ch from hook and in each of next 3 chs, hdc in each

of next 3 chs, dc in next ch, 5 dc in next ch, working on opposite side of ch, dc in next ch, hdc in each of next 3 chs, sc in each of next 4 chs. Fasten off.

Rnd 2: With RS facing, join yellow with sc in first sc, sc in each of next 9 sts, 3 sc in next st, sc in each of last 10 sts. Fasten off.

Outer Ear
Rnd 1 (RS): With yellow, ch 10, sc in 2nd ch from hook and in each of next 3 chs, hdc in each of next 3 chs, dc in next ch, 5 dc in next ch, working on opposite side of ch, dc in next ch, hdc in each of next 3 chs, sc in each of last 4 chs, **turn**.

Row 2: Now working in rows, ch 1, sc in each of first 10 sts, 3 sc in next st, sc in each of last 10 sts, **turn**.

Row 3: Place Inner Ear on top of Outer Ear, working through both pieces at same time, sl st in each of next 12 sts, ch 1, sl st in each of last 11 sts. Fasten off.

Tail
With yellow, work same as Cheek.

Finishing
1. Stuff Legs with fiberfill and

sew to Body as shown in photo. Stuff Arms and sew to Body as shown in photo.

2. Stuff Cheeks with fiberfill and sew to Head as shown in photo. Stuff Nose and sew between Cheeks.

3. Sew Ears to top of Head.

4. Stuff Tail and sew to back of Body.

5. With black, use satin stitch *(see Fig. 1)* to make eyes as shown in photo. ■

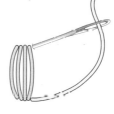

Satin Stitch
Fig. 1

Awesome Afghans

Chapter Contents

Scraps Extraordinaire

DESIGN BY MARTHA BROOKS STEIN

Use a different family of colors for each diagonal row in this amazing afghan! Lots of small squares of your favorite scrap colors turn into a beautiful creation when you stitch them together.

SKILL LEVEL ■■□□
EASY

FINISHED SIZE
55 x 70 inches

MATERIALS

Medium (worsted)
weight yarn:
36 oz/1,800 yds/1,021g in
assorted shades of green,
yellow, purple, orange,
red and blue
21 oz/1,050 yds/595g black
Size I/9/5.5mm crochet hook or
size needed to obtain gauge
Tapestry needle

GAUGE
Square = 2¾ inches

INSTRUCTIONS

AFGHAN
Square
Make 48 in each green, yellow, red and purple shades.
Make 46 each orange and blue shades.
Rnd 1 (RS): With scrap color, ch 4, sl st in first ch to form ring, ch 2, 2 dc in ring, [ch 2, 3 dc in ring] 3 times, join with hdc in 2nd ch of beg ch-2 forming last ch sp.

Rnd 2: Ch 2 (counts as first dc), 2 dc in ch sp just made, [ch 1, (3 dc, ch 2, 3 dc) in next ch-2 sp] around, ch 1, 3 dc in same ch as beg ch-2, ch 2, join with sl st in 2nd ch of beg ch-2. Fasten off.

Rnd 3: Join black with sc in any corner ch-2 sp, *sc in each of

next 3 dc, in next ch-1 sp and in each of next 3 dc**, (sc, ch 2, sc) in corner ch-2 sp (corner), rep from * around, ending last rep at **, sc in next ch-2 sp, ch 2, join with sl st in beg sc. Fasten off.

Assembly
To join, hold 2 Squares with RS tog, carefully matching sts, working in **back lps** (see Stitch Guide) only, sew Squares tog, beg in 2nd ch of first corner ch-2 sp and ending in first ch of last corner ch-2 sp according to diagram.

Join rem Squares in same manner, making sure all 4-corner joinings are secure.

Border
Rnd 1 (RS): Hold Afghan with

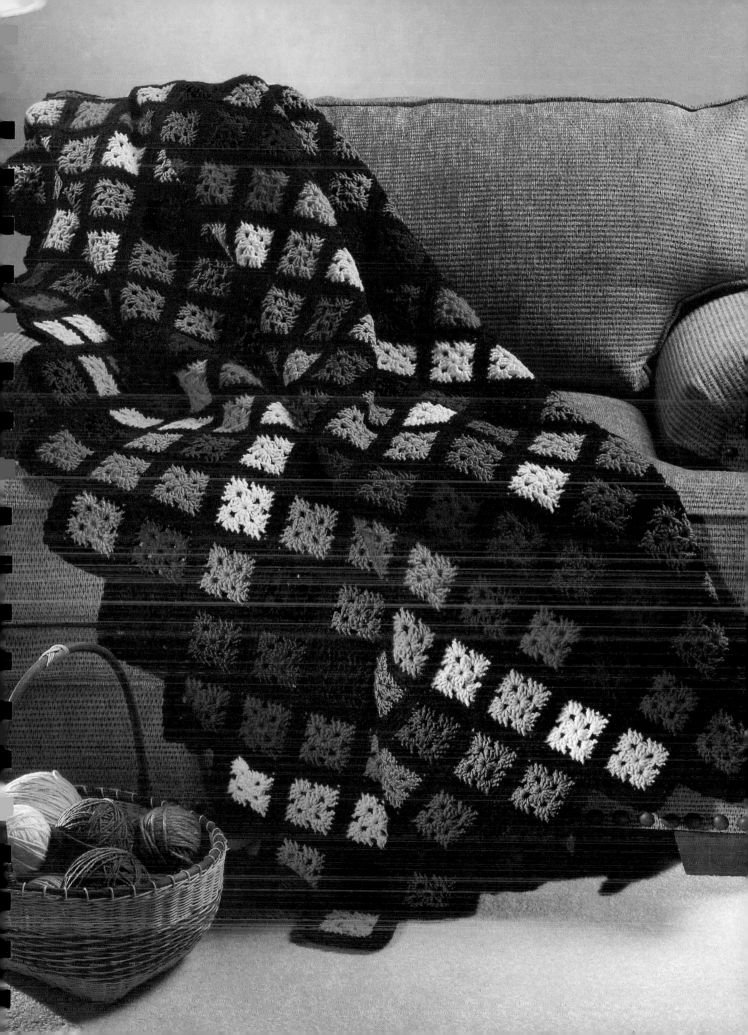

RS facing, join black with sc in back lp of 2nd ch of top corner ch-2 sp of Square in upper right-hand corner, working in back lps only, sc in each of next 9 sc, sc in next joining, sc in each of next 9 sc, sc in first ch of next corner ch-2 sp, *ch 2, sc in next ch, sc in each of next 9 sc, sc in next joining, sc in each of next 9 sc, sc in first ch of next corner ch-2 sp, rep from * 8 times, ch 2, sc in next ch, sc in each of next 9 sc, sc in first ch of next corner ch-2 sp, **ch 2, sc in next ch, sc in each of next 9 sc, sc in next joining, sc in each of next 9 sc, sc in first ch of next corner ch-2 sp, rep from ** 12 times, ch 2, sc in next ch, sc in each of next 9 sc, sc in first ch of next corner ch-2 sp, ***ch 2, sc in next ch, sc in each of next 9 sc, sc in next joining, sc in each of next 9 sc, sc in first ch of next corner ch-2 sp, rep from *** 9 times, ch 2, sc in next ch, sc in each of next 9 sc, sc in first ch of next corner ch-2 sp, ****ch 2, sc in next ch, sc in each of next 9 sc, sc in next joining, sc in each of next 9 sc, sc in first ch of next corner ch-2 sp, rep from **** 12 times, ch 2, sc in next ch, sc in each of next 9 sc, sc in first ch of next corner ch-2 sp, join with hdc in first sc.

Rnd 2: *[Ch 3, sk next sc, sl st in next sc] 5 times, sk next sc, [sl st in next sc, ch 3, sk next sc] 5 times, ch 3, sl st in next corner ch-2 sp, rep from * 9 times, [ch 3, sk next sc, sl st in next sc] 5 times, ch 3, sk next sc, sc in next corner ch-2 sp, **[ch 3, sk next

Scraps Extraordinaire Assembly Diagram

COLOR KEY
◆ Shades of orange
◆ Shades of purple
◇ Shades of yellow
◆ Shades of green
◆ Shades of red
◆ Shades of blue

sc, sl st in next sc] 5 times, sk next sc, [sl st in next sc, ch 3, sk next sc] 5 times, ch 3, sl st in next corner ch-2 sp, rep from ** 12 times, [ch 3, sk next sc, sl st in next sc] 5 times, ch 3, sk next sc, sl st in next corner ch-2 sp, ***[ch 3, sk next sc, sl st in next sc] 5 times, sk next sc, [sl st in next sc, ch 3, sk next sc] 5 times, ch 3, sl st in next corner ch-2 sp, rep from *** 9 times, [ch 3, sk

next sc, sl st in next sc] 5 times, ch 3, sk next sc, sl st in next corner ch-2 sp, ****[ch 3, sk next sc, sl st in next sc] 5 times, sk next sc, [sl st in next sc, ch 3, sk next sc] 5 times, ch 3, sl st in next corner ch-2 sp, rep from **** 12 times, [ch 3, sk next sc, sl st in next sc] 5 times, ch 3, sk next sc, join with sl st in base of beg ch-3. Fasten off. ∎

Woven Ribbons

DESIGN BY ANNE HALLIDAY

Rich jewel tones in dusky tweed yarns create the colorful palette in this gem of an afghan. It would make a beautiful holiday or housewarming gift.

SKILL LEVEL ◼◻◻◻
BEGINNER

FINISHED SIZE
49 x 66 inches

MATERIALS

Medium (worsted) weight yarn:
    16 oz/800 yds/454g soft white
Tweed medium (worsted) weight yarn:
    4 oz/200 yds/113g each moss, mulberry, denim, coffee, cranberry, frosty green and charcoal
    2 oz/100 yds/57g lavender
Size I/9/5.5mm crochet hook or size needed to obtain gauge
Tapestry needle

GAUGE
1 pattern rep = 2¾ inches; 5 cl rows = 3½ inches

PATTERN NOTES
Leave an 8-inch length of yarn when joining and fastening off each yarn.

Afghan is crocheted vertically.

SPECIAL STITCHES
Cluster (cl): Holding back last lp of each st on hook, 3 dc in same st, yo, pull through all lps on hook.

Join with hdc: With slip knot on hook, yo, insert hook in indicated st, yo, pull up lp, complete as hdc.

INSTRUCTIONS

AFGHAN
Row 1: With soft white, ch 215, sc in 2nd ch from hook, [ch 3, sk next 2 chs, sc in next ch] across, turn. Fasten off. *(71 ch-3 sps)*

Row 2 (WS): Using soft white, **join with hdc** *(see Special Stitches)* in first sc, ch 1, sc in first ch-3 sp, [ch 3, sc in next ch-3 sp] across to last sc, ch 1, hdc in last sc, turn. Fasten off.

Row 3 (RS): Join moss with sc in hdc, ch 3, sk first ch-1 sp, working in front of next ch-3 sp of row 2, **cl** *(see Special Stitches)* in sc directly below on row 1, ch 3, *[sc in next ch-3 sp, ch 3]

twice, working in front of ch-3 sp of row 2, cl in next sc directly below on row 1, ch 3, rep from * across to last ch-1 sp, sk ch-1 sp, sc in last hdc, turn. Fasten off.

Row 4 (WS): Join soft white with hdc in first sc, ch 1, sc in first ch-3 sp, [ch 3, sc in next ch-3 sp] across to last sc, ch 1, hdc in last sc, turn. Fasten off.

Row 5 (RS): Join mulberry with sc in hdc, ch 3, sk next ch-1 sp, working in front of next ch-3 sp, cl in cl directly below, ch 3, *[sc in next ch-3 sp, ch 3] twice, working in front of next ch-3 sp, cl in cl directly below, ch 3, rep from * across to last ch-1 sp, sk ch-1 sp, sc in last hdc, turn. Fasten off.

Row 6: Rep row 4.

Row 7: Rep row 5 with denim.

Row 8: Rep row 4.

Row 9: Rep row 5 with coffee.

Row 10: Rep row 4.

Row 11: Rep row 5 with cranberry.

Row 12: Rep row 4.

Row 13: Rep row 5 with frosty green.

Row 14: Rep row 4.

Row 15: Rep row 5 with charcoal.

Row 16: Rep row 4.

Row 17: Rep row 5 with moss.

Next rows: [Rep rows 4–17 consecutively] 8 times.

Next row: Rep rows 4–14 once.

Last row (RS): Join charcoal with sc in first hdc, ch 2, sk next ch-1 sp, working in front of next ch-3 sp, cl in cl directly below, ch 2, *[sc in next ch-3 sp, ch 2] twice, working in front of next ch-3 sp, work cl in cl directly below, ch 2, rep from * across to last ch-1 sp, sk ch-1 sp, sc in last hdc. Fasten off.

Edging

Row 1 (RS): Working in last worked row of Afghan, join lavender with sl st in first sc, ch 2, dc in same sc, sk next 2 chs, *(sl st, ch 2, dc) in next st, sk next 2 chs, rep from * across to last sc, sl st in last sc. Fasten off.

Row 2 (RS): Working in starting ch on opposite side of row 1, join lavender with sl st in first ch, ch 2, dc in same ch, sk next 2 chs, *(sl st, ch 2, dc) in next ch, sk next 2 chs, rep from * across to last ch, sl st in last ch. Fasten off.

FRINGE

Cut 2 strands of matching color each 16 inches in length for each row. Fold 2 matching strands in half, pull fold through, pull all ends, including ends from each row, through fold. Pull ends to tighten. Attach Fringe with matching colors on each end of Afghan. Trim ends evenly. ■

Just Geese

DESIGN BY DIANE POELLOT

What a wonderful scrap solution! Bring out your inner quilter when you stitch this afghan, made in the flying geese tradition. The multitude of colors on a black background gives the impression of a stained glass window.

SKILL LEVEL
INTERMEDIATE

FINISHED SIZE
35 x 58 inches

MATERIALS
Red Heart Super Saver medium (worsted) weight yarn (7 oz/364 yds/198g per skein):
  3 skeins #312 black
  6 skeins of desired geese colors—shown are: #661 frosty green, #356 amethyst, #319 cherry red, #363 pale green, #358 lavender, #254 pumpkin, #389 hunter green, #327 light coral, #385 royal, #886 blue, #373 petal pink, #530

orchid, #324 bright yellow, #354 vibrant orange, #579 pale plum, #885 delft blue, #774 light raspberry, #321 gold, #320 cornmeal, #376 burgundy, #368 paddy green, #381 light blue
Size G/6/4mm crochet hook or size needed to obtain gauge
Tapestry needle

GAUGE
7 sc = 2 inches; 7 sc rows = 2 inches

PATTERN NOTES
For color change, always change in last st made, drop last color, pick up again when needed.

Do not work over dropped color unless otherwise stated.

Use separate strand for each section of color.

INSTRUCTIONS

AFGHAN
Strip
Make 11.
Row 1: With first goose color, ch 12, sc in 2nd ch from hook and in each ch across, **changing colors** (see Stitch Guide and Pattern Notes) to black, turn. (11 sc)

Row 2: Ch 1, sc in first st changing to goose color, sc in each of next 9 sts changing to separate strand black, sc in last st, turn.

Row 3: Ch 1, sc in each of first 2 sts, changing to same goose color in last st, sc in each of next 7 sts, changing to black, sc in each of last 2 sts, turn.

Row 4: Ch 1, sc in each of first 3 sts, changing to same goose color in last st, sc in each of next 5 sts, changing to black, sc in each of last 3 sts, turn.

Row 5: Ch 1, sc in each of first 4 sts, changing to same goose color in last st, sc in each of next 3 sts, changing to black, sc in each of last 4 sts, turn.

Row 6: Ch 1, sc in each of first 5 sts, changing to same goose color in last st, sc in next st changing to black, sc in each of last 5 sts, turn. Fasten off goose color.

Row 7: Working over dropped black on each side, join next goose color with sc in first st, sc in each st across, turn.

Next rows: Using each of the separate goose colors before repeating any colors, rep rows 2–7 consecutively until there are 34 geese in Strip, ending with row 6. At end of last row, fasten off black.

Assembly
Arrange Strips matching first row on 1 Strip to last row on next Strip so color pattern is inverted on alternate Strips.

Using tapestry needle and black, sew ends of rows tog, pulling end sts flush and snug without forming a ridge.

EDGING
Working around entire outer edge of assembled Strips, join black with sc in any st, sc in each st or ch and in end of each row around with 3 sc in each corner, join with sl st in beg sc. Fasten off. ■

Hot-Cross Granny

DESIGN BY GLENDA WINKLEMAN

Grandma always had something wonderful baking in the oven and was always willing to share. Stitch this gorgeous afghan and give it to a friend or family member as a tribute to your Grandma!

SKILL LEVEL ■■■□
INTERMEDIATE

FINISHED SIZE
48½ x 66 inches

MATERIALS
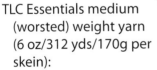
TLC Essentials medium (worsted) weight yarn (6 oz/312 yds/170g per skein):
  5 skeins #2101 white
  1 skein each #2915 cranberry, #2772 light country rose, #2883 country blue, #2533 dark plum, #2531 light plum, #2220 butter, #2673 medium thyme, #2675 dark thyme
Size K/10½/6.5mm crochet hook or size needed to obtain gauge
Tapestry needle

GAUGE
3 rnds = 4 inches

SPECIAL STITCHES
Popcorn (pc): 5 dc in indicated st, drop lp from hook, insert hook in top of first dc of dc group, pull dropped lp through.

Cross-stitch (cross-st): Sk next 2 dc, dc in next dc, dc in 2nd sk dc.

INSTRUCTIONS

AFGHAN
Block
Make 63 blocks, using different combinations of five colors per block.

Rnd 1 (RS): With color of choice, ch 5, sl st in first ch to form ring, ch 2 *(does not count*

as a st), [**pc** *(see Special Stitches)* in ring, ch 5, sl st in top of pc, ch 3] 4 times, join with sl st in top of first pc. Fasten off. *(4 pc)*

Rnd 2: Join color of choice with sl st in any ch-5 sp, ch 3 *(counts as first dc)*, (2 dc, ch 2, 3 dc) in same ch sp, *working over ch-3 sp between pc sts, work 2 tr between next 2 pc sts pulling tr up to current level of work** (3 dc, ch 2, 3 dc) in next ch-5 sp, rep from * around, ending last rep at **, join with sl st in 3rd ch of beg ch-3. Fasten off. *(24 dc, 8 tr)*

Rnd 3: Join white with sl st in corner ch-2 sp, ch 3, (dc, ch 2, 2 dc) in same ch sp, ***cross-st** *(see Special Stitches)*, sk next tr, dc in next tr, dc in sk tr, sk next dc, dc in next dc, dc in sk dc**, (2 dc, ch 2, 2 dc) in corner ch sp, rep from * around, ending last rep at **, join with sl st in 3rd ch of beg ch-3. Fasten off.

Rnd 4: Join color of choice with sc in corner ch-2 sp, ch 2, sc in same ch sp, * [ch 1, sk next dc, sc in next dc] 5 times**, (sc, ch 2, sc) in corner ch sp, rep from * around, ending last rep at **, join with sl st in beg sc. Fasten off. *(28 sc)*

Rnd 5: Join color of choice with sl st in corner ch-2 sp, ch 3, (2 dc, ch 2, 3 dc) in same ch sp, *sk next sc, [sk next ch-1 sp, dc in next sc, dc in next sk ch-1 sp] 5 times, sk next sc**, (3 dc, ch 2, 3 dc) in corner ch sp, rep from * around, ending last rep at **, join with sl st in 3rd ch of beg ch-3. Fasten off. *(64 dc)*

Rnd 6: Join white with sl st in any corner ch-2 sp, ch 3, (2 dc, ch 2, 3 dc) in same ch sp, *work 2 dc between each set of dc across to next corner *(6 sets of 2 dc)***, (3 dc, ch 2, 3 dc) in corner ch sp, rep from * around, ending last rep at **, join with sl st in 3rd ch of beg ch-3. Fasten off. *(72 dc)*

Assembly

With white, working in **back lps** *(see Stitch Guide)* only, sl st Blocks tog in 9 rows of 7 Blocks each.

When joining Blocks, make sure that each junction of 4 Blocks and all other corners are evenly spaced so design will not be distorted.

Border

Rnd 1: Join white with sl st in upper right corner ch-2 sp, ch 3, (2 dc, ch 2, 3 dc) in same ch-2 sp, work 2 dc between each 2-dc group around, 2 dc in each ch sp on each side of each joining seam, and (3 dc, ch 2, 3 dc) in each corner ch-2 sp, join with sl st in 3rd ch of beg ch-3. Fasten off.

Rnd 2: Join color of choice with sl st in corner ch-2 sp, ch 3, (dc, ch 5, sl st in top of last dc) 3 times in same ch sp, *(dc, ch 5, sl st in top of last dc, dc) in sp between each 2-dc group across, changing color before working next corner**, (2 dc, ch 5, sl st in top of last dc) 3 times in corner ch sp, rep from * around, ending last rep at **, join with sl st in 3rd ch of beg ch-3. Fasten off. ∎

Flower Power

DESIGN BY ANNE HALLIDAY

Big, colorful flowers created with puffy clusters bring to mind the fanciful floral designs that artfully decorated the "peace mobile" vans of the free-spirited hippie era. Stitch it for your favorite "flower child."

SKILL LEVEL ◼◼◼◻
INTERMEDIATE

FINISHED SIZE
49 x 68 inches

MATERIALS
Red Heart Super Saver
  medium (worsted)
  weight yarn (7 oz/364
  yds/198g per skein):
    3 skeins #312 black (MC)
    1 skein each #774 light
      raspberry (A), #406
      medium thyme (B), #322
      pale yellow (C) and #530
      orchid (D)
Size I/9/5.5mm crochet hook or
  size needed to obtain gauge
Tapestry needle
2 safety pins

GAUGE
Motif corner to corner = 5
inches; rnds 1 and 2 = 2½ inches

PATTERN NOTES
Work the following color
sequence and quantity of motifs:

Motif A: Make 50, rnds 1 and
2 with A, rnd 3 with MC, rnd 4
with A and rnd 5 with MC.

Motif B: Make 49, rnds 1 and
2 with B, rnd 3 with MC, rnd 4
with B and rnd 5 with MC.

Motif C: Make 40, rnds 1 and
2 with C, rnd 3 with MC, rnd 4
with C and rnd 5 with MC.

Motif D: Make 40, rnds 1 and
2 with D, rnd 3 with MC, rnd 4
with D and rnd 5 with MC.

SPECIAL STITCH
Cluster (cl): Ch 3, yo, insert
hook in 3rd ch from hook, yo,
pull up lp, yo, pull through 2
lps on hook, yo, insert hook in
same ch, yo, pull up lp, yo, pull
through 2 lps on hook, yo, pull
through all lps on hook.

INSTRUCTIONS

AFGHAN
Motif
Rnd 1 (RS): Ch 2, 6 sc in 2nd ch
from hook, join with sl st in beg
sc, **turn.**

Rnd 2 (WS): Ch 1, (sc, **cl**—see
Special Stitch) in first sc, [sc in
next sc, cl] 5 times, join with
sl st in beg sc, turn. Fasten off.
(6 cls)

Rnd 3 (RS): Join MC with sl st in any sc, ch 4 *(counts as first dc and ch-1)*, working behind next cl, tr in sc on rnd 1 to left of sc on rnd 2, ch-1, [dc in next sc on rnd 2, ch 1, working behind next cl, tr in sc on rnd 1 to left of sc on rnd 2, ch 1] around, join with sl st in 3rd ch of beg ch-4, turn. Remove lp from hook and place on safety pin. *(12 ch-1 sps)*

Note: *Keep MC and safety pin on WS.*

Rnd 4 (WS): Join with sc in same ch as joining, cl, sk next ch, [sc in next st, cl, sk next ch] around, join with sl st in beg sc, turn. Fasten off. *(12 cls)*

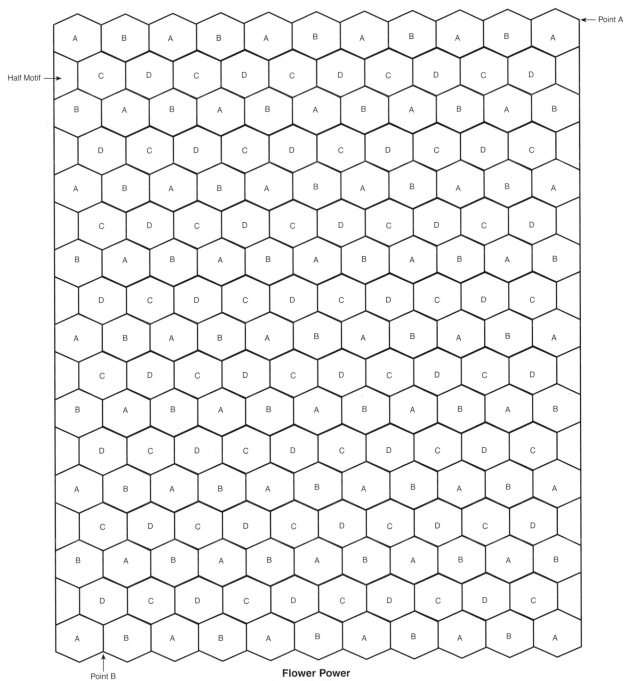

**Flower Power
Assembly Diagram**

Rnd 5 (RS): Remove safety pin, insert hook in dropped lp of MC, ch 2, sl st in sc in front of ch-2, ch 4, *working behind next cl, tr in ch-1 sp 1 rnd below cl, (tr, ch 1, tr) in next sc (corner), working behind next cl, tr in ch-1 sp 1 rnd below cl, ch 1**, dc in next sc, ch 1, rep from * around, ending last rep at **, join with sl st in 3rd ch of beg ch-4. Fasten off. (6 dc, 24 tr, 18 ch-1 sps)

Half Motif
Make 16.
Row 1 (WS): With MC, ch 4, 6 dc in 4th ch from hook (first 3 chs count as first dc), turn. (7 dc)

Row 2: Ch 2 (counts as first hdc), hdc in same st, 2 hdc in each of next 5 sts, hdc in last st, turn. (13 hdc)

Row 3: Ch 3 (counts as first dc), dc in same st, [dc in next st, 2 dc in next st] 5 times, dc in each of next 2 sts, turn. (19 dc)

Row 4: Ch 3, dc in same st, hdc in next st, sc in each of next 3 sts, hdc in next st, *(dc, ch 1, dc) in next st, hdc in next st, sc in each of next 3 sts, hdc in next st, rep from * once, 2 dc in last st. Fasten off. (23 sts, 2 corner ch-1 sps)

Assembly
When sewing Motifs tog, beg and end in corner ch-1 sps. When sewing Half Motifs, match first and last dc sts on rnd 4 to single corner ch sp on Motifs.

Thread yarn needle with MC, whipstitch Motifs and Half Motifs tog according to diagram.

Edging
Rnd 1 (RS): Starting at point A as indicated on diagram, join MC with sl st in tr to right of corner ch-1 sp, ch 3 (counts as first dc and ch-1, mark this dc with safety pin), dc in next corner ch-1 sp, *ch 1, dc in next tr, ch 1, sk next st, [dc in next ch-1 sp, ch 1, sk next st] twice, dc in next tr, ch 1, dc in next corner ch-1 sp, ch 1, dc in next tr, ch 1, sk next st, [dc in next ch-1 sp, ch 1, sk next st] twice, dc in next tr, [**dc dec** (see Stitch Guide) in next 2 ch sps, sk seam between, dc in next tr, ch 1, sk next st, {dc in next ch-1 sp, ch 1, sk next st} twice, dc in next tr, ch 1, dc in next corner ch-1 sp, ch 1, dc in next tr, ch 1, sk next st, {dc in next ch-1 sp, ch 1, sk next st} twice, dc in next tr] 10 times, ch 1, dc in next corner ch-1 sp, ch 1, dc in next tr, ch 1, sk next st, [dc in next ch-1 sp, ch 1, sk next st] twice, [dc in next tr, ch 1, working across next Half Motif and working in end of rows, {hdc in next row, ch 1} 8 times, working across next Motif, dc in next unworked tr, ch 1, sk next st, {dc in next ch-1 sp, ch 1, sk next st} twice] across to first corner of last Motif*, dc in next tr, ch 1, dc in next corner ch-1 sp (mark last dc made with safety pin for st placement), rep between * once, join with sl st in 2nd ch of beg ch-3.

Rnd 2: Ch 1, sc in next ch-1 sp, ch 1, *sc in next dc, ch 1, [sc in next ch-1 sp, ch 1] 5 times, sc in next dc, [{ch 1, sc in next ch-1 sp} 4 times, sk next dc, sc in next dc dec, sk next dc, {sc in next ch-1 sp} 4 times, sc in next dc] 10 times, ch 1, [sc in next ch-1 sp, ch 1] 5 times, sc in next dc, ch 1, [sc in next ch-1 sp, ch 1] across to next marked dc, rep from * around, join with sl st in beg sc, remove safety pins.

Rnd 3: Ch 1, [sc in next ch-1 sp, ch 1] 11 times, sk next sc, sc in next sc, *ch 1, sk next sc, [{sc in next ch-1 sp, ch 1} 8 times, sk next sc, sc in next sc, ch 1, sk next sc] 9 times*, [sc in next ch-1 sp, ch 1] across to first sc of 3-sc group at point B, sk next sc, sc in next sc (mark sc just made with safety pin), rep between * once, [sc in next ch-1 sp, ch 1] across to beg of rnd, join with sl st in beg sc.

Rnd 4: Sl st in next ch-1 sp, [ch 2, sl st in next ch-1 sp] 10 times, [sl st in next ch-1 sp, {ch 2, sl st in next ch-1 sp} 8 times] 9 times, sl st in next ch-1 sp, [ch 2, sl st in next ch-1 sp] across to marked st, [sl st in next ch-1 sp, {ch 2, sl st in next ch-1 sp} 8 times] 9 times, [sl st in next ch-1 sp, ch 2] across to beg of rnd, join with sl st in beg sl st. Fasten off. ■

Color Bands

DESIGN BY KATHLEEN GAREN

Start this beauty in the center and radiate your shades of color out from there. We've used three shades each of four complimentary colors, bordered by a band of black, stitched with a rickrack look, giving this afghan a broad appeal.

SKILL LEVEL ◼◼◻◻
EXPERIENCED

FINISHED SIZE
54 x 60 inches

MATERIALS
Medium (worsted)
   weight yam:
   18½ oz/925 yds/524g white
   8½ oz/425 yds/241g black
   5 oz/250 yds/142g each
   light blue, medium blue,
   dark blue, light red, medium
   red and dark red
   3½ oz/175 yds/100g each light
   purple, medium purple, dark
   purple, light brown, medium
   brown and dark brown
   1 oz/50 yds/28g each
   light teal, medium teal and
   dark teal

Size I/9/5.5mm crochet hook or
   size required for gauge
Tapestry needle
Stitch markers

GAUGE
3 cls = 2 inches

SPECIAL STITCH
Cluster (cl): Holding back last
lp of each dc on hook, 2 dc in st
or ch sp indicated or dc in 2 ch
sps indicated, yo, pull through
all lps on hook.

---INSTRUCTIONS---

AFGHAN
Row 1 (RS): With dark teal, ch
24, sc in 5th ch from hook, [ch
1, sk next ch, sc in next ch] 8

times, ch 1, sk next 2 chs, sl st
in last ch, working on opposite
side of ch, (sl st, ch 2, dc, ch 1,
cl—*see Special Stitch*, ch 2, cl)
in sp formed by last 2 sk chs of
beg ch *(partial beg corner, mark
ch-2)*, ch 1, [cl in same sp and
sp formed by next sk ch, ch 1] 8
times, cl in same ch-1 sp and sp
formed by beg 4 sk chs of beg
ch, ch 1, (cl, ch 2, cl, ch 1, cl, ch
2, cl) in same sp *(corner)*, ch 1,
[cl in same sp and next ch-1 sp,
ch 1] 8 times, cl in same ch-1 sp
and sp where beg corner was
worked, ch 1, cl in same sp, ch
2 *(completed beg corner)*, join
with sl st in 2nd ch of marked
ch-2. Fasten off.

Rnd 2: With RS facing, join

same ch-1 sp and next ch-1 sp, ch 1] across to last ch-1 sp before next corner, cl in same ch sp and next corner ch-2 sp, (cl, ch 2, cl) in same ch sp, ch 1, cl in same ch sp and next ch-1 sp, ch 1, [cl in same ch-1 sp and next ch-1 sp, ch 1] across to last ch-1 sp before next corner, cl in same ch sp and next corner ch-2 sp, ch 1*, (cl, ch 2, cl) in same ch sp, rep between *, join with sl st in 2nd ch of beg ch-2.

Rnds 4–42: Rep rnd 3 in following color sequence:

* 1 row white, 1 row black, 1 row white*, 1 row light brown, 1 row medium brown, 2 rows dark brown, 1 row medium brown, 1 row light brown, rep between * once, 1 row light purple, 1 row medium purple, 2 rows dark purple, 1 row medium purple, 1 row light purple, rep between * once, 1 row light red, 1 row medium red, 2 rows dark red, 1 row medium red, 1 row light red, rep between * once, 1 row light blue, 1 row medium blue, 2 rows dark blue, 1 row medium blue, 1 row light blue, rep between * once. At end of last rnd, **do not fasten off**.

Rnd 43: Sl st in next ch-2 sp, ch 1, 4 sc in same ch sp, *2 sc in each ch-1 sp across to next corner ch-2 sp, 4 sc in corner ch-2 sp, rep from * twice, 2 sc in each ch-1 sp across to first sc, join with sl st in beg sc.

Rnd 44: Sl st in each sc, join with sl st in beg sl st. Fasten off. ■

medium teal with sl st in first ch-2 sp of 1 corner, ch 2, (dc, ch 2, cl) in same ch sp (*beg corner*), *ch 1, cl in same ch sp and next ch-1 sp, ch 1, cl in same ch sp and next ch-2 sp, ch 1, (cl, ch 2, cl) in same ch sp (*corner*), ch 1, cl in same ch sp and next ch-1 sp, ch 1, [cl in same ch sp and next ch-1 sp, ch 1] 9 times, cl in same ch sp and next corner ch-2 sp, ch 1*, (cl, ch 2, cl) in same ch sp (*corner*), rep between *, join with sl st in 2nd ch of beg ch-2. Fasten off.

Rnd 3: With RS facing, join light teal with sl st in first ch-2 sp of 1 corner, ch 2, (dc, ch 2, cl) in same ch sp, *ch 1, cl in same sp and next ch-1 sp, ch 1, [cl in

Blooms at the Beach

DESIGN BY KATHERINE ENG

A sandy background with beautiful blooms in your favorite colors makes a pretty scrap solution. This striking pattern, created with hexagonal blocks, give this afghan a unique edge and stylish look.

SKILL LEVEL ■■■□
INTERMEDIATE

FINISHED SIZE
42 x 62 inches

MATERIALS
Medium (worsted) weight yarn:
    14 oz/700 yds/397g light
      beige
    1 oz/50 yds/28g each
      various scrap colors
Sizes G/6/4mm and H/8/5mm
    crochet hook or size needed
    to obtain gauge
Tapestry needle

GAUGE
Size H hook: Rnds 1 and 2 = 3 inches; Completed Motif = 5¾ inches point to point

PATTERN NOTES
Rounds 1 and 2 are each worked with a different scrap color. Rounds 3 and 4 are worked with a 3rd scrap color.

Round 5 of all Hexagon Motifs is worked with light beige.

Hexagon Motifs are joined as work progresses in round 5.

Arrange Hexagon Motifs in 5 rows of 12 Motifs with 4 rows of 11 Hexagon Motifs between, scattering colors evenly.

SPECIAL STITCHES
Popcorn (pc): Ch 3, 3 dc in same sc, drop lp from hook, insert hook in top of beg ch-3, pull dropped lp through st on hook, ch 3, sl st in same sc.

Shell: [2 dc, ch 2, 2 dc] in indicated st.

INSTRUCTIONS

AFGHAN
First Motif
Rnd 1: With size H hook and scrap color, ch 4, sl st in first ch to form ring, ch 1, 12 sc in ring, join with sl st in beg sc. Fasten off. *(12 sc)*

Rnd 2: Join scrap color with sl st in any sc, [**pc** *(see Special Stitches)* in sc, ch 1, sk next sc, sl st in next sc] 6 times, ending with sl st in beg sc. Fasten off. *(6 pc sts)*

Rnd 3: Working in **back lp** *(see Stitch Guide)* of pc, join scrap color with sc in same st, *ch 2, dc in next ch-1 sp, ch 2**, sc in back lp of next pc, rep from * around, ending last rep at **, join with sl st in beg sc.

Rnd 4: Ch 1, (sc, ch 2, sc) in first sc, *2 sc in next ch-2 sp, ch 1, sk next dc, 2 sc in next ch-2 sp**, (sc, ch 2, sc) in next sc, rep from * around, ending last rep at **, join with sl st in beg sc. Fasten off.

Rnd 5: Join light beige with sc in any corner ch-2 sp, ch 4, sc in same ch-2 sp, *ch 1, sk next sc, sc in next sc, ch 1, sk next sc, (sc, ch 2, sc) in next ch-1 sp, ch 1, sk next sc, sc in next sc, ch 1, sk next sc**, (sc, ch 4, sc) in next ch-2 sp, rep from * around, ending last rep at **, join with sl st in beg sc. Fasten off.

Remaining Motifs
Make 103.
Rnds 1–4: Rep rnds 1–4 of First Motif.

Rnd 5: Rep rnd 5 of First Motif, joining to previous Motif at corner ch-4 sps by working: [ch 2, drop lp from hook, pull dropped lp through corresponding ch-4 sp, ch 2], and joining at center ch-2 sps by working: [ch 1, drop lp from hook, pull dropped lp through corresponding ch-2 sp, ch 1].

To join where 3 corners meet, work: [ch 2, drop lp from hook pull dropped lp through corresponding ch-4 sp, ch 1, drop lp from hook, pull dropped lp through corresponding ch-4 sp, ch 2] continue in established pattern.

Border
Note: *Rnd 1 is worked in ch-2 sps, ch 4 sps, joining seams and in sc to the right and left of center ch-2 sps on side edge of Motif. Do not work in other sc sts.*

Rnd 1 (RS): With size G hook, join light beige with sc in sc at center between ch-4 sp and ch-2 sp, *shell (see Special Stitches) in next ch-4 sp (or ch-2 sp or joining seam)**, sc in next sc, rep from * around, ending last rep at **, join with sl st in beg sc.

Rnd 2: [Ch 3, (sl st, ch 3, sl st) in next ch-2 sp, ch 3, sl st in next sc] around, ending with sl st in same st as beg ch-3. Fasten off.

With WS facing, block lightly. ∎

Square Dance

DESIGN BY NORMA GALE

Instead of "Grab your partner and do-si-do," how about "grab your hook and off you go," to crochet this striking afghan stitched in a lively arrangement of colors! It's a uniquely casual plaid that's sure to please.

SKILL LEVEL ◼◼◼◻
INTERMEDIATE

FINISHED SIZE
48¾ x 51 inches, excluding Fringe

MATERIALS
Red Heart Super Saver medium (worsted) weight yarn (7 oz/364 yds/198g per skein):
  2 skeins #312 black
  1 skein #311 white
  50 oz/2,500 yds/1,418g assorted scrap colors
Size F/5/3.75mm crochet hook or size needed to obtain gauge
Tapestry needle

GAUGE
4 sc = 1 inch; 9 sc rows = 2 inches

PATTERN NOTES
Work with as many colors as desired. Rows 2–21 and 182–201 have 10 color sections, remaining sections have 11 color sections.

A full-size Square requires approximately 25 yards or ½ ounce.

Change colors in last stitch made.

Do not work over color not in use.

Drop old color to wrong side of Afghan.

INSTRUCTIONS

AFGHAN
Row 1 (RS): With black, ch 203, sc in 2nd ch from hook, sc in each of next 8 chs, [ch 1, sk next ch, sc in next ch] 3 times, *sc in each of next 14 chs, [ch 1, sk next ch, sc in next ch] 3 times, rep from * across to last 7 chs, sc in each of last 7 chs, turn. *(202 sts)*

Rows 2–21: Work as indicated for even- and odd-numbered rows, with the exception of rows 10, 12 and 14.

Even-Numbered Rows
Ch 1, sc in first sc, **change color** *(see Stitch Guide and Pattern Notes)*, *sc in each of next 7 sts, [ch 1, sk next ch, sc in next st] 3 times, sc in each of next 7 sts, change color, rep from * across to last st, changing to black at end of last rep, sc in last st, turn.

Odd-Numbered Rows

Ch 1, sc in first st, change color, *sc in each of next 8 sts, [ch 1, sk next ch, sc in next st] 3 times, sc in each of next 6 sts, change color, rep from * across to last st, changing to black at end of last rep, sc in last st, turn.

Rows 10, 12 & 14: With black, ch 1, sc in each of next 8 sts, [ch 1, sk next ch, sc in next st] 3 times, *sc in each of next 14 sts, [ch 1, sk next ch, sc in next st] 3 times, rep from * across to last 8 sts, sc in each of next 8 sts, turn.

Rows 22–41: Work as indicated for even- and odd-numbered rows, with the exception of rows 30, 32 and 34.

Even-Numbered Rows

Ch 1, sc in first st, change color, sc in each of next 5 sts, change color, *sc in each of next 2 sts, [ch 1, sk next ch, sc in next st] 3 times, sc in each of next 12 sts, change color, rep from * across 8 times, sc in each of next 2 sts, [ch 1, sk next ch, sc in next st] 3 times, sc in each of next 7 sts, change to black, sc in last st, turn.

Odd-Numbered Rows

Ch 1, sc in first st, change color, *sc in each of next 8 sts, [ch 1, sk next ch, sc in next st] 3 times, sc in next st, change color, rep from * across to last 6 sts, sc in each of next 5 sts, changing to black, sc in last st, turn.

Rows 30, 32 & 34: Ch 1, sc in first st, change to white, sc in each of next 7 sts, [ch 1, sk next ch, sc in next st] 3 times, *sc

in each of next 14 sts, [ch 1, sk next ch, sc in next st] 3 times, rep from * across to last 8 sts, sc in each of next 7 sts, change to black, sc in last st, turn.

Rows 42–61: Work as indicated for even- and odd-numbered rows, with the exception of rows 50, 52 and 54.

Even-Numbered Rows

Ch 1, sc in first st, change color, sc in each of next 7 sts, [ch 1, sk next ch, sc in next st] 3 times, sc in each of next 2 sts, change color, *sc in each of next 12 sts, [ch 1, sk next ch, sc in next st] 3 times, sc in each of next 2 sts, change color, rep from * across to last 6 sts, sc in each of next 5 sts, change to black, sc in last st, turn.

Odd-Numbered Rows

Ch 1, sc in first st, change color, sc in each of next 5 sts, change color, *sc in each of next 3 sts, [ch 1, sk next ch, sc in next st] 3 times, sc in each of next 11 sts, change color, rep from * 8 times, sc in each of next 3 sts, [ch 1, sk next ch, sc in next st] 3 times, sc in each of next 6 sts, change to black, sc in last st, turn.

Rows 50, 52 & 54: Rep rows 10, 12 and 14.

Rows 62–81: Work as indicated for even- and odd-numbered rows, with the exception of rows 70, 72 and 74.

Even-Numbered Rows

Ch 1, sc in first st, change color, sc in each of next 7 sts, *ch 1,

sk next ch, sc in next st, change color *(pull lp of new color through lp on hook, counts as ch-1)*, sk next ch, sc in next st, ch 1, sk next ch, sc in each of next 15 sts, rep from * 8 times, ch 1, sk next ch, sc in next st, change color to create ch-1 sp, sk next ch, sc in next st, ch 1, sk next ch, sc in each of next 8 sts, change to black, sc in last sc, turn.

Odd-Numbered Rows

Ch 1, sc in first st, change color, sc in each of next 8 sts, *ch 1, sk next ch, sc in next st, change color to create ch-1 sp, sk next ch, sc in next st, ch 1, sk next ch, sc in each of next 15 sts, rep from * 9 times, ch 1, sk next ch, sc in next st, change color to create ch-1 sp, sk next ch, sc in next st, ch 1, sk next ch, sc in each of next 7 sts, change to black, sc in last st, turn.

Rows 70, 72 & 74: Rep rows 30, 32 and 34.

Rows 82–101: Work same as rows 22–41, with the exception of rows 90, 92 and 94.

Rows 90, 92 & 94: Rep rows 10, 12 and 14.

Rows 102–121: Work same as rows 42–61, with the exception of rows 110, 112 and 114.

Rows 110, 112 & 114: Rep rows 30, 32 and 34.

Rows 122–141: Work same as rows 62–81, with the exception of rows 130, 132 and 134.

Rows 130, 132 & 134: Rep rows 10, 12 and 14.

Rows 142–161: Work same as rows 22–41, with the exception of rows 150, 152 and 154.

Rows 150, 152 & 154: Rep rows 30, 32 and 34.

Rows 162–181: Work same as rows 42–61, with the exception of rows 170, 172 and 174.

Rows 170, 172 & 174: Rep rows 10, 12 and 14.

Rows 182–201: Work same as rows 2–21, with the exception of rows 190, 192 and 194,

Rows 190, 192 & 194: Rep rows 30, 32 and 34.

Row 202: With black, rep row 10. Fasten off.

Vertical Stripes
Using white, ch 1, hold yarn at back of Afghan, insert hook from front into first ch sp of row 1, yo, pull lp through ch sp and lp on hook *(as for sl st)*, [insert hook in next ch sp directly above, yo, pull up lp and pull through st on hook] across to top of Afghan. Fasten off.

Rep using white in each of next 2 ch-sp rows.

Use black for each of next 3 ch-sp rows. Continue to alternate 3 vertical white and black rows across Afghan.

Border
Join black with sc in first st of row 202, sc in same st as beg sc, sc in each st across to last st, 2 sc in last st, working in ends of rows, 2 sc in end of first row, sc in end of each row across to last row, 2 sc in last row, working in starting ch on opposite side of row 1, 2 sc in first ch, sc in each ch across to last ch, 2 sc in last ch, working up opposite edge, 2 sc in end of first row, sc in end of each row across to last row, 2 sc in last row, join with sl st in beg sc. Fasten off.

Fringe
Fringe is worked in each sc of Border.

Cut 14-inch strand of black yarn, fold strand in half, insert hook in sc st, pull fold through, pull ends through fold. Pull to tighten. Trim ends even. ∎

Repeating Rainbows

DESIGN BY CAROLYN PFEIFER

A bright rainbow of color and bands of visual texture give this afghan an ageless appeal, and, using only 5 ounces of each color, it makes economical sense, too! Use it to bring color into a dull space or to brighten a friend's face.

SKILL LEVEL ■□□□
BEGINNER

FINISHED SIZE
40 x 45 inches

MATERIALS
Medium (worsted)
 weight yarn:
  5 oz/250 yds/142g each red,
  orange, yellow, green,
  blue and lavender
Size I/9/5.5mm crochet hook or
 size needed to obtain gauge

GAUGE
7 sc = 2 inches; 7 sc rows =
2 inches

INSTRUCTIONS

AFGHAN
Row 1: With red, ch 143, sc in 2nd ch from hook and in each ch across, turn. *(142 sc)*

Row 2: Ch 1, sc in each st across, turn. Fasten off.

Row 3: Join orange with sc in first st, sc in each st across, turn.

Row 4: Ch 1, sc in each st across, turn. Fasten off.

Row 5: Join yellow with sc in first st, sc in each st across, turn.

Row 6: Ch 1, sc in each st across, turn. Fasten off.

Row 7: Join green with sc in first st, sc in each st across, turn.

Row 8: Ch 1, sc in each st across, turn. Fasten off.

Row 9: Join blue with sc in first st, sc in each st across, turn.

Row 10: Ch 1, sc in each st across, turn. Fasten off.

Row 11: Join lavender with sc in first st, sc in each st across, turn.

Row 12: Ch 1, sc in each st across, turn. Fasten off.

Row 13: Join red with sc in first st, sc in each of next 3 sts, [ch 3, sk

next 2 sts, sc in next st] 44 times, ch 3, sk next 2 sts, sc in each of last 4 sts, turn. *(45 ch-3 sps)*

Row 14: Ch 1, working in **front lps** *(see Stitch Guide)*, sc in each of first 4 sts, 3 sc in next ch sp, sc in next ch sp, [5 sc in next ch sp, sc in next ch sp] across with 4 sc in last ch sp, sc in front lp of each of last 4 sts, turn. Fasten off. *(142 sc)*

Row 15: Join orange with sc in first st, sc in each of next 3 sts, [ch 3, sk next 2 sts, sc in next st] 44 times, ch 3, sk next 2 sts, sc in each of last 4 sts, turn.

Row 16: Ch 1, working in front lps, sc in each of first 4 sts, 3 sc in next ch sp, sc in next ch sp, [5 sc in next ch sp, sc in next ch sp] across with 4 sc in last ch sp, sc in front lp in each of last 4 sts, turn. Fasten off.

Row 17: Join yellow with sc in first st, sc in each of next 3 sts, [ch 3, sk next 2 sts, sc in next st] 44 times, ch 3, sk next 2 sts, sc in each of last 4 sts, turn.

Row 18: Ch 1, working in front lps, sc in each of first 4 sts, 3 sc

in next ch sp, sc in next ch sp, [5 sc in next ch sp, sc in next ch sp] across with 4 sc in last ch sp, sc in front lp in each of last 4 sts, turn. Fasten off.

Row 19: Join green with sc in first st, sc in each of next 3 sts, [ch 3, sk next 2 sts, sc in next st] 44 times, ch 3, sk next 2 sts, sc in each of last 4 sts, turn.

Row 20: Ch 1, working in front lps, sc in each of first 4 sts, 3 sc in next ch sp, sc in next ch sp, [5 sc in next ch sp, sc in next ch sp] across with 4 sc in last ch sp, sc in front lp of each of last 4 sts, turn. Fasten off.

Row 21: Join blue with sc in first st, sc in each of next 3 sts, [ch 3, sk next 2 sts, sc in next st] 44 times, ch 3, sk next 2 sts, sc in each of last 4 sts, turn.

Row 22: Ch 1, working in front lps, sc in each of first 4 sts, 3 sc in next ch sp, sc in next ch sp, [5 sc in next ch sp, sc in next ch sp] across with 4 sc in last ch sp, sc in front lp of each of last 4 sts, turn. Fasten off.

Row 23: Join lavender with sc in first st, sc in each of next 3 sts, [ch 3, sk next 2 sts, sc in next st] 44 times, ch 3, sk next 2 sts, sc in each of last 4 sts, turn.

Row 24: Ch 1, working in front lps, sc in each of first 4 sts, 3 sc in next ch sp, sc in next ch sp, [5 sc in next ch sp, sc in next ch sp] across with 4 sc in last ch sp, sc in front lp of each of last 4 sts, turn. Fasten off.

Row 25: Join red with sc in first st, sc in each st across, turn.

Rows 26–145: [Rep rows 2–25 consecutively] 5 times.

Rows 146–156: Rep rows 2–12. At end of last row, fasten off.

Fringe
Cut 2 strands each 8 inches in length, holding both strands tog, fold in half, pull fold through st, pull ends through fold. Pull to tighten.

Matching colors, attach Fringe in every other st across short ends of Afghan. ■

Dimensional Squares

DESIGN BY ELAINE BARTLETT

Stitch a scrap-a-holic's dream project! Use as many or as few colors as you wish in this handsome afghan made with motifs of popcorn stitches in granny squares. It's a great blanket to snuggle under while watching a movie.

SKILL LEVEL
EASY

FINISHED SIZE
40 x 60 inches

MATERIALS
Medium (worsted)
  weight yarn:
    28 oz/1,400 yds/794g navy
    3 oz/150 yds/85g each of 12
      different scrap colors
Size J/10/6mm crochet hook
  or size needed to obtain
  gauge
Tapestry needle

GAUGE
Motif = 5 inches

SPECIAL STITCHES
Beginning Popcorn (beg pc):
Ch 3, 3 dc in same ch sp, drop lp from hook, insert hook in top of beg ch-3, pull dropped lp through.

Popcorn (pc): 4 dc in ch sp indicated, drop lp from hook, insert hook in first dc made, pull dropped lp through.

INSTRUCTIONS

AFGHAN
Motif
Make 8 of each color.
Rnd 1 (RS): With scrap color, ch 4, sl st in first ch to form ring, ch 3 (counts as first dc), 2 dc in ring, ch 2, [3 dc in ring, ch 2] 3 times, join with sl st in 3rd ch of beg ch-3. (12 dc)

Rnd 2: Sl st in next dc, **beg pc** (see Special Stitches) in same dc, *ch 2, sk next dc, (**pc**—see Special Stitches, ch 2, pc) in next ch-2 sp (corner), ch 2, sk next dc, pc in next dc, rep from * twice, ch 2, sk next dc, (pc, ch 2, pc) in next ch-2 sp (corner), ch 2, sk next dc, join with sl st in beg pc. (12 pc)

Rnd 3: Sl st in next ch-2 sp, ch 3, 2 dc in same ch sp, *sk next pc, (3 dc, ch 2, 3 dc) in next corner ch-2 sp, sk next pc, 3 dc in next ch-2 sp, sk next pc, 3 dc in next ch-2 sp, rep from * twice, sk next pc, (3 dc, ch 2, 3 dc) in next corner ch-2 sp, sk next pc, 3 dc in next ch-2 sp, sk next pc, join with sl st in 3rd ch of beg ch-3. Fasten off.

Rnd 4: Join navy with sc in first st, *sc in each dc across to next corner ch-2 sp, (sc, ch 2, sc) in corner ch-2 sp, rep from * twice, sc in each dc across to first sc, join with sl st in beg sc. Fasten off.

Assembly
Hold 2 Motifs with WS tog, join navy with sc in corner ch-2 sps of both Motifs, sc in each sc across to next corner ch-2 sp, sc in next corner ch-2 sp. **Do not** fasten off. Hold next 2 Motifs tog and sc across in same manner.

Join 8 rows of 12 Motifs in random order. Fasten off at the end of each row or column.

Edging
Rnd 1: Hold Afghan with RS facing and 1 short end at top, join navy with sc in ch-2 sp in upper right-hand corner, ch 2, sc in same ch sp, *[ch 2, sk next 2 sc, sc in next sc] 4 times, ch 2, sc in next ch-2 sp, ch 2, sk next joining, sc in next ch-2 sp, rep from * 6 times, [ch 2, sk next 2 sc, sc in next sc] 4 times, ch 2, (sc, ch 2, sc) in next corner ch-2 sp, **[ch 2, sk next 2 sc, sc in next sc] 4 times, ch 2, sc in next ch-2 sp, ch 2, sk next joining, sc in next ch-2 sp, rep from ** 10 times, [ch 2, sk next 2 sc, sc in next sc] 4 times, ch 2, (sc, ch 2, sc) in next corner ch-2 sp, ***[ch 2, sk next 2 sc, sc in next sc] 4 times, ch 2, sc in next ch-2 sp, ch 2, sk next joining, sc in next ch-2 sp, rep from *** 6 times, [ch 2, sk next 2 sc, sc in next sc] 4 times, ch 2, (sc, ch 2, sc) in next corner ch-2 sp, ****[ch 2, sk next 2 sc, sc in next sc] 4 times, ch 2, sc in next ch-2 sp, ch 2, sk next joining, sc in next ch-2 sp, rep from **** 10 times, [ch 2, sk next 2 sc, sc in next sc] 4 times, ch 2, join with sl st in beg sc.

Rnd 2: Sl st in next ch-2 sp, (beg pc, ch 2, pc) in same ch sp, *ch 2, pc in next ch-2 sp, rep from * across to next corner ch-2 sp, ch 2, (pc, ch 2, pc) in corner ch-2 sp, **ch 2, pc in next ch-2 sp, rep from ** across to next corner ch-2 sp, ch 2, (pc, ch 2, pc) in next corner ch-2 sp, ***ch 2, pc in next ch-2 sp, rep from *** across to next corner ch-2 sp, ch 2, (pc, ch 2, pc) in next corner ch-2 sp, ****ch 2, pc in next ch-2 sp, rep from **** across to beg corner, ch 2, join with sl st in beg pc.

Rnd 3: Sl st in next ch-2 sp, ch 3, 4 dc in same ch sp, *2 dc in each ch-2 sp across to next corner ch-2 sp, 5 dc in next corner ch-2 sp, rep from * twice, 2 dc in each ch-2 sp across to beg ch-3, join with sl st in 3rd ch of beg ch-3.

Rnd 4: Ch 1, sc in each of first 2 sts, *3 sc in next dc, sc in each dc across to 3rd dc of next corner, rep from * twice, 3 sc in next dc, sc in each dc across to first sc, join with sl st in beg sc. Fasten off. ■

Heartfelt Home

Chapter Contents

Scrappy Stripes

DESIGN BY CYNTHIA ADAMS

Need a quick hostess or housewarming gift? Who can't use more pot holders, especially when they're lovingly stitched in the recipient's favorite colors? It's a useful gift that will surely be appreciated.

SKILL LEVEL ■■□□
EASY

FINISHED SIZE
10 x 10 inches

MATERIALS
Medium (worsted)
   weight cotton yarn:
      1½ oz/75 yds/42g each blue
      (A), lime green (B), teal (C),
      off-white (D) or orange
      (A), dark orange (B),
      yellow (C), off-white (D)
Size G/6/4mm crochet hook or
   size needed to obtain gauge
Tapestry needle

GAUGE
5 st groups = 4 inches

INSTRUCTIONS

POT HOLDER
Front/Back
Make 2.

Row 1 (RS): With A, ch 32, (sc, 2 dc) in 2nd ch from hook, sk next 2 chs, [(sc, 2 dc) in next ch, sk next 2 chs] across to last ch, sc in last ch, **changing colors** (*see Stitch Guide*) to B in last st made, drop A, turn.

Row 2: Ch 1, (sc, 2 dc) in first sc, sk next 2 dc, [(sc, 2 dc) in next sc, sk next 2 dc] across to last sc, sc in last sc, changing to C in last st, drop B, turn.

Row 3: Rep row 2, changing to A in last sc, drop C, turn.

Row 4: Rep row 2, changing to B in last sc, drop A, turn.

Rows 5–22: [Rep rows 2–4 consecutively] 6 times. At end of last row, do not change colors.

Fasten off all colors.

Assembly
Hold pieces with WS tog, working through both pieces at same time, join D with sc in first sc of row 22, 2 dc in same sc, (sc, 2 dc) in next sc, sk next dc, (sc, 2 dc) in next dc, working across next side in ends of rows, in row 22 work (sc, 2 dc), [sk next row, (sc, 2 dc) in next row] 10 times, (sc, 2 dc) in next row, working in starting ch on opposite side of row 1, (sc, 2 dc) at base of each (sc, 2 dc) group, working across next side in ends of rows, (sc, 2 dc) in row 1, [sk next row, (sc, 2 dc) in next row] 10 times, (sc, 2 dc) in next row, join with sl st in beg sc. Fasten off. ■

Picnic Mats

DESIGN BY KATHERINE ENG

Add a bright splash of tropical colors to a summer picnic with these festive, beaded table mats. They're oh-so-quick and easy to stitch when made with your fun, fabulous microfiber scraps.

SKILL LEVEL ■□□□ BEGINNER

FINISHED SIZE
7¼ inches in diameter

MATERIALS

Lion Brand Microspun light (light worsted) weight yarn (2½ oz/168 yds/70g per skein):
  1 skein each #194 lime, #148 turquoise and #186 mango
Size 10/1.15mm steel crochet hook
Size E/4/3.5mm crochet hook or size needed to obtain gauge
Tapestry needle
¼-inch faceted beads: 16 each lime, orange and blue

GAUGE
Rnds 1 and 2 = 1¾ inches

PATTERN NOTES
Size 10 steel hook is used only to thread beads onto sport weight yarn.

Each yarn color makes 1 Mat.

SPECIAL STITCH
Shell: (2 dc, ch 2, 2 dc) as indicated.

INSTRUCTIONS

MAT
Make 3.

Rnd 1 (RS): With size E hook, ch 6, sl st in first ch to form ring, ch 1, [sc in ring, ch 2] 8 times, join with sl st in beg sc. *(8 sc, 8 ch-2 sps)*

Rnd 2: Sl st in ch-2 sp, ch 1, (sc, ch 2, sc) in same ch sp, ch 2, [(sc, ch 2, sc) in ch-2 sp, ch 2] around, join with sl st in beg sc. *(16 sc)*

Rnd 3: Sl st in next ch-2 sp, ch 1, (sc, ch 2, sc) in same ch sp, ch 3, [(sc, ch 2, sc) in ch-2 sp, ch 3] around, join with sl st in beg sc.

Rnd 4: Sl st in ch-2 sp, ch 1, (sc, ch 2, sc) in same ch sp, ch 1, sc in next ch-3 sp, ch 1, [(sc, ch 2, sc) in ch-2 sp, ch 1, sc in next ch-3 sp, ch 1] around, join with sl st in beg sc. *(24 sc)*

Rnd 5: Sl st in ch-2 sp, ch 1, (sc, ch 2, sc) in same ch sp, ch 1, (sc, ch 2, sc) in next sc between ch-1 sps, ch 1, [(sc, ch 2, sc) in ch-2 sp, ch 1, (sc, ch 2, sc) in next sc between ch-1 sps, ch 1] around, join with sl st in beg sc. *(32 sc)*

Rnds 6–8: Rep rnds 2–4. *(48 sc at end of last rnd)*

Rnd 9: Sl st in ch-2 sp, ch 1, [(sc, ch 2, sc) in ch-2 sp, ch 6] 16 times, join with sl st in beg sc.

Rnd 10: Sl st in ch-2 sp, ch 1, [sc in ch-2 sp, **shell** *(see Special Stitch)* in next ch-5 sp] 16 times. Fasten off.

Note: *With size 10 steel crochet hook, thread 16 matching faceted beads on sport weight yarn.*

Rnd 11: With size E hook, join with sl st in any sc between shells, *ch 3, sc in ch-2 sp, ch 1, pull bead down and forward, ch 2 over bead, sc in same ch 2 sp, ch 3, sl st in next sc, rep from * around. Fasten off. ■

Treasured Bouquet

DESIGN BY HAZEL HENRY

Whip this doily up in five hours and have a beautiful last-minute gift for someone special. It's dainty and a great project for crocheters of all skill levels to stitch. If you can't resist the finished project, just make two!

SKILL LEVEL ◼☐☐☐
BEGINNER

FINISHED SIZE
8 inches in diameter

MATERIALS
Size 10 crochet cotton:
    35 yds tan
    28 yds green
    21 yds rose
Size 9/1.25mm steel crochet
    hook or size needed to
    obtain gauge
Pinning board
Plastic wrap
Rustproof pins
Starch

GAUGE
Rnds 1 and 2 = 1 inch

SPECIAL STITCHES
Beginning treble crochet cluster (beg tr cl): Ch 4, holding back last lp of each st on hook, 2 tr as indicated, yo, pull through all lps on hook.

Treble crochet cluster (tr cl): Holding back last lp of each st on hook, 3 tr as indicated. Yo, pull through all lps on hook.

INSTRUCTIONS

DOILY
First Motif
Rnd 1 (RS): With rose, ch 12, sl st in first ch to form ring, **beg tr cl** (see Special Stitches) in ring, [ch 3, **tr cl** (see Special Stitches) in ring] 11 times, ch 3, join with sl st in top of beg tr cl. Fasten off. (12 cls, 12 ch-3 sps)

Rnd 2: Join green with sl st in any ch-3 sp, (beg tr cl, ch 3, tr cl) in same ch sp, *ch 5, sc in next ch-3 sp, ch 5**, [tr cl, ch 3, tr cl] in next ch-3 sp, rep from * around, ending last rep at **, join with sl st in top of beg cl. Fasten off. (12 cls)

Rnd 3: Join tan with sl st in any ch-3 sp between cls, (beg tr cl, ch 5, tr cl) in same ch sp, *ch 4, sc in next ch sp, ch 9, sc in next ch sp, ch 4**, (tr cl, ch 5, tr cl) in next ch-3 sp between cls, rep from * around, ending last rep at **, join with sl st in top of beg cl. Fasten off.

2nd Motif
Rnds 1 & 2: Rep rnds 1 and 2 of First Motif.

Rnd 3: Join tan with sl st in any ch-3 sp between cl, (beg tr cl, ch 5, tr cl) in same ch sp, ch 4, sc in next ch sp, ch 9, sc in next ch sp,

ch 4, tr cl in next ch sp, ch 2, sl st in corresponding ch-5 sp between cls of previous Motif, ch 2, tr cl in same ch-3 sp on working Motif, ch 4, sc in next ch sp, ch 4, sl st in ch-9 sp on previous Motif, ch 4, sc in next ch sp on working Motif, ch 4, tr cl in next ch-3 sp, ch 2, sl st in ch-5 sp between cls of previous Motif, ch 2, tr cl in same

ch-3 sp on working Motif, *ch 4, sc in next ch sp, ch 9, sc in next ch sp, ch 4**, (tr cl, ch 5, tr cl) in next ch-3 sp, rep from * around, ending last rep at **, join with sl st in top of beg cl. Fasten off.

Remaining 5 Motifs
Rnds 1–3: Rep rnds 1–3 of 2nd Motif.

When working last Motif, join to previous and first Motifs to close ring.

Cover pinning board with plastic wrap, starch Doily and pin to pinning board in all outer ch sps. ■

Bath Boutique

DESIGN BY SUE CHILDRESS

Dress up your guest bathroom with accessories edged with pretty watercolor motifs. Stitched in easy-care cotton sport weight yarn, they're ideal for almost any gift-giving occasion.

SKILL LEVEL ◼◼◼▢
INTERMEDIATE

FINISHED SIZE
Each Motif is 3½ inches square

MATERIALS
Fine (sport) weight
  cotton yarn:
    3 oz/270 yds/85g blue/
      green variegated
    1½ oz/135 yds/43g each of
      blue and lilac
Size E/4/3.5mm crochet hook
  or size needed to obtain
  gauge
Tapestry needle
3 yds loop braid
14-inch-wide washcloth
17½-inch-wide hand towel
70-inch-wide shower curtain

GAUGE
Each Motif is 3½ inches square.

INSTRUCTIONS

MOTIF
Rnd 1: With lilac, ch 4, sl st in first ch to form ring, ch 1, [sc in ring, ch 3] 8 times, join with sl st in beg sc. *(8 ch sps)*

Rnd 2: (Sl st, ch 1, sc) in first ch sp, (hdc, 3 dc, hdc) in next ch sp, *sc in next ch sp, (hdc, 3 dc, hdc) in next ch sp, rep from * around, join with sl st in beg sc. Fasten off.

Rnd 3: Join blue/green variegated with sl st in any sc, (ch 3, 2 dc) in same st, sk next 2 sts, (2 dc, ch 2, 2 dc) in center dc, sk next 2 sts, *3 dc in next sc, sk next 2 sts, (2 dc, ch 2, 2 dc) in center dc, sk next 2 sts, rep from * around, join with sl st in 3rd ch of beg ch-3.

Rnd 4: (Sl st, ch 3, 4 dc) in next st, (3 dc, ch 2, 3 dc) in next ch sp, *5 dc in center dc of next 3-dc group, (3 dc, ch 2, 3 dc) in next ch sp, rep from * around, join with sl st in 3rd ch of beg ch-3. Fasten off.

Rnd 5: Join blue with sc in any st, sc in each st around with 3 sc in each ch sp, join with sl st in beg sc. Fasten off.

Shower Curtain

Cut off desired length from bottom of curtain. Turn raw edge under ½ inch and sew to braid.

Make 20 Motifs. Sew tog making 1 long strip.

Sew to bottom of curtain.

Washcloth

Make 4 Motifs.
Sew tog in a strip and sew strip to 1 end of cloth.

Hand Towel

Make 5 Motifs.
Sew tog in a strip and sew strip to 1 end of towel.

Edging

Join lilac with sc in first st on Motif next to right-hand sewn edge, sc in each st across to left-hand sewn edge with 3 sc in each of the 2 corners across to last st. Fasten off.

Work edging on all pieces. ■

Dig-It Flowerpot Cover

DESIGN BY TAMMY HILDEBRAND

Dress up an inexpensive flowerpot with a simple cover made from four large granny squares, joined in a cylinder and finished with an easy single crochet edging. Cotton worsted yarn makes it durable and easy to care for.

SKILL LEVEL ■■□□
EASY

FINISHED SIZE
Fits flowerpot 5½ inches tall x 5½ inches across bottom and 7½ inches across top

MATERIALS
Lion Brand Lion Cotton
    medium (worsted)
    weight yarn (5 oz/236
    yds/140g per ball):
    1 ball #098 natural
    1 oz/47 yds/28g each #140
        rose and #131 fern green
Size I/9/5.5mm crochet hook or
    size needed to obtain gauge
Tapestry needle

4 MEDIUM

GAUGE
Rnd 1 of Motif = 1½ inches; 7 sc = 2 inches

SPECIAL STITCH
Cluster (cl): Holding back last lp of each st on hook, 3 dc in ring, yo, pull through all lps on hook.

INSTRUCTIONS

COVER
First Motif
Rnd 1: With rose, ch 3, sl st in first ch to form ring, ch 3, **cl** *(see Special Stitch)* in ring, ch 1, cl in ring, ch 2, [cl in ring, ch 1, cl in ring, ch 2] 3 times, join with sl st in 3rd ch of beg ch-3. Fasten off. *(8 cl)*

Rnd 2: Join fern green with sc in any ch-1 sp, (3 dc, ch 3, 3 dc) in next ch-2 sp, [sc in next ch-1 sp, (3 dc, ch 3, 3 dc) in next ch-2

sp] around, join with sl st in beg sc. Fasten off. *(4 ch-3 sps, 4 sc, 24 dc)*

Rnd 3: Join natural with sl st in any ch-3 sp, ch 8 *(counts as first dc and ch-5)*, dc in same ch sp as beg ch-8, sk next st, (dc, ch 1, dc) in next st, sk next st, working over next sc, tr in ch-1 sp on rnd 1, sk next st, (dc, ch 1, dc) in next st, [(dc, ch 5, dc) in next ch-3 sp, sk next st, (dc, ch 1, dc) in next st, tr in next ch-1 sp on rnd 1, sk next st, (dc, ch 1, dc) in next st] around, join with sl st in 3rd ch of beg ch-8. *(4 tr, 4 ch-5 sps, 8 ch-1 sps, 24 dc)*

Rnd 4: Ch 1, sc in first st, 5 sc in next ch-5 sp, sc in each st and in each ch-1 sp around with 5 sc in each ch-5 sp, join with sl st in beg sc. Fasten off. *(56 sc)*

Rnd 5: Join fern green in center sc of any 5-sc group, ch 1, (sc, ch 3, sc) in same sc as beg ch-1, sc in each of next 13 sts, (sc, ch 3, sc) in next st, (ch 1, sc) in each of next 13 sts, ch 1, (sc, ch 3, sc) in next st, sc in each of next 13 sts, (sc, ch 3, sc) in next

st, (ch 1, sc) in each of next 13 sts, ch 1, join with sl st in beg sc. Fasten off.

Joined Motif
Rnds 1–4: Rep rnds 1–4 of First Motif.

Rnd 5: Join fern green with sl st in center sc of any 5-sc group, ch 1, (sc, ch 3, sc) in same sc,

*sc in each of next 13 sts, sc in next st, ch 1, drop lp from hook, insert hook in corresponding ch-3 sp of Last Motif, pull dropped lp through, ch 1, sc in same st on working Motif, [drop lp from hook, insert hook in corresponding ch-1 sp of Last Motif, pull dropped lp through, sc in next st on working Motif] 13 times, drop

lp from hook, insert hook in corresponding ch-1 sp of Last Motif, pull dropped lp through, (sc, ch 1) in next st, drop lp from hook, insert hook in corresponding ch-3 sp of Last Motif, pull dropped lp through, ch 1, sc in same st on working Motif, sc in each of next 13 sts, (sc, ch 3, sc) in next st, ch 1, (sc, ch 1) in each st around, join with sl st in beg sc. Fasten off.

Rep Joined Motif once for total of 3 Motifs.

Last Motif
Rnds 1–4: Rep rnds 1–4 of First Motif.

Rnd 5: Join fern green with sc in center sc of any 5-sc group, drop lp from hook, insert hook in corresponding ch-3 sp of First Motif, pull dropped lp through, ch 1, sc in same sc, *sc in each of next 13 sts, (sc, ch 1, sc) in next st, drop lp from hook, insert hook in corresponding ch-3 sp of Last Motif, pull dropped lp through, ch 1, sc in same st as last sc on working Motif, [drop lp from hook, insert hook in corresponding ch-1 sp of Last Motif, pull dropped lp through, sc in next st] 13 times, drop lp from hook, insert hook in corresponding ch-1 sp of last Motif, pull dropped lp through*, sc in next st, ch 1, drop lp from hook, insert hook in corresponding ch-3 sp of Last Motif, pull dropped lp through, ch 1, sc in same st as last sc on working Motif, rep between * joining to

First Motif, join with sl st in beg sc. Fasten off.

Bottom Edging
Rnd 1: Working around bottom edge in **back lps** (see Stitch Guide), join natural with sc in any st, sc in each st around, join with sl st in beg sc.

Rnd 2: Ch 1, sc in each st around, join with sl st in beg sc. Fasten off.

Top Edging
Rnd 1: Working around top edge in back lps, join natural with sc in any st, sc in each st around, join with sl st in beg sc.

Rnds 2 & 3: Ch 1, sc in each st around, join with sl st in beg sc. At the end of last rnd, fasten off. ∎

Tempting Textures

DESIGN BY ANNE HALLIDAY

Soft, super bulky yarn and dimensional stitches give this plush, cozy rug delicious texture your bare feet will love! Stitched with a large hook, it works up quickly and looks great in an entryway!

SKILL LEVEL
INTERMEDIATE

FINISHED SIZE
21 x 25 inches

MATERIALS
Super bulky (super chunky) weight yarn:
    10 oz/230 yds/284g each linen (MC) and white (CC)
Size N/13/9mm crochet hook or size needed to obtain gauge
Tapestry needle
Stitch marker

GAUGE
2-dc cl and 2 ch-3 sps = 4 inches

PATTERN NOTE
When changing yarn color, leave an 8-inch length of yarn at beginning and end of row to be worked into fringe.

SPECIAL STITCHES
2-double crochet cluster (2-dc cl): Ch 3, [yo, insert hook in first ch of ch-3, yo, pull up lp, yo, pull through 2 lps on hook] twice, yo, pull through all lps on hook.

Bobble: Ch 4, sc in 2nd ch from hook, sc in each of next 2 chs, fold 3-sc group in half toward you from right to left, sl st in the single lp at edge of first sc made.

INSTRUCTIONS

RUG
Row 1 (RS): With MC, ch 62, sc in 2nd ch from hook, [ch 3, sk next 2 chs, sc in next ch] across, turn. Fasten off. (20 ch 3 sps)

Note: Place st marker on right side of row 1.

Row 2 (WS): Join CC with sl st in first sc, ch 3 (counts as first hdc and ch-1), sc in first ch-3 sp, **2-dc cl** (see Special Stitches), sc in next ch-3 sp, *[ch 3, sc in next ch-3 sp] twice, 2-dc cl, sc in next ch-3 sp, rep from * across to last sc, ch 1, hdc in last sc, turn. Fasten off. (7 dc cls)

Row 3 (RS): Join MC with sc in first hdc, ch 3, working behind next 2-dc cl, dc in sc 1 row below 2-dc cl, ch 3, *sc in next ch-3 sp, **bobble** *(see Special Stitches)*, sc in next ch-3 sp, ch 3, working behind next 2-dc cl, dc in sc 1 row below 2-dc cl, ch 3, rep from * across to last ch-3, sc in 2nd ch of last ch-3, turn. Fasten off. *(6 bobbles)*

Row 4 (WS): Join CC with sl st in first sc, ch 3 *(counts as first hdc and ch-1)*, sc in first ch-3 sp, 2-dc cl, sc in next ch-3 sp, *ch 3, working in front of next bobble, dc in sc 1 row below bobble, ch 3, sc in next ch-3 sp, 2-dc cl, sc in next ch-3 sp, rep from * across to last sc, ch 1, hdc in last sc, turn. Fasten off. *(7 cls)*

Row 5 (RS): Join MC with sc in first hdc, ch 3, working behind next 2-dc cl, dc in dc 1 row below 2-dc cl, ch 3, *sc in next ch-3 sp, bobble, sc in next ch-3 sp, ch 3, working behind next 2-dc cl, dc in dc 1 row below

2-dc cl, ch 3, rep from * across to last ch-3, sc in 2nd ch of ch-3, turn. Fasten off. *(6 bobbles)*

Row 6 (WS): Join CC with sl st in first sc, ch 3 *(counts as first hdc and ch-1)*, sc in first ch-3 sp, 2-dc cl, sc in next ch-3 sp, *ch 3, working in front of next bobble, dc in dc 1 row below bobble, ch 3, sc in next ch-3 sp, 2-dc cl, sc in next ch-3 sp, rep from * across to last sc, ch 1, hdc in last sc, turn. Fasten off. *(7 cls)*

Rows 7–36: Rep rows 5 and 6, ending last rep with row 6. Fasten off.

Row 37 (RS): Join MC with sc in first hdc, ch 2, working behind next 2-dc cl, dc in dc 1 row below 2-dc cl, *[ch 2, sc in next ch-3 sp] twice, ch 2, working behind next 2-dc cl, dc in dc 1 row below 2-dc cl, rep from * across to last ch-3, ch 2, sc in 2 ch of ch-3. Fasten off.

Edging
With RS facing, attach MC with sl st in first sc, ch 2, dc in same st, sk next 2 chs, *(sl st, ch 2, dc) in next st, sk next 2 chs, rep from * across to last sc, sl st in last sc, fasten off.

Foundation Edging
With RS facing and working in starting ch on opposite side of foundation ch, join MC with sl st in first ch, ch 2, dc in same st, sk next 2 chs, *(sl st, ch 2, dc) in next ch, sk next 2 chs, rep from * across to last ch, sl st in last ch. Fasten off.

Fringe
Combine three 12-inch lengths for 1 Fringe. Holding all strands tog, fold in half, pull fold through, pull all ends through fold. Pull to tighten.

Matching color of Fringe to row color, attach 1 Fringe in single lp of each row across top and bottom edges. Trim ends even on each end. ■

Flower Coasters

DESIGN BY JUDY TEAGUE TREECE

Mini doilies are the perfect answer to a shortage of coasters, and these are positively lovely. Stitch them up with your scraps of size 10 cotton thread for a different take on decorating with doilies!

SKILL LEVEL
BEGINNER

FINISHED SIZE
4¾ inches in diameter

MATERIALS
Crochet cotton size 10:
    20 yds each color A and B
Size 6/1.80mm steel crochet
    hook or size needed to
    obtain gauge

GAUGE
Rnds 1–3 = 1¾ inches across

PATTERN NOTE
Coaster may ruffle until blocked.

SPECIAL STITCHES
Beginning shell (beg shell):
Ch 3 *(counts as first dc)*, (dc, ch 2, 2 dc) in same ch sp.

Shell: (2 dc, ch 2, 2 dc) in next ch sp.

Beginning cluster (beg cl): Ch 3, holding back on hook last lp of each st, 2 dc in same st, yo, pull through all lps on hook.

Cluster (cl): Holding back last lp of each st on hook, 3 dc in next ch sp, yo, pull through all lps on hook.

INSTRUCTIONS

COASTER
Rnd 1: With A, ch 5, sl st in first ch to form ring, ch 4 *(counts as first dc and ch-1)*, [dc in ring, ch 1] 7 times, join with sl st in 3rd ch of beg ch-4. *(8 dc, 8 ch sps)*

Rnd 2: Sl st in next ch sp, **beg shell** *(see Special Stitches)*, ch 1, [**shell** *(see Special Stitches)* in next ch sp, ch 1] around, join with sl st in 3rd ch of beg ch-3. *(8 shells, 8 ch-1 sps)*

Rnd 3: Sl st in next st, sl st in next ch sp, beg shell, ch 2, sc in next ch-1 sp, ch 2, [shell in ch sp of next shell, ch 2, sc in next ch-1 sp, ch 2] around, join with sl st in 3rd ch of beg ch-3. Fasten off. *(16 ch-2 sps, 8 shells)*

Rnd 4: Join B with sl st in first shell, (**beg cl**—*see Special Stitches*, ch 2, **cl**—*see Special Stitches*) in same shell, ch 6, sk next 2 ch-2 sps, *(cl, ch 2, cl) in next shell, ch 6, sk next 2 ch-2 sps, rep from * around, join with sl st in top of beg cl. *(16 cls, 8 ch-6 sps, 8 ch-2 sps)*

Rnd 5: Sl st in first ch sp, (beg cl, ch 2, cl, ch 2, cl) in same ch sp, ch 6, sk next ch-6 sp, *(cl, ch 2, cl, ch 2, cl) in next ch-2 sp, ch 6, sk next ch-6 sp, rep from * around, join with sl st in top of beg cl. *(24 cls)*

Rnd 6: Sl st in next ch-2 sp, beg cl, *ch 2, cl in same ch sp, ch 2, (cl, ch 2, cl) in next ch-2 sp, ch 6, sk next ch-6 sp**, cl in next ch 2 sp, rep from * around, ending last rep at **, join with sl st in top of beg cl. *(32 cls)*

Rnd 7: Sl st in next ch sp, beg cl, *ch 2, cl in same ch sp, ch 2, cl in next ch-2 sp, ch 2, (cl, ch 2, cl) in next ch-2 sp, ch 5, sc around all 3 ch-6 sps of last 3 rnds at same time, ch 5**, cl in next ch-2 sp, rep from * around, ending last rep at **, join with sl st in top of beg cl. Fasten off. *(40 cls)*

Rnd 8: Join A with sc in first ch 2 sp, *ch 2, [sc in next ch 2 sp, ch 2] 3 times, 5 sc in each of next 2 ch-5 sps, ch 2**, sc in next ch-2 sp, rep from * around, ending last rep at **, join with sl st in first sc.

Rnd 9: Sl st in next ch-2 sp, ch 1, (sc, ch 3, sc) in same ch sp, (sc, ch 3, sc) in each of next 3 ch-2 sps, *sk next st, sc in next st, ch 3, sc in next st, sl st in each of next 2 sts, sc in next st, [ch 3, sk next st, sc in next st] twice**, (sc, ch 3, sc) in each of next 5 ch 2 sps, rep from * around, ending last rep at **, (sc, ch 3, sc) in last ch-2 sp, join with sl st in beg sc. Fasten off. ■

Wildflowers

DESIGN BY BRENDA STRATTON

Three of life's pleasures are a cool drink, beautiful weather and elegant crochet—especially when the elegant crochet sings to our thrifty natures!

SKILL LEVEL INTERMEDIATE

FINISHED SIZE
13 inches in diameter

MATERIALS
Size 10 crochet cotton:
   100 yds each white and blue variegated
   25 yds each pink and green
Size 5/1.90mm steel crochet hook or size needed to obtain gauge

GAUGE
Rnds 1–3 of Motif = 1¾ inches across

Each Motif = 4⅜ inches across.

SPECIAL STITCHES
Leaf: Holding back last lp of each st on hook, ch 3, 2 tr in same st, yo, pull through all lps on hook.

Beginning cluster (beg cl):
Ch 3 (counts as first dc), holding back last lp of each st on hook, 2 dc in same place, yo, pull through all lps on hook.

Cluster (cl): Holding back last lp of each st on hook, 3 dc as indicated, yo, pull through all lps on hook.

INSTRUCTIONS

CENTER MOTIF
Rnd 1: With pink, ch 4, sl st in first ch to form ring, ch 1, [sc in ring, ch 3] 6 times, join with sl st in beg sc. (6 sc, 6 ch sps)

Rnd 2: (Sl st, hdc, 3 dc, hdc) in first ch sp and in each ch sp around, join with sl st in beg sl st. Fasten off. (6 petals)

Rnd 3: Join green with sl st in any sl st, *leaf (see Special Stitches), ch 4, sl st in same st, working behind next petal, ch 3**, sl st in next sl st, rep from * around, ending last rep at **, join with sl st in top of leaf. Fasten off. (6 leaves, 6 ch-3 sps)

Rnd 4: Join white with sc in tip of any leaf, ch 5, sc in next ch sp between leaves, ch 5, [sc in tip of next leaf, ch 5, sc in next ch sp between leaves, ch 5] around, join with sl st in beg sc. (12 ch sps)

Rnd 5: Sl st in first ch sp, ch 1, sc in same ch sp, ch 5, [sc in next ch sp, ch 5] around, join with sl st in beg sc. Fasten off.

Rnd 6: Join blue with sl st in any ch sp, **beg cl** (see Special Stitches), ch 3, **cl** (see Special

Stitches) in same ch sp, ch 3, (cl, ch 3) twice in each ch sp around, join with sl st in top of beg cl. *(24 ch sps)*

Rnd 7: Sl st in first ch sp, ch 1, 5 sc in same ch sp, 4 sc in next ch sp, 3 sc in next ch sp, 4 sc in next

ch sp, [5 sc In next ch sp, 4 sc in next ch sp, 3 sc in next ch sp, 4 sc in next ch sp] around, join with sl st in beg sc. Fasten off. *(96 sc)*

Rnd 8: Join white with sl st in center sc of any 5-sc group, ch 3, dc in same st, dc in next 15

sts, [3 dc in next st, dc in each of next 15 sts] around, dc in same st as first st, join with sl st in 3rd ch of beg ch-3. *(108 dc)*

Rnd 9: Ch 1, 2 sc in first st, sc in each of next 17 sts, [3 sc in next st, sc in each of next 17 sts] around, sc in same st as first st, join with sl st in beg sc. Fasten off. *(120 sc)*

Rnd 10: Join blue with sc in center sc of any 3-sc group, ch 3, sc in same st, [ch 3, sk next 2 sts, sc in next st] 6 times, ch 3, sk next st, *(sc, ch 3, sc) in next st, [ch 3, sk next 2 sts, sc in next st] 6 times, ch 3, sk next st, rep from * around, join with sl st in beg sc. *(48 ch sps)*

Rnd 11: Sl st in first ch sp, ch 1, (sc, ch 3, sc) in same ch sp, ch 3, [sc in next ch sp, ch 3] 7 times, *(sc, ch 3, sc) in next ch sp, ch 3, [sc in next ch sp, ch 3] 7 times, rep from * around, join with sl st in beg sc. Fasten off. *(54 ch sps)*

FIRST MOTIF

Rnds 1–10: Rep rnds 1–10 of Center Motif.

Rnd 11: Sl st in first ch sp, ch 1, sc in same ch sp, to join to Center Motif, ch 1, sl st in any corner ch sp on other Motif, ch 1, sc in same ch sp on this Motif, ch 1, sl st in next ch sp on other Motif, ch 1, [sc in next ch sp on this Motif, ch 1, sl st in next ch sp on other Motif, ch 1] 7 times, sc in next ch sp on this Motif, ch 1, sl st in next ch sp on other Motif, ch 1, sc in same sp on this Motif, ch 3, (sc in next ch sp, ch 3] 7 times, *(sc, ch 3, sc) in next ch sp, ch 3, [sc in next ch sp, ch 3] 7 times, rep from * around, join with sl st in beg sc. Fasten off.

2ND MOTIF

Rnds 1–10: Rep rnds 1–10 of Center Motif.

Rnd 11: Sl st in first ch sp, ch 1, sc in same ch sp, to join to First Motif, ch 1, sl st in next unworked corner ch sp on other Motif, ch 1, sc in same ch sp on this Motif, *ch 1, sl st in next ch sp on other Motif, ch 1, [sc in next ch sp on this Motif, ch 1, sl st in next ch sp on other Motif, ch 1] 7 times, sc in next ch sp on this Motif*, ch 1, sl st in joining between Motifs, ch 1, sc in same ch sp on this Motif, to join to Center Motif, rep between *, ch 1, sl st in next ch sp on other Motif, ch 1, sc in same ch sp on this Motif, ch 3, [sc in next ch sp, ch 3] 7 times, **(sc, ch 3, sc) in next ch sp, ch 3, (sc in next ch sp, ch 3) 7 times, rep from ** around, join with sl st in beg sc. Fasten off.

Rep 2nd Motif 3 times for a total of 5 Motifs around Center Motif.

6TH MOTIF

Rnds 1–10: Rep rnds 1–10 of Center Motif.

Rnd 11: Sl st in first ch sp, ch 1, sc in same ch sp, to join to First Motif, ch 1, sl st in next unworked corner ch sp on other Motif, ch 1, sc in same ch sp on this Motif, ◊* ch 1, sl st in next ch sp on other Motif, ch 1, [sc in next ch sp on this Motif, ch 1, sl st in next ch sp on other Motif,

ch 1] 7 times, sc in next ch sp on this Motif*, ch 1, sl st in joining between Motifs, ch 1, sc in same ch sp on this Motif◊, to join to Center Motif, rep between ◊◊, to join to other side of First Motif, rep between *, ch 1, sl st in next ch sp on other Motif, ch 1, sc in same ch sp on this Motif, ch 3, [sc in next ch sp, ch 3] 7 times, **(sc, ch 3, sc) in next ch sp, ch 3, [sc in next ch sp, ch 3] 7 times, rep from **, join with sl st in beg sc. Fasten off.

OUTER EDGING

Rnd 1: Working around outer edge, join blue with sc in first ch sp after any 2 joined ch sps, ch 3, [sc in next ch sp, ch 3] 7 times, ◊*(sc, ch 3, sc) in next ch sp, ch 3, [sc in next ch sp, ch 3] 8 times, rep from ◊, **sc dec** *(see Stitch Guide)* in next 2 joined ch sps, ch 3**, [sc in next ch sp, ch 3] 8 times, rep from * around, ending last rep at **, join with sl st in beg sc.

Rnd 2: Ch 1, sl st in first ch sp, ch 1, sc in same ch sp, [ch 3, sc in next ch sp] 7 times, *3 sc in next ch sp, sc in next ch sp, [ch 3, sc in next ch sp] 8 times, 3 sc in next ch sp, [sc in next ch sp, ch 3] 8 times, sc next 2 ch sps tog**, [ch 3, sc in next ch sp] 8 times, rep from * around, ending last rep at **, ch 3, join with sl st in beg sc. Fasten off. ■

Kitchen Helpers

DESIGNS BY ELAINE BARTLETT

Put your scraps of cotton yarn to work with these handy kitchen aids. The dishcloth is great for your more delicate dishes and the towel has a hanger so it's always close and just where you need it!

SKILL LEVEL ◼◻◻
EASY

FINISHED SIZES
Hanging towel: 10 x 13½ inches, excluding hanging strap

Dishcloth: 8½ x 9½ inches

MATERIALS
Medium (worsted) weight cotton yarn:
    4 oz/200 yds/113g assorted scrap colors
    2½ oz/125 yds/70g white
Size H/8/5mm crochet hook or size needed to obtain gauge
Tapestry needle
Sewing needle
Sewing thread
¾-inch shank button

GAUGE
15 sc = 4 inches

INSTRUCTIONS

HANGING TOWEL
Row 1 (RS): With scrap color, ch 40, sc in 2nd ch from hook and in each ch across, turn. *(39 sc)*

Row 2: Ch 1, sc in first sc, [ch 1, sk next sc, sc in next sc] across. Fasten off. *(20 sc)*

Row 3: With RS facing, join white with sc in first sc, [sc in next ch-1 sp, ch 1, sk next sc] across, sc in last sc, turn. *(21 sc)*

Row 4: Ch 1, sc in each sc and in each ch sp across, turn. *(39 sc)*

Row 5: Rep row 2. Fasten off.

Rows 6 & 7: With scrap color, rep rows 3 and 4.

Row 8: Ch 1, hdc in first sc, [ch 1, sk next sc, hdc in next sc] across, turn. *(20 hdc)*

Row 9: Ch 1, sc in first hdc, sc in each hdc and in each ch-1 sp across, turn. *(39 sc)*

Rows 10 & 11: Rep rows 8 and 9.

Row 12: Rep row 2. Fasten off.

Rows 13–52: [Rep rows 3–12 consecutively] 4 times.

Row 53: With RS facing, join white with sc in first sc, sc in each ch-1 sp across, with sc in last sc. *(21 sc)*

Row 54: Ch 1, **sc dec** *(see Stitch Guide)* in first 2 sc, sc in next sc, [sc dec in next 2 sc, sc in next sc] across, turn. *(14 sc)*

Row 55: Ch 1, sc in first sc, [sc dec in next 2 sc, sc in next sc] 4 times, sc in last sc, turn. *(10 sc)*

Row 55: Ch 1, sc in first sc, [sc dec in next 2 sts] 4 times, sc in last sc, turn. Fasten off. *(6 sc)*

Row 57: With RS facing, join scrap color with sc in first sc, sc in next sc, sc dec in next 2 sc, sc in each of last 2 sc, turn. *(5 sc)*

Row 58: Ch 1, sc in each sc across, turn.

Rows 59–78: Rep row 58.

Row 79: Ch 1, sc dec in first 2 sc, ch 5, sk next sc, sc dec in last 2 sc. Fasten off.

Finishing
With sewing needle and sewing thread, sew button to center of row 57 on RS of towel.

DISHCLOTH
Row 1 (RS): With white, ch 32, sc in 2nd ch from hook and in each ch across. Fasten off. *(31 sc)*

Row 2: With RS facing, join scrap color with sc in first sc, [sc in next ch-1 sp, ch 1, sk next sc] across, sc in last sc, turn. *(16 sc)*

Row 3: Ch 1, sc in first sc, sc in each sc and in each ch-1 sp across, turn. *(31 sc)*

Row 4: Ch 1, sc in first sc, [ch 1, sk next sc, sc in next sc] across. Fasten off. *(16 sc)*

Row 5: With RS facing, join white with sc in first sc, [sc in next ch-1 sp, ch 1, sk next sc] across, sc in last sc, turn. *(17 sc)*

Row 6: Rep row 3.

Row 7: Ch 1, hdc in first sc, [ch 1, sk next sc, hdc in next sc] across. Fasten off. *(16 hdc)*

Row 8: Ch 1, sc in first hdc, sc in each hdc and in each ch-1 sp across, turn. *(31 sc)*

Rows 9 & 10: Rep rows 7 and 8.

Row 11: Rep row 4. Fasten off.

Rows 12–14: Rep rows 2–4.

Rows 15–34: [Work rows 5–14 consecutively] twice.

Row 35: With RS facing, join white with sc in first sc, sc in each ch-1 sp and in each sc across. Fasten off.

Border
Rnd 1 (RS): With RS facing and row 35 at top, join scrap color with sc in first sc, ch 2, sc in same st, *[ch 1, sk next sc, sc in next sc] 14 times, ch 1, sk next sc, (sc, ch 2, sc) in next sc *(corner)*, ch 1, working across next side in ends of rows, evenly sp [sc, ch 1] 16 times across, working across next side in starting ch on opposite side of row 1, (sc, ch 2, sc) in first ch, sc in each ch across with (sc, ch 2, sc) in last ch, ch 1, working across next side in ends of rows, evenly sp [sc, ch 1] 16 times across to first sc, join with sl st in joining sc.

Rnd 2: Ch 1, sc in first sc, sc in each sc and in each ch-1 sp around with 3 sc in each ch-2 sp, join with sl st in beg sc. Fasten off. ∎

Cat in the Window

DESIGN BY BEVERLY MEWHORTER

A cute kitty surrounded by four joined squares appears to be looking out a window at pretty blue skies in these decorative and whimsical pot holders. They will make a delightful gift for a special cat-loving friend.

SKILL LEVEL ■■■□
INTERMEDIATE

FINISHED SIZE
7½ inches square

MATERIALS
Red Heart Super Saver medium (worsted) weight yarn (7 oz/364 yds/198g per skein for solids, 5 oz/278 yds/141g per skein for prints):
  2½ oz/130 yds/71g #336 warm brown
  ½ oz/26 yds/14g each #381 light blue, #312 black and #305 aspen print
Size H/8/5mm crochet hook or size needed to obtain gauge
Tapestry needle
1-inch plastic ring

GAUGE
3 sc = 1 inch; 3 sc rows = 1 inch

Each Block = 3 inches square

INSTRUCTIONS

POT HOLDER
Front
Block
Make 4.
Rnd 1: With light blue, ch 4, sl st in first ch to form ring, ch 3 *(counts as first dc)*, 2 dc in ring, ch 2, (3 dc, ch 2) 3 times in ring, join with sl st in 3rd ch of beg ch-3. Fasten off. *(4 ch sps)*

Rnd 2: Join aspen print with sl st in any ch sp, ch 3, (2 dc, ch 2, 3 dc) in same ch sp, ch 3, (3 dc, ch 2, 3 dc, ch 3) in each ch sp around, join with sl st in 3rd ch of beg ch-3. Fasten off. *(8 ch sps)*

Rnd 3: Join brown with sc in any st, sc in each st and 3 sc in each ch sp around, join with sl st in beg sc. Fasten off.

Sew Blocks tog as shown in photo.

Kitty
Row 1: Starting at bottom of body, with black, ch 5, sc in 2nd ch from hook, sc in each ch across, turn. *(4 sc)*

Row 2: Ch 1, 2 sc in first st, sc in each st across with 2 sc in last st, turn. *(6 sc)*

Row 3: Ch 1, sc in each st across, turn.

Row 4: Ch 1, **sc dec** *(see Stitch Guide)* in first 2 sts, sc in each

of next 2 sts, sc dec in last 2 sts, turn. *(4 sc)*

Row 5: Ch 1, sc dec in first 2 sts, sc dec in last 2 sts, turn *(2 sc)*

Row 6: Ch 1, sc in each st across, turn.

Row 7: Ch 1, 2 sc in each st across, turn. *(4 sc)*

Row 8: Ch 1, sc dec in first 2 sts, sc dec in last 2 sts, turn. *(2 sc)*

Row 9: For ears, ch 3, (hdc, sl st) in same st as beg ch-3, (sl st, hdc, ch 3, sl st) in last st, **do not turn**.

Rnd 10: Now working in rnds,

working around entire outer edge, sl st in end of each row and in each st around, join with sl st in first sl st. Fasten off.

Tail
With black, ch 12. Fasten off.

Sew 1 end of Tail to center bottom of Kitty.

Center and sew Kitty to Front as shown in photo.

Back
Row 1: With brown, ch 23, sc in 2nd ch from hook, sc in each ch across, turn. *(22 sc)*

Rows 2–23: Ch 1, sc in each st

across, turn. At end of last row, fasten off.

Hold Front and Back tog, with Front facing, working through both thicknesses, join aspen print with sc in any st, sc in each st around with 3 sc in each corner, join with sl st in first sc. Fasten off.

Hanging Loop
Working around plastic ring, join aspen print with sc around ring, work 29 more sc around ring, join with sl st in first sc. Fasten off.

Center and sew Hanging Loop to Front as shown in photo. ∎

Glorious Gifts

Chapter Contents

Girly-Girl Pillows

DESIGNS BY MICHELE WILCOX

Trendy young ladies with fashion flair will love these fun, fanciful pillows that show off their girly sense of style! Stitch them in the favorite colors of your favorite tween or teen to accent her bedroom.

SKILL LEVEL ◖■□□
EASY

FINISHED SIZE
Each pillow is 9½ inches square

MATERIALS
TLC Cotton Plus medium
   (worsted) weight yarn
   (3½ oz/178 yds/100g per skein):
   2 skeins each #3222 yellow
      and #3752 hot pink
   1 skein #3002 black
Size G/6/4mm crochet hook or
   size needed to obtain gauge
Tapestry needle
⅜-inch rhinestone buttons: 2
8-inch pillow forms: 2

GAUGE
4 sc = 1 inch; 4 rows = 1 inch

INSTRUCTIONS

PILLOW
Side
Make 2 hot pink & 2 yellow.
Row 1: Ch 35, sc in 2nd ch from hook and in each ch across, turn. *(34 sc)*

Rows 2–33: Ch 1, sc in each st across, turn.

Rnd 34: Now working in rnds, ch 1, sc in each st and in end of each row around with 3 sc in each corner, join with sl st in beg sc. Fasten off.

SHOE
Heel
Row 1: With hot pink, ch 3, sc in 2nd ch from hook and in next ch, turn. *(2 sc)*

Row 2: Ch 1, **sc dec** *(see Stitch Guide)* in next 2 sts, turn. *(1 sc)*

Rows 3–5: Ch 1, sc in sc, turn.

Row 6: Ch 1, 2 sc in sc, turn. *(2 sc)*

Row 7: Ch 1, sc in first st, 2 sc in next st, turn. *(3 sc)*

Row 8: Ch 1, sc in each st across, turn.

Row 9: Ch 1, sc in each of first 2 sts, 2 sc in last st, turn. *(4 sc)*

Row 10: Ch 2 *(counts as first hdc)*, sc in each of next 2 sts, sl st in last st, turn.

Row 11: Sk sl st, sl st in next st, hdc in each of last 2 sts. Fasten off.

Foot
Row 1: With hot pink, ch 11, sc in 2nd ch from hook and in each ch across, turn. *(10 sc)*

Row 2: Ch 1, sc in each st across, turn.

Row 3: Ch 1, 2 sc in first st, sc in each of next 7 sts, sc dec in last 2 sts, turn.

Row 4: Ch 1, sc dec in first 2 sts, sc in each st across, turn. *(9 sc)*

Row 5: Ch 1, sc in each of first 7 sts, sc dec in last 2 sts, turn. *(8 sc)*

Row 6: Ch 1, sc dec in first 2 sts, sc in each st across, turn. *(7 sc)*

Row 7: Ch 1, 2 sc in first st, sc in each of next 3 sts, sc dec in next 2 sts, leaving last st unworked, turn. *(6 sc)*

Row 8: Ch 1, sc dec in first 2 sts, sc in each of last 4 sts, turn. *(5 sc)*

Row 9: Ch 1, sc in each of first 3 sts, sc dec in last 2 sts, turn. *(4 sc)*

Row 10: Ch 1, sc dec in first 2 sts, sc in next st, 2 sc in last st, turn.

Row 11: Ch 1, 2 sc in first st, sc in next st, sc dec in last 2 sts, turn.

Row 12: Ch 1, sc dec in first 2 sts, sc in each of last 2 sts, turn. *(3 sc)*

Row 13: Ch 1, 2 sc in first st, sc dec in last 2 sts, turn.

Row 14: Ch 1, sc dec in first 2 sts, 2 sc in next st, turn.

Row 15: Ch 1, sc in each st across, turn.

Rnd 16: Ch 1, sc dec in 3 sts, working around outer edge, evenly sp sc around with 3 sc in top of toe, join with sl st in beg sc. Fasten off.

Sew Foot and Heel to 1 yellow Pillow Side as shown in photo.

Flower
Rnd 1: With black, ch 2, 6 sc in 2nd ch from hook, **do not join** rnds. *(6 sc)*

Rnd 2: Working in **front lps** *(see Stitch Guide)*, (sl st, ch 1, 2 hdc, ch 1) in each st around.

Rnd 3: Working in **back lps** *(see Stitch Guide)* of rnd 1, (sl st, ch 1, 2 dc, ch 1) in each st around, join with sl st in beg sl st. Fasten off.

Sew Flower with rhinestone button in center to Shoe as shown in photo.

PURSE
Front
Row 1: With black, ch 13, sc in 2nd ch from hook and in each ch across, turn. *(12 sc)*

Rows 2 & 3: Ch 1, 2 sc in first st, sc in each st across with 2 sc in last st, turn. *(16 sc at end of last row)*

Rows 4 & 5: Ch 1, sc in each st across, turn.

Row 6: Ch 1, sc dec in first 2 sts, sc in each of next 12 sts, sc dec in last 2 sts, turn. *(14 sc)*

Row 7: Ch 1, sc in each st across, turn.

Row 8: Ch 1, sc dec in first 2 sts, sc in each of next 10 sts, sc dec in last 2 sts, turn. *(12 sc)*

Row 9: Ch 1, sc in each st across, turn.

Row 10: Ch 1, sc dec in first 2 sts, sc in each st across with sc dec in last 2 sts, turn. *(10 sc)*

Row 11: Ch 1, sc in each st across, turn.

Rnd 12: Now working in rnds, ch 1, sc dec in first 2 sts, sc in each st across with sc dec in last 2 sts, working in ends of rows and in starting ch on opposite side of row 1, evenly sp sc around, join with sl st in beg sc. Fasten off.

Clasp
With black, ch 5, sc in 2nd ch from hook and in each of next 2 chs, 3 sc in last ch, working on opposite side of ch, sc in each ch across. Fasten off.

Handle
With yellow, ch 22, sl st in 2nd ch from hook and in each ch across. Fasten off.

Sew ends of Handle to top edge of Purse Front

Sew Purse Front and Handle to hot pink Pillow Side as shown in photo.

Sew Clasp to center top edge of Purse Front. Sew button to Clasp as shown in photo.

PILLOW TRIM
Rnd 1: Holding 1 yellow and 1 hot pink Pillow Side *(1 front and 1 back)* with WS tog, working through both thicknesses and in back lps, join black with sc in first st, sc in each st around with 3 sc in each corner, insert pillow form before closing, join with sl st in beg sc.

Rnd 2: Ch 1, sl st in first st, ch 3, sk next st, [sl st in next st, ch 3, sk next st] around, join with sl st in beg sl st. Fasten off.

Rep with rem Pillow Sides. ■

Book Cover

DESIGN BY ALICE HEIM

Never lose your place again with this nifty book cover and its attached bookmark! The cover works up quickly and easily in your favorite crochet cotton for a gift any booklover would love to own.

SKILL LEVEL ▰▰▰▱
INTERMEDIATE

FINISHED SIZE
Fits 5 x 7-inch book

MATERIALS
Size 10 crochet cotton:
 250 yds red
 100 yds each white and blue
Size 5/1.90mm steel hook or
 size needed to obtain gauge

GAUGE
Rnds 1–3 of Granny Square =
1½ inches across; 7 V-sts = 2
inches; 4 V-st rows = 1 inch.

Each Granny Square = 2¼
inches square

SPECIAL STITCH
V-stitch (V-st): (Dc, ch 1, dc) in
indicated st.

INSTRUCTIONS

FIRST ROW
First Granny Square
Rnd 1: With red, ch 6, sl st
in first ch to form ring, ch 3
(counts as first dc), 2 dc in ring,
ch 3, [3 dc in ring, ch 3] 3 times,
join with sl st in 3rd ch of beg
ch-3. Fasten off. *(12 dc, 4 ch sps)*

Rnd 2: Join white with sl st in
any ch sp, (ch 3, 2 dc) in same
ch sp, ch 1, [(3 dc, ch 3, 3 dc) in
next ch sp, ch 1] around, 3 dc
in same ch sp as first 3 dc, join
with dc in 3rd ch of beg ch-3
forming last ch sp. Fasten off.

Rnd 3: Join blue with sl st in
any corner ch-3 sp, (ch 3, 2 dc)
in same ch sp, ch 1, 3 dc in next
ch sp, ch 1, [(3 dc, ch 3, 3 dc) in

next corner ch sp, ch 1, 3 dc in
next ch sp, ch 1] around, 3 dc
in same ch sp as first 3 dc, join
with dc in 3rd ch of beg ch-3
forming last ch sp. Fasten off.

Rnd 4: Join white with sl st in
any corner ch-3 sp, (ch 3, 2 dc)
in same ch sp, ch 1, [3 dc in
next ch sp, ch 1] twice, *(3 dc,
ch 3, 3 dc) in next corner ch sp,
ch 1, [3 dc in next ch sp, ch 1]
twice, rep from * around, 3 dc
in same ch sp as first 3 dc, join
with dc in 3rd ch of beg ch-3
forming last ch sp. Fasten off.

Rnd 5: Join red with sl st in any
corner ch-3 sp, (ch 3, 2 dc) in
same ch sp, ch 1, [3 dc in next
ch sp, ch 1] 3 times, *(3 dc, ch
3, 3 dc) in next corner ch sp, ch
1, [3 dc in next ch sp, ch 1] 3
times, rep from * around, 3 dc
in same ch sp as first 3 dc, join
with dc in 3rd ch of beg ch-3
forming last ch sp. Fasten off.

2nd Granny Square
Rnds 1–4: Rep rnds 1–4 of First
Granny Square.

Rnd 5: Join red with sl st in any
corner ch-3 sp, (ch 3, 2 dc) in
same sp, ch 1, [3 dc in next ch
sp, ch 1] 3 times, 3 dc in next
corner ch sp, joining to side of
First Granny Square, ch 1, sc in
corresponding corner ch sp on
other Square, sc in next ch sp on this Square, sc in next
ch sp on other Square, [3 dc in
next ch sp on this Square, sc in
next ch sp on other Square] 3
times, 3 dc in next corner ch sp
on this Square, ch 1, sc in next
corner ch sp on other Square,

ch 1, 3 dc in same ch sp on this
Square, ch 1, [3 dc in next ch sp,
ch 1] 3 times, (3 dc, ch 3, 3 dc)
in next corner ch sp, ch 1, [3 dc
in next ch sp, ch 1] 3 times, 3 dc
in same ch sp as first 3 dc, join
with dc in 3rd ch of beg ch-3
forming last ch sp. Fasten off.

2ND ROW
First Granny Square
Joining to bottom of First
Granny Square on First Row,
work same as First Row 2nd
Granny Square.

2nd Granny Square
Rnds 1–4: Rep rnds 1–4 of First
Row First Granny Square.

Rnd 5: Join red with sl st in any
corner ch-3 sp, (ch 3, 2 dc) in
same ch sp, ch 1, [3 dc in next
ch sp, ch 1] 3 times, 3 dc in next
corner ch sp, joining to bottom
of 2nd Granny Square on last
row, ch 1, sc in corresponding
corner ch sp on other Square,
ch 1, 3 dc in same ch sp on this
Square, *sc in next ch sp on
other Square, [3 dc in next ch
sp on this Square, sc in next ch
sp on other Square] 3 times,
3 dc in next corner ch sp on

this Square, ch 1, sc in next corner ch sp on other Square, ch 1, 3 dc in same ch sp on this Square*, joining to side of First Granny Square on this row, rep between * once, ch 1, [3 dc in next ch sp, ch 1] 3 times, 3 dc in same ch sp as first 3 dc, join with dc in 3rd ch of beg ch-3 forming last ch sp. Fasten off.

Rep 2nd Row once for a total of 3 rows.

GRANNY SQUARE EDGING

Working around entire outer edge of Granny Squares, join red with sc in any st, sc in each st and in each ch-1 sp around with 5 sc in each corner ch sp, join with sl st in beg sc. Fasten off.

BACK

Row 1: Join red with sl st in center st of corner 5-dc group before 1 long edge, ch 3, sk next 2 sts, **V-st** *(see Special Stitch)* in next st, sk next 2 sts, [V-st in next st, sk next 2 sts] 20 times, dc in last st, turn. *(21 V-sts, 2 dc)*

Rows 2–29 or until entire piece including Granny Squares reaches around your book plus 8 rows: Ch 3, V-st in ch sp of each V-st across with dc in last st, turn. At end of last row, fasten off.

Fold under last 8 rows to form back pocket.

FRONT POCKET

Row 1: Working across opposite long edge of Granny Squares, rep row 1 of Back.

Rows 2–8: Ch 3, V-st in ch sp of each V-st across with dc in last st, turn. At end of last row, fasten off.

Fold under 8 rows of Front Pocket.

BOOK COVER EDGING

Working around entire outer edge, through both thicknesses of Back/Pocket, Granny Squares/Pocket and folded edges, join red with sc in any corner st, 2 sc in same st, sc in each st and in each ch sp around with 2 sc in end of each row and 3 sc in each corner and sk sts at top and bottom of Granny Squares as necessary for piece to lie flat, join with sl st in beg sc. Fasten off.

BOOKMARK

Rnd 1: With red, ch 6, sl st in first ch to form ring, ch 3, 2 dc in ring, ch 3, [3 dc in ring, ch 3] 3 times, join with sl st 3rd ch of beg ch-3 ch-3. Fasten off. *(12 dc, 4 ch sps)*

Rnd 2: Join white with sl st in any ch sp, (ch 3, 2 dc) in same ch sp, ch 1, *(3 dc, ch 3, 3 dc) in next ch sp, ch 1, rep from * around, 3 dc in same ch sp as first 3 dc, join with dc in 3rd ch of beg ch-3. Fasten off.

Rnd 3: Join blue with sc in any corner ch sp, 2 sc in same ch sp, sc in each st and in each ch-1 sp around with 3 sc in each corner ch sp, join with sl st in beg sc. Fasten off.

Rnd 4: Join red with sc in any center corner st, 2 sc in same st, sc in each st around with 3 sc in each center corner st, join with sl st in beg sc, ch 40, sl st in 2 sts at center top of Book Cover, sc in 2nd ch from hook, sc in each ch across, sl st in next st on Bookmark. Fasten off.

HANDLES

For **front Handle**, join red with sc in st above joining between 2 Granny Squares, ch 25, sc in st above joining between next 2 Granny Squares, turn, sc in each ch across, sl st in first sc. Fasten off.

Work **back Handle** in same manner, placing Handle in sts corresponding to Front and sk sts in between. ■

Scrapbooking Keeper

DESIGN BY CINDY CARLSON

Scrapbooking and crochet go hand-in-hand with this convenient holder. It's great to take along on vacation to keep photos and mementos organized in one easy place until you create your page.

SKILL LEVEL ●□□□
BEGINNER

FINISHED SIZE
5 x 7½ inches across

MATERIALS
Fine (sport) weight yarn:
   100 yds each red, white and navy
Size C/2/2.75mm crochet hook or size needed to obtain gauge
Tapestry needle
1-inch wooden heart shape button

GAUGE
10 hdc = 2 inches; 6 hdc rows = 2 inches

INSTRUCTIONS

KEEPER
Pocket
Make 1 each red, white and navy.
Row 1: Beg at bottom, ch 37, sc in 2nd ch from hook, sc in each ch across, turn. *(36 sc)*

Row 2: Ch 2 *(counts as first hdc)*, hdc in each st across, turn.

Rows 3–12: Rep row 2.

Row 13: Rep row 2, **do not turn for red and white Pockets**.

Red & White Pockets Only
Row 14: Working across top edge from left to right, ch 1, **reverse sc** *(see Fig. 1)* in each hdc across. Fasten off.

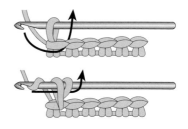

Reverse Sc
Fig. 1

Navy Pocket Only
Row 14: Working across top edge, ch 1, sc in each hdc across. Fasten off.

Flap
Row 1: With red, ch 17, sc in 2nd ch from hook, sc in each ch across, turn. *(16 sc)*

Row 2: Ch 1, sc in each sc across, turn. Fasten off.

Row 3: Join white with sc in first sc, sc in each sc across, turn.

Row 4: Rep row 2.

Row 5: Join navy with sc in first sc, sc in each sc across, turn.

Row 6: Rep row 2.

Row 7: Join red with sc in first sc, sc in each sc across, turn.

Rows 8–36: [Rep rows 2-7 consecutively] 5 times, ending last rep with row 6.

Button Loop
Join white with sl st in side edge of Flap between rows 18 and 19, ch 8, sl st in same sp. Fasten off.

Finishing
Place navy Pocket on flat surface, place white Pocket on top of navy and then red Pocket on top of white Pocket. Because of the sc row at top edge, navy Pocket will be slightly larger at top edge.

Join white with sc in end of row 14 of navy section, ch 1, working through all thicknesses, evenly sp [sc in side edge of Pocket, ch 1] 14 times down side edge to corner, work 3 sc in center sc of corner, evenly sp 34 sc across opposite side of foundation ch, 3 sc in next corner, evenly sp [ch 1, sc in side edge of Pocket] 14 times up opposite side edge, ch 1, sc in navy section only in side edge of row 14. Fasten off.

Thread tapestry needle with length of navy, holding side edge of Flap rows to row 14 of navy Pocket and with button lp at opposite edge, whipstitch side edge of Flap rows to row 14 of navy Pocket.

Sew button to center front of red Pocket between rows 7 and 8. ■

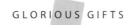

Bee Tidy

DESIGN BY SUE PENROD

This whimsical little fellow will help kids tidy up their room by providing a quick, easy place to hang up their jackets and bags. He works up quick-as-a-wink in medium weight yarn and makes a great gift for parents.

SKILL LEVEL ■□□□
BEGINNER

FINISHED SIZE
4 x 5 inches

MATERIALS
Red Heart Super Saver medium (worsted) weight yarn (3 oz/160 yds/85g per skein):
  ½ oz/27 yds/14g #312 black
  ¼ oz/40 yds/7g each #324 bright yellow and #354 vibrant orange
  1 yd each #319 cherry red and #311 white
Size G/6/4mm crochet hook or size needed to obtain gauge
Tapestry needle
3-inch plastic peel and stick wall hook
Craft glue
Scrap of fiberfill
Stitch markers

GAUGE
4 sc = 1 inch; 4 sc rows = 1 inch

PATTERN NOTES
Do not join rounds unless otherwise stated.

Mark first stitch of each round.

INSTRUCTIONS

BEE
Body
Rnd 1: Beg at bottom, with black, ch 4, sl st in first ch to form ring, ch 1, 2 sc in each ch around, **do not join** (see Pattern Notes). (8 sc)

Rnds 2–12: Ch 1, sc in each sc around.

Rnd 13: Sc in next sc, ch 4, sk next 4 sc, sc in each of next 3 sc. (4 sc, 1 ch-4 sp)

Rnd 14: 2 sc in each st and ch around. (16 sc)

Rnds 15–20: Rep rnd 2.

Rnd 21: Sc in every other sc. (8 sc)

Head
Rnd 22: 2 sc in each sc around. (16 sc)

Rnds 23–25: Rep rnd 2.

Stuff Head lightly with fiberfill.

Rnd 26: Rep rnd 21. (8 sc)

Rnd 27: Sl st in every other sc. Fasten off. (4 sl sts)

Feelers
Cut 4-inch length of black yarn. Fold strand in half, insert hook in center top of Head, pull fold through to form lp on hook, pull ends through lp on hook. Tie in knot 1 inch from Head on each end, trim ends beyond each knot.

Left Side Upper Wing
Row 1: Working in side edge of Body, join bright yellow in sp between rnds 19 and 20 with sl st, ch 8, sc in 2nd ch from hook, sc in each of next 6 chs, sl st in same st between rnd 19 and 20, turn. (7 sc)

Row 2: Sk first sc, sc in each sc across, turn. (6 sc)

Row 3: Ch 1, sc in each of first 6 sc, sl st in next st of Body between rnds 20 and 21, turn. (6 sc)

Row 4: Rep row 2. (5 sc)

Row 5: Ch 1, sc in each of first 5 sc, sl st in same st of Body between rnds 20 and 21. Fasten off. (5 sc)

Left Side Lower Wing
Row 1: Working in side edge of Body below Upper Wing, join vibrant orange with sl st between rnds 17 and 18, ch 5, sc in 2nd ch from hook, sc in each of next 3 chs, sl st in same st between rnds 17 and 18, turn. (4 sc)

Row 2: Sc in each sc across, turn.

Row 3: Ch 1, sc in each sc across, sl st in sp between rnds 18 and 19, turn. (4 sc)

Row 4: Ch 1, **sc dec** (see Stitch Guide) in next 2 sc, sc in each of last 2 sc. Fasten off. (3 sc)

Right Side Lower Wing
Row 1: Working in side edge of Body opposite left side of Lower Wing, join vibrant orange with sl st between rnds 18 and 19, ch 4, sc in 2nd ch from hook, sc in each of next 2 chs, sl st in same st between rnds 18 and 19, turn. (3 sc)

Row 2: Ch 1, 2 sc in first sc, sc in each of next 2 sc, turn. (4 sc)

Row 3: Ch 1, sc in each of first 4 sc, sl st in sp between rnds 17 and 18, turn.

Row 4: Ch 1, sc in each of next 4 sc. Fasten off.

Right Side Upper Wing
Row 1: Working in side edge of Body above Lower Wing opposite Left Side Upper Wing, join bright yellow with sl st in sp between rnds 20 and 21, ch 6, sc in 2nd ch from hook, sc in each ch across, sl st in same sp between rnds 20 and 21, turn. (5 sc)

Row 2: Sc in each sc across, turn.

Row 3: Ch 1, 2 sc in first sc, sc in each sc across, sl st in sp between rnds 19 and 20, turn. (6 sc)

Row 4: Rep row 2.

Row 5: Ch 1, 2 sc in first sc, sc in each sc, sl st in same sp between rnds 19 and 20. Fasten off. (7 sc)

French knot *(see Fig. 1)* and black French knot centered over white between rnds 24 and 25 as shown in photo.

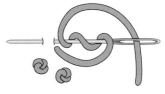

**French Knot
Fig. 1**

With cherry red, embroider nose with French knot centered below eyes between rnds 23 and 24 and cherry red V-shape mouth centered below nose as shown in photo.

With cherry red, embroider V-shape on upper Body over rnds 18 and 19 as shown in photo.

Place small amount of glue on wall hook, slide rnds 1–12 of Body over hook.

Place a small amount of glue on flat portion of 3-inch plastic hook and press Body to plastic to secure Body to piece.

Shape each Wing and allow glue to dry. ■

Wing Trim
Join black with sl st in side edge of Wing next to Body, ch 1, evenly sp sc around outer edge of Wing, working 2 sc in each outer corner and ending Wing Trim at side edge of Wing next to Body. Fasten off. Rep on rem Wings.

Finishing
Embroider eyes with white and

Pretty Tissues

DESIGN BY AGNES RUSSELL

Keep your packet of tissues close at hand inside this lovely tissue holder, specially sized for your purse! It makes a beautiful gift for friends and family, while still serving a practical purpose.

SKILL LEVEL ●□□□
BEGINNER

FINISHED SIZE
2¾ x 4¾ inches

MATERIALS
Opera size 5 crochet cotton
 (191 yds per ball):
  1 ball #503 ecru
Size 20 crochet cotton:
  20 yds each coral, spruce,
   orchid and dusty rose
Sizes 11/1.10mm and
 8/1.50mm steel crochet
 hooks or size needed to
 obtain gauge
Tapestry needle
Sewing needle
Ecru sewing thread
Clear 6mm bead
Silver 3mm beads: 9
Size 4/0 snap fasteners: 2
15-tissue pocket pack

GAUGE
Size 8 hook & ecru crochet
cotton: 7 sts = 1 inch; 3 pattern
rows = ½ inch

SPECIAL STITCH
Split decrease (split dec):
Holding back last lp of each
st on hook, sc in next st, sk
next st, sc in next st, [yo, pull
through 2 lps on hook] twice.

INSTRUCTIONS

COVER
Body
Row 1: With size 8 hook and ecru,
ch 33, sc in 2nd ch from hook, sc
in each ch across, turn. *(32 sc)*

Row 2: Ch 1, sc in first sc, dc in
next sc, [sc in next sc, dc in next
sc] across, turn.

Rows 3–9: Ch 1, sc in first dc,
dc in next sc, [sc in next dc, dc
in next sc] across, turn.

Row 10: Ch 1, sc in first dc, dc
in next sc, [sc in next dc, dc in
next sc] twice, ch 19, sk next 19
sts, dc in next sc, [sc in next dc,
dc in next sc] 3 times, turn.

Row 11: Ch 1, sc in first dc, [dc
in next sc, sc in next dc] 3 times,
[dc in next ch, sc in next ch] 9
times, dc in next ch, [sc in next
dc, dc in next sc] 3 times, turn.

Rows 12–19: Rep row 3. At the
end of last row, fasten off.

Row 20: With ecru, ch 6, [sc in
next dc, dc in next sc] 16 times,
ch 7, turn.

Row 21: Sc in 2nd ch from
hook, [dc in next ch, sc in next
ch] twice, dc in next ch, [sc in
next dc, dc in next sc] 16 times,
[sc in next ch, dc in next ch] 3
times, turn. *(44 sts)*

Rows 22–32: Rep row 3.

Row 33: Sl st in each of first 6
sts, (sl st, ch 1, sc) in next dc, dc
in next sc, [sc in next dc, dc in
next sc] 15 times, leaving rem 6
sts unworked, turn. *(32 sts)*

Rows 34–42: Rep row 3.

Row 43: Ch 1, sc in next dc,
[dc in next sc, sc in next dc]
14 times, **split dec** *(see Special
Stitch)*, turn. *(30 sts)*

Rows 44–51: Ch 1, sc in first
dc, [dc in next sc, sc in next dc]

across to last 3 sts, split dec,
turn. *(14 sts at end of last row)*

Row 52: Ch 1, sc in first dc,
[dc in next sc, sc in next dc] 3
times, ch 8, sl st in top of last sc
(button lp), [dc in next sc, sc in
next dc] 3 times, ending with sc
in last st. Fasten off.

With tapestry needle and
length of ecru, sew ends of rows
1–19 to ends of rows 20–32.

Rep on opposite edge.

With sewing needle and thread,
sew snap fasteners evenly spaced
across row 1 and row 33.

Trim
With RS facing and size 8 hook,
join ecru with sl st in end of row
33, working down side edge to
within button lp, evenly sp [5 dc,
sl st] 7 times, 16 sc in ch-8 button
lp, sl st in next st, evenly sp [5
dc, sl st] 7 times across opposite
edge ending in end of row 33.
Fasten off.

Insert tissue pack and snap
the fasteners.

Button
Rnd 1: With size 8 hook and ecru,
ch 2, 6 sc in 2nd ch from hook,
join with sl st in beg sc. *(6 sc)*

Rnd 2: Ch 1, 2 sc in first st, sc
in next sc, [2 sc in next sc, sc in
next sc] around, join with sl st
in beg sc. *(9 sc)*

Rnd 3: Ch 1, sc in each sc
around, join with sl st in beg sc.
Leaving long end, fasten off.

With tapestry needle, thread long end and weave through sc sts of rnd 3, place 6mm bead in center of piece, pull woven length gently to close opening, knot to secure, **do not fasten off**.

Fold flap closed to find placement of Button. Sew Button to tissue cover.

Flowers

Make 3 each of coral, orchid and dusty rose.
With size 11 hook and size 20 crochet cotton, ch 5, sl st in first ch to form ring, ch 1, sc in ring, [ch 2, 2 dc in ring, ch 2, sc in ring] 5 times. Fasten off.

Leaf

Make 5.
With size 11 hook and spruce,

ch 8, sl st in 2nd ch from hook, sl st in next ch, sc in next ch, dc in each of next 3 chs, sc in last ch. Fasten off.

Sew Leaves and Flowers to front flap of tissue holder as desired. Sew 3mm bead to the center of each Flower. ■

Snipper Keeper

DESIGN BY SUE CHILDRESS

Keep your scissors close at hand with this charming little bunny dressed in a sweet romper. Quilting and crocheting friends will also enjoy this handy solution to lost scissors while crafting!

SKILL LEVEL ■□□□
BEGINNER

FINISHED SIZE
To fit 5 inch soft-sculpture bunny

MATERIALS

Light (light worsted) weight yarn:
    ½ oz/50 yds/14g
Size D/3/3.25 crochet hook or size needed to obtain gauge
5 inch soft-sculpture bunny
Small pair scissors
⅛-inch-wide ribbon in desired color: 24 inches
Craft glue

GAUGE
6 hdc = 1 inches

INSTRUCTIONS

KEEPER
Romper
Row 1: Ch 24, hdc in 3rd ch from hook *(first 2 chs count as first hdc)* and in each ch across, turn. *(23 hdc)*

Row 2 (RS): Ch 3 *(counts as first dc)*, dc in each of next 2 sts, *ch 6, sk next 5 sts for armhole*, dc in each of next 3 sts, 3 dc in next st, dc in each of next 3 sts, rep between * once, dc in each of last 3 sts, turn. *(15 dc, 2 ch-6 sps)*

Row 3: Ch 2 *(counts as first hdc)*, hdc in each dc and 6 hdc in each ch-6 sp across, turn. *(27 hdc)*

Rnd 4: Now working in rnds, ch 2, hdc in each st around, join with sl st in 2nd ch of beg ch-2. *(27 hdc)*

Rnd 5: Ch 2, hdc in each of next 12 hdc, 2 hdc in next hdc, hdc in each hdc around, join with sl st in 2nd ch of beg ch-2. *(28 hdc)*

First Leg
Rnd 6: Ch 2, hdc in each of next 13 hdc, leaving rem sts unworked, join with sl st in 2nd ch of beg ch-2. *(14 hdc)*

Rnd 7: Ch 1, sc in first st, sc in each hdc around, join with sl st in beg sc, sl st into next

unworked hdc of rnd 5, **do not fasten off**.

2nd Leg

Rnd 6: Working in rem unworked hdc of rnd 5, rep rnd 6 of First Leg.

Rnd 7: Rep rnd 7 of First Leg, ending with join with sl st in beg sc. Fasten off.

Headpiece & Scissors Holder

[Ch 6, sl st in 6th ch from hook] 5 times, sl st in sl st at base of beg ch-6, ch 60, place scissors on ch, sc in 5th ch from hook and in each ch across, sl st in Headpiece. Fasten off.

Finishing

Glue Headpiece on top of bunny's head.

Cut ribbon in half, weave 1 length through rnd 6 on each Leg of Romper and tie into bow at outer edge of Leg if desired.

Glue back opening of bunny's romper tog. ■

Floral Jar Covers

DESIGNS BY PATRICIA HALL

Dress up your canned jellies, jams and layered dessert mixes with dainty jar toppers. Roses and posies on frilly skirted covers turn plain canning jars into lovely gifts.

SKILL LEVEL ◼◼◼◻
INTERMEDIATE

FINISHED SIZES
Off-White Cover: 6 inches across

Light Yellow Cover: 6 inches across

White Cover: 6¾ inches across

MATERIALS
Medium (worsted) weight yarn:
    1 oz/50 yds/28g each off-white, light yellow and white
Size 10 crochet cotton:
    42 yds avocado
    21 yds purple
    16 yds red
    10 yds orange
    3 yds yellow
Size 4/2.00mm steel crochet hook or size needed to obtain gauge

Size G/6/4mm crochet hook or size needed to obtain gauge
Tapestry needle
⅝-inch-wide satin ribbon:
    24 inches each off-white, orange and white

GAUGE
Size 4 steel hook: Red Flower = 1¾ inches across; Orange Flower = 1½ inches across; Purple Flower = 1¼ inches across

Size G hook: Rnds 1–3 of Top = 3½ inches across

PATTERN NOTES
Use size G hook with medium weight yarn.

Use size 4 steel hook with crochet cotton.

SPECIAL STITCHES
Beginning treble crochet cluster (beg tr cl): Ch 3, holding back last lp of each st on hook, 2 tr in same place, yo, pull through all lps on hook.
Treble crochet cluster (tr cl): Holding back last lp of each st on hook, 3 tr as indicated, yo, pull through all lps on hook.
Picot: Ch 4, sl st in top of st just made.
Beginning double treble crochet cluster (beg dtr cl): Ch 4, holding back last lp of each st on hook, 3 dtr in same st, yo, pull through all lps on hook.
Double treble crochet cluster (dtr cl): Holding back last lp of each st on hook, 4 dtr in same st, yo, pull through all lps on hook, yo, pull through all lps on hook.

OFF-WHITE COVER
Top
Rnd 1: With size G hook and off-white, ch 4, 11 dc in 4th ch from hook *(first 3 chs count as first dc)*, join with sl st in 3rd ch of ch-3. *(12 dc)*

Rnds 2 & 3: Ch 3 *(counts as first dc)*, dc in same st, 2 dc in each st around, join with sl st in 3rd ch of beg ch-3. *(48 dc at end of last rnd)*

Rnd 4: Working this rnd in **back lps** *(see Stitch Guide)* only, ch 4 *(counts as first dc and ch-1)*, sk next st, [dc in next st, ch 1, sk next st] around, join with sl st in 3rd ch of beg ch-4. *(24 dc, 24 ch-1 sps)*

Rnd 5: Ch 1, sc in each st and in each ch around, join with sl st in beg sc. *(48 sc)*

Rnd 6: Beg tr cl *(see Special Stitches)* in first st, ch 9, **tr cl** *(see Special Stitches)* in next st, sk next 2 sts, [tr cl in next st, ch 9, tr cl in next st, sk next 2 sts] around, join with sl st in top of beg tr cl. Fasten off. *(24 tr cls, 12 ch sps)*

Rnd 7: For edging, with size 4 hook, join red with sc in sp between last and first tr cls, ch 7, (sc, hdc, dc, tr, **picot**— see Special Stitches, tr, dc, hdc, sc) in next ch sp, ch 7, *sc in sp between next 2 tr-cls, ch 7, (sc, hdc, dc, tr, picot, tr, dc, hdc, sc) in next ch sp, ch 7, rep from * around, join with sl st in beg sc. Fasten off.

Leaves
Rnd 1: With size 4 hook and avocado, ch 12, sl st in first ch to form ring, ch 3, 23 dc in ring, join with sl st in 3rd ch of beg ch-3. *(24 dc)*

Rnd 2: Ch 1, sc in first st, [ch 5, sk next st, sc in next st] around, join with ch 2, sk last st, dc in first sc forming last ch sp. *(12 sc, 12 ch sps)*

Rnd 3: Ch 1, sc in ch sp just made, [ch 5, sc in next ch sp] around, join with ch 2, dc in first sc forming last ch sp.

Rnd 4: Ch 1, sc in ch sp just made, ch 5, [sc in next ch lp, ch 5] around, join with sl st in beg sc.

Rnd 5: Beg dtr cl (see Special Stitches), ch 6, sc in next ch sp, ch 6, [(**dtr cl** (see Special Stitches) in next sc, ch 6, sc in next ch sp, ch 6)] around, join with sl st in top of beg dtr cl. Fasten off.

Tack Leaves over rnds 1–3 of Top.

Red Flower
Rnd 1: With size 4 hook and red, ch 6, sl st in first ch to form ring, ch 3, 23 dc in ring, join with sl st in top of ch-3. (24 dc)

Rnd 2: Ch 6, sk next 7 sts, [sl st in next st, ch 6, sk next 7 sts] around, join with sl st in first ch of first beg ch-6. (3 ch sps)

Rnd 3: Sl st in first ch sp, ch 1, (sc, hdc, dc, 5 tr, dc, hdc, sc) in same ch sp and in each ch sp around, join with sl st in beg sc. Fasten off.

Rnd 4: Fold petals forward, join with sl st in 4th dc of any sk 7-dc group on rnd 1, ch 6, [sl st in 4th dc on next sk 7-dc group, ch 6] around, join with sl st in beg sl st. (3 ch sps)

Rnd 5: Rep rnd 3.

Rnd 6: Fold petals forward, join with sl st in 2nd dc of any sk 3-dc group on rnd 1, ch 6, sk

next 3-dc group, [sl st in 2nd dc of next sk 3-dc group, ch 6, sk next 3-dc group] around, join with sl st in beg sl st.

Rnd 7: Sl st in first ch sp, (sc, ch 2, 2 tr, 10 dtr, 2 tr, ch 2, sc) in same ch sp and in each ch sp around, join with sl st in beg sl st. Fasten off.

For center of Flower, with size 4 steel hook and yellow, ch 3, (2 dc, sl st) in 3rd ch from hook. Fasten off. Tack to center of Flower.

Tack Red Flower to center of Leaves.

Weave off-white ribbon through ch sps of rnd 4 of Top.

Tie ends into a bow.

LIGHT YELLOW COVER
Top
Rnd 1: With size G hook and light yellow, ch 4, 11 dc in 4th ch from hook (first 3 chs count as first dc), join with sl st in 3rd ch of ch-3. (12 dc)

Rnds 2 & 3: Ch 3 (counts as first dc), dc in same st, 2 dc in each st around, join with sl st in 3rd ch of beg ch-3. (48 dc at end of last rnd)

Rnd 4: Working this rnd in back lps only, ch 4 (counts as first dc and ch-1), sk next st, [dc in next st, ch 1, sk next st] around, join with sl st in 3rd ch of beg ch-4. (24 dc, 24 ch-1 sps)

Rnd 5: Ch 1, sc in each st and in each ch around, join with sl st in beg sc. (48 sc)

Rnd 6: Ch 1, sc in first st, ch 6, sk next st, **tr cl** (see Special Stitches) in next st, ch 8, tr cl in next st, ch 6, sk next 2 sts, [sc in next st, ch 6, sk next 2 sts, tr cl in next st, ch 8, tr cl in next st, ch 6, sk next 2 sts] around, join with sl st in beg sc. Fasten off. (14 tr cls, 14 ch-6 sps, 7 sc, 7 ch-8 sps)

Rnd 7: With size 4 steel hook and orange, join with sc in first sc, ch 10, 2 sc in next tr cl, ch 14, 2 sc in next tr cl, ch 10, [sc in next sc, ch 10, 2 sc in next tr cl, ch 14, 2 sc in next tr cl, ch 10] around, join with sl st in beg sc. Fasten off.

Leaves
Rnd 1: With size 4 hook and avocado, ch 12, sl st in first ch to form ring, ch 3, 23 dc in ring, join with sl st in 3rd ch of beg ch-3. (24 dc)

Rnd 2: Ch 1, sc in first st, [ch 5, sk next st, sc in next st] around, join with ch 2, sk last st, dc in first sc forming last ch sp. (12 sc, 12 ch sps)

Rnd 3: Ch 1, sc in ch sp just made, ch 11, [sc in next ch sp, ch 11] around, join with sl st in beg sc.

Rnd 4: Ch 1, sc in first st, *ch 6, (sc, ch 4, sc) in next ch sp, ch 6**, sc in next st, rep from * around, ending last rep at **, join with sl st in beg sc. Fasten off.

Tack Leaves over rnds 1–3 of Top.

Orange Flower
Rnd 1: With size 4 hook and orange, ch 5, sl st in first ch to

form ring, ch 2 *(counts as first hdc)*, 13 hdc in ring, join with sl st in 2nd ch of beg ch-2. *(14 hdc)*

Rnd 2: Ch 3, sk next st, [sl st in next st, ch 3, sk next st] around, join with sl st in first ch of beg ch-3. *(7 ch sps)*

Rnd 3: (Sl st, ch 2, 2 dc, ch 2, sl st) in each ch sp around, join with sl st in beg sl st. Fasten off.

Rnd 4: Fold petal forward, join with sl st in any sk st on rnd 1, ch 4, [sl st in next sk st, ch 4] around, join with sl st in beg sl st.

Rnd 5: Sl st in first ch sp, ch 1, (sc, ch 1, dc, 3 tr, dc, ch 1, sc) in same ch sp and in each ch sp around, join with sl st in beg sc. Fasten off.

For center of Flower, with size 4 hook and yellow, ch 3, (2 dc, sl st) in 3rd ch from hook. Fasten off. Tack to center of Flower.

Tack Orange Flower to center of Leaves.

Weave orange ribbon through ch sps of rnd 4 of Top.

Tie ends into a bow.

WHITE COVER
Rnd 1: With size G hook and white, ch 4, 11 dc in 4th ch from hook *(first 3 chs count as first dc)*, join with sl st in 3rd ch of ch-3. *(12 dc)*

Rnds 2 & 3: Ch 3 *(counts as first dc)*, dc in same st, 2 dc in each st around, join with sl st in 3rd ch of beg ch-3. *(48 dc at end of last rnd)*

Rnd 4: Working this rnd in back lps only, ch 4 *(counts as first dc and ch-1)*, sk next st, [dc in next st, ch 1, sk next st] around, join with sl st in 3rd ch of beg ch-4. *(24 dc, 24 ch-1 sps)*

Rnd 5: Ch 1, sc in each st and in each ch around, join with sl st in beg sc. *(48 sc)*

Rnd 6: Ch 1, sc in first st, ch 9, sk next 3 sts, [sc in next st, ch 9, sk next 3 sts] around, join with sl st in beg sc. *(12 sc, 12 ch-9 sps)*

Rnd 7: Ch 1, sc in first st, (5 dc, ch 2, sc, ch 2, 5 dc) in next ch sp, [sc in next sc, (5 dc, ch 2, sc, ch 2, 5 dc) in next ch sp] around, join with sl st in beg sc. Fasten off. *(120 dc, 24 ch-2 sps, 24 sc)*

Rnd 8: With size 4 steel hook and purple, join with sc in first sc, *ch 9, sk next 4 dc, sc in next dc, ch 5, (sc, ch 4, sc) in next sc, ch 5, sc in next dc, ch 9, sk next 4 dc**, sc in next sc, rep from * around, ending last rep at **, join with sl st in beg sc. Fasten off.

Leaves
Rnd 1: With size 4 hook and avocado, ch 12, sl st in first ch to form ring, ch 3, 23 dc in ring, join with sl st in 3rd ch of beg ch-3. *(24 dc)*

Rnd 2: Ch 1, sc in first st, [ch 4, sk next st, sc in next st] around, join with ch 2, sk last st, dc in first sc forming last ch sp. *(12 sc, 12 ch sps)*

Rnd 3: Ch 1, sc in ch sp just made, [ch 5, sc in next ch sp] around, join with ch 2, dc in first sc forming last ch sp.

Rnd 4: Ch 1, sc in ch sp just made, ch 7, [sc in next ch sp, ch 7] around, join with sl st in beg sc.

Rnd 5: Sl st in first ch sp, ch 1, (sc, hdc, dc, 2 tr, **picot**—*see Special Stitches*, tr, dc, hdc, sc) in same ch sp and in each ch sp around, join with sl st in beg sc. Fasten off.

Tack over rnds 1–3 of Top.

Purple Flower
Make 3.
Rnd 1: With size 4 hook and purple, ch 5, sl st in first ch to form ring, ch 2 *(counts as first hdc)*, 9 hdc in ring, join with sl st in 2nd ch of beg ch-2. *(10 hdc)*

Rnd 2: ◊Ch 4, *yo twice, insert hook in same st, yo, pull lp through, [yo, pull through 2 lps on hook] twice*, rep between *, yo twice, insert hook in next st, yo, pull lp through, [yo, pull through 2 lps on hook] twice, rep between *, yo, pull through all lps on hook, ch 4, sl st in same st◊, [sl st in next st, rep between ◊] around, join with sl st in beg sl st. Fasten off.

For center of flower *(make 3)*, with size 4 hook and yellow, ch 3, (2 dc, sl st) in 3rd ch from hook. Fasten off.

Tack to center of each Flower.

Tack Purple Flowers to rnds 1–3 of Leaves.

Weave white ribbon through ch sps of rnd 4 of Top.

Tie ends into a bow. ■

Vineyard Wine Set

DESIGN BY SANDY ABBATE

Treat your favorite wine lover to an elegant accessory set. When paired with a bottle of wine or sparkling juice, it makes a fabulous gift for weddings, birthdays or holidays.

SKILL LEVEL ■□□□
BEGINNER

FINISHED SIZES
Caddy: 5 inches in diameter x 6 inches tall

Coaster: 5 inches in diameter

MATERIALS
Medium (worsted)
  weight yarn:
    3 oz/150 yds/85g
      deep crimson
    1 oz/50 yds/28g each violet
      and woodsy green
Size F/5/3.75mm crochet hook or
  size needed to obtain gauge
Tapestry needle
  ⅛-inch-wide gold ribbon:
  1⅔ yds

GAUGE
9 dc = 2 inches; 5 dc rnds = 2 inches

SPECIAL STITCHES
Beginning cross-stitch (beg cross-st): Ch 3, working in front of beg ch, dc in dc before beg ch.
Cross-stitch (cross-st): Sk next dc, dc in next dc, working in front of last dc, dc in dc just sk.

INSTRUCTIONS

COASTER
Make 2.
First Grape
With violet, ch 3, 11 hdc in 3rd ch from hook *(first 2 chs count as first hdc)*, join with sl st in 2nd ch of beg ch-2. Fasten off. *(12 hdc)*

2nd Grape
Rep First Grape, **do not fasten off**, sl st in **back lp** *(see Stitch Guide)* of joining of First Grape. Fasten off.

3rd Grape
With violet, ch 3, 9 hdc in 3rd ch from hook, sl st in 2nd st from joining on First Grape, hdc in same ch on this Grape, sl st in 2nd st from joining on 2nd Grape, hdc in same ch on this Grape, join with sl st in 2nd ch of beg ch-2. Fasten off.

Vine
Rnd 1 (RS): Join woodsy green with sl st in sp between Grapes, ch 1, *(sc, ch 9, sc) in sp between Grapes, ch 6, working in back lps,

sk next 4 hdc, (sc, ch 6, sc) in next hdc, ch 6, rep from * twice, join with sl st in beg sc. Fasten off.

Rnd 2 (RS): Join woodsy green with sl st in any ch-9 sp, ch 1, sc in same ch sp, *ch 4, [sc in next ch-6 sp, ch 3] 3 times**, sc in next ch-9 sp, rep from * around, ending last rep at **, join with sl st in beg sc. Fasten off. *(12 ch-4 sps)*

Rnd 3 (RS): Join deep crimson with sl st in any ch-4 sp, ch 3 *(counts as first dc)*, 3 dc in same ch sp, dc in next sc, [4 dc in next ch-4 sp, dc in next sc] around, join with sl st in 3rd ch of beg ch-3. Fasten off. *(60 dc)*

Rnd 4 (RS): Join violet with sl st in any dc, ch 1, **sc dec** *(see Stitch Guide)* in first 2 sts, ch 3, [sc dec in next 2 sts, ch 3] around, join with sl st in beg sc dec. Fasten off.

Cut 8-inch length of ribbon. Tie in bow around any dc of rnd 3.

WINE CADDY
Rnd 1 (RS): Beg at bottom with deep crimson, ch 4, 15 dc in 4th ch from hook *(first 3 chs count as first dc)*, join with sl st in 3rd ch of beg ch-43. *(16 dc)*

Rnd 2: Ch 3 *(counts as first dc)*, dc in same st, 2 dc in each st around, join with sl st in 3rd ch of beg ch-3. *(32 dc)*

Rnd 3: Ch 3, 2 dc in next dc, [dc in next dc, 2 dc in next dc] around, join with sl st in 3rd ch of beg ch-3. *(48 dc)*

Rnd 4: Working in back lps for this rnd only, ch 3, dc in each st around, join with sl st in top of beg ch-3.

Rnd 5: Ch 3, dc in each dc around, join with sl st in 3rd ch of beg ch-3, pull up lp of woodsy green, drop deep crimson to WS, **do not fasten off.**

Rnd 6: With woodsy green, **beg cross-st** *(see Special Stitches)*, **cross-st** *(see Special Stitches)* around, join with sl st in 3rd ch of beg ch-3. Fasten off woodsy green. *(24 cross-sts)*

Rnd 7: Pull up lp of deep crimson and sl st in joining, ch 3, dc in each dc around, join with sl st in 3rd ch of beg ch-3. *(48 dc)*

Rnds 8–13: Ch 3, dc in each dc around, join with sl st in 3rd ch of beg ch-3.

Rnds 14–17: Rep rnds 5–8. At end of last rnd, fasten off.

Rnd 18: Join violet with sl st in any dc, ch 1, sc dec in first 2 dc, ch 3, [sc dec in next 2 sts, ch 3] around, join with sl st in beg sc dec. Fasten off.

Bottom Trim
Rnd 1: Join deep crimson in unworked lps of rnd 3, ch 3, dc in next st, 2 dc in next st, [dc in each of next 2 sts, 2 dc in next st] around, join with sl st in 3rd ch of beg ch-3. *(64 dc)*

Rnd 2: Ch 3, dc in each of next 2 sts, 2 dc in next st, [dc in each of next 3 sts, 2 sc in next st] around, join with sl st in 3rd ch

of beg ch-3. Fasten off. *(80 dc)*

Rnd 3: Join violet with sl st in any dc, ch 1, sc dec in first 2 dc, ch 3, [sc dec in next 2 dc, ch 3] around, join with sl st in beg sc dec. Fasten off.

APPLIQUÉS
Leaf Group
With woodsy green, ch 10, *sc in 2nd ch from hook, hdc in next ch, dc in next ch, hdc in next ch, sc in next ch, sl st in next ch**, ch 7, rep from * across, ending 2nd rep at **, sc in each of last 3 chs of beg ch-10. Leaving long end, fasten off.

Grape
Make 9.
With violet, ch 3, 11 hdc in 3rd ch from hook, join with sl st in 2nd ch of beg ch-3. Leaving long end, fasten off.

Finishing
1. Grapes and Leaf Group are sewn to Caddy between rnds 5–14. Sew first Grape over rnd 5, 2 Grapes centered over previous Grape, 3 Grapes centered above previous Grapes and sew rem 2 Grapes centered above previous Grapes leaving center sp free.

2. Sew stem of Leaf Group in sp between last 2 Grapes at top and Leaves above.

3. Cut 2 lengths of gold ribbon each 22 inches. Weave first length over and under sts of rnd 4, gather slightly, tie ends in bow. Weave 2nd length over and under sts of rnd 17, tie ends in bow. ■

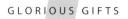

Tissue Holder

DESIGN BY SHIRLEY SOUCH

A lady is never without a tissue, and what lady wants to carry a plain packaged pack? Stitch this holder to carry in your pocket or purse for times when you're feeling under the weather.

SKILL LEVEL ◼◻◻ EASY

FINISHED SIZE
Fits 2½ x 4¼-inch tissue pack

MATERIALS
Size 10 crochet cotton:
   100 yds blue
   10 yds white
Size 4/2.00mm steel crochet hook or size needed to obtain gauge
Tapestry needle
2½ x 4¼-inch tissue pack

GAUGE
7 patterns = 2 inches; 8 rows = 1 inch

INSTRUCTIONS

TISSUE HOLDER
Row 1: With blue, ch 39, sc in 2nd ch from hook, sc in each ch across, turn. *(38 sc)*

Row 2: Ch 1, sk first sc, (sc, hdc) in next sc, [sk next sc, (sc, hdc in next sc] for pattern across, turn. *(19 patterns)*

Row 3: Ch 1, sk first hdc, (sc, hdc) in next sc, [sk next hdc, (sc, hdc) in next sc] across, turn.

Next rows: Rep row 3 until piece measures 6¾ inches from beg.

Row 4: Working across last pattern row, sl st in each st across. Fasten off.

Row 5: Join blue with sl st in opposite side of foundation ch, sl st in each ch across. Fasten off.

Trim
Row 1: With row 4 of sl sts facing, join white with sl st in **back lp** *(see Stitch Guide)*, sl st in same st, ch 3, sk next st, sl st in next st, [ch 3, sk next 2 sts, sl st in next back lp of sl st] 11 times, ch 3, sk next st, sl st in last st, turn. *(13 ch-3 sps)*

Row 2: [Ch 3, sl st in next ch-3 sp] 13 times, turn.

Row 3: [Ch 4, sl st in 3rd ch from hook for picot, ch 2, sl st in next ch-3 sp] across. Fasten off.

Working across sl sts of row 5, rep rows 1–3 on opposite edge.

Finishing
Holder is sewn tog on WS. With tapestry needle and blue, place Holder on flat surface with trim rows showing, fold each trim edge to center of Holder, sew side seams across edge, sew edges of rows 4 and 5 tog at each end ¾ inch in from outer edge.

Turn Holder RS out and insert tissue pack. ◼

Golf Club Covers

DESIGNS BY SHARON FOTTA ANDERSON

Show your patriotic pride while walking the back nine with this trio of club covers. They're super simple to crochet from worsted weight yarn and are sure to please your favorite player.

SKILL LEVEL ■□□□
BEGINNER

FINISHED SIZE
4 x 9 inches, excluding pompom

MATERIALS

Medium (worsted) weight yarn:
    4 oz/200 yds/113g burgundy
    2 oz/100 yds/57g each soft white and country blue
Size F/5/3.75mm crochet hook or size needed to obtain gauge
Tapestry needle
Sewing needle
Sewing thread
1-inch white sew-on stars: 9
4-inch piece cardboard

GAUGE
4 dc = 1 inch; 2 dc rows = 1 inch

INSTRUCTIONS

GOLF CLUB COVER
Make 3.
Row 1: With burgundy, ch 37, hdc in 2nd ch from hook, hdc in each of next 15 chs, dc in each of next 20 chs, turn. *(16 hdc, 20 dc)*

Row 2: Ch 3 *(counts as first dc)*, dc in each of next 19 dc, working in **back lps** *(see Stitch Guide)* only, hdc in each of last 16 sts, turn.

Row 3: Ch 2 *(counts as first hdc)*, working in back lps only, hdc in each of next 15 sts, working in both lps, dc in each of last 20 dc, turn.

Rows 4–15: [Rep rows 2 and 3 alternately] 6 times.

Row 16: Rep row 2.

Row 17: Holding opposite side of foundation ch to row 16, matching sts, sl st in each st across. Leaving long end, fasten off.

Weave long end through ends of dc rows, pull gently to close opening, knot to secure. Fasten off.

POMPOM
Make 3.
Holding 1 strand each burgundy, soft white and country blue tog, wrap around the 4-inch cardboard 30 times, cut yarn. Gently slide lps off cardboard and tie length of yarn tightly around the center of the bundle. Cut lps at each end of bundle, fluff and trim ends.

Attach 1 Pompom to center top of each Golf Club Cover.

FINISHING
Sew 5 stars to center of first Cover, 3 stars to 2nd Cover and last star to 3rd Cover. ■

Double-Decker Card Set

DESIGNS BY JENNIFER MOIR

Pretty single and double-deck card holders, stitched in size 10 thread and accented with dainty flowers, add a feminine touch to the ladies' bridge club get-together. Tuck in a score card and you're ready to play!

SKILL LEVEL ▮▮▮▯
INTERMEDIATE

FINISHED SIZES
Single deck case: ¾ x 4 inches

Double-deck case: 1½ x 4 inches

MATERIALS
Size 10 crochet cotton:
    350 yds blue
    25 yds dark blue
    5 yds green
Size 7/1.65mm steel crochet hook or size needed to obtain gauge
Tapestry needle
10mm blue novelty buttons: 2
Stitch markers: 4

GAUGE
4 shells = 1¾ inches; 6 shell rnds = 1½ inches

SPECIAL STITCHES
Shell: (2 dc, ch 2, 2 dc) in indicated st.
Beginning shell (beg shell): (Ch 3, dc, ch 2, 2 dc) in indicated st.
Picot: Ch 3, sl st in top of last st.

INSTRUCTIONS

SINGLE-DECK CASE
Base
Row 1: With blue, ch 26, hdc in 3rd ch from hook *(first 2 chs count as first hdc)*, hdc in each ch across, turn. *(25 hdc)*

Row 2: Ch 2 *(counts as first hdc)*, hdc in each hdc across, turn.

Rows 3 & 4: Rep row 2. At the end of last row, **do not turn**.

Rnd 5: Now working in rnds, ch 1, evenly sp 7 sc across ends of rows, 3 sc in corner st *(place st marker in center corner sc of each corner 3-sc group)*, evenly sp 23 sc across long edge, 3 sc in corner st, evenly sp 6 sc across ends of rows, 3 sc in corner st, evenly sp 23 sc across long edge, 2 sc in same st as beg sc to complete last 3-sc corner group, join with sl st in beg sc. *(70 sc)*

Side
Rnd 6: Working in **back lps** *(see Stitch Guide)* for this rnd only, ch 2, hdc in each st around, moving st markers at each corner as rnd progresses, join with sl st in 2nd ch of beg ch-2.

Rnd 7: Sl st to 3rd st on short edge, **beg shell** *(see Special*

Stitches) in same st, **fpdc** *(see Stitch Guide)* around center corner hdc, sk next 2 sts, **shell** *(see Special Stitches)* in next st, [sk next 3 sts, shell in next st] 5 times, sk next 2 sts, fpdc around center corner hdc, sk next 3 hdc, shell in next hdc on side edge, sk next 4 hdc, fpdc around center corner hdc, sk next 2 hdc, shell in next hdc, [sk next 3 sts, shell in next st] 5 times, sk next 2 sts, fpdc around center corner hdc, join with sl st in 3rd ch of beg ch-3. *(14 shells, 4 fpdc)*

Rnd 8: Sl st into ch-2 sp of shell, beg shell in same ch sp, fpdc around next fpdc, shell in ch-2 sp of each of next 6 shells, fpdc around next fpdc, shell in next shell, fpdc around next fpdc, shell in ch-2 sp of each of next 6 shells, fpdc around next fpdc, join with sl st in 3rd ch of beg ch-3.

Rnds 9–20: Rep rnd 8.

Note: The following row is worked across front and sides only, do not work across back.

Row 21 (RS): Now working in rows, ch 3 *(counts as first dc)*, 3 dc in next ch-2 sp of next shell, dc in next fpdc, [3 dc in ch-2 sp of next shell, dc in sp between shells] 5 times, [3 dc in ch-2 sp of next shell, dc in next fpdc] twice, turn. *(33 dc)*

Row 22 (WS): Ch 1, sc in first dc, sc in each of next 32 sts. Fasten off. *(33 sc)*

Flap
Row 23 (RS): With back facing,

join blue with sl st in first sc of previous row, shell in ch-2 sp of each of next 6 shells across back, sl st in last sc of previous row, turn. *(6 shells)*

Row 24: Sl st into ch-2 sp of shell, beg shell in same ch sp, shell in ch-2 sp of each of next 5 shells, turn.

Row 25: Rep row 24.

Row 26: Sl st into ch-2 sp of shell, ch 3, dc in same ch-2 sp, shell in ch-2 sp of each of next 4 shells, 2 dc in ch-2 sp of last shell, turn. *(4 shells, 2 dc each end)*

Row 27: Ch 3, shell in ch-2 sp of each of next 4 shells, dc in last dc of row, turn. *(4 shells, 2 dc)*

Row 28: Sl st into ch-2 sp of shell, ch 3, dc in same ch-2 sp, shell in ch-2 sp of each of next 2 shells, 2 dc in ch-2 sp of last shell, turn. *(2 shells, 4 dc)*

Row 29: Ch 3, shell in ch-2 sp of each of next 2 shells, dc in last dc, turn. *(2 shells, 2 dc)*

Row 30: Sl st into ch-2 sp of shell, ch 3, dc in same ch-2 sp, ch 4 *(button lp)*, 2 dc in ch-2 sp of next shell. Fasten off.

Edging
Row 31: With RS facing, working in ends of rows, join blue with sc in first sc of row 22, evenly sp 20 sc across edge to ch-4 button lp, work 4 sc over button lp, evenly sp 20 sc across opposite ends of rows, ending with sc in last sc of row 22, turn. *(46 sc)*

Row 32: Ch 1, [sc in each of next 2 sc, **picot** *(see Special Stitches)*] across edge. Fasten off.

Flower
Rnd 1: With dark blue, ch 2, 6 sc in 2nd ch from hook. *(6 sc)*

Rnd 2: (Sl st, ch 2, 3 dc, ch 2, sl st) in each sc around, join with sl st in beg sl st. Leaving long end, fasten off. *(6 petals)*

Leaf
With green, ch 8, sc in 2nd ch from hook, dc in next ch, tr in each of next 2 chs, dc in next ch, sc in next ch, sl st in next ch, *ch 7, sc in 2nd ch from hook, dc in next ch, tr in each of next 2 chs, dc in next ch, sc in next ch, sl st in same ch as last st, rep from * once. Fasten off.

Using photo as guide, sew Leaf group and Flower centered over rnds 11 and 12 of front. Sew button centered over rnd 15.

DOUBLE-DECK CASE
Base
Row 1: Rep row 1 of Single-Deck Case. *(25 hdc)*

Rows 2–8: Rep row 2 of Single-Deck Case. At the end of last row, **do not turn.**

Rnd 9: Now working in rnds, ch 1, [evenly sp 11 sc across side edge of rows, 3 sc in corner *(place st marker in center corner sc of each corner 3-sc group)*, evenly sp 23 sc across long edge, 3 sc in corner] twice, join with sl st in beg sc. *(80 sc)*

Side

Rnd 10: Working in back lps for this rnd only, ch 2, hdc in each st around, moving st markers at each corner, join with sl st in 2nd ch of beg ch-2.

Rnd 11: Sl st into next st, **beg shell** (see Stitch Guide) in same st, *[sk next 3 sts, **shell** (see Special Stitches) in next st] twice, sk next 2 sts, fpdc around next st, sk next 2 sts, shell in next st, [sk next 3 sts, shell in next st] 5 times, sk next 2 sts, fpdc around next st**, sk next 2 sts, shell in next st, rep from * around, ending last rep at **, join with sl st in 3rd ch of beg ch-3. (18 shells, 4 fpdc)

Rnd 12: Sl st into ch-2 sp, beg shell in ch-2 sp of shell, shell in ch-2 sp of each of next 2 shells, fpdc around next fpdc, shell in ch-2 sp of each of next 6 shells, fpdc around next fpdc, shell in ch-2 sp of each of next 3 shells, fpdc around next fpdc, shell in ch-2 sp of each of next 6 shells, fpdc around fpdc, join with sl st in 3rd ch of beg ch-3.

Rnds 13–24: Rep rnd 12.

Row 25: Now working in rows, ch 3, 3 dc in ch-2 sp of next shell, [dc in sp between shells, 3 dc in ch-2 sp of next shell] twice, dc in next fpdc, [3 dc in ch-2 sp of next shell, dc in sp between shells] 5 times, dc in next fpdc, [3 dc in ch-2 sp of next shell, dc in sp between shells] twice, 3 dc in ch-2 sp of next shell, dc in next fpdc, turn. (49 dc)

Row 26: Ch 1, sc in first st, sc in each of next 48 sc. Fasten off. (49 sc)

Flap

Row 27: Rep row 23 of Single-Deck Case. (6 shells)

Rows 28–33: Rep row 24 of Single-Deck Case.

Row 34: Rep row 26 of Single-Deck Case. (4 shells, 4 dc)

Rows 35–38: Rep rows 27–30 of Single-Deck Case.

Edging

Row 39: With RS facing and working in ends of rows, join blue with sc in first sc of row 26, evenly sp 28 sc in ends of rows to ch-4 button lp, work 4 sc over button lp, evenly sp 28 sc across opposite edge of rows, sc in last sc of row 26, turn. (62 sc)

Row 40: Ch 1, [sc in each of next 2 sc, **picot** (see Special Stitches)] across. Fasten off.

Flower

Rnds 1 & 2: Rep Single-Deck Case Flower.

Leaf

Rep Leaf of Single-Deck Case.

Using photo as a guide, sew Leaf group and Flower centered on over rnds 15 and 16 of front.

Sew button centered over rnd 20. ■

Pampered Pets

Chapter Contents

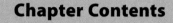

Kitty Toys

DESIGNS BY MICHELE WILCOX

This enticing pair of cute and cuddly toys will keep your cat engaged in fun-filled games sure to entertain you as well. Dangle the fish from a pole and "fish for a kitty" or toss the mouse to begin a hunt!

SKILL LEVEL ■□□□
BEGINNER

FINISHED SIZES
Mouse: 4 inches long, excluding Tail

Fish: 6½ inches long

MATERIALS
Medium (worsted) weight yarn:
   1 oz/50 yds/28g gray
   1 oz/50 yds/28g orange
Size 10 crochet cotton:
   25 yds black
   25 yds white/metallic
Size G/6/4mm crochet hook or size needed to obtain gauge
Tapestry needle
Orange 8mm animal eyes with washers: 2
Orange 5mm animal eyes with washers: 2
2¾-inch suction cup

Stitch markers
Polyester fiberfill

GAUGE
4 sc = 1 inch; 4 sc rows = 1 inch

PATTERN NOTES
Do not join or turn rounds unless otherwise stated.

Mark first stitch of each round.

INSTRUCTIONS

MOUSE
Body
Rnd 1: Beg at tip of nose, with gray, ch 2, 6 sc in 2nd ch from hook, **do not join** (see Pattern Notes). (6 sc)

Rnd 2: [Sc in each of next 2 sts, 2 sc in next st] around. (8 sc)

Rnd 3: [Sc in each of next 3 sts, 2 sc in next st] around. (10 sc)

Rnd 4: [Sc in each of next 4 sts, 2 sc in next st] around. (12 sc)

Rnds 5 & 6: Sc in each st around.

Rnd 7: 2 sc in each of first 6 sts, sc in each of last 6 sts. (18 sc)

Attach 5mm eyes 3 sts apart between rnds 2 and 3, centered under the 6 inc of rnd 7.

Rnds 8–14: Sc in each st around. At end of last rnd, stuff, continue stuffing as you work.

Rnd 15: [Sc in next st, **sc dec** (see Stitch Guide) in next 2 sts] around. (12 sc)

Rnd 16: [Sc dec in next 2 sts] around, join with sl st in beg sc. Leaving long strand for weaving, fasten off. *(6 sc)*

Weave strand through sts of last rnd, pull to gather; secure end.

Ear
Make 2.
With gray, ch 2, 4 sc in 2nd ch from hook, join with sl st in beg sc. Leaving long strand for sewing, fasten off.

Sew Ears to top of head between rnds 4 and 5 as shown in photo.

Tail
With gray, ch 21, sl st in 2nd ch from hook and in each ch across. Leaving long strand for sewing, fasten off.

Sew Tail to back of Body.

With black crochet cotton, using satin st *(see Fig. 1)*, embroider nose as shown in photo. With black, using straight st *(see Fig. 2)*, embroider mouth lines centered below nose.

**Satin Stitch
Fig. 1**

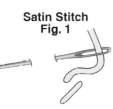

**Straight Stitch
Fig. 2**

FISH
Body Side
Make 2.
Row 1: With orange, ch 2, 3 sc in 2nd ch from hook, turn. *(3 sc)*

Row 2: Ch 1, sc in first st, 2 sc in next st, sc in last st, turn. *(4 sc)*

Rows 3 & 4: Ch 1, 2 sc in first st, sc in each st across with 2 sc in last st, turn. *(8 sc at end of last row)*

Row 5: Ch 1, sc in each st across, turn.

Rows 6 & 7: Rep row 3. *(12 sc at end of last row)*

Rows 8–14: Ch 1, sc in each st across, turn.

Rows 15 & 16: Ch 1, sc dec in first 2 sts, sc in each st across to last 2 sts, sc dec in last 2 sts, turn. *(8 sc at end of last row)*

Row 17: Ch 1, sc dec in first 2 sts, [sc dec in next 2 sts] across, turn. *(4 sc)*

Row 18: Ch 1, sc in each st across, turn.

Row 19: Ch 1, sc dec in first 2 sts, sc dec in last 2 sts, turn. *(2 sc)*

Row 20: Ch 1, sc in each st across, turn.

Rows 21 & 22: Ch 1, 2 sc in each st across, turn. *(8 sc at end of last row)*

Row 23: Ch 1, 2 sc in first st, sc in each of next 2 sts, sl st in each of next 2 sts, sc in each of next 2 sts, 2 sc in last st, turn. *(10 sts)*

Row 24: Ch 2 *(counts as first hdc),* hdc in same st, 2 hdc in next st, hdc in next st, ch 1, sl st in each of next 4 sts, ch 1, hdc in next st, 2 hdc in each of last 2 sts, turn. *(14 sts, 2 ch sps)*

Row 25: Ch 2, hdc in each of next 4 sts, ch 1, sl st in next ch sp, sl st in each of next 4 sts, sl st in next ch-1 sp, ch 1, hdc in

each of last 5 sts, turn. *(16 sts, 2 ch sps)*

Rnd 26: Now working in rnds around outer edge, ch 1, sc in each of first 5 sts, sk next ch sp, sc in each of next 2 sl sts, sc dec in next 2 sl sts, sc in each of next 2 sl sts, sk next ch sp, sc in each of next 4 sts, 3 sc in last st, evenly sp 26 sc across ends of rows, 3 sc in starting ch on opposite side of row 1, evenly sp 26 sc across ends of rows, 2 sc in same st as first sc, join with sl st in beg sc. Fasten off. *(74 sts)*

Attach 1 eye centered between rows 4 and 5 on each Body Side.

Sew Body Sides tog through **back lps** *(see Stitch Guide),* stuffing before closing.

With black, using straight st *(Fig. 2, p. 227),* embroider mouth lines as shown in photo.

Top Fin
Row 1: With orange, ch 6, sc in 2nd ch from hook and in each ch across, turn. *(5 sc)*

Rows 2 & 3: Working in back lps only on these rows and on each rem row, ch 1, sc in each st across, turn.

Row 4: Ch 1, sc in each of first 4 sts, leaving rem st unworked, turn. *(4 sc)*

Row 5: Ch 1, sc in each st across, turn.

Row 6: Ch 1, sc in each of first 3 sts, leaving rem st unworked, turn. *(3 sc)*

Rows 7–9: Ch 1, sc in each st across, turn. At end of last row, fasten off.

Sew to top of Fish over seam as shown in photo.

Side Fin
Make 2.
With orange, ch 6, 2 sc in 3rd ch from hook, hdc in next ch, sc in next ch, sl st in last ch. Fasten off.

Sew 1 Side Fin centered on each side of Body.

Bottom Fin
Make 2.
With orange, ch 6, 2 sc in 3rd ch from hook, hdc in next ch, sc in next ch, sl st in last ch. Fasten off.

Sew Bottom Fins side by side to center bottom of Body.

Attach 1 end of strand of white/ metallic crochet cotton to mouth of fish and other end to post of suction cup.

Attach suction cup to table, door or window as desired for cat to play with toy. ■

Crawly Critters

DESIGNS BY LORI ZELLER

When your dog spies these wiggly creatures, he'll be ready to play tug-of-war, or toss one in the yard as a great throw-and-fetch toy. Your pampered pooch will love his new treats!

SKILL LEVEL ■□□□
BEGINNER

FINISHED SIZES
Snake: 19 inches long

Caterpillar: 13½ inches long

MATERIALS
Medium (worsted)
weight yarn:
2 oz/100 yds/57g green
1 oz/50 yds/28g each light
blue, royal blue and navy blue

Size F/5/3.75mm crochet hook or
size needed to obtain gauge
Tapestry needle
Black and red dimensional
fabric paint
Fiberfill
Stitch markers

GAUGE
5 sc = inch; 5 sc rnds = 1 inch

PATTERN NOTES
Do not join rounds unless
otherwise stated.

Mark first stitch of each round.

INSTRUCTIONS

SNAKE
Rnd 1: Starting at head, with green, ch 2, 5 sc in 2nd ch from hook, **do not join** (see Pattern Notes). (5 sc)

Rnd 2: 2 sc in each sc around. (10 sc)

Rnd 3: [Sc in next sc, 2 sc in next sc] around. (15 sc)

Rnd 4: [Sc in each of next 2 sc, 2 sc in next sc] around. (20 sc)

Rnds 5–11: Sc in each sc around.

Rnd 12: Sc in each sc around, join with sl st in next st. Fasten off.

Row 13: Stuff head with fiberfill and flatten last rnd, working through both thicknesses, join royal blue with sc in first st, sc in each st across, turn. (10 sc)

Rnd 14: Now working in rnds, in **front lps** (see Stitch Guide) only, sc in each st across, **turn**, working in **back lps** (see Stitch Guide) only of same sts, sc in each st across. (20 sc)

Rnds 15–20: Rep rnd 5.

Rnd 21: [**Sc dec** (see Stitch Guide) in next 2 sc, sc in each of next 8 sc] twice. (18 sc)

Rnd 22: Rep rnd 12.

Row 23: Stuff section just made with fiberfill and flatten, through both thicknesses, join

green with sc in first st, sc in each st across, turn. (9 sc)

Rnd 24: Rep rnd 14. (18 sc)

Rnds 25–30: Rep rnd 5.

Rnd 31: [Sc dec in next 2 sc, sc in each of next 7 sc] twice. (16 sc)

Rnd 32: Rep rnd 12.

Row 33: With light blue, rep row 23. (8 sc)

Rnd 34: Rep rnd 14. (16 sc)

Rnds 35–40: Rep rnd 5.

Rnd 41: [Sc dec in next 2 sc, sc in each of next 6 sc] twice. (14 sc)

Rnd 42: Rep rnd 12.

Row 43: With green, rep row 23. (7 sc)

Rnd 44: Rep rnd 14. (14 sc)

Rnds 45–50: Rep rnd 5.

Rnd 51: [Sc dec in next 2 sc, sc in next 5 sc] twice. (12 sc)

Rnd 52: Rep rnd 12.

Row 53: With navy blue, rep row 23. (6 sc)

Rnd 54: Rep rnd 14. (12 sc)

Rnds 55–60: Rep rnd 5.

Rnd 61: [Sc dec in next 2 sc, sc in each of next 4 sc] twice. (10 sc)

Rnd 62: Rep rnd 12.

Row 63: With green, rep row 23. (5 sc)

Rnd 64: Rep rnd 14. (10 sc)

Rnd 65–70: Rep rnd 5.

Rnd 71: [Sc dec in next 2 sc, sc in each of next 3 sc] twice. (8 sc)

Rnd 72: Rep rnd 12.

Row 73: With light blue, rep row 23. (4 sc)

Rnd 74: Rep rnd 14. (8 sc)

Rnds 75–80: Rep rnd 5.

Rnd 81: [Sc dec in next 2 sc, sc in next 2 sc] twice. (6 sc)

Rnd 82: Rep rnd 12.

Row 83: With green, rep row 23. (3 sc)

Rnd 84: Rep rnd 14. (6 sc)

Rnds 85–90: Rep rnd 5.

Rnd 91: [Sc dec in next 2 sc, sc in next sc] twice. *(4 sc)*

Rnd 92: Sc in each sc around. Leaving long end, fasten off.

Stuff last section with fiberfill; sew opening closed.

For eyes, paint 2 small black dots on top of head.

For mouth, with red, paint a smile centered below eyes.

CATERPILLAR

Rnd 1: Starting at top of head, with green, ch 2, 5 sc in 2nd ch from hook. *(5 sc)*

Rnd 2: 2 sc in each sc around. *(10 sc)*

Rnd 3: [Sc in next sc, 2 sc in next sc] around. *(15 sc)*

Rnd 4: [Sc in each of next 2 sc, 2 sc in next sc] around. *(20 sc)*

Rnds 5–8: Sc in each sc around.

Rnd 9: [Sc dec in next 2 sc] around, stuff section with fiberfill. *(10 sc)*

Rnd 10: Rep rnd 5. Fasten off.

Rnd 11: Join royal blue with sc in any sc, sc in same st, 2 sc in each sc around. *(20 sc)*

Rnds 12–17: Rep rnd 5.

Rnd 18: Rep rnd 9. *(10 sc)*

Rnd 19: Rep rnd 5. Fasten off.

Rnd 20: With green, rep rnd 11. *(20 sc)*

Rnds 21–26: Rep rnd 5.

Rnd 27: Rep rnd 9. *(10 sc)*

Rnd 28: Rep rnd 5. Fasten off.

Rnd 29: With light blue, rep rnd 11. *(20 sc)*

Rnds 30–46: Rep rnds 12–28.

Rnd 47: With navy blue, rep rnd 11. *(20 sc)*

Rnds 48–59: Rep rnds 12–23.

Rnd 60: [Sc in each of next 2 sc, sc dec in next 2 sc] around. *(15 sc)*

Rnds 61 & 62: Rep rnd 5.

Rnd 63: [Sc in next sc, sc dec in next 2 sc] around. *(10 sc)*

Rnd 64: Rep rnd 5.

Rnd 65: [Sc dec in next 2 sc] around. Leaving long end, fasten off. *(5 sc)*

Sew opening closed.

Leg
Make 2 each royal blue, navy blue and light blue.
Make 4 green.
Rnd 1: Ch 2, 8 sc in 2nd ch from hook. *(8 sc)*

Rnds 2–4: Sc in each sc around.

Rnd 5: Sc in each of next 2 sc, [sc dec in next 2 sc] twice, sc in each of next 2 sc. Leaving long end, fasten off.

Stuff Legs with fiberfill. Sew on opposite sides of body to sections matching Leg colors.

For eyes, paint 2 small black dots on top of head.

With red, paint a smile centered below eyes. ■

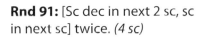

Diamond Dog Collar

DESIGN BY STACEY GRAHAM

Larger dogs often need a collar that reflects their size and build. This bold, broad-banded collar will make your dog look quite handsome, especially when stitched in colors to complement his coat.

SKILL LEVEL ◼☐☐☐
BEGINNER

FINISHED SIZE
1½ x 16 inches

MATERIALS
Size 18 crochet nylon:
    22 yds country blue
    10 yds natural
Size D/3/3.25mm crochet hook
  or size needed to obtain gauge
Tapestry needle
Heavy duty slide lock for 1-inch
  strapping

GAUGE
Scallop and 1 sc = 1¼ inches

PATTERN NOTE
Collar length can be increased or decreased by adding or subtracting multiples of 6 chains from beginning foundation chain.

SPECIAL STITCH
Scallop: 5 dc in indicated st.

INSTRUCTIONS

COLLAR
Rnd 1 (RS): With country blue, ch 98, sc in 2nd ch from hook, *sk next 2 chs, **scallop** *(see Special Stitch)* in next ch, sk next 2 chs, sc in next ch*, rep between * 15 times, working on opposite side of ch, sc in same ch as last sc, rep between * 16 times, join with sl st in beg sc. Fasten off.

Row 2 (RS): Now working in rows, position half of slide lock between first and 2nd scallop, join natural with sc in center dc of 2nd scallop and center dc of first scallop, [3 dc in next sc, sc in center dc of next scallop] 12 times, 3 dc in next sc, position other half of slide lock between last 2 scallops, working through both thicknesses, sc in center dc of scallop. Fasten off.

Row 3 (RS): Working on opposite side of rnd 1, join natural with sl st in center dc of scallops folded over slide lock, ch 1, working through both thicknesses of end scallops, sc in same dc, [3 dc in next sc, sc in center dc of next scallop] 12 times, 3 dc in next sc, working through both thicknesses, sc in center dc of scallops folded over slide lock. Fasten off.

With WS facing, thread tapestry needle with country blue, sew under side scallop at center to next scallop of Collar.

Rep on opposite end of Collar. ◼

Doggy Barbells

DESIGNS BY BELINDA "BENDY" CARTER

Dogs and puppies will have hours of fun playing with this intriguing and versatile barbell toy! With the "weights" in place, you can enjoy a tug-of-war game with your favorite canine. For additional fun, you can remove the weights and toss them like Frisbees, or use the center bar like a stick for a game of fetch.

SKILL LEVEL ■□□□
BEGINNER

FINISHED SIZES
Small barbell: 12 inches long
Large barbell: 18 inches long

MATERIALS

Medium (worsted)
    weight yarn:
        10 oz/500yds/284g each
            red, blue and yellow
        5 oz/250 yds/142g green
Size G/6/4mm crochet hook or
    size needed to obtain gauge
Tapestry needle
½-inch-diameter wooden dowel:
    12 inches *(small barbell)*
1-inch-diameter wooden dowel:
    18 inches *(large barbell)*
Fiberfill

GAUGE
4 sc = 1 inch; 6 sc rnds =
1½ inches

INSTRUCTIONS

SMALL DOGGY BARBELL
Red Disk
Make 2.
Rnd 1: With red, ch 12, sl st in first ch to form ring, ch 1, sc in each sc around, join with sl st in beg sc. *(12 sc)*

Rnd 2: Ch 1, 2 sc in each sc around, join with sl st in beg sc. *(24 sc)*

Rnd 3: Ch 1, sc in each sc around, join with sl st in beg sc.

Rnd 4: Ch 1, sc in each of first 2 sc, 2 sc in next sc, [sc in each of next 2 sc, 2 sc in next sc] around, join with sl st in beg sc. *(36 sc)*

Rnd 5: Rep rnd 3.

Rnd 6: Ch 1, sc in each of first 3 sc, 2 sc in next sc, [sc in each of

next 3 sc, 2 sc in next sc] around, join with sl st in beg sc. *(48 sc)*

Rnds 7–10: Rep rnd 3.

Rnd 11: Ch 1, sc in each of first 3 sc, **sc dec** *(see Stitch Guide)* in next 2 sts, [sc in each of next 3 sc, sc dec in next 2 sc] around, join with sl st in beg sc. *(36 sc)*

Rnd 12: Rep rnd 3.

Rnd 13: Ch 1, sc in each of first 2 sc, sc dec in next 2 sc, [sc in each of next 2 sc, sc dec in next 2 sc] around, join with sl st in beg sc. *(24 sc)*

Rnd 14: Rep rnd 3.

Rnd 15: Ch 1, sc dec in first 2 sc, [sc dec in next 2 sc] around, join with sl st in beg sc. Leaving long end, fasten off. *(12 sc)*

Blue Disk
Make 2.
Rnd 1: With blue, ch 12, sl st into first ch to form ring, ch 1, sc in each ch around, join with sl st in beg sc. *(12 sc)*

Rnds 2–4: Rep rnds 2–4 of Red Disk. *(36 sc)*

Rnds 5–8: Ch 1, sc in each sc around, join with sl st in beg sc.

Rnds 9–11: Rep rnds 13–15 of Red Disk. *(12 sc)*

Yellow Disk
Make 2.
Rnd 1: With yellow, ch 12, sl st into first ch to form ring, ch 1, sc in each ch around, join with sl st in beg sc. *(12 sc)*

Rnd 2: Rep rnd 2 of Red Disk. *(24 sc)*

Rnds 3–6: Ch 1, sc in each sc around, join with sl st in beg sc.

Rnd 7: Rep rnd 11 of Red Disk. Leaving long end, fasten off. *(12 sc)*

For each Disk, sew last rnd to opposite side of starting ch, stuffing with fiberfill as work progresses.

Bar
Rnd 1 (RS): With green, leaving long end at beg, ch 2, 6 sc in 2nd ch from hook, join with sl st in beg sc. *(6 sc)*

Rnd 2: Ch 1, 2 sc in each sc around, join with sl st in beg sc. *(12 sc)*

Rnd 3: Ch 1, sc in first sc, 2 sc in next sc, [sc in next sc, 2 sc in next sc] around, join with sl st in beg sc. *(18 sc)*

Note: *Pull rem beg length from rnd 1 and secure on WS of Bar.*

Rnd 4: Ch 1, sc in each sc around, join with sl st in beg sc.

Rnd 5: Ch 1, sc in first sc, sc dec in next 2 sc, [sc in next sc, sc dec in next 2 sc] around, join with sl st in beg sc. *(12 sc)*

Rnds 6–28: Rep rnd 4. At the end of last rep, pull up lp, remove hook.

Insert 12-inch wooden dowel into opening, stuffing with fiberfill around dowel. Continue stuffing with fiberfill as work progresses. Pick up dropped lp.

Rnds 29–51: Rep rnd 4.

Rnd 52: Rep rnd 3. *(18 sc)*

Rnd 53: Rep rnd 4.

Rnd 54: Rep rnd 5. *(12 sc)*

Rnd 55: Ch 1, sc dec in first 2 sc, [sc dec in next 2 sc] around, join with sl st in beg sc. Leaving long end, fasten off. *(6 sc)*

Weave long end through sts of last rnd, pull opening closed, secure end.

Place 3 weight Disks, 1 of each color, on each end of Bar.

LARGE DOGGY BARBELL
Red Disk
Make 2.
Rnd 1: With red, ch 24, sl st in first ch to form ring, ch 1, sc in

each ch around, join with sl st in beg sc. *(24 sc)*

Rnd 2: Ch 1, 2 sc in first st and in each sc around, join with sl st in beg sc. *(48 sc)*

Rnd 3: Ch 1, sc in each sc around, join with sl st in beg sc.

Rnd 4: Ch 1, sc in each of first 2 sc, 2 sc in next sc, [sc in each of next 2 sc, 2 sc in next sc] around, join with sl st in beg sc. *(64 sc)*

Rnd 5: Rep rnd 3.

Rnd 6: Ch 1, sc in each of first 3 sc, 2 sc in next sc, [sc in each of next 3 sc, 2 sc in next sc] around, join with sl st in beg sc. *(80 sc)*

Rnd 7: Rep rnd 3.

Rnd 8: Ch 1, sc in each of first 4 sc, 2 sc in next sc, [sc in each of next 4 sc, 2 sc in next sc] around, join with sl st in beg sc. *(96 sc)*

Rnds 9–14: Rep rnd 3.

Rnd 15: Ch 1, sc in each of first 4 sc, sc dec in next 2 sc, [sc in each of next 4 sc, sc dec in next 2 sc] around, join with sl st in beg sc. *(80 sc)*

Rnd 16: Rep rnd 3.

Rnd 17: Ch 1, sc in each of first 3 sc, sc dec in next 2 sc, [sc in each of next 3 sc, sc dec in next 2 sc] around, join with sl st in beg sc. *(64 sc)*

Rnd 18: Rep rnd 3.

Rnd 19: Ch 1, sc in each of first 2 sc, sc dec in next 2 sc, [sc in each of next 2 sc, sc dec in next 2 sc] around, join with sl st in beg sc. *(48 sc)*

Rnd 20: Rep rnd 3.

Rnd 21: Ch 1, sc dec in first 2 sc, [sc dec in next 2 sc] around, join with sl st in beg sc. Leaving long end, fasten off. *(24 sc)*

Blue Disk
Make 2.
Rnd 1: With blue, ch 24, sl st in first ch to form ring, ch 1, sc in each ch around, join with sl st in beg sc. *(24 sc)*

Rnds 2–6: Rep rnds 2–6 of Red Disk. *(80 sc)*

Rnds 7–12: Ch 1, sc in each sc around, join with sl st in beg sc.

Rnds 13–17: Rep rnds 17–21 of Red Disk. *(24 sc)*

Yellow Disk
Make 2.
Rnd 1: With yellow, ch 24, sl st in first ch to form ring, ch 1, sc in each sc around, join with sl st in beg sc. *(24 sc)*

Rnds 2–4: Rep rnds 2–4 of Red Disk. *(64 sc)*

Rnds 5–10: Ch 1, sc in each sc around, join with sl st in beg sc.

Rnds 11–13: Rep rnds 19–21 of Red Disk. *(24 sc)*

For each Disk, sew last rnd to opposite side of starting ch, stuffing with fiberfill as work progresses.

Bar
Rnd 1 (RS): With green, leaving long end at beg, ch 2, 6 sc in 2nd ch from hook, join with sl st in beg sc. *(6 sc)*

Rnd 2: Ch 1, 2 sc in each sc around, join with sl st in beg sc. *(12 sc)*

Rnd 3: Ch 1, sc in first sc, 2 sc in next sc, [sc in next sc, 2 sc in next sc] around, join with sl st in beg sc. *(18 sc)*

Note: *Pull rem beg length from rnd 7 and secure on WS of Bar.*

Rnd 4: Ch 1, sc in each of first 2 sc, 2 sc in next sc, [sc in each of next 2 sc, 2 sc in next sc] around, join with sl st in beg sc. *(24 sc)*

Rnd 5: Ch 1, sc in each of first 3 sc, 2 sc in next sc, [sc in each of next 3 sc, 2 sc in next sc] around, join with sl st in beg sc. *(30 sc)*

Rnd 6: Ch 1, sc in each of first 4 sc, 2 sc in next sc, [sc in each of next 4 sc, 2 sc in next sc] around, join with sl st in beg sc. *(36 sc)*

Rnd 7: Ch 1, sc in first sc and in each sc around, join with sl st in beg sc.

Rnd 8: Rep rnd 7.

Rnd 9: Ch 1, sc in each of first 4 sc, sc dec in next 2 sc, [sc in each of next 4 sc, sc dec in next 2 sc] around, join with sl st in beg sc. *(30 sc)*

Rnd 10: Ch 1, sc in each of first 3 sc, sc in dec in next 2 sc, [sc in each of next 3 sc, sc dec in next 2 sc] around, join with sl st in beg sc. *(24 sc)*

Rnds 11–40: Rep rnd 7. At end of last rnd, pull up lp, remove hook.

Insert 18-inch wooden dowel into opening, stuffing with fiberfill around dowel. Continue stuffing with fiberfill as work progresses. Pick up dropped lp.

Rnds 41–71: Rep rnd 7.

Rnds 72–77: Rep rnds 5–10. *(24 sc)*

Rnd 78: Ch 1, sc in each of first 2 sc, sc dec in next 2 sc, [sc in each of next 2 sc, sc dec in next 2 sc] around, join with sl st in beg sc. *(18 sc)*

Rnd 79: Ch 1, sc in first sc, sc dec in next 2 sc, [sc in next sc, sc dec in next 2 sc] around, join with sl st in beg sc. *(12 sc)*

Rnd 80: Ch 1, sc dec in first 2 sc, [sc dec in next 2 sc] around, join with sl st in beg sc. Leaving long end, fasten off. *(6 sc)*

Weave long end through sts of last rnd, pull to gather. Secure end.

Place 3 weight Disks, 1 of each color, on each end of Bar. ∎

Tennis Ball Snake

DESIGN BY STACEY GRAHAM

Fuzzy, fun-shaped and ready to play, this perky snake toy will give your dog plenty of exercise and entertainment. Throw it down and watch it bounce, or toss it in the yard; either way your dog will have a ball!

SKILL LEVEL ■□□□
BEGINNER

FINISHED SIZE
20 inches long

MATERIALS
Lion Brand Homespun **5** BULKY
   bulky (chunky) weight
   yarn (6 oz/185 yds/170g
   per skein):
      1 skein #318 sierra
Medium (worsted) **4** MEDIUM
   weight yarn:
      ¼ oz/13 yds/7g red
Size J/10/6mm crochet hook or
   size needed to obtain gauge
Tapestry needle
Small amount red and white felt
Craft glue
Fiberfill
Tennis ball

GAUGE
3 hdc sts = 1 inch; 2 hdc rnds =
1 inch

INSTRUCTIONS

SNAKE
Rnd 1 (RS): With sierra, ch 3,
7 hdc in 3rd ch from hook *(first
2 chs count as first hdc)*, join
with sl st in 3rd ch of beg ch-3.
(8 hdc)

Rnds 2 & 3: Ch 2 *(counts as first
hdc)*, hdc in same st, 2 hdc in
each st around, join with sl st in
2nd ch of beg ch-2. *(16 hdc at
end of last rnd)*

Rnd 4: Ch 2, hdc in next st, **hdc
dec** *(see Stitch Guide)* in next 2
sts, [hdc in each of next 2 sts,

hdc dec in next 2 sts] around,
join with sl st in 2nd ch of beg
ch-2. *(24 hdc)*

Rnd 5: Ch 2, hdc in each st
around, join with sl st in 2nd ch
of beg ch-2.

Rnd 6: Rep rnd 5.

Rnd 7: Rep rnd 4. *(18 hdc)*

Pull up lp, remove hook.

Fold 6-inch length of red yarn
in half, knot ½ inch from fold,
insert folded end RS to WS
through center of rnd 1, sew at
inside of Snake head over rnd 1.

Rnd 8: Pick up dropped lp, ch
2, hdc in each of next 3 sts, **hdc

dec *(see Stitch Guide)* in next 2 sts, [hdc in each of next 4 sts, hdc dec in next 2 sts] around, join with sl st in 2nd ch of beg ch-2. *(15 hdc)*

Insert tennis ball into head.

Rnd 9: Hdc in each hdc around, **do not join**.

Next rnds: Rep rnd 9 until Snake measures 18 inches, stuffing with fiberfill as work progresses.

Next rnds: [Hdc dec in next 2 sts, hdc in each of next 6 sts] around for several rnds until only 6 hdc rem. Leaving long end, fasten off.

Weave long end through sts of last rnd, pull to close opening, secure end.

Eyes
From white felt, cut 2 circles 1-inch in diameter. From red felt, cut 2 circles ½-inch in diameter. Glue white eyes to Snake, center red pupils over eye, glue pupils to eyes. ■

Beaded Elegance

DESIGNS BY BELINDA "BENDY" CARTER

Stitch a fantastic collar and leash for a prince or princess of a pooch, or a fabulous feline. Your pet will step out in glamorous fashion for walks in the park or lounging around the house.

SKILL LEVEL ◼◼◻◻
EASY

FINISHED SIZES
Collar: 8½-inch [9½-inch, 10½-inch] neck

Pattern is written for smallest Collar size with changes for larger sizes in brackets

Leash: 43½ inches long

MATERIALS
Size 10 crochet cotton:
    350 yds black
Size 5/1.90mm crochet hook or
    size needed to obtain gauge.
Tapestry needle
Sewing needle
Beading needle
Black sewing thread
⅞-inch lanyard hook
Package blue mix seed beads

¼-inch wide elastic
8mm jingle bell
Stitch marker

GAUGE
4 sc = ½ inch; 4 sc rows = ½ inch

PATTERN NOTES
Do not join or turn rounds unless otherwise stated.

Mark first stitch of each round.

INSTRUCTIONS

LEASH
Rnd 1: String 262 seed beads onto crochet cotton, push back until needed, ch 2, 7 sc in 2nd ch from hook, **do not join** (see Pattern Notes). (7 sc)

Rnd 2: Pull up bead, sc in each of next 7 sts.

Next rnds: Rep rnd 2 until all beads are used. **Do not fasten off**.

Handle
Rnd 1: 2 sc in each st around. (14 sc)

Rnd 2: Sc in each of first 4 sts, sk next 7 sts, sc in each of last 3 sts. (7 sc)

Rnd 3: Sc in each st around.

Next rnds: Rep rnd 3 until Handle measures 12 inches. At end of last rnd, fasten off.

Sew sts of last rnd to 7 sk sts on rnd 1. Sew lanyard hook to end of Leash.

COLLAR
Top Side
Notes: *Cut elastic ½ inch larger than pet's neck size. Overlap ends ½ inch and sew tog.*

Row 1: String 164 [180, 196] beads onto crochet cotton, push back until needed, ch 5, sc in 2nd ch from hook and in each ch across, turn. *(4 sc)*

Row 2: Ch 1, [pull up 1 bead, sc in next st] across, turn.

Row 3: Ch 1, sc in each st across, turn.

Next rows: Rep rows 2 and 3 alternately until all beads are used or to desired length to fit comfortably around pet's neck. At end of last row, fasten off.

Sew first and last rows tog.

Bottom Side
Row 1: Ch 5, sc in 2nd ch from hook and in each ch across, turn. *(4 sc)*

Row 2: Ch 1, sc in each st across, turn.

Next rows: Rep row 2 until piece measures same length

as Top Side. At end of last row, fasten off.

Sew first and last rows tog.

Hold Top and Bottom sides tog with elastic piece between, sew edges tog.

Ch 12, place ch around Collar, sl st in first ch to form ring around Collar. Fasten off. Attach lanyard hook from leash to ring.

Tack bell to center front of Collar. ∎

Fishbowl Place Mat

DESIGN BY BEVERLY MEWHORTER

Crochet this cute little mat for a great accent in an underwater-themed bathroom or as a wonderful water-catcher for your fishbowl.

SKILL LEVEL ◼☐☐☐
BEGINNER

FINISHED SIZE
9½ inches

MATERIALS
Medium (worsted)
   weight yarn:
      1½ oz/75 yds/43g light blue
      ½ oz/25 yds/14g orange
Size G/6/4mm crochet hook or
   size needed to obtain gauge
Tapestry needle
8mm half-round black beads: 3
3mm pearl beads: 9
White sequins: 9
Hot-glue gun

GAUGE
4 dc = 1 inch

INSTRUCTIONS

PLACE MAT
Rnd 1 (RS): With light blue, ch 4, 11 dc in 4th ch from hook *(first 3 chs count as first dc)*, join with sl st in 4th ch of ch-4. *(12 dc)*

Rnd 2: Ch 3 *(counts as first dc)*, dc in same st, 2 dc in each dc around, join with sl st in 3rd ch of beg ch-3. *(24 dc)*

Rnd 3: Ch 3, dc in same st, dc in next dc, [2 dc in next dc, dc in next dc] around, join with sl st in 3rd ch of beg ch-3. *(36 dc)*

Rnd 4: Ch 3, dc in same st, dc in each of next 2 dc, [2 dc in next dc, dc in each of next 2 dc] around, join with sl st in 3rd ch of beg ch-3. *(48 dc)*

Rnd 5: Ch 3, dc in same st, dc in each of next 3 dc, [2 dc in next dc, dc in each of next 3 dc] around, join with sl st in 3rd ch of beg ch-3. *(60 dc)*

Rnd 6: Ch 3, dc in same st, dc in each of next 4 dc, [2 dc in next dc, dc in each of next 4 dc] around, join with sl st in 3rd ch of beg ch-3. *(72 dc)*

Rnd 7: Ch 3, dc in same st, dc in each of next 5 dc, [2 dc in next dc, dc in each of next 5 dc] around, join with sl st in 3rd ch of beg ch-3. *(84 dc)*

Rnd 8: Ch 1, sl st in first dc, *sc in next dc, dc in next dc, 2 tr in next dc, dc in next dc, sc in next dc, sl st in next dc**, sl st in next dc, rep from * around, ending last rep at **. Fasten off. *(12 scallops)*

Goldfish
Make 3.
Row 1: With orange, ch 4, sc in 2nd ch from hook, sc in each of last 2 chs, turn. *(3 sc)*

Row 2: Ch 1, 2 sc in first sc, sc in next sc, 2 sc in last sc, turn. *(5 sc)*

Rows 3–6: Ch 1, sc in each sc across, turn.

Row 7: Ch 1, **sc dec** *(see Stitch Guide)* in first 2 sc, sc in next sc, sc dec in last 2 sc, turn. *(3 sc)*

Row 8: Ch 1, sc dec in first 2 sc, sc in next sc, turn. *(2 sc)*

Row 9: Ch 1, sc dec in next 2 sc. Fasten off. *(1 sc)*

Tail

Row 10: Working in starting ch on opposite side of row 1, join orange with sc in first ch, ch 1, sc in each of next 2 chs, turn. *(3 sc)*

Row 11: Ch 3, (dc, hdc, sc) in same sc, sl st in next sc, (sc, hdc, dc, ch 3, sl st) in last sc. Fasten off.

Fin

Make 3.
With orange, ch 4, (dc, ch 3, sl st) in 4th ch from hook. Fasten off.

Sew Fin to body between rows 5 and 6.

Finishing

Glue or sew Fish evenly spaced around Place Mat.

For eye, glue black bead to row 10 of Goldfish.

For bubbles at front of each Fish, glue 3 white sequins with pearl bead in each center. ■

I Love My Pet Mat & Toys

DESIGNS BY BELINDA "BENDY" CARTER

This versatile, pet-pleasing mat can be customized for cats or dogs with interchangeable mouse and bone appliqués. It's cozy and chic in sport-weight yarn, and even includes two stuffed toys.

SKILL LEVEL ■□□□
BEGINNER

FINISHED SIZE
Mat: 19 inches square

MATERIALS
Fine (sport) weight yarn:
  7 oz/700 yds/198g white
  3½ oz/350 yds/99g light green
  1¾ oz/175 yds/50g pink
Sizes D/3/3.25mm and H/8/5mm crochet hooks or size needed to obtain gauge
Tapestry needle
Fiberfill

GAUGE
Size H hook: 5 sc = 1½ inches; 5 sc rows = 1½ inches

INSTRUCTIONS

DOG BONE TOY
Rnd 1: With size D hook and white, ch 6, sc in 2nd ch from hook, sc in each of next 4 chs, working on opposite side of ch, sc in each of next 5 chs, **do not join.** *(10 sc)*

Rnd 2: Sc in each of next 10 sc, **do not join**.

Next rnds: Rep rnd 2 until tube measures 14 inches from beg. Leaving long end, fasten off.

Using first 6 inches of tube, fold beg end down, around, then tuck under fold and sew in place.

Stuff next 2 inches of tube with fiberfill.

Sew end of tube closed, using last 6 inches of tube, fold end down, around, and tuck under beg fold and sew in place.

MOUSE TOY
With size D hook and white, ch 2, 4 sc in 2nd ch from hook, working in rnds without joining and working continuously around, sc in first st, 2 sc in each of next 2 sc, sc in each of next 3 sts, 2 sc in each of next 2 sc, sc in each of next 5 sts, 2 sc in each of next 2 sc, sc in each of next 7 sts, 2 sc in each of next 2 sc, sc in each of next 9 sts, 2 sc in each of next 2 sc, sc in each of next 38 sts, [**sc dec** *(see Stitch Guide)* in next 2 sts] twice, sc in each of next 8 sts, [sc dec in next 2 sts] 3 times, pull up lp, remove hook, **do not fasten off**.

Eye

With pink, embroider satin stitch (see Fig 1) eyes as shown in photo.

**Satin Stitch
Fig. 1**

Ear

Make 2.

With size D hook and pink, ch 4, sl st in first ch. Fasten off. Sew Ears to head. Stuff Mouse with fiberfill.

Pick up dropped lp and continue on with Mouse, sc in each of next

4 sts, [sc dec in next 2 sts] 3 times, sc in each of next 2 sts, sl st in next st. Leaving long end, fasten off. Weave long end through sts, pull to close opening and secure.

Tail

With size D hook and white, ch 13, sl st in 2nd ch from hook, sl st in each ch across. Fasten off.

Attach Tail to back body of Mouse.

DOG BONE APPLIQUE

Make 5.

Row 1: With size D hook and white, ch 4, sc in 2nd ch from hook, sc in each ch across, turn. *(3 sc)*

Rows 2–12: Ch 1, sc in each of next 3 sc, turn.

Rnd 13: Ch 4 *(counts as first tr)*, (dc, sc) in same sc, sl st in next sc, (sc, dc, tr) in next sc, *working down side in ends of rows, 2 dtr in end of first row, (tr, dc, sc) in end of next row, sc in each of next 8 rows, (sc, dc, tr) in end of next row, 2 dtr in end of last row **, working across opposite side of ch, (tr, dc, sc) in first ch, sl st in next ch, (sc, dc, tr) in next ch, rep from *, ending last rep at **, join with sl st in 4th ch of beg ch-4. Leaving long end, fasten off.

MOUSE APPLIQUE

Make 5.

Row 1 (RS): With size D hook

and white, ch 31, sc in 2nd ch from hook, sc in each of next 11 chs, leaving rem chs unworked for tail, turn. *(12 sc)*

Row 2: Ch 1, sc in each sc across to last 2 sc, sc dec in next 2 sc, turn. *(11 sc)*

Row 3: Ch 1, sc dec in first 2 sc, sc in each sc across to last 2 sc, sc dec in last 2 sc, turn. *(9 sc)*

Row 4: Rep row 2. *(8 sc)*

Row 5: Rep row 3. Fasten off. *(6 sc)*

Rnd 6 (RS): Join white with sl st at bottom of Mouse at tail, working across bottom of Mouse, then around top of Mouse, evenly sp sl st around and sl st in each ch of starting ch. Leaving long end, fasten off.

Eye
With pink, embroider cross-stitch *(see Fig. 2)* on Mouse for Eye.

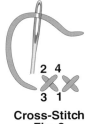

**Cross-Stitch
Fig. 2**

Ear
Make 1.
Rep Ear as for Mouse Toy and sew to head.

HEART APPLIQUÉ
Make 4.
Row 1: With size D hook and pink, ch 2, sc in 2nd ch from hook, turn. *(1 sc)*

Row 2: Ch 1, 3 sc in sc, turn. *(3 sc)*

Rows 3–6: Ch 1, 2 sc in first sc, sc in each sc across to last sc, 2 sc in last sc, turn. *(11 sc at end of last row)*

Rows 7 & 8: Ch 1, sc in each st across, turn.

First Lobe
Row 1: Ch 1, sc in each of next 5 sc, leaving rem sc unworked, turn. *(5 sc)*

Row 2: Sl st in each of first 2 sts, ch 1, sc in same st as last sl st and in each sc across, turn. *(4 sc)*

Row 3: Sl st in each of first 2 sts, ch 1, sc in same st as last sl st, sc in next st, leaving last st unworked. Fasten off. *(2 sc)*

2nd Lobe
Row 1: Sk next sc of row 8, join pink with sc in next st, sc in each of next 4 sc, turn. *(5 sc)*

Row 2: Ch 1, sc in each of next 4 sc, leaving last st unworked, turn. *(4 sc)*

Row 3: Rep row 3 of First Lobe, turn.

Rnd 4: Ch 1, working around outer edge, evenly sp sc around, join with sl st in beg sc. Leaving long end, fasten off.

BLANKET SQUARE
Make 4 white.
Make 5 light green.
Row 1: With size H hook and 2 strands held tog, ch 16, sc in 2nd ch from hook, sc in each ch across, turn. *(15 sc)*

Rows 2–16: Ch 1, sc in each sc across, turn.

Row 17: Ch 1, sc in each sc across.

Rnd 18: Now working in rnds around outer edge of Square, ch 1, evenly sp 15 sc across each edge with ch 2 in each corner, join with sl st in beg sc. Fasten off.

Note: Use 1 strand of each white and pink held tog on white Squares and 1 strand of each white and light green held tog on light green Squares.

Rnd 19: Join with sc in any st, sc in each sc around, with (sc, ch 2, sc) in each corner ch-2 sp, join with sl st in beg sc. Fasten off.

Rnd 20: Using 2 strands of

white held tog for each Square, join white with sc in **back lp** *(see Stitch Guide)* of any st, ch 1, sc in back lp of each st around, with (dc, ch 1, dc) in ch-2 sp of rnd 18 and working sts behind ch-2 sp of rnd 19, join with sl st in beg sc. Fasten off.

Assembly
Sew 1 Heart Appliqué to center of each white Square, sew 1 Bone or Mouse Appliqué to center of each light green Square.

Sew 3 Squares tog for first row: light green, white and light green.

Sew 3 Squares tog for 2nd row: white, light green and white.

The 3rd row of Squares is the same as the first row.

Sew rows tog.

Edging
Rnd 1: With size H hook, join 2 strands of white with sc in corner ch-1 sp, *evenly sp 57 sc across edge to next corner ch-1 sp**, (sc, ch 2, sc) in corner ch-1 sp, rep from * around, ending last rep at **, sc in same ch-1 sp as beg sc, ch 2, join with sl st in beg sc.

Rnd 2: Ch 1, sc in first st, *[ch 3, sl st in first ch of ch-3, sk next st, sc in next st] 29 times, ch 3, sl st in first ch, sc in corner ch-2 sp, ch 3, sl st in first ch**, sc in next st, rep from * around, ending last rep at **, join with sl st in beg sc. Fasten off. ∎

Happy Holidays

Chapter Contents

Say it With Hearts

DESIGNS BY AMY BREWER

Stitch these hearts to send a friend a valentine or to decorate a package. They work for any occasion—just change the colors: make blue hearts for a baby boy, yellow hearts for a spring day, or whatever suits your fancy!

SKILL LEVEL ◼◼◼◻
INTERMEDIATE

FINISHED SIZES
Large Heart: approximately 2¼ inches

Small Heart: approximately 1 x 1¼ inches

MATERIALS
Size 10 crochet cotton:
    50 yds each pink and white
Size 6/1.80mm steel crochet hook or size needed to obtain gauge
5 x 7-inch blank greeting card
1½-inch-wide sheer floral ribbon: ⅓ yd
Tacky craft glue

GAUGE
4 dc = ½ inch

SPECIAL STITCHES
14-roll stitch (14-roll st): Yo 14 times, insert hook in st indicated, pull up lp, yo, pull through all lps on hook, ch 1.
12-roll stitch (12-roll st): Yo 12 times, insert hook in st indicated, pull up lp, yo, pull through all lps on hook, ch 1.
10-roll stitch (10-roll st): Yo 10 times, insert hook in st indicated, pull up lp, yo, pull through all lps on hook, ch 1.
7-roll stitch (7-roll st): Yo 7 times, insert hook in st indicated, pull up lp, yo, pull through all lps on hook, ch 1.
5-roll stitch (5-roll st): Yo 5 times, insert hook in st indicated, pull up lp, yo, pull through all lps on hook, ch 1.
3-roll stitch (3-roll st): Yo 3 times, insert hook in st indicated, pull up lp, yo, pull through all lps on hook, ch 1.

INSTRUCTIONS

LARGE HEART
Foundation rnd: With pink, ch 5, dc in 5th ch from hook, ch 3, **turn**, sc around next ch of beg ch-5, ch 3, sl st in next ch, turn.

Rnd 1 (RS): Ch 3, (4 **10-roll sts**—*see Special Stitches,* **7-roll st**—*see Special Stitches,* **5-roll st**—*see Special Stitches*) in next ch-3 sp, sc in next st, (5-roll st, 7-roll st, 4 10-roll sts) in next ch-3 sp, (2 10-roll sts, **12-roll st**—*see Special Stitches,* **14-roll st**—*see Special Stitches,* 12-roll st, 2 10-roll sts) in sp formed by beg dc of foundation row, join with sl st in first roll st.

Rnd 2: Ch 1, 2 sc in each of first 6 roll sts, sk next sc, 2 sc in each of next 9 roll sts, 3 sc in next roll st, 2 sc in each of next 3 roll sts, join with sl st in first sc. Fasten off.

Rnd 3: Join white in first sc, [ch 4, sk next sc, sl st in next sc] 5 times, sk next 2 sc, sl st in next sc, [ch 4, sk next sc, sl st in next sc] 12 times, ch 1, join with dc in joining sl st forming last ch sp.

Rnd 4: Ch 1, sc in ch sp formed, [ch 3, sc in next ch-4 sp] 5 times, ch 1, sc in next ch-4 sp, [ch 3, sc next ch-4 sp] 11 times, ch 3, join with sl st in beg sc.

Rnd 5: [(**3-roll st**—*see Special Stitches*, 5-roll st, 3-roll st) in next ch-3 sp, sl st in next sc] 5 times, sk next ch-1 sp, sl st in next sc, [(3-roll st, 5-roll st, 3-roll st) in next ch-3 sp, sl st in next sc] 11 times, (3-roll st, 5-roll st, 3-roll st) in next ch-3 sp, join in joining sl st. Fasten off.

SMALL HEART
Make 3.
Rnd 1: With pink, ch 4, (2 dc, hdc, sc, hdc, 6 dc, tr, 3 dc) in 4th ch from hook *(first 3 chs count as first dc)*, join with sl st in 3rd ch of beg ch-4.

Rnd 2: Ch 2, 5-roll st in first st, 5-roll st in each of next 2 dc, 2 5-roll sts in next dc, 3-roll st in next hdc, sl st in next sc, 3-roll st in next hdc, 2 5-roll sts in next dc, 5-roll st in each of next 5 dc, (5-roll st, 7-roll st, 5-roll st) in next tr, 5 roll st in each of last

2 dc, join with sl st in first roll st. Fasten off.

Finishing
1. Glue ends of ribbon to inside front of card as shown in photo.

2. Glue Hearts as desired to front of card. ■

Sweetheart Coasters

DESIGN BY DIONNE BARRATT

Set the mood for an informal gathering of intimate friends on Valentine's Day with these adorable heart coasters worked in crochet cotton. They make a great accent when stitched in shades of red and pink.

SKILL LEVEL ◼◻◻
EASY

FINISHED SIZE
4½ inches across

MATERIALS FOR 1 COASTER
Size 10 crochet cotton:
    75 yds red
    25 yds white
Size 7/1.65mm steel hook or
    size needed to obtain gauge

GAUGE
9 dc = 1 inch; 2 dc rows and 1 sc row = ½ inch

INSTRUCTIONS

COASTER
Row 1 (RS): With red, ch 4, 5 dc in 4th ch from hook *(first 3 chs count as first dc)*, turn. *(6 dc)*

Row 2: Ch 1, sc in each st across, turn. *(6 sc)*

Row 3: Ch 3 *(counts as first dc)*, dc in same st, 2 dc in each st across, turn. *(12 dc)*

Row 4: Rep row 2. *(12 sc)*

Row 5: Ch 3, dc in same st, [dc in next st, 2 dc in next st] twice, dc in each of next 2 sts, [2 dc in next st, dc in next st] twice, 2 dc in last st, turn. *(18 dc)*

Row 6: Rep row 2. *(18 sc)*

Row 7: Ch 3, [2 dc in next st, dc in next st] 3 times, dc in each of next 5 sts, [2 dc in next st, dc in next st] 3 times, turn. *(24 dc)*

Row 8: Rep row 2. *(24 sc)*

Row 9: Ch 3, dc in each st across, turn. *(24 dc)*

Row 10: Rep row 2. *(24 sc)*

Row 11: Ch 3, dc in each of next 2 sts, [2 dc in next st, dc in each of next 3 sts] twice, 2 dc in each of next 2 sts, [dc in each of next 3 sts, 2 dc in next st] twice, dc in each of last 3 sts, turn. *(30 dc)*

Row 12: Rep row 2. *(30 sc)*

Row 13: Ch 3, dc in next st, [2 dc in next st, dc in each of next 2 sts] 3 times, dc in each of next 10 sts, [2 dc in next st, dc in each of next 2 sts] 3 times, turn. *(36 dc)*

Row 14: Rep row 2. **Do not fasten off**. *(36 sc)*

First Side
Row 1 (RS): Ch 2 *(does not count as st)*, **dc dec** *(see Stitch Guide)* in first 2 sts, [dc dec in next 2 sts, dc in next st, dc dec in next 2 sts, dc in each of next 2 sts] twice, hdc in next st, sc in next st, leaving rem sts unworked, turn. *(13 sts)*

Row 2: Ch 1, sc in each st across turn. *(13 sc)*

Row 3: Ch 3, dc in each of next 2 sts, dc dec in next 2 sts, [dc in next st, dc dec in next 2 sts] twice, hdc in next st, sc in last st, turn. *(10 sts)*

Row 4: Rep row 2. *(10 sc)*

Row 5: Ch 2 *(does not count as a st)*, dc dec in next 2 sts, dc in next st, [dc dec in next 2 sts] twice, dc in each of last 2 sts, turn. *(6 dc)*

Row 6: Rep row 2. Fasten off.

2nd Side
Row 1 (RS): With RS facing, join red with sc in first unworked st on last row of Coaster, hdc in next st, [dc in each of next 2 sts, dc dec in next 2 sts, dc in next st, dc dec in next 2 sts] twice, dc dec in last 2 sts, turn. *(13 sts)*

Row 2: Ch 1, sc in each st across, turn. *(13 sc)*

Row 3: Ch 1, sc in first st, hdc in next st, [dc dec in next 2 sts, dc in next st] twice, dc dec in next 2 sts, dc in each of last 3 sts, turn. *(10 dc)*

Row 4: Rep row 2. *(10 sc)*

Row 5: Ch 3, dc in next st, [dc dec in next 2 sts] twice, dc in next st, dc dec in next 2 sts, leaving last st unworked, turn. *(6 dc)*

Row 6: Rep row 2.

Rnd 7: Now working in rnds around outer edge in sts and ends of rows, ch 1, evenly sp 38 sc on each side of heart with 3 sc at tip of heart, join with sl st in beg sc. *(79 sc)*

Rnd 8: Sl st in next st, ch 3, dc in same st, [dc in next st, 2 dc in next st] around to 3 center bottom sts, dc in next st, 3 dc in next st, [dc in next st, 2 dc in next st] around to last st, dc dec in last st and first st, join with sl st in 3rd ch of beg ch-3. Fasten off. *(118 dc)*

Edging
Rnd 1: Join white with sc in first dc of 3-dc group at point, ch 5, sk next st, sc in next st, [ch 5, sk next 2 sts, sc in next st] around to dec at center of heart, ch 3, sk next dec, [sc in next st, ch 5, sk next 2 sts] around, join with sl st in beg sc. *(40 ch sps)*

Rnd 2: Ch 1, (sc, ch 4, sc) in first ch sp, [ch 5, (sc, ch 4, sc) in next ch sp] around to ch-3 sp at top center of heart Sides, ch 2, sc in next ch-3 sp, ch 2, (sc, ch 4, sc) in next ch sp, [ch 5, (sc, ch 4, sc) in next ch sp] around, ch 5, join with sl st in beg sc. Fasten off. ∎

Pot o' Gold

DESIGN BY CINDY HARRIS

Tempt a wee leprechaun with this enchanting holiday basket worked in bright colors of worsted weight yarn. Fill it with chocolate gold coins as a surprise treat for the lucky finder of the end of the rainbow.

SKILL LEVEL ●□□□
BEGINNER

FINISHED SIZE
4 inches tall x 6 inches in diameter, not including Handle

MATERIALS
Red Heart Super Saver medium (worsted) weight yarn (7 oz/364 yds/198g per skein):
- 1 skein #312 black
- 1 oz/50 yds/28g #368 paddy green
- 10 yds #319 cherry red
- 10 yds #385 royal
- 10 yds #356 amethyst
- 10 yds #324 bright yellow

Red Heart Classic medium (worsted) yarn (3½ oz/190 yds/99g per skein):
- 10 yds #245 orange

Size G/6/4mm crochet hook or size needed to obtain gauge

Tapestry needle
⅛-inch wide ribbon:
   ⅔ yd each orange and green
Fiberfill
Craft glue or hot-glue gun
Stitch markers
Clean soda can

GAUGE
4 sc = 1 inch; 4 sc rows = 1 inch

PATTERN NOTE
Do not join or turn rounds unless otherwise stated.

Mark first stitch of each round.

INSTRUCTIONS

BASE
Rnd 1: With black, ch 3, sl st in beg ch to form ring, ch 1, 2 sc in each ch around. *(6 sc)*

Rnds 2 & 3: 2 sc in each st around. *(24 sc at end of last rnd)*

Rnd 4: [Sc in each of next 2 sts, 2 sc in next st] around, join with sl st in beg sc. Fasten off. *(32 sc)*

front lps (see Stitch Guide) of Base, sc in each st around, join with sl st in beg sc, **turn**.

Rnds 6–17: Sc in each st around.

Rnd 18: Working this rnd in **back lps** (see Stitch Guide) only, [sc in each of next 3 sts, 2 sc in next st] around. (40 sc)

Rnd 19: [Sc in each of next 7 sts, 2 sc in next st] around. (45 sc)

Rnd 20: [Sc in each of next 8 sts, 2 sc in next st] around. (50 sc)

Rnds 21–32: Sc in each st around.

Rnds 33 & 34: [Sc in each of next 3 sts, **sc dec** (see Stitch Guide) in next 2 sts] around. (32 sc at end of last rnd)

Place soda can inside Basket, stuff sides firmly, spreading fiberfill evenly around can to round out basket.

Rnd 35: Working through both thicknesses in both lps of last rnd on Basket and rem lps of rnd 4 on Base, sc in each st around, join with sl st in beg sc. Fasten off. Remove soda can.

LEG
Make 4.
Rnd 1: With black, ch 3, sl st in first ch to form ring, ch 1, 2 sc in each ch around. (6 sc)

Rnd 2: 2 sc in each st around. (12 sc)

Rnd 3: [Sc in next st, 2 sc in next st] around. (18 sc)

BASKET
Rnd 1: With black, ch 3, sl st in beg ch to form ring, ch 1, 2 sc in each ch around. (6 sc)

Rnds 2 & 3: 2 sc in each st around. (24 sc at end of last rnd)

Rnd 4: [Sc in each of next 2 sts, 2 sc in next st] around, join with sl st in beg sc. (32 sc)

Rnd 5: Holding Base and Basket WS tog, working through both lps of Basket and

Rnds 4 & 5: Sc in each st around.

Rnd 6: [Sc dec in next 2 sts] around, join with sl st in beg sc. Fasten off. Stuff. *(9 sc)*

Sew last row of 2 Legs to each side on bottom of Basket as shown in photo.

HANDLE SIDE
Make 2.
Row 1: With amethyst, ch 41, sc in 2nd ch from hook and in each ch across, turn. Fasten off. *(40 sc)*

Row 2: Join royal with sc in first st, sc in each of next 6 sts, 2 sc in next st, [sc in each of next 7 sts, 2 sc in next st] across, turn. Fasten off. *(45 sc)*

Row 3: Join cherry red with sc in first st, sc in each of next 7

sts, 2 sc in next st, [sc in each of next 8 sts, 2 sc in next st] across, turn. Fasten off. *(50 sc)*

Row 4: Join orange with sc in first st, sc in each of next 8 sts, 2 sc in next st, [sc in each of next 9 sts, 2 sc in next st] across, turn. Fasten off. *(55 sc)*

Row 5: Join bright yellow in first st, sc in each of next 9 sts, 2 sc in next st, [sc in each of next 10 sts, 2 sc in next st] across, turn. Fasten off. *(60 sc)*

Row 6: Join paddy green with sc in first st, sc in each of next 10 sts, 2 sc in next st, [sc in each of next 11 sts, 2 sc in next st] across. Fasten off. *(65 sc)*

Matching colors, sew Handle Sides tog, leaving ends unsewn. Stuff.

With black, sew Handle ends to sides of Basket at top as shown in photo.

SHAMROCK
Make 3.
With paddy green, ch 4, sl st in first ch to form ring, (ch 3, 2 dc, ch 3, sl st) in same ch, (sl st, ch 3, 2 dc, ch 3, sl st) in each ch around, for **stem**, ch 7, working in back lps, sl st in 2nd ch from hook and in each ch across, join with sl st in joining sl st. Fasten off.

Sew Shamrock to 1 side of Handle *(see photo)*.

With green and orange ribbons held tog, tie into a bow leaving long ends for streamers. Glue to Handle above Shamrock. ■

Shamrock Pin

DESIGN BY ROSETTA HARSHMAN

Show your Irish pride with this simple little pin—and keep from getting pinched on St. Patrick's Day! It works up quickly with just a bit of thread and looks adorable on any jacket lapel.

SKILL LEVEL ◼◼◻◻
EASY

FINISHED SIZE
1¾ x 1½ inches

MATERIALS
Aunt Lydia's Classic Crochet size 10 crochet cotton (350 yds per ball):
  1 ball #484 myrtle green
Size C/2/2.75mm crochet hook
1-inch pin back
Craft glue

PATTERN NOTE
Divide crochet cotton into 2 balls to yield 2 working strands, or use 2 balls of crochet cotton.

INSTRUCTIONS

SHAMROCK
Holding 2 strands tog as 1, for

stem, ch 7, sc in 2nd ch from hook, sc in each of next 5 chs, [for **leaves**, ch 5, dc in top of stem, ch 5, sc in top of stem] 3 times, **turn**, ch 1, (sc, 5 hdc) in first ch sp, (5 hdc, sc) in next ch sp, *(sc, 5 hdc) in next ch sp, (5 hdc, sc) in next ch sp, rep from * once. Fasten off.

Glue pin back to back of Shamrock. ◼

Bunny Purse

DESIGN BY SHEILA LESLIE

A friendly, floppy-eared bunny peeks from the front of this quick-to-stitch purse. It's just big enough for a little wallet, handkerchief and a few of her favorite things.

SKILL LEVEL ■■□□
EASY

FINISHED SIZE
6½ inches deep

MATERIALS
Medium (worsted)
 weight yarn:
  4 oz/200 yds/114g yellow
  1 oz/50 yds/28g white
  10 yds each pink and black
Size G/6/4mm crochet hook or
  size needed to obtain gauge
Tapestry needle
Sewing needle
Pompoms:
  1-inch: 2 white
  ½-inch: 1 pink
1-inch square hook-and-loop
  tape
White sewing thread
Stitch markers

GAUGE
4 sc = 1 inch; 4 sc rows = 1 inch

PATTERN NOTES
Do not join or turn rounds unless otherwise stated.

Mark first stitch of each round.

INSTRUCTIONS

PURSE
Rnd 1: With yellow, ch 10, 3 sc in 2nd ch from hook, sc in each of next 7 chs, 3 sc in last ch, working on opposite side of ch, sc in each of next 7 chs, **do not join** (see Pattern Notes). (20 sc)

Rnd 2: [2 sc in each of next 3 sts, sc in each of next 7 sts] around. (26 sc)

Rnd 3: [2 sc in next st, sc in next st] 3 times, sc in each of next 7 sts, [2 sc in next st, sc in next st] 3 times, sc in each of last 7 sts. (32 sc)

Rnd 4: Sc in each of first 2 sts, [2 sc in next st, sc in next st] 3 times, sc in each of next 10 sts, [2 sc in next st, sc in next st] 3 times, sc in each of last 8 sts. (38 sc)

Rnd 5: Sc in each of first 2 sts, [2 sc in next st, sc in each of next 2 sts] 3 times, sc in each of next 10 sts, [2 sc in next st, sc in each of next 2 sts] 3 times, sc in each of last 8 sts. (44 sc)

Rnd 6: Sc in each of first 4 sts, [2 sc in next st, sc in each of next 2 sts] 3 times, sc in each of next 13 sts, [2 sc in next st, sc in each of next 2 sts] 3 times, sc in each of last 9 sts. *(50 sc)*

Rnd 7: Sc in each of first 5 sts, [2 sc in next st, sc in each of next 2 sts] 3 times, sc in each of next 16 sts, [2 sc in next st, sc in each of next 2 sts] 3 times, sc in each of last 11 sts. *(56 sc)*

Rnd 8: Sc in each of first 6 sts, [2 sc in next st, sc in each of next 3 sts] 3 times, sc in each of next 16 sts, [2 sc in next st, sc in each of next 3 sts] 3 times, sc in each of last 10 sts. *(62 sc)*

Rnd 9: Sc in each of first 8 sts, [2 sc in next st, sc in each of next 3 sts] 3 times, sc in each of next 18 sts, [2 sc in next st, sc in each of next 3 sts] 3 times, sc in each of last 12 sts. *(68 sc)*

Rnds 10–28: Sc in each st around.

Rnd 29: Sc in each st around, join with sl st in beg sc. Fasten off.

BUNNY
Face
Row 1 (RS): Starting at top of Face, with white, ch 13, sc in 2nd ch from hook and in each ch across, turn. *(12 sc)*

Rows 2–12: Ch 1, sc in each st across, turn.

Rows 13–15: Ch 1, **sc dec** *(see Stitch Guide)* in first 2 sts, sc in each st across to last 2 sts, sc dec in last 2 sts, turn. At end of last row, **do not turn.** *(6 sc at end of last row)*

Rnd 16: Now working in rnds around outer edge, sc in end of each row across, working in starting ch on opposite side of row 1, sc in each ch across, sc in end of each row across, 2 sc in next st, sc in each of next 4 sts, 2 sc in last st, join with sl st in beg sc. Fasten off.

For front, sew Face centered to Purse with top edge of Face even with top edge of Purse.

Ear
Make 2.
Row 1: With white, ch 14, sc in 2nd ch from hook and in each of next 6 chs, hdc in each of next 3 chs, dc in each of next 2 chs, 6 dc in last ch, working on opposite side of ch, dc in each of next 2 chs, hdc in each of next 3 chs, sc in each of last 7 chs, turn. *(30 sts)*

Row 2: Ch 1, sc in each of first 14 sts, 2 sc in next st, ch 1, 2 sc in next st, sc in each of last 14 sts. Fasten off.

Sew Ears to top edge of Purse on back, centered above Face *(see photo)*.

Sew white pompoms for cheeks and pink pompom for nose to Face as shown in photo.

With black, using satin stitch *(see Fig. 1)*, embroider eyes to face on each side of nose" or "on each side of nose as shown.

Satin Stitch
Fig. 1

FLOWER
With pink, ch 6, sl st in 6th ch from hook, [ch 6, sl st in same ch] 5 times. Fasten off.

With yellow, using French knot *(see Fig. 2)*, embroider center of Flower.

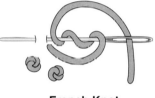

French Knot
Fig. 2

Sew Flower to top of Face as shown in photo.

HANDLE
Make 2.
Row 1: With yellow, ch 5, sc in 2nd ch from hook and in each ch across, turn. *(4 sc)*

Rows 2–61: Ch 1, sc in each st across, turn. Fasten off at end of last row.

Sew ends of 1 Handle to top edge of front 4½ inches apart. Rep with other Handle on back.

Sew hook-and-loop tape to center top of Purse on inside. ∎

Easter Celebration

DESIGNS BY LOUISE PUCHATY

When planning your Easter table decorations, consider this charming basket full of eggs and accompanying coasters. Stitch them in a variety of colors to bring the beauty of spring to your party.

SKILL LEVEL ◼◼◻◻
EASY

FINISHED SIZES
Basket: 3½ inches tall x
7 inches in diameter, excluding
Handles

Egg: 3 x 6¼ inches in
circumference

Coaster: 3½ inches square

MATERIALS
Caron Simply Soft
  medium (worsted)
  weight yarn (6 oz/330
  yds/170g per skein):
    1 skein #9701 white
    1¾ oz/96 yds/50g
      each #9739 soft green,
      #9712 soft blue and
      #9719 soft pink

4 MEDIUM

Sizes F/5/3.75mm and
  G/6/4mm crochet hooks or
  sizes needed to obtain gauge
Tapestry needle
Safety pins
Stitch markers
6-inch-diameter plastic
  canvas circle
3 x 22-inch strip of plastic canvas
Fiberfill

GAUGE
Size F hook: 7 sc = 1½ inches; 7
sc rnds = 1½ inches

Size G hook: 4 sc = 1 inch; 4 sc
rnds = 1 inch

PATTERN NOTES
Do not join rounds unless
otherwise stated.

Mark first stitch of each round.

INSTRUCTIONS

BASKET
Inner Bottom
Rnd 1: With size G hook and
white, ch 4, sl st in first ch to
form ring, ch 1, 8 sc in ring, **do
not join** (see Pattern Notes). (8 sc)

Rnd 2: 2 sc in each sc around.
(16 sc)

Rnd 3: [2 sc in next sc, sc in
next sc] around. (24 sc)

Rnd 4: [2 sc in next sc, sc in
each of next 2 sc] around. (32 sc)

Rnd 5: [2 sc in next sc, sc in
each of next 3 sc] around. (40 sc)

Rnd 6: [2 sc in next sc, sc in
each of next 4 sc] around. (48 sc)

Rnd 7: [2 sc in next sc, sc in each of next 5 sc] around. *(56 sc)*

Rnd 8: [2 sc in next sc, sc in each of next 6 sc] around. *(64 sc)*

Rnd 9: [2 sc in next sc, sc in each of next 7 sc] around. *(72 sc)*

Rnd 10: [2 sc in next sc, sc in each of next 8 sc] around. *(80 sc)*

Rnd 11: [2 sc in next sc, sc in each of next 9 sc] around. *(88 sc)*

Rnd 12: Sc in each sc around.

Inner Side
Rnd 13: Working in **front lp** *(see Stitch Guide)* only of each st, sc in each st around.

Rnds 14–28: Rep rnd 12. At the end of last rnd, fasten off.

Outer Side
First Vertical Slat
Row 1: With Inner Side upright and working in rem lps of rnd 12, beg First Vertical Slat, join white with sl st in any unworked lp, loosely sl st in each of next 3 sts, leaving rem sts unworked, turn. *(4 sl sts)*

Row 2: Ch 1, working in front lps for this row only, sc in each of next 4 sts, turn.

Rows 3–15: Ch 1, sc in each of next 4 sc. At the end of last row, fasten off.

2nd Vertical Slat
Row 1: Attach white with sl st in next rem free lp of rnd 12, sl st loosely in each of next 3 sts, leaving rem sts unworked, turn. *(4 sl sts)*

Rows 2–15: Rep rows 2–15 of First Vertical Slat.

Rep 2nd Vertical Slat until 22 Slats are completed.

Outer Bottom
Rnds 1–12: Rep rnds 1–12 on Inner Bottom. *(88 sc)*

Rnd 13: Holding Outer Bottom to Inner Bottom with plastic canvas circle between layers, working in sl sts of row 1 of

Outer Side and back lps of rnd 12 of Outer Bottom, sc in each st around. Fasten off.

Joining Inner & Outer Sides
Working with 3 x 22-inch strip of plastic canvas, overlap 3-inch ends by 1 inch, sew ends tog.

Insert plastic canvas circle between layers of Inner Side and Outer Side.

Working through both thicknesses in sc sts of row 15 of Vertical Slats and rnd 28 of Inner Side, matching sts, join white with sl st in any st, sl st in each sc around. Fasten off.

Horizontal Strip
Make 1 each soft pink, soft green & soft blue.
Row 1: Ch 5, sc in 2nd ch from hook, sc in each ch across, turn. *(4 sc)*

Rows 2–102: Ch 1, sc in each sc across, turn. At the end of row last row, leaving long end, fasten off.

Beg with soft pink Horizontal Strip, weaving under and over Vertical Slats around the Basket. Sew beg and end of Strip tog.

Rep weaving with soft green and soft blue Strips, weaving each in opposite direction of previous Strip.

Handle
Make 2.
Row 1: With white, leaving long end at beg, ch 16, sc in 2nd ch from hook, sc in each ch across, turn. *(15 sc)*

Row 2: Ch 1, sc in each sc across, turn.

Row 3: Rep row 2. Leaving long end, fasten off.

Fold Handle in half lengthwise, sew row 3 to opposite side of starting ch on row 1.

Sew 1 Handle to each side of Basket as shown in photo.

Solid Egg
Make 1 each soft pink, soft green & soft blue.
Rnd 1: Ch 2, 4 sc in 2nd ch from hook. *(4 sc)*

Rnd 2: 2 sc in each sc around. *(8 sc)*

Rnd 3: Rep rnd 2. *(16 sc)*

Rnd 4: [2 sc in next sc, sc in next sc] around. *(24 sc)*

Rnd 5: Sc in each sc around.

Rnds 6–11: Rep rnd 5.

Rnd 12: [Sc in each of next 4 sc, **sc dec** *(see Stitch Guide)* in next 2 sc] around. *(20 sc)*

Stuff Egg with fiberfill, continue to stuff as work progresses.

Rnd 13: Rep rnd 5.

Rnd 14: [Sc in each of next 3 sc, sc dec in next 2 sc] around. *(16 sc)*

Rnd 15: [Sc in each of next 2 sc, sc dec in next 2 sc] around. *(12 sc)*

Rnd 16: [Sc in next sc, sc dec in next 2 sc] around. *(8 sc)*

Rnd 17: [Sc dec in next 2 sc] around, join with sl st in next sc. Leaving long end, fasten off. *(4 sc)*

Sew opening closed.

Striped Egg
Make 1 each soft pink, soft green & soft blue.
Rnd 1: With soft pink [soft green, soft blue], ch 2, 4 sc in 2nd ch from hook. *(4 sc)*

Rnds 2–8: Rep rnds 2–8 of Solid Egg. At end of last rnd,

fasten off. *(24 sc)*

Rnd 9: Join white with sc in any st, sc in each sc around. Fasten off.

Rnd 10: Join soft green [soft blue, soft pink] with sc in any st, sc in each sc around. Fasten off.

Rnd 11: Rep rnd 9.

Rnd 12: Join soft pink [soft green, soft blue], rep rnd 12 of Solid Egg.

Rnds 13–17: Rep rnds 13–17 of Solid Egg.

COASTER
Make 4.
White Strip
Make 3.
Row 1: With white, ch 5, sc in 2nd ch from hook, sc in each ch across, turn. *(4 sc)*

Row 2: Ch 1, sc in each sc across, turn.

Rows 3–15: Rep row 2. At the end of last row, fasten off.

Pastel Strip
Make 1 each soft pink, soft green & soft blue.
Rows 1–15: Rep rows 1–15 of White Strip.

Thread tapestry needle with white, place 3 White Strips next to 1 another, weave 3 Pastel Strips through the White Strips. Pin with safety pin as needed to hold in place while sewing. Sew pieces tog around outer edge. ■

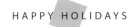

Butterflies

DESIGN BY DOT DRAKE

These delicate butterflies alight and sit still as long as you need a page marked. Though it looks intricate and impossible, it's a deceptively easy-to-do design that will delight anyone who receives it.

SKILL LEVEL ⬛⬛⬛◻
INTERMEDIATE

FINISHED SIZE
9 Inches long, excluding Fringe

MATERIALS
Size 10 crochet cotton:
    50 yds each green,
      white, yellow, aqua,
      pink and lilac
Size 9/1.25mm steel hook or
    hook size needed to obtain
    gauge
Sewing needle
Lilac sewing thread
Seed beads:
    5 each of 3 different colors
Craft glue or hot-glue gun

GAUGE
10 sts = 1 inch; 5 sc back lp
rows = ½ inch

Butterfly = 1½ x 2 inches

Flower = ⅝-inch across

INSTRUCTIONS

VINE
Row 1: With green, ch 111, sc in 2nd ch from hook, sc in each of next 9 chs, [sk next 2 chs, sc in each of next 11 chs, 3 sc in next ch, sc in each of next 11 chs] across, turn. *(110 sc)*

Row 2: Working the following rows in **back lps** *(see Stitch Guide)*, ch 2 *(does not count as first st)*, sk first 2 sts, sc in each of next 10 sts, 3 sc in next st, sc in each of next 11 sts, sk next 2 sts, [sc in each of next 11 sts, 3 sc in next st, sc in each of next 11 sts, sk next 2 sts] 3 times, sc in each of last 9 sts, turn. *(108 sc)*

Row 3: Ch 1, sc in each of first 8 sts, sk next 2 sts, sc in each of next 11 sts, 3 sc in next st, [sc in each of next 11 sts, sk next 2 sts, sc in each of next 11 sts, 3 sc in next st] 3 times, sc in each of last 11 sts, turn.

Row 4: Ch 2, sk first 2 sts, sc in each of next 11 sts, (ch 8, sl st in top of last sc made) 3 times, sc in each of next 11 sts, sk next 2 sts, *sc in each of next 12 sts, (ch 8, sl st in top of last sc made) 3 times, sc in each of next 11 sts, sk next 2 sts, rep from * twice, sc in each of last 7 sts, **do not turn**. Fasten off.

Row 5: Working in starting ch on opposite side of row 1, join green with sc in first ch, sc in each of next 9 chs, *2 sc in next ch sp, (ch 8, sl st in top of last sc made) 3 times, sc in same ch sp, sc in each of next 11 chs, sk next ch, sc in each of next 11 chs, rep from * across, sc in end of row 1, (ch 8, sl st in top of last sc made) 3 times, sl st in same row. Fasten off.

FLOWER
Make 3.
Rnd 1: With lilac, ch 2, 5 sc in 2nd ch from hook, join with sl st in beg sc. *(5 sc)*

Rnd 2: Ch 6, sl st in same st, (sl st, ch 6, sl st) in each st around, join with sl st in joining sl st of last rnd. Fasten off.

With sewing thread and needle, sew 5 seed beads of same color to center of each Flower.

PINK BUTTERFLY
Large Ring
Make 2.
With white, ch 10, sl st in first ch to form ring, ch 1, 23 sc in ring, join with sl st in beg sc. Fasten off.

Small Ring
Make 2.
With white, ch 7, sl st in first ch to form ring, ch 1, 16 sc in ring, join with sl st in beg sc. Fasten off.

Inner Joining Round
Join pink with sc in any st on either Large Ring, sc in each of next 4 sts, ch 2, sc in any st on either Small Ring, sc in each of next 2 sts, ch 1, sc in any st on other Small Ring, sc in each of next 2 sts, ch 1, sc in ch-2 sp between first Large Ring and adjoining Small Ring, ch 1, sc in any st on other Large Ring, sc in each of next 4 sts, ch 1, drop lp from hook, insert hook in first sc, pull dropped lp through.

Outer Round
Ch 1, (sc, ch 5, sc) in ch sp just made, sc in each of next 6 sts, *ch 3, sl st in top of last sc made, sc in next st, ch 4, sl st in top of last sc made, sc in next st, ch 3, sl st in top of last sc made*, sc in each of next 7 sts, sk next 3 unworked sts on next Small Ring, sc in each of next 4 sts, rep between * once, sc in each of next 4 sts, (sc, ch 3, sc) in next ch sp, sc in each of next 4 unworked sts on next Small Ring, rep between * once, sc in each of next 4 sts, sk next 3 unworked sts on next Large Ring, sc in each of next 7 sts, rep between * once, sc in each of last 6 sts, join with sl st in beg sc. Fasten off.

Antennae
Cut a 4-inch strand of pink. Tie center of strand to back side of ch-5 sp at center top of Butterfly. Trim ends to 1 inch.

AQUA BUTTERFLY
Using aqua instead of pink, work same as Pink Butterfly.

YELLOW BUTTERFLY
Using yellow instead of pink, work same as Pink Butterfly.

ASSEMBLY
Glue Butterflies and Flowers alternately across Vine as shown in photo.

FRINGE
Cut 4 strands green each 10 inches in length. With all strands held together, fold in half, insert hook in bottom corner of Vine, pull all loose ends through fold, tighten. Trim. ■

Star Sparklers

DESIGNS BY KATHRYN CLARK

Add some fun to your holiday celebration with these easy-to-make sparklers! They can be placed anywhere for just the right touch for a patriotic picnic and party, then sent home with your younger guests.

SKILL LEVEL ◆■□□
EASY

FINISHED SIZE
4 inches square

MATERIALS
Size 10 crochet cotton:
　　50 yds red
　　50 yds blue
　　50 yds white/silver
　　　metallic
Size 7/1.65mm steel crochet
　　hook or size needed to
　　obtain gauge
Fiberfill
Pencils in desired colors: 3
Red, blue and silver metallic
　　gift-wrapping shreds
Matching sewing thread

GAUGE
8 dc = 1 inch; 4 dc rows = 1 inch

4 MEDIUM

INSTRUCTIONS

BLUE SPARKLER
Center
Make 2.
Rnd 1: With blue, ch 6, sl st in first ch to form ring, ch 3 *(counts as first dc)*, (tr, dc) in ring, ch 1, *(dc, tr, dc) in ring, ch 1, rep from * 3 times, join with sl st in 3rd ch of beg ch-3. *(15 sts, 5 ch-1 sps)*

Rnd 2: Ch 3, (2 dc, tr, 2 dc) in next st, dc in next st, ch 1, *dc in next st, (2 dc, tr, 2 dc) in next st, dc in next st, rep from * around, join with sl st in 3rd ch of beg ch-3. *(35 sts, 5 ch sps)*

Rnd 3: Sl st in next st, ch 2 *(counts as first hdc)*, hdc in next st, *5 hdc in next st, hdc in each of next 2 sts, ch 1, sk next 2

sts**, hdc in each of next 2 sts, rep from * around, ending last rep at **, join with sl st in 2nd ch of beg ch-2. *(45 sts, 5 ch sps)*

Rnd 4: Sl st in next st, ch 2, hdc in next st, *2 hdc in next st, 5 dc in next st, 2 hdc in next st, hdc in each of next 2 sts, ch 1, sk next 2 sts**, hdc in each of next 2 sts, rep from * around, ending

last rep at **, join with sl st in 2nd ch of beg ch-2. Fasten off. *(65 sts, 5 ch sps)*

Border
Rnd 1: Holding Centers WS tog, matching sts and working through both thicknesses, join blue with sc in first st, *ch 3, sk next 2 sts, sc in next st, ch 3, sk next 2 sts, (sc, ch 3, sc) in next st, [ch 3, sk next 2 sts, sc in next st] twice, sk next ch sp**, sc in next st, rep from * around, ending last rep at **, join with sl st in beg sc.

Rnd 2: (Sl st, ch 1, 3 sc) in first ch sp, *ch 1, 3 hdc in next ch sp, ch 1, (3 dc, ch 1, 3 dc) in next ch sp, ch 1, 3 hdc in next ch sp, ch 1, 3 sc in next ch sp, ch 1**, 3 sc in next ch sp, rep from * around, ending last rep at **, join with sl st in beg sc.

Rnd 3: Ch 1, sc in first st, [ch 4, sc in next ch sp] twice, *ch 4, (sc, ch 4, sc) in next ch sp, [ch 4, sc in next ch sp] 5 times,

rep from * 4 times, ch 4, (sc, ch 4, sc) in next ch sp, [ch 4, sc in next ch sp] twice, ch 4, join with sl st in beg sc. Fasten off.

Tie
With blue, ch 75. Fasten off.

Finishing
Stuff Star through opening between sts with small amount of fiberfill.

Tie several strands of red, blue and white/silver metallic gift-wrapping shreds tog with sewing thread. Tie shreds to pencil 1 inch below top edge. Insert top of pencil into Center at back of Center.

Thread ends of Tie from back to front through sts around pencil. Tie ends into a bow.

SILVER SPARKLER
Center
Make 2.
Rnds 1–4: With white/silver, work rnds 1–4 of Blue Sparkler Center.

Border
Rnd 1: Holding Centers WS tog, matching sts and working through both thicknesses, join white/silver with sc in first st, *ch 1, sk next st, hdc in next st, ch 1, sk next st, dc in next st, ch 1, sk next st, (dc, ch 1) 5 times in next st, sk next st, dc in next st, ch 1, sk next st, hdc in next st,

ch 1, sk next st, sc in next st, sk next ch sp**, sc in next st, rep from * around, ending last rep at **, join with sl st in beg sc.

Rnd 2: (Sl st, ch 1, sc) in first ch sp, *[ch 3, sc in next ch sp] 9 times**, sc in next ch sp, rep from * around, ending last rep at **, join with sl st in beg sc.

Rnd 3: (Sl st, ch 1, sc) in first ch sp, *[ch 3, sc in next ch sp] 3 times, ch 3, (sc, ch 5, sc) in next ch sp, [ch 3, sc in next ch sp] 4 times**, sc in next ch sp, rep from * around, ending last rep at **, join with sl st in beg sc. Fasten off.

Tie
With white/silver, ch 75. Fasten off.

Finishing
Work same as Blue Sparkler using only white/silver gift-wrapping shreds.

RED SPARKLER
Center
Make 2.
Rnds 1–4: With red, work rnds 1–4 of Blue Sparkler Center.

Border
Rnd 1: Holding Centers WS tog, matching sts and working through both thicknesses, join red with sc in first st, *ch 1, sk next st, hdc in next st, ch 1, sk next st, dc in next st, ch 1, sk

next st, (dc, ch 1) 3 times in next st, sk next st, dc in next st, ch 1, sk next st, hdc in next st, ch 1, sk next st, sc in next st**, ch 1, sk next ch sp, sc in next st, rep from * around, ending last rep at **, join with sc in beg sc.

Rnd 2: Ch 1, sc around joining sc, *[ch 1, sk next ch sp, hdc in next st] twice, ch 1, sk next ch sp, dc in next st, ch 1, sk next ch sp, (dc, ch 1) 3 times in next st, sk next ch sp, dc in next st, [ch 1, sk next ch sp, hdc in next st] twice, ch 1**, sc in next ch sp, rep from * around, ending last rep at **, join with sl st in beg sc.

Rnd 3: Ch 2, *sc in next st, [ch 1, sk next ch sp, hdc in next st] twice, ch 1, sk next ch sp, dc in next st, ch 1, sk next ch sp, (dc, ch 2, dc, ch 3, sl st in top of last dc made, ch 2, dc) in next st, ch 1, sk next ch sp, dc in next st, [ch 1, sk next ch sp, hdc in next st] twice, ch 1, sk next ch sp, sc in next st**, hdc in next st, rep from * around, ending last rep at **, join with sl st in 2nd ch of beg ch-2. Fasten off.

Tie
With red, ch 75. Fasten off.

Finishing
Work same as Blue Sparkler using only blue gift-wrapping shreds. ■

Patriotic Picnic Set

DESIGNS BY JOCELYN SASS

Every potluck dinner contributor faces the same problem: How to get my dish there before it gets cold? Wonder no more with this patriotic set: the casserole cozy keeps the food warm while the pot holder and towel protect your hands!

SKILL LEVEL ■■□□
EASY

FINISHED SIZES
Pot holder: 8 x 8½ inches

Casserole cover: 9 inches in diameter x 3 inches high

Towel top: 5½ x 6 inches

MATERIALS

Medium (worsted) weight yarn:
    4 oz/200 yds/113g each white and red
    3 oz/150 yds/85g royal blue
Sizes C/2/2.75mm and G/6/4mm crochet hooks or size needed to obtain gauge
Tapestry needle
Sewing needle

Sewing thread
White 1-inch plastic rings: 2
White ¾-inch star buttons: 8
⅛-inch white ribbon: 1½ yds
Kitchen terry towel, cut in half

GAUGE
Size G hook: 4 sc = 1 inch; 4 sc rnds = 1 inch

INSTRUCTIONS

POT HOLDER
Front
Row 1 (RS): With size G hook and red, ch 30, sc in 4th ch from hook *(first 3 chs count as first dc)*, [dc in next ch, sc in next ch] 13 times, turn. *(28 sts)*

Row 2: Ch 3 *(counts as first dc)*, sc in next sc, [dc in next sc, sc in next dc] across **changing colors** *(see Stitch Guide)* to white in last st, turn.

Row 3: Ch 3, sc in next sc, [dc in next sc, sc in next dc] across, turn.

Row 4: Rep row 2 changing to red.

Rows 5 & 6: Rep rows 3 and 2 changing to white.

Rows 7 & 8: Rep rows 3 and 2 changing to royal blue.

Rows 9–16: Rep row 3.

Row 17: Rep row 2 changing to white.

Rows 18 & 19: Rep rows 3 and 2 changing to red.

Rows 20 & 21: Rep rows 3 and 2 changing to white.

Rows 22 & 23: Rep rows 3 and 2 changing to red.

Rows 24 & 25: Rep row 3.

Rnd 26: Working around entire outer edge, changing color according to rows, evenly sp sc around, working 3 sc in each corner st, join with sl st in beg sc. Fasten off.

Back
Work same as Front.

Joining
With Front and Back WS tog and working through **back lps** (see Stitch Guide) and both thicknesses, with size G hook, join white with sl st in any st, ch 3, 2 dc in same st, sl st in next st, [3 dc in next st, sl st in next st] around, join with sl st in beg sl st. Fasten off.

Sew 2 star buttons evenly spaced between rows 13 and 14 across.

Sew 1 plastic ring to top left corner.

CASSEROLE COVER
Bottom
Rnd 1 (RS): With size G hook and red, ch 2, 6 sc in 2nd ch from hook, join with sl st in beg sc. (6 sc)

Rnd 2: Ch 1, 2 sc in each sc around, join with sl st in beg sc, **turn**. (12 sc)

Rnd 3: Ch 1, sc in first st, 2 sc in next st, [sc in next st, 2 sc in next st] around, join with sl st in beg sc, turn. (18 sc)

Rnd 4: Ch 1, sc in each of first 2 sc, 2 sc in next sc, [sc in each of next 2 sc, 2 sc in next sc] around, join with sl st in beg sc, turn. (24 sc)

Rnd 5: Ch 1, sc in each of first 3 sc, 2 sc in next sc, [sc in each of next 3 sc, 2 sc in next sc] around, join with sl st in beg sc, turn. (30 sc)

Rnd 6: Ch 1, sc in each of first 4 sc, 2 sc in next sc, [sc in each of next 4 sc, 2 sc in next sc] around, join with sl st in beg sc, turn. (36 sc)

Rnd 7: Ch 1, sc in each of first 5 sc, 2 sc in next sc, [sc in each of next 5 sc, 2 sc in next sc] around, join with sl st in beg sc, turn. (42 sc)

Rnd 8: Ch 1, sc in each of first 6 sc, 2 sc in next sc, [sc in each of next 6 sc, 2 sc in next sc] around, join with sl st in beg sc, turn. (48 sc)

Rnd 9: Ch 1, sc in each of first 7 sc, 2 sc in next sc, [sc in each of next 7 sc, 2 sc in next sc] around, join with sl st in beg sc, turn. (54 sc)

Rnd 10: Ch 1, sc in each of first 8 sc, 2 sc in next sc, [sc in each of next 8 sc, 2 sc in next sc] around, join with sl st in beg sc, turn. (60 sc)

Rnd 11: Ch 1, sc in each of first 9 sc, 2 sc in next sc, [sc in each of next 9 sc, 2 sc in next sc] around, join with sl st in beg sc, turn. (66 sc)

Rnd 12: Ch 1, sc in each of first 10 sc, 2 sc in next sc, [sc in each of next 10 sc, 2 sc in next sc] around, join with sl st in beg sc, turn. (72 sc)

Rnd 13: Ch 1, sc in each of first 11 sc, 2 sc in next sc, [sc in each of next 11 sc, 2 sc in next sc] around, join with sl st in beg sc, turn. (78 sc)

Rnd 14: Ch 1, sc in each of first 12 sc, 2 sc in next sc, [sc in each of next 12 sc, 2 sc in next sc] around, join with sl st in beg sc, turn. (84 sc)

Rnd 15: Ch 1, sc in each of first 13 sc, 2 sc in next sc, [sc in each of next 13 sc, 2 sc in next sc] around, join with sl st in beg sc, turn. (90 sc)

Rnd 16: Ch 1, sc in each of first 14 sc, 2 sc in next sc, [sc in each of next 14 sc, 2 sc in next sc] around, join with sl st in beg sc, turn. (96 sc)

Rnd 17: Ch 1, sc in each of first 2 sc, 2 sc in next sc, [sc in each of next 2 sc, 2 sc in next sc] around **changing colors** (see Stitch Guide) to white in last st, join with sl st in beg sc, turn. (102 sc)

Rnd 18: Ch 1, [sc in next sc, dc in next sc] around changing to red in last st, join with sl st in beg sc, turn.

Rnd 19: Ch 1, [sc in next dc, dc in next sc] around, changing to white in last st, join with sl st in beg sc, turn.

Rnd 20: Ch 1, [sc in next dc, dc in next sc] around changing to royal blue in last st, join with sl st in beg sc, turn.

Rnds 21 & 22: Ch 1, [sc in next dc, dc in next sc] around, join with sl st in beg sc, turn.

Rnd 23: Ch 1, [sc in next dc, dc in next sc] around changing to white in last st, join with sl st in beg sc, turn.

Rnd 24: Ch 1, [sc in next dc, dc in next sc] around changing to red in last st, join with sl st in beg sc, turn.

Rnd 25 (RS): Ch 1, [sc in next dc, dc in next sc] around, join with sl st in beg sc. Fasten off.

Trim
Rnd 26 (RS): Join white with sl st in any st, ch 3 *(counts as first dc)*, 2 dc in same st, sl st in next st, sk next st, [3 dc in next st, sl st in next st, sk next st] around, join with sl st in top of beg ch-3. Fasten off.

Over center of rnd 22, sew 5 star buttons with 3½ inches between each button.

Starting at center front button, weave white ribbon

through sts of rnd 25, tie ends in bow.

TOWEL
Towel Trim
Row 1: With size C hook, join white to cut edge of towel, ch 1, evenly sp 40 sc across edge of towel, turn. *(40 sc)*

Rows 2–4: Ch 3 *(counts as first dc)*, dc in each st across, turn.

Row 5: Ch 2, sk next dc, [**dc dec** *(see Stitch Guide)* in next 2 dc] across, turn. *(20 dc)*

Rows 6 & 7: Ch 3, dc in each dc across, turn. At end of last row, leaving long end, fasten off.

Sew ends of rows 4–7 tog.

Front Towel Top
Row 1: With size G hook, and red, ch 22, sc in 4th ch from hook, [dc in next ch, sc in next ch] 9 times, turn. *(20 sts)*

Row 2: Ch 3 *(counts as first dc)*, sc in next dc, [dc in next sc, sc in next dc] across changing to white in last st, turn.

Row 3: Ch 3, sc in next dc, [dc in next sc, sc in next dc] across, turn.

Row 4: Ch 3, sc in next dc, [dc in next sc, sc in next dc] across changing to royal blue in last st, turn.

Rows 5–9: Ch 3, sc in next dc, [dc in next sc, sc in next dc] across, turn.

Row 10: Ch 3, sc in next dc, [dc

in next sc, sc in next dc] across changing to white in last st, turn.

Row 11: Ch 3, sc in next dc, [dc in next sc, sc in next dc] across, turn.

Row 12: Ch 3, sc in next dc, [dc in next sc, sc in next dc] across changing to hot red in last st, turn.

Rows 13 & 14: Ch 3, sc in next dc, [dc in next sc, sc in next dc] across, turn. At end of last row, do not turn.

Rnd 15: Working around entire outer edge, changing color according to rows, evenly sp sc around, working 3 sc in each corner st, join with sl st in beg sc. Fasten off.

Back Towel Top
Work same as Front Towel Top.

Trim
With Front and Back WS tog and working through **back lps** *(see Stitch Guide)* and both thicknesses, with G hook, join white with sl st in any st, ch 3, 2 dc in same st, sl st in next st, [3 dc in next st, sl st in next st] around, join with sl st in beg sl st. Fasten off.

Sew 1 star button to front center between rows 7 and 8.

Sew rows 4–7 of Towel Trim to Back Towel Top over rows 1–4.

Sew plastic ring to top center back of towel top, centered on rnd 15. ∎

Spooky Spiders

DESIGN BY ANGELA TATE

Spooky spiders climbing a crocheted web make this doily perfect for scaring your Halloween guests! Drape it across your food table as a deliciously disgusting spidery-surprise!

SKILL LEVEL ■■■□
INTERMEDIATE

FINISHED SIZE
14½ inches in diameter

MATERIALS
Size 10 crochet cotton:
    60 yards each pumpkin
      and black
Size 6/1.80mm steel crochet
    hook or size needed to
    obtain gauge
Sewing needle
Black sewing thread
Fabric stiffener

GAUGE
Web motif = 4½ inches in diameter

PATTERN NOTES
For larger Doily, add sufficient cotton on a basis of 8 yards

pumpkin and 4 yards black per motif and 5 yards black for each spider.

INSTRUCTIONS

DOILY
Spider Web Motif
Make 7.
Rnd 1 (RS): With pumpkin, ch 12, sl st in first ch to form ring, ch 6 *(counts as first dc and ch-3)*, [dc in next ch, ch 3] 11 times, join with sl st in 3rd ch of beg ch-6. *(12 ch-3 sps)*

Rnd 2: Ch 9 *(counts as first tr and ch-5)*, [tr in next dc, ch 5] around, join with sl st in 4th ch of beg ch-9.

Rnd 3: Ch 11 *(counts as first tr and ch-7)*, [tr in next tr, ch 7]

around, join with sl st in 4th ch of beg ch-11.

Rnd 4: Ch 13 *(counts as first tr and ch-9)*, [tr in next tr, ch 9] around, join with sl st in 4th ch of beg ch-13. Fasten off.

First Spider Web Motif Trim
Rnd 5: Join black with sl st in first ch of any ch-9 sp, ch 1, sc in same ch, sc in each of next 3 chs, [ch 7, sk next ch, sc in each of next 4 chs, sk next tr, sc in each of next 4 chs] around, ch 7, sk next ch, sc in each of next 4 chs, join with sl st in beg sc. Fasten off.

Remaining Spider Web Motifs Trim
Rnd 5: Join black with sl st in first ch of any ch-9 sp, ch 1, sc

in same ch, sc in each of next 3 chs, ch 3, sl st in center of unworked ch-7 sp of adjacent Motif, ch 3, sk next ch on working Motif, sc In each of next 4 chs, sk tr, sc in each of next 4 chs, ch 3, sl st in center of next unworked ch-7 sp on adjacent Motif, ch 3, sk next ch on working Motif, sc in each of next 4 chs, continue working as for rnd 5 of First Spider Web Motif Trim, joining 2 ch-7 sps per side along 1, 2 or 3 adjacent Motifs.

Spider
Make 6.
Rnd 1: With black, ch 4, 15 dc in 4th ch from hook *(first 3 chs count as first dc)*, join with sl st in 4th ch of beg ch-4. *(16 dc)*

Rnd 2: Ch 3, (3 dc, ch 3, sl st) in same st *(head)*, sc in each of next 2 dc, *[ch 10, sl st in 2nd ch from hook, sl st in each of next 8 chs, sc in next dc of rnd 1] 4 times *(4 legs)**, sc in each of next 4 dc, rep between *, sc in each of next 2 dc, join with sl st in beg sc. Fasten off.

Finishing
Saturate Spiders with fabric stiffener, place on flat surface and shape. Allow to dry completely.

Press Doily with steam iron. Position Spiders to center of each outer Spider Web Motif and sew in place. ◼

Halloween Garland

DESIGNS BY BEVERLY MEWHORTER

With happy pumpkins, googly-eyed black cats and silent ghosts, this versatile little garland will add a festive touch to your Halloween party. Use it to dress up your door in whimsical style to delight trick-or-treaters of all ages!

SKILL LEVEL ■■■□ INTERMEDIATE

FINISHED SIZE
62½ inches across

MATERIALS

Medium (worsted) weight yarn:
1 oz/50 yds/28g each black, orange, white and green
Size H/8/5mm crochet hook or size needed to obtain gauge
Tapestry needle
Hot-glue gun
11mm round wiggle eyes: 3 pair
10 x 15mm oval wiggle eyes: 4 pairs
8mm half round black beads: 6
4-inch square black felt

GAUGE
7 sc = 2 inches; 7 sc rows = 2 inches

INSTRUCTIONS

GARLAND
Row 1: With black, ch 220, sc in 11th ch from hook, sc in each ch across, ch 10, sl st in last sc. Fasten off. *(210 sc, 2 ch-10 sps)*

Row 2: Working in starting ch on opposite side of row 1, sk first ch-10 sp, join orange with sc in next ch, sc in each ch across, leaving last ch-10 sp unworked. Fasten off.

PUMPKIN
Make 4.
Rnd 1: With orange, ch 2, 6 sc in 2nd ch from hook, join with sl st in beg sc. *(6 sc)*

Rnd 2: Ch 1, 2 sc in each sc around, join with sl st in beg sc. *(12 sc)*

Rnd 3: Ch 1, sc in first sc, 2 sc in next sc, [sc in next sc, 2 sc in next sc] around, join with sl st in beg sc. *(18 sc)*

Rnd 4: Ch 1, sc in each of first 2 sc, 2 sc in next sc, [sc in each of next 2 sc, 2 sc in next sc] around, join with sl st in beg sc. *(24 sc)*

Rnd 5: Ch 1, sc in each of first 3 sc, 2 sc in next sc, [sc in each of next 3 sc, 2 sc in next sc] around, join with sl st in beg sc. Fasten off. *(30 sc)*

Row 6: Now working in rows, for stem, join green with sc in first sc of previous rnd, ch 5, sc in 2nd ch from hook, sc in each of next 3 chs, sl st in same sc as joining sc. Fasten off.

Finishing
Glue 2 oval wiggle eyes ⅜ inch apart over rnds 2 and 3.

From black felt for nose, cut ⅜ x ½-inch wide triangle. Glue to center of rnd 1.

For mouth, cut a ¼-inch x 1⅜-inch-wide curved piece from black felt as shown in photo. Glue centered below nose.

CAT
Make 3.
Body
Rnds 1–4: With black, rep rnds 1–4 of Pumpkin. *(24 sc)*

Rnd 5: For **tail**, ch 10, sl st in 2nd ch from hook, sl st in each ch across, sl st in next sc of rnd 4. Fasten off.

Head
Rnds 1–3: With black, rep rnds 1–3 of Pumpkin. *(18 sc)*

Rnd 4: Ch 1, sc in first st, ch 2, sl st in 2nd ch from hook *(first ear)*, sl st in each of next 4 sts, ch 2, sl st in 2nd ch from hook *(2nd ear)*, sl st in next st, leave rem sts unworked. Fasten off.

Sew Head over top of rnd 4 on Body as shown in photo.

Finishing
Glue 2 round wiggle eyes over top of rnd 2 on Head ⅛ inch apart.

For whiskers, tie a 3-inch piece of white into knot around center of rnd 1 on Head. Separate plies of yarn, trim whiskers to ¾ inch.

GHOST
Make 3.
Head
Rnds 1–3: With white, rep rnds 1–3 of Pumpkin. *(18 sc)*

Body
Row 4: Now working in rows, ch 1, sc in each of next 6 sc, leaving rem sts unworked, turn. *(6 sc)*

Rows 5 & 6: Ch 1, 2 sc in first sc, sc in each sc across to last sc, 2 sc in last sc, turn. *(10 sc)*

Rows 7–12: Ch 1, sc in each sc across, turn.

Row 13: Ch 1, sc in first sc, [ch 2, sc in next sc] across. Fasten off.

Glue half round beads to top of rnds 1 and 2 on Head ⅛ inch apart.

TIES
For each Pumpkin, cut 1 strand of black 6 inches long.

For each Cat, cut 1 strand of green 6 inches long.

For each Ghost, cut 1 strand of orange 6 inches long.

Draw each Tie through center top of each piece.

Sk first 6 sts on row 2 of Garland, [attach 1 Pumpkin to next st of Garland, tie ends in a bow, sk next 21 sts, attach 1 Ghost to next st of Garland, tie ends in a bow, sk next 21 sts, attach 1 Cat to next st of Garland, tie ends in a bow, sk next 21 sts] 3 times, attach 1 Pumpkin to next st of Garland, leaving last 5 sts unworked. ■

Turkey Basket

DESIGN BY CINDY HARRIS

This turkey basket is just the right size for a handful of treats. Set him on a table in your house, or use him as a gift basket to give a friend some seasonal cheer. Either way, he's sure to please.

SKILL LEVEL ◼◼◻◻
EASY

FINISHED SIZE
Approximately 4 inches deep

MATERIALS
Red Heart Super Saver
    medium (worsted) weight yarn
    (3 oz/160 yds/85g per skein):
        3 skeins #328 brown
Red Heart Super Saver medium
    (worsted) weight yarn (7
    oz/364 yds/198g per skein):
        1 oz/50 yds/28g each #319
            cherry red and #324
            bright yellow
Red Heart Classic medium
    (worsted) weight yarn (3½
    oz/190 yds/99g per skein):
        1 oz/50 yds/28g #245 orange
Size G/6/4mm crochet hook or
    size needed to obtain gauge
Tapestry needle
10mm x 12mm oblong wiggly
    eyes: 1 pair
Clean glass or soda can

Fiberfill
Craft glue or hot glue gun
Stitch markers

GAUGE
4 sc = 1 inch

PATTERN NOTES
Project is worked in continuous rounds, do not join unless
specified.

Mark first stitch of each round.

INSTRUCTIONS

BASKET BASE
Rnd 1 (RS): With brown, ch 3, sl
st in first ch to form ring, ch 1, 2
sc in each ch around. *(6 sc)*

Rnd 2: 2 sc in each sc
around. *(12 sc)*

Rnd 3: 2 sc in each sc
around. *(24 sc)*

Rnd 4: [Sc in each of next 2 sc, 2 sc in next sc] around, join with sl st in beg sc. Fasten off. *(32 sc)*

BASKET
Rnds 1–3: Rep rnds 1–3 of Base.

Rnd 4: [Sc in each of next 2 sc, 2 sc in next sc] around. *(32 sc)*

Rnd 5: Hold WS of Base facing WS of piece, working through both lps of Basket and **front lps** *(see Stitch Guide)* of piece at same time, sc in each sc around.

Rnds 6–17: Sc in each sc around.

Rnd 18: Working in **back lps** *(see Stitch Guide)* only, [sc in each of next 3 sc, 2 sc in next sc] around. *(40 sc)*

Rnd 19: [Sc in each of next 7 sc, 2 sc in next sc] around. *(45 sc)*

Rnd 20: [Sc in each of next 8 sc, 2 sc in next sc] around. *(50 sc)*

Rnds 21–32: Rep rnd 6.

Rnd 33: [Sc in each of next 3 sc, **sc dec** *(see Stitch Guide)* in next 2 sc] around. *(40 sc)*

Rnd 34: [Sc in each of next 3 sc, sc dec in next 2 sts] around. *(32 sc)*

Place soda can or glass inside Basket, stuff sides firmly, spreading fiberfill to round out Basket.

Rnd 35: Working through both lps of last rnd on piece and rem lps of rnd 4 on Base at same time, sc in each sc around, join with sl st in first sc. Fasten off.

Remove glass or soda can.

Head & Neck
Rnd 1: With brown, ch 3, sl st in first ch to form ring, ch 1, 2 sc in each ch around. *(6 sc)*

Rnd 2: 2 sc in each sc. *(12 sc)*

Rnd 3: [Sc in next sc, 2 sc in next sc] around. *(18 sc)*

Rnd 4: [Sc in each of next 2 sc, 2 sc in next sc] around. *(24 sc)*

Rnds 5–10: Sc in each sc around.

Rnd 11: [Sc dec in next 2 sts, sc in each of next 2 sc] around. *(18 sc)*

Rnd 12: [Sc dec in next 2 sts, sc in next sc] around. *(12 sc)*

Rnds 13–15: Rep rnd 5.

Rnd 16: [Sc in each of next 3 sc, 2 sc in next sc] around. *(15 sc)*

Rnd 17: [Sc in each of next 4 sts, 2 sc in next st] around. *(18 sc)*

Rnd 18: [Sc in each of next 5 sts, 2 sc in next st] around. *(21 sc)*

Rnd 19: [Sc in each of next 6 sts, 2 sc in next st] around. *(24 sc)*

Rnd 20: Sl st in each of first 12 sc, sc in each of next 12 sc. *(24 sts)*

Rnd 21: Sl st in each of first 12 sc, sc in each of next 12 sc, join with sl st in beg sl st. Fasten off.

Stuff Head and Neck with fiberfill. Sew to Basket as shown in photo with sl sts of rnds 20 and 21 at back of Neck.

Large Feather
Make 2.
Rnd 1: With bright yellow, ch 3, sl st in first ch to form ring, ch 1, 2 sc in each ch around. *(6 sc)*

Rnd 2: 2 sc in each sc around. *(12 sc)*

Rnd 3: Sc in each sc around.

Rnds 4 & 5: Rep rnd 3.

Rnd 6: Sc in each sc around, join with sl st in beg sc. Fasten off.

Rnd 7: Join orange with sc in first sc, sc in each sc around.

Rnds 8–10: Rep rnd 3.

Rnd 11: Sc in each sc around, join with sl st in beg sc. Fasten off.

Rnd 12: Join cherry red with sc in first sc, sc in each sc around.

Rnds 13–15: Rep rnd 3.

Rnd 16: Sc in each sc around, join with sl st in beg sc. Fasten off.

Medium Feather
Make 2.
Rnd 1: With bright yellow, ch 3, sl st in first ch to form ring, ch 1, 2 sc in each ch. *(6 sc)*

Rnd 2: 2 sc in each sc around. *(12 sc)*

Rnd 3: Sc in each sc around.

Rnd 4: Rep rnd 3.

Rnd 5: Sc in each sc around, join with sl st in beg sc. Fasten off.

Rnd 6: Join orange with sc in first sc, sc in each sc around.

Rnds 7 & 8: Rep rnd 3.

Rnd 9: Sc in each sc around, join with sl st in beg sc. Fasten off.

Rnd 10: Join cherry red with sc in first sc, sc in each sc around.

Rnds 11 & 12: Rep rnd 3.

Rnd 13: Sc in each sc around, join with sl st in beg sc. Fasten off.

Small Feather
Make 2.
Rnd 1: With bright yellow, ch 3, sl st in first ch to form ring, ch 1, 2 sc in each ch around. *(6 sc)*

Rnd 2: 2 sc in each sc around. *(12 sc)*

Rnd 3: Sc in each sc around.

Rnd 4: Sc in each sc around, join with sl st in beg sc. Fasten off.

Rnd 5: Join orange with sc in first sc, sc in each sc around.

Rnd 6: Rep rnd 3.

Rnd 7: Sc in each sc around, join with sl st in beg sc. Fasten off.

Rnd 8: Join cherry red with sc in first sc, sc in each sc around.

Rnd 9: Rep rnd 3.

Rnd 10: Sc in each sc around, join with sl st in beg sc. Fasten off.

Stuff Feathers and sew to back of Basket with Large Feathers at center back, Medium Feathers on each side of Large Feathers and Small Feathers on each side of Medium Feathers.

Wing
Make 2.
Row 1: With brown, ch 2, 2 sc in 2nd ch from hook, turn. *(2 sc)*

Row 2: Ch 1, 2 sc in each sc across, turn. *(4 sc)*

Row 3: Ch 1, sc in each sc across, turn.

Row 4: Ch 1, 2 sc in first sc, sc in each sc across to last sc, 2 sc in last sc, turn. *(6 sc)*

Rows 5–8: [Rep rows 3 and 4 alternately] twice. *(10 sc at end of last row)*

Rows 9–11: Rep row 3.

Row 12: Ch 1, sc dec in first 2 sc, sc in each of next 6 sc, sc dec in last 2 sc, turn. *(8 sc)*

Row 13: Ch 1, sc dec in first 2 sc, sc in each of next 4 sc, sc dec in last 2 sc, turn. *(6 sc)*

Row 14: Ch 1, sc dec in first 2 sc, sc in each of next 2 sc, sc dec in last 2 sc, turn. *(4 sc)*

Row 15: Ch 1, sc in each sc and in end of each row around with 3 sc in tip of Wing, join with sl st in beg sc. Fasten off.

Sew 1 Wing to each side of Basket, with tips pointing back.

Comb
With cherry red, ch 10, sl st in 4th ch from hook, [ch 5, sl st in next ch] across. Fasten off.

Sew across top of Head as shown in photo.

Beak
Rnd 1: With orange, ch 2, 4 sc in 2nd ch from hook. *(4 sc)*

Rnd 2: 2 sc in each sc around. *(8 sc)*

Rnd 3: Sc in each sc around.

Rnd 4: Sc in each sc around, join with sl st in beg sc. Fasten off.

Stuff with fiberfill and sew to front of Head as shown in photo.

Wattle
With cherry red, ch 7, dc in 4th ch from hook, hdc in next ch, sc in next ch, sl st in last ch. Fasten off.

Sew to Head below Beak.

Foot
Make 2.
With orange, ch 10, sl st in 2nd ch from hook and in each of next 3 chs, [ch 5, sl st in 2nd ch from hook, sl st in each of next 3 chs] twice, sl st in each of last 5 chs. Fasten off.

Sew to bottom front of Basket 2 inches apart as shown in photo.

Glue eyes to Head centered above Beak, ¼ inch apart. ■

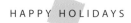

Turkey Hot Pad

DESIGN BY MARY LAYFIELD

This gobbler is a great accent for your Thanksgiving table! He'll hold your hot items while you delight in the feast—and look cute while the food is passed! Stitch him for yourself or for a deserving friend.

SKILL LEVEL ■■■□
INTERMEDIATE

FINISHED SIZE
6½ wide x 7 inches high

MATERIALS
Elmore-Pisgah Peaches & Crème medium (worsted) weight cotton yarn (2½ oz/122 yds/71g per ball):
  1 ball #121 chocolate
  ½ ball each #2 black, #3 cream, #7 ivory, #11 sunburst, #95 red, #48 mauve, #89 camel, #26 light blue and #20 teal blue
Size E/4/3.5mm crochet hook or size needed to obtain gauge
Tapestry needle

GAUGE
5 sts = 1 inch; rnd 1 = 1 inch across

INSTRUCTIONS

TAIL
Rnd 1: Work in **back lps** (see Stitch Guide) unless otherwise stated, with cream, ch 6, sl st in first ch to form ring, ch 3 (counts as first dc), (2 dc, 10 tr, 3 dc, 4 sc) in ring, join with sl st in 3rd ch of beg ch-3. Fasten off. (20 sts)

Row 2: Now working in rows, join sunburst with sc in first st, sc in each of next 15 sts leaving last 4 sc unworked, **do not turn**. Fasten off. (16 sc)

Row 3: Join camel with sl st in first st, ch 3 (counts as first dc), dc in same st, dc in next st, 2 dc in next st, dc in next st, [2 tr in next st, 3 tr in next st] 4 times, [dc in next st, 2 dc in next st] twice. Fasten off. (32 sts)

Row 4: Join red with sc in first st, sc in each st across. Fasten off.

Row 5: Join cream with sl st in first st, ch 3, 2 dc in next st, dc in next st, 2 dc in next st, 2 tr in each st across to last 4 sts, [2 dc in next st, dc in next st] across. Fasten off. (60 sts)

Row 6: Join sunburst with sc in first st, sc in each st across. Fasten off.

Row 7: Join camel with sl st in first st, ch 3, 2 dc in next st, [dc in next st, 2 dc in next st] 3 times, [2 tr in next st, tr in next st] across to last 8 sts, [2 dc in next st, dc in next st] across. Fasten off. *(90 sts)*

Row 8: Join chocolate with sc in first st, sc in each of next 5 sts, [sl st in next st, sc in each of next 5 sts] across. Fasten off.

Using straight stitches *(see Fig. 1)* and couching stitches *(see Fig. 2)*, embroider Tail according to illustration.

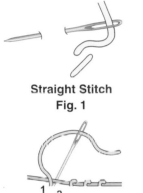

Straight Stitch
Fig. 1

Couching Stitch
Fig. 2

HEAD

Beg at neck, with cream, ch 16, sc in 2nd ch from hook, sc in each of next 5 chs, hdc in next ch, dc in each of next 2 chs, tr in each of next 3 chs, dc in each of next 2 chs, ch 2, sl st in last ch, ch 2, working on opposite side of ch, dc in each of next 2 chs, tr in each of next 3 chs, dc in each of next 2 chs, hdc in next ch, sc in each of last 6 chs. Fasten off.

Beak

With sunburst, ch 3, (dc, ch 2, sl

st) in 3rd ch from hook. Leaving 6-inch end for sewing, fasten off.

Wattles
Large Wattle

With red, ch 10, dc in 3rd ch from hook, dc in each of next 3 chs, sc in each of last 4 chs. Leaving 6-inch end for sewing, fasten off.

Small Wattle

With red, ch 6, dc in 3rd ch from hook, dc in next ch, sc in each of last 2 chs. Leaving 6-inch end for sewing, fasten off.

Head Finishing

1. With black yarn, embroider French knots *(see Fig. 3)* for eyes centered on each side of Head between 11th and 12th sts from neck end.

French Knot
Fig. 3

2. Sew Beak, with back of sts facing out, to center of Head

between 8th and 9th sts from neck end.

3. Sew end of Small Wattle, with back of sts facing out, directly under Beak, tack other end to center of Head at neck end.

4. Sew end of Large Wattle, with back to sts facing out, directly over Beak, bring other end of Wattle around Beak and tack to Head next to Small Wattle.

5. Tack Head to Tail centered over rows 1–6.

BODY

Row 1: Beg at neck edge, with teal blue, ch 6, sc in 2nd ch from hook, [2 dc in next ch, sc in next ch] twice, turn. *(7 sts)*

Row 2: Ch 3, 2 dc in same st, [sc in next st, sk next st, 3 dc in next st] twice, turn. Fasten off. *(11 sts)*

Row 3: Sk first st, join light blue with sc in next st, [sk next st, 2 dc in next st, sk next st, sc in next st] twice, leaving last st unworked, turn. *(7 sts)*

Row 4: Ch 3, 2 dc in same sc, sc in next dc, sk next dc, 3 dc in next sc, sk next dc, sc in next dc, 3 dc in next sc, sc in last st on row 2, turn. Fasten off. *(12 sts)*

Row 5: Join mauve with sc in first sc, sk next dc, 3 dc in next dc, sk next dc, sc in next sc, sk next dc, 4 dc in next dc, sk next dc, sc in next sc, sk next st, 3 dc in next st, sc in last dc, turn. Fasten off. *(14 sts)*

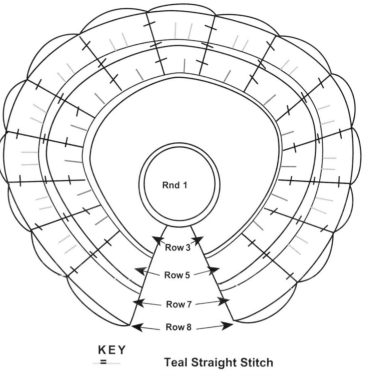

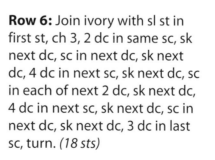

KEY
=   **Teal Straight Stitch**
—   **Mauve Straight Stitch**
+   **Black Couching Stitch**

Row 6: Join ivory with sl st in first st, ch 3, 2 dc in same sc, sk next dc, sc in next dc, sk next dc, 4 dc in next sc, sk next dc, sc in each of next 2 dc, sk next dc, 4 dc in next sc, sk next dc, sc in next dc, sk next dc, 3 dc in last sc, turn. *(18 sts)*

Row 7: Ch 3, 2 dc in same dc, sk next 2 dc, sc in next sc, *sk next 2 dc, 4 dc in sp between 2nd and 3rd dc of next 4-dc group, sk next 2 dc*, sc in sp between next 2 sc, rep between *, sc in next sc, sk next 2 dc, 3 dc in last dc, turn. Fasten off. *(17 sts)*

Row 8: Join camel with sl st in first dc, ch 3, 2 dc in same dc, sk next 2 dc, 4 dc in next sc, sk next dc, sc in next dc, sk next 2 dc, 4 dc in next sc, sk next 2 dc, sc in next dc, sk next dc, 4 dc in next sc, sk next 2 dc, 3 dc in last dc, turn. Fasten off. *(20 sts)*

Row 9: Join chocolate with sc in first st, sk next 2 dc, 3 dc in next sp between dc groups, [sk next 2 dc, sc in next dc, sk next dc, 4 dc in next sc] twice, sk next 2 dc, sc in next dc, sk next dc, 3 dc in next sp between dc groups, sk next 2 dc, sc in last dc, turn. *(19 sts)*

Row 10: Ch 3, sk next dc, sc in next dc, [sk next dc, 3 dc in next sc, sk next 2 dc, sc in next dc] twice, sk next dc, 3 dc in next sc, sk next dc, sc in next dc, ch 3, sl st in last sc. Fasten off.

Front of row 10 is RS of work. Sew ends of rows on Body over ends of rows on Tail with row 1 centered directly below Head *(Head and Body should touch)*.

SHOES

Row 1: With black yarn, ch 13, sc in 2nd ch from hook, sc in next ch, dc in each of next 3 chs, sc in each of next 2 chs, dc in each of next 3 chs, sc in each of last 2 chs, turn. *(12 sts)*

Row 2: Ch 3, sk next st, dc in each of next 3 sts, sk next 2 sts, dc in each of next 3 sts, sk next st, sc in last st. Fasten off.

Buckles

With sunburst, embroider 4 straight sts on each side according to illustration.

Sew top of row 2 to back of row 9 on Body.

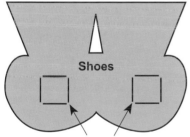

Sunburst Straight Stitches

WING

Make 2.
Upper Section
Row 1: With camel, ch 4, sl st in first ch to form ring, ch 5 *(counts as first dc and ch-2)*, dc in ring, [ch 2, dc in ring] 4 times, turn. *(5 ch sps)*

Row 2: Ch 1, (sc, 3 dc, sc) in each ch sp across. Fasten off.

Lower Section
Rnd 1: With ivory, ch 4, sl st in first ch to form ring, ch 1, 4 sc in ring, ch 3, 10 tr in ring, ch 3, join with sl st in beg sc. *(4 sc, 2 dc— each ch-3 counts as 1 dc, 10 tr)*

Rnd 2: Ch 1, sc in each of first 4 sc, ch 3, sc in top of ch-3, ch 1, [2 dc in next tr, dc in next tr] twice, 2 dc in next tr, (dc, sc) in next tr, ch 2, for **scallops**, (3 tr, ch 2, sc, ch 2) in each of next 5 sts, join with sl st in beg sc. Fasten off. Scallops are at bottom of Wing.

Wings Assembly
1. On Upper Section, sew ends of rows 1 and 2 tog.

2. With seam at top, sew Upper Section over Lower Section with Scallops extended at bottom.

3. Matching outer edges on Tail and Wings, sew Wings to Tail with sc on Wings touching edges of Body and end scallops covering edges of Body.

COLLAR
Side
Make 2.
Row 1 (WS): With ivory, ch 8, sc in 2nd ch from hook, sc in each ch across, turn. *(7 sc)*

Row 2: Ch 3, dc in same st, dc in each st across with 2 dc in last st, turn. *(9 sts)*

Row 3: Ch 1, sc in each st across. Fasten off.

Row 4: With RS of both pieces facing, working on opposite

side of ch on row 1, join with sc in first ch on 1 Side, sc in each ch across first Side, sc in each ch across 2nd Side. Fasten off.

With row 4 at top, shape Collar in a V-shape and sew to Head, Body and Tail, with center of V-shape covering top of Body and ends of row 4 on Collar touching edges of Head.

Tie
For **bow**, with chocolate, ch 3, (2 dc, ch 2, sl st) in 3rd ch from hook *(sl st is at center of bow)*, (ch 2, 2 dc, ch 2, sl st) in same ch as last sl st made. Fasten off.

For **ends**, with chocolate, beg at center of ends, leaving 6-inch strand, [ch 8, sc in 2nd ch from hook, dc in each of next 2 chs, sc in each of last 4 chs] twice. Leaving 6-inch strand, fasten off. Wrap 6-inch strand on ends around center of bow, tie 6-inch strands tog on back of bow.

Sew assembled Tie to center of row 4 on Collar.

HAT
Crown
Row 1: With black, ch 5, sc in 2nd ch from hook, sc in each of next 2 chs, (sc, ch 1, sl st) in last ch, continuing on opposite side of ch, ch 1, sc in same ch, sc in each of last 3 chs, turn. *(4 sc on each side of ch)*

Row 2: Ch 1, 2 sc in first st, sc in each of next 2 sts, 2 sc in last st, leaving 4 sc on other side of ch unworked, **do not turn**. Fasten off. *(6 sts)*

Row 3: Join ivory with sc in first st of row 2, sc in same st, sc in each of next 4 sts, 2 sc in last st, turn. *(8 sts)*

Row 4: Ch 1, sc in each st across, turn. Fasten off.

Row 5: Join black with sc in first st, sc in each st across, turn. Fasten off.

Brim
Row 1: With black, ch 9, 2 sc in 2nd ch from hook, sc in each ch across with 2 sc in last ch, turn. *(11 sc)*

Row 2: Ch 1, (sc, ch 1, 2 dc) in first st, 3 dc in next st, sc in each of next 7 sts, 3 dc in next st, (2 dc, ch 1, sc, sl st) in last st. Fasten off.

With black, sew row 1 of Brim to row 5 of Crown.

With sunburst, embroider straight stitches on center of Crown over rows 3–5 according to illustration.

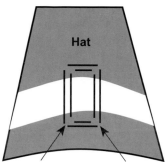

Hat

Sunburst Straight Stitches

Sew Hat to Tail covering top of Head, pulling ends of Brim around to sides of Head and tacking in place.

BACK
Rnd 1: With chocolate, ch 5, sl st in first ch to form ring, ch 3, 11 dc in ring, join with sl st in 3rd ch of beg ch-3. *(12 dc)*

Rnd 2: Ch 3, dc in same st, 2 dc in each st around, join with sl st in 3rd ch of beg ch-3. *(24 dc)*

Rnd 3: Ch 3, 2 dc in next st, [dc in next st, 2 dc in next st] around, join with sl st in 3rd ch of beg ch-3. *(36 dc)*

Rnd 4: Ch 3, dc in next st, 2 dc in next st, [dc in each of next 2 sts, 2 dc in next st] around, join with sl st in 3rd ch of beg ch-3. *(48 dc)*

Rnd 5: Ch 3, dc in each of next 2 sts, 2 dc in next st, [dc in each of next 3 sts, 2 dc in next st around, join with sl st in 3rd ch of beg ch-3. *(60 dc)*

Rnd 6: Ch 1, sc in each st around, join with sl st in beg sc. Leaving 20-inch end, fasten off.

Using end, sew Back to WS of Tail. ■

Country Mini Stocking

DESIGN BY SANDY ABBATE

Small enough to hang on your tree, this delightful little stocking is a charming holiday accent! If you leave out the potpourri, you can also use it as a gift bag for small items, or to hold your place setting flatware at a special holiday meal.

SKILL LEVEL ■□□□
BEGINNER

FINISHED SIZE
2¾ x 6½ inches

MATERIALS
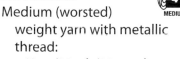

Medium (worsted)
   weight yarn with metallic
   thread:
      ½ oz/25 yds/14g each
         cranberry, green, off-white
Size H/8/5mm crochet hook or
   size needed to obtain gauge
Tapestry needle
7-inch circle cream tulle
Small amount potpourri
⅜-inch-wide wire-edge gold
   ribbon: 18 inches
¾-inch red star button

GAUGE
4 sc = 4 inch; 4 sc rnds = 1 inch

INSTRUCTIONS

STOCKING
Heel

Rnd 1 (RS): With green, ch 7, 3 sc in 2nd ch from hook, sc in each of next 4 chs, 3 sc in next ch, working on opposite side of ch, sc in each of next 4 chs, join with sl st in beg sc. *(14 sc)*

Rnd 2: Ch 1, sc in first sc, 3 sc in next sc, sc in each of next 6 sc, 3 sc in next sc, sc in each of last 5 sc, join with sl st in beg sc. *(18 sc)*

Rnd 3: Ch 1, sc in each sc around, join with sl st in beg sc. Fasten off.

Foot

Rnd 1: Join cranberry with sc in center sc of 3-sc group, sc in

each of next 9 sc, ch 10, leaving rem sts unworked, join with sl st in beg sc. *(10 sc, 1 ch-10 sp)*

Rnd 2: Ch 1, sc in each of first 10 sc, sc in each of next 10 chs,

join with sl st in beg sc. Fasten off. *(20 sc)*

Rnd 3: Join off-white with sc in first sc, sc in each sc around, join with sl st in beg sc. *(20 sc)*

Rnd 4: Ch 1, sc in each sc around, join with sl st in beg sc. Fasten off.

Rnds 5 & 6: With cranberry, rep rnds 3 and 4.

Rnds 7 & 8: Rep rnds 3 and 4.

Toe
Rnds 9 & 10: With green, rep rnds 3 and 4. At end of last rnd, **do not fasten off**.

Rnd 11: Ch 1, **sc dec** *(see Stitch Guide)* in first 2 sc, [sc dec in next 2 sc] around, join with sl st in beg sc. *(10 sc)*

Rnd 12: Rep rnd 11. Leaving long end, fasten off. *(5 sc)*

Weave long end through sts of rnd 12, close opening and secure.

Leg
Rnd 1: Join off-white with sc in end of rnd 1 of Foot, working in starting ch on opposite side of rnd 1, sc in each of next 10 chs, sc in end of rnd 1, sc in each of next 8 sc of Heel, join with sl st in beg sc. *(20 sc)*

Rnd 2: Ch 1, sc in each sc around, join with sl st in beg sc. Fasten off.

Rnds 3 & 4: With cranberry, rep rnds 3 and 4 of Foot.

Rnds 5 & 6: Rep rnds 3 and 4 of Foot.

Rnds 7 & 8: Rep rnds 3 and 4.

Cuff
Rnd 1: Join green with sl st in first st, ch 2 *(does not count as first dc)*, dc in first st, dc in each sc around, join with sl st in beg dc. *(20 dc)*

Rnd 2: Ch 2, dc in first dc and in each dc around, join with sl st in first dc, **turn**.

Rnd 3: Ch 2, working in **back lps** *(see Stitch Guide)* only, dc in each dc around, join with sl st in beg dc, **do not turn**.

Rnd 4: Rep rnd 2. Fasten off.

Rnd 5: With WS facing, join cranberry with sl st in joining st, [ch 2, sl st in next st] around, ch 2, join with sl st in beg sl st. Fasten off. Fold Cuff down at rnd 3.

Hanger
Join green with sl st in back at top of Cuff, ch 13, sl st in same st. Fasten off.

Finishing
Sew star button to center front of Cuff.

Place potpourri in center of tulle circle, gather circle around potpourri, tie with gold ribbon and make a bow and crimp ends of ribbon.

Place potpourri in top of stocking. ■

Snowman Stocking

DESIGN BY MICHELE GUYAN

Fill this adorable stocking with deliciously sweet treats, and hang it with care for a tempting holiday morning surprise! He'll greet you with a smile and promise not to eat Santa's cookies!

SKILL LEVEL ■■□□
EASY

FINISHED SIZE
22 inches long

MATERIALS

Red Heart Classic medium (worsted) weight yarn (3½oz/190 yds/99g per skein):
  2 skeins #1 white
  1 skein #827 light periwinkle
  25 yds #245 orange
  2 yds #12 black
Sizes G/6/4mm and H/8/5mm crochet hooks or sizes needed to obtain gauge
Tapestry needle
Fiberfill
3-inch square piece of cardboard
1-inch metal or plastic ring

GAUGE
Size G hook: 4 sc = 1 inch; 4 sc rows = 1 inch

Size H hook: 7 sc = 2 inches; 7 sc rows = 2 inches

INSTRUCTIONS

SNOWMAN
Head
Rnd 1: With size H hook and white, ch 12, 2 sc in 2nd ch from hook, 2 sc in next ch, sc in each of next 8 chs, 4 sc in last ch, working on opposite side of ch, sc in each of next 8 chs, 2 sc in each of last 2 chs, join with sl st in beg sc, **turn.** *(28 sc)*

Rnd 2: Ch 1, 2 sc in each of first 2 sts, sc in each of next 10 sts, 2 sc in each of next 4 sts, sc in

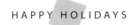

Rnd 19: Ch 1, sc in each of first 8 sts, sc dec in next 2 sts, [sc in each of next 8 sts, sc dec in next 2 sts] around, join with sl st in beg sc, turn. *(36 sc)*

Rnd 20: Ch 1, sc in each st around, join with sl st in beg sc, turn.

Rnd 21: Ch 1, sc in each of first 7 sts, sc dec in next 2 sts, [sc in each of next 7 sts, sc dec in next 2 sts] around, join with sl st in beg sc, turn. *(32 sc)*

Rnd 22: Ch 1, sc in each st around, join with sl st in beg sc, turn.

Rnd 23: Ch 1, sc in each of first 6 sts, sc dec in next 2 sts, [sc in each of next 6 sts, sc dec in next 2 sts] around, join with sl st in beg sc, turn. *(28 sc)*

Rnd 24: Ch 1, sc in each st around, join with sl st in beg sc. Fasten off.

Stuff Head. Sew opening closed.

With tapestry needle and black, using satin stitch *(see Fig. 1)*, embroider eyes over rnds 11 and 12 of Head 1½ inches apart, embroider mouth over rnds 17–20 centered below eyes as shown in photo.

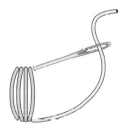

Satin Stitch
Fig. 1

Nose
Row 1: With size H hook and orange, ch 2, 2 sc in 2nd ch from hook, turn. *(2 sc)*

Row 2: Ch 1, sc in first st, 2 sc in last st, turn. *(3 sc)*

Row 3: Ch 1, sc in first st, 2 sc in next st, sc in last st, turn. *(4 sc)*

Row 4: Ch 1, sc in first st, 2 sc in next st, sc in each of last 2 sts, turn. *(5 sc)*

Row 5: Ch 1, sc in each of first 2 sts, 2 sc in next st, sc in each of last 2 sts, turn. *(6 sc)*

Row 6: Ch 1, sc in each of first 2 sts, 2 sc in next st, sc in each of last 3 sts, turn. *(7 sc)*

Row 7: Ch 1, sc in each of first 3 sts, 2 sc in next st, sc in each of last 3 sts. Fasten off. *(8 sc)*

Sew ends of rows tog, stuff. Sew to Head centered below eyes over rnds 14 and 15.

HAT
Cuff
Row 1: With size G hook and light periwinkle, ch 6, sc in 2nd ch from hook and in each ch across, turn. *(5 sc)*

Rows 2–40: Working these rows in **back lps** only *(see Stitch Guide)*, ch 1, sc in each st across, turn. At end of last row, **do not turn** or fasten off.

Crown
Rnd 1: Working in ends of rows on Cuff, ch 1, sc in each row around, join with sl st in beg sc. *(40 sc)*

Rnd 2: Ch 1, sc in back lp of first st, sc in **front lp** *(see Stitch Guide)* of next st, [sc in back lp of next st, sc in front lp of next st] around, join with sl st in beg sc.

Rnd 3: Ch 1, sc in front lp of first st, sc in back lp of next st, [sc in front lp of next st, sc in back lp of next st] around, join with sl st in beg sc.

Rnds 4–16: Rep rnds 2 and 3 alternately, ending with rnd 2. At end of last rnd, leaving 12-inch end for weaving, fasten off.

Weave end through sts of last rnd, pull to gather tightly, secure end.

Sew first and last rows of Cuff tog.

Pompom
Wrap light periwinkle yarn around cardboard 60 times, slide lps off cardboard, tie

separate strand of light periwinkle tightly around center of all lps. Cut lps, trim ends.

Sew Pompom to top of Hat. Sew Hat to top of Head.

MITTENS & ARMS

Rnd 1: Starting at **Mitten**, with size H hook and light periwinkle, ch 2, 6 sc in 2nd ch from hook, join with sl st in beg sc. *(6 sc)*

Rnd 2: Ch 1, 2 sc in each st around, join with sl st in beg sc. *(12 sc)*

Rnd 3: Ch 1, sc in first st, 2 sc in next st, [sc in next st, 2 sc in next st] around, join with sl st in beg sc. *(18 sc)*

Rnd 4: Ch 1, sc in each of first 2 sts, 2 sc in next st, [sc in each of next 2 sts, 2 sc in next st] around, join with sl st in beg sc. *(24 sc)*

Rnds 5–14: Ch 1, sc in each st around, join with sl st in beg sc. At end of last rnd, fasten off.

Rnd 15: For **Arms**, join white with sc in first st, sc in next st, sc dec in next 2 sts, [sc in each of next 2 sts, sc dec in next 2 sts] around, join with sl st in beg sc. *(18 sc)*

Stuff. Continue stuffing as you work.

Rnds 16–46: Ch 1, sc in each st around, join with sl st in beg sc.

Rnd 47: Ch 1, sc in each of first 2 sts, 2 sc in next st, [sc in each of next 2 sts, 2 sc in next st] around, join with sl st in beg sc. Fasten off. *(24 sc)*

Rnd 48: For **Mitten**, join light periwinkle with sc in first st, sc in each st around, join with sl st in beg sc.

Rnds 49–56: Ch 1, sc in each st around, join with sl st in beg sc.

Rnd 57: Ch 1, sc in each of first 2 sts, sc dec in next 2 sts, [sc in each of next 2 sts, sc dec in next 2 sts] around, join with sl st in beg sc. *(18 sc)*

Rnd 58: Ch 1, sc in first st, sc dec in next 2 sts, [sc in next st, sc dec in next 2 sts] around, join with sl st in beg sc. *(12 sc)*

Rnd 59: Ch 1, sc dec in first 2 sts, [sc dec in next 2 sts] around, join with sl st in beg sc. Leaving 12-inch end for weaving, fasten off.

Weave end through sts of last rnd, pull to gather tightly, secure end.

Cuff
Make 2.
Row 1: With size G hook and light periwinkle, ch 5, sc in 2nd ch from hook and in each ch across, turn. *(4 sc)*

Rows 2–24: Ch 1, sc in each st across, turn. At end of last row, fasten off.

Sew rows 1 and 24 tog.

Tack 1 Cuff over rnd 14 and other over rnd 47 of Mittens and Arms.

Tack Head to center 6 rows at top of Arms *(see photo)*.

SCARF
Row 1: With size G hook and light periwinkle, ch 8, sc in 2nd ch from hook and in each ch across, turn. *(7 sc)*

Rows 2–70: Ch 1, sc in back lp of first st, [sc in front lp of next st, sc in back lp of next st] across, turn. At end of last row, fasten off.

Fringe
For **each Fringe**, cut 1 strand light periwinkle, 4 inches long.

Fold strand in half, insert hook in st, pull fold through st, pull all loose ends through fold, tighten. Trim.

Attach fringe in each st on each short end of Scarf.

Tie Scarf around Neck, tack in place.

SOCK SIDE
Make 2.
Row 1: With size H hook and white, ch 27, sc in 2nd ch from hook and in each ch across, turn. *(26 sc)*

Rows 2–4: Ch 1, 2 sc in first st, sc in each st across with 2 sc in last st, turn. *(32 sc at end of last row)*

Rows 5–7: Ch 1, 2 sc in first st, sc in each st across, turn. *(35 sc at end of last row)*

Rows 8–12: Ch 1, sc in each st across, turn.

Row 13: Ch 1, sc dec in first 2 sts, sc in each st across, turn. *(34 sc)*

Row 14: Ch 1, sc in each st across to last 2 sts, sc dec in last 2 sts, turn. *(33 sc)*

Rows 15–21: Rep rows 13 and 14 alternately, ending with row 13. *(26 sc at end of last row)*

Row 22: Ch 1, sc in each of first 20 sts, leaving last 6 sts unworked, turn. *(20 sc)*

Rows 23–47: Ch 1, sc in each st across, turn. At end of last row, fasten off.

Matching shaping, sew Sock Sides tog.

Easing to fit, sew Sock opening to bottom of Arms *(see photo)*, leaving Mittens and 10 sts at front of Sock unsewn.

Tack Mittens tog in front. Sew plastic or metal ring to top back of Hat. ■

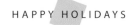

Peppermint People

DESIGNS BY ANGELA WINGER

These peppermint people couldn't be sweeter, especially since Christmas and peppermint seem to go so well together! These delightful folks make the perfect Christmas tree or package trims!

SKILL LEVEL ◧▢▢ EASY

FINISHED SIZES
Snowman: 3¾ inches tall

Gingerbread man: 3½ inches tall

MATERIALS
Aunt Lydia's Classic Crochet size 10 crochet cotton (350 yds per ball):
    60 yds #1 white
    40 yds #131 fudge brown
    25 yds #492 burgundy
    10 yds #449 forest green
    5 yds #12 black
    ½ yd #431 pumpkin
Size 7/1.65mm steel crochet hook or size needed to obtain gauge
Tapestry needle
Fiberfill
12 inches nylon thread

9mm green pompoms: 2
Stitch markers
Hot-glue gun

GAUGE
6 rnds = ½ inch

PATTERN NOTES
Do not join rounds unless otherwise stated.

Mark first stitch of each round.

When not working with a color, carry along the back of work loosely, do not pull tightly or piece will pucker.

Always change color in last stitch made.

INSTRUCTIONS

SNOWMAN
Body
Make 2.
Rnd 1: With white, ch 2, 6 sc in 2nd ch from hook, **do not join** *(see Pattern Notes)*. *(6 sc)*

Rnd 2: Changing colors *(see Stitch Guide and Pattern Notes)*, sc with each white and burgundy in each sc around. *(12 sc)*

Rnd 3: [With white, 2 sc in next white sc, with burgundy, sc in next burgundy sc] 6 times. *(18 sc)*

Rnd 4: [With white, sc in each of next 2 sc, with burgundy, 2 sc in next sc] 6 times. *(24 sc)*

Rnd 5: [With white, sc in next sc, 2 sc in next sc, with burgundy, sc in next sc, 2 sc in next sc] 6 times. *(36 sc)*

Rnd 6: [With white, sc in next sc, 2 sc in next sc, sc in next sc, with burgundy, sc in next sc, 2 sc in next sc, sc in next sc] 6 times. *(48 sc)*

Rnd 7: [With white, sc in each of next 2 sc, 2 sc in next sc, sc in next sc, with burgundy, sc in each of next 2 sc, 2 sc in next sc, sc in next sc] 6 times. *(60 sc)*

Rnd 8: Working in **back lp** (see Stitch Guide) only of each st,

[with white, sc in each of next 5 sc, with burgundy, sc in each of next 5 sc] 6 times, join with sl st in next st. Fasten off.

Matching sts and using same color as sts, sew Body pieces tog, stuffing lightly with fiberfill before closing.

Head Side
Make 2.
Rnd 1: With white, ch 2, 6 sc in 2nd ch from hook, **do not join**. *(6 sc)*

Rnd 2: 2 sc in each sc around. *(12 sc)*

Rnd 3: [Sc in next sc, 2 sc in next sc] 6 times. *(18 sc)*

Rnd 4: [Sc in each of next 2 sc, 2 sc in next sc] 6 times. *(24 sc)*

Rnd 5: [Sc in each of next 3 sc, 2 sc in next sc] 6 times. *(30 sc)*

Rnd 6: Working in back lp only, sc in each st around, join with sl st in next st. Leaving long end on first Head Side only, fasten off.

Holding both sections WS tog, sew pieces tog, stuffing lightly with fiberfill before closing.

Sew Head to top of Body.

Arm
Make 2.
Rnd 1: With white, ch 2, 6 sc in 2nd ch from hook, **do not join**. *(6 sc)*

Rnd 2: 2 sc in each sc around. *(12 sc)*

Rnd 3: Sc in each sc around.

Rnd 4: Rep rnd 3.

Rnd 5: 5 dc in first sc *(thumb)*, sc in each of next 11 sc. *(16 sts)*

Rnd 6: Sc dec *(see Stitch Guide)* in next 5 dc, ch 1, sc in each of next 11 sc.

Rnd 7: Sc in next sc, sk next ch-1 sp, sc in next 11 sc. *(12 sc)*

Rnds 8 & 9: Rep rnd 3. At the end of last rnd, leaving long end, fasten off.

Stuff lightly with fiberfill making sure the thumb sticks out. With thumbs pointing upward, sew Arms to sides of Body.

Leg
Make 2.
Rnd 1: With white, ch 6, sc in 2nd ch from hook, sc in each of next 3 chs, 3 sc in last ch *(toe)*, working on opposite side of ch, sc in each of next 3 chs, 2 sc in same ch as first sc, **do not join**. *(12 sc)*

Rnd 2: [2 sc in next sc, sc in next sc] 6 times. *(18 sc)*

Rnd 3: Working in back lps only, sc in each sc around.

Rnd 4: Sc in each sc around.

Rnd 5: Sc in each of next 3 sc, [sc dec in next 2 sc] 6 times, sc in each of last 3 sc. *(12 sc)*

Rnds 6–9: Rep rnd 4. At the end of last rnd, join with sl st in next sc. Leaving long end, fasten off.

Stuff lightly with fiberfill, with toes pointing to the outside.

Sew Legs to bottom of Body.

Scarf
With forest green, ch 31, sc in 2nd ch from hook, sc in each ch across. Fasten off.

Place around neckline and tack in place.

Hat
Rnds 1–4: With black, rep rnds 1–4 of Head Side. *(24 sc)*

Rnd 5: Working in back lps only, sc in each st around.

Rnd 6: Sc in each sc around, change to forest green in last sc.

Rnd 7: Sc in each sc around, change to black in last sc. Fasten off forest green.

Rnd 8: Rep rnd 6.

Rnd 9: Working in **front lp** *(see Stitch Guide)* only of each st, 2 hdc in each st around, join with sl st in beg hdc. Fasten off.

Stuff lightly and sew to top of Head.

Facial Features
1. For nose, with pumpkin, embroider 1 French knot *(see Fig. 1)* over center of rnd 1 of Head.

**French Knot
Fig. 1**

2. With black, embroider 1 French knot for each eye slightly above nose with ¼ inch between eyes.

3. With black, embroider straight stitch *(see Fig. 2)* mouth centered below nose.

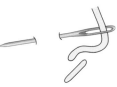

**Straight Stitch
Fig. 2**

Finishing
Cut 6-inch length of nylon thread, attach to center top of ornament, knot ends tog.

GINGERBREAD MAN BODY
Make 2.
Rnds 1–8: Rep rnds 1–8 of Snowman Body.

Head Side
Make 2.
Rnds 1–6: With fudge brown, rep Snowman Head Side.

Arm
Make 2.
Rnds 1–9: With fudge brown, rep Snowman Arm.

Leg
Make 2.
Rnds 1–9: With fudge brown, rep Snowman Leg.

Scarf
With forest green, rep Snowman Scarf.

Earmuff Band
With white, ch 16, sc in 2nd ch from hook, sc in each ch across. Fasten off. *(15 sc)*

Sew centered over top of Head.

Glue 1 pompom to each end of Earmuff Band.

Facial Features & Icing
1. For nose, with burgundy, embroider 1 French knot over center of rnd 1 of Head.

2. With white, embroider 1 French knot for each eye slightly above nose with ¼ inch between eyes.

3. With white, embroider straight stitch mouth centered below nose.

4. With white, embroider long straight stitches in zigzag fashion around Arms and Legs for icing as shown in photo.

Finishing
Cut 6-inch length of nylon thread, attach to center top of ornament, knot ends tog. ■

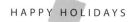

String of Lights

DESIGN BY GLORIA GRAHAM

Just like real Christmas lights, these cheerful bulbs have a glowing beauty all their own! Use them to decorate a tree, or string them across a doorway or mantel for a holiday display.

SKILL LEVEL ◼◻◻◻
BEGINNER

FINISHED SIZE
1¼ x 2½ inches

MATERIALS
Size 10 crochet cotton:
  24 yds gray
  20 yds each red, blue, green, gold, orange and white
Size 7/1.65mm steel crochet hook or size needed to obtain gauge
Tapestry needle
8mm jump rings: 12
6mm jump rings: 12
1½-inch eye pins: 12
Gold craft cord
Craft glue
Fiberfill

GAUGE
9 hdc = 1 inch

PATTERN NOTES
Begin each round with chain 2 to count as first half double crochet, pattern will simply indicate half double crochet.

Materials listed will make a set of 12 lights.

Each bulb requires 10 yards bulb color and 2 yards gray.

INSTRUCTIONS

BULB
Rnd 1 (RS): Starting at tip of Bulb with Bulb color, ch 3, 5 hdc in 3rd ch from hook *(first 2 chs count as first hdc)*, join with sl st in top of beg ch-3. *(6 hdc)*

Rnd 2: Ch 2 *(counts as first hdc, see Pattern Note)*, hdc in same st, 2 hdc in each hdc around, join with sl st in top of beg ch-2. *(12 hdc)*

Rnd 3: Hdc in each hdc around, join with sl st in top of beg ch-2.

Rnd 4: Hdc in each of first 3 hdc, 2 hdc in next hdc, [hdc in each of next 3 hdc, 2 hdc in next hdc] around, join with sl st in top of beg ch-2. *(15 hdc)*

Rnd 5: Hdc in each of first 4 hdc, 2 hdc in next hdc, [hdc in each of next 4 hdc, 2 hdc in next hdc] around, join with sl st in top of beg ch-2. *(18 hdc)*

Rnd 6: 2 hdc in first hdc, hdc in each of next 2 hdc, [2 hdc in next st, hdc in each of next 2 hdc] around, join with sl st in top of beg ch-2. *(24 hdc)*

Rnd 7: 2 hdc in first hdc, hdc in each of next 5 hdc, [2 hdc in next hdc, hdc in each of next 5 hdc] around, join with sl st in top of beg ch-2. *(28 hdc)*

Rnd 8: Rep rnd 3.

Rnd 9: 2 hdc in first hdc, hdc in each of next 6 hdc, [2 hdc in next hdc, hdc in each of next 6 hdc] around, join with sl st in top of beg ch-2. *(32 hdc)*

Rnd 10: Rep rnd 3.

Rnd 11: Hdc in each of first 2 hdc, **hdc dec** *(see Stitch Guide)* in next 2 hdc, [hdc in each of next 2 hdc, hdc dec in next 2 hdc] around, join with sl st in top of beg ch-2. *(24 hdc)*

Rnd 12: Hdc in each of first 2 hdc, hdc dec in next 2 hdc, [hdc in each of next 2 hdc, hdc dec in next 2 hdc] around, join with sl st in top of beg ch-2. *(18 hdc)*

Rnd 13: Hdc in first hdc, hdc dec in next 2 hdc, [hdc in next hdc, hdc dec in next 2 hdc] around, join with sl st in top of beg ch-2. Fasten off.

Stuff firmly with fiberfill.

Rnd 14: Join gray with sl st in any hdc, ch 2, hdc in each st around, join with sl st in top of beg ch-2. *(12 hdc)*

Rnds 15–17: Ch 1, sc in each st around, join with sl st in beg sc.

At the end of last rnd, leaving long end, fasten off.

Stuff firmly with fiberfill. Weave long end through sts, knot to secure. Fasten off.

Finishing
Twisting sideways, open 6mm jump ring, slide on eye pin and 8mm jump ring, close 6mm jump ring.

Dot glue on eye pin and insert into gray end of Bulb, allow to dry completely.

String Bulbs on gold cord through 8mm jump rings, spacing Bulbs 5 inches apart, tie knot over each jump ring to secure Bulb on cord. ■

General Instructions

Please review the following information before working the projects in this book. Important details about the abbreviations and symbols used are included.

HOOKS

Crochet hooks are sized for different weights of yarn and thread. For thread crochet, you will usually use a steel crochet hook. Steel crochet hook sizes range from size 00 to 14. The higher the number of the hook, the smaller your stitches will be. For example, a size 1 steel crochet hook will give you much larger stitches than a size 9 steel crochet hook. Keep in mind that the sizes given with the pattern instructions were obtained by working with the size thread or yarn and hook given in the materials list. If you work with a smaller hook, depending on your gauge, your project size will be smaller; if you work with a larger hook, your finished project's size will be larger.

GAUGE

Gauge is determined by the tightness or looseness of your stitches and affects the finished size of your project. If you are concerned about the finished size of the project matching the size given, take time to crochet a small section of the pattern and then check your gauge. For example, if the gauge called for is 10 dc = 1 inch, and your gauge is 12 dc to the inch, you should switch to a larger hook. On the other hand, if your gauge is only 8 dc to the inch, you should switch to a smaller hook.

If the gauge given in the pattern is for an entire motif, work one motif and then check your gauge.

UNDERSTANDING SYMBOLS

As you work through a pattern, you'll quickly notice several symbols in the instructions. These symbols are used to clarify the pattern for you: brackets [], curlicue braces {}, parentheses () and asterisks *.

Brackets [] are used to set off a group of instructions worked a specific number of times. For example, "[ch 3, sc in next ch-3 sp] 7 times" means to work the instructions inside the [] seven times.

Occasionally, a set of instructions inside a set of brackets needs to be repeated, too. In this case, the text within the brackets to be repeated will be set off with curlicue braces {}. For example, "[dc in each of next 3 sts, ch 1, {shell in next ch-1 sp} 3 times, ch 1] 4 times." In this case, in each of the four times you work the instructions included in the brackets, you will work the section included in the curlicue braces three times.

Parentheses () are used to set off a group of stitches to be worked all in one stitch, space or loop. For example, the parentheses () in this set of instructions, "Sk 3 sc, (3 dc, ch 1, 3 dc) in next st", indicate that after skipping 3 sc, you will work 3 dc, ch 1 and 3 more dc all in the next stitch.

Single asterisks * are also used when a group of instructions is repeated. For example, "*Sc in each of next 5 sc, 2 sc in next sc, rep from * around, join with a sl st in beg sc" simply means you will work the instructions from the first * around the entire round.

Double asterisks ** are used to indicate when a partial set of repeat instructions are to be worked. For example, "*Ch 3, (sc, ch 3, sc) in next ch-2 sp, ch 3**, shell in next dc, rep from * 3 times, ending last rep at **" means that on the third repeat of the single asterisk instructions, you stop at the double asterisks.

Stitch Guide

ABBREVIATIONS

beg	begin/beginning
bpdc	back post double crochet
bpsc	back post single crochet
bptr	back post treble crochet
CC	contrasting color
ch	chain stitch
ch-	refers to chain or space previously made (i.e., ch-1 space)
ch sp	chain space
cl	cluster
cm	centimeter(s)
dc	double crochet
dec	decrease/decreases/decreasing
dtr	double treble crochet
fpdc	front post double crochet
fpsc	front post single crochet
fptr	front post treble crochet
g	gram(s)
hdc	half double crochet
inc	increase/increases/increasing
lp(s)	loop(s)
MC	main color
mm	millimeter(s)
oz	ounce(s)
pc	popcorn
rem	remain/remaining
rep	repeat(s)
rnd(s)	round(s)
RS	right side
sc	single crochet
sk	skip(ped)
sl st	slip stitch
sp(s)	space(s)
st(s)	stitch(es)
tog	together
tr	treble crochet
trtr	triple treble
WS	wrong side
yd(s)	yard(s)
yo	yarn over

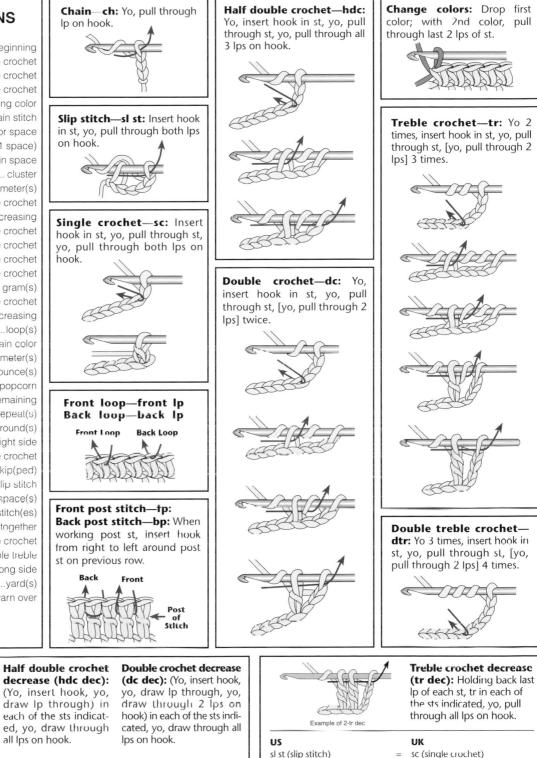

Chain—ch: Yo, pull through lp on hook.

Slip stitch—sl st: Insert hook in st, yo, pull through both lps on hook.

Single crochet—sc: Insert hook in st, yo, pull through st, yo, pull through both lps on hook.

**Front loop—front lp
Back loop—back lp**

Front Loop   Back Loop

**Front post stitch—fp:
Back post stitch—bp:** When working post st, insert hook from right to left around post st on previous row.

Back   Front

Post of Stitch

Half double crochet—hdc: Yo, insert hook in st, yo, pull through st, yo, pull through all 3 lps on hook.

Double crochet—dc: Yo, insert hook in st, yo, pull through st, [yo, pull through 2 lps] twice.

Change colors: Drop first color; with 2nd color, pull through last 2 lps of st.

Treble crochet—tr: Yo 2 times, insert hook in st, yo, pull through st, [yo, pull through 2 lps] 3 times.

Double treble crochet—dtr: Yo 3 times, insert hook in st, yo, pull through st, [yo, pull through 2 lps] 4 times.

Single crochet decrease (sc dec): (Insert hook, yo, draw up a lp) in each of the sts indicated, yo, draw through all lps on hook.

Example of 2-sc dec

Half double crochet decrease (hdc dec): (Yo, insert hook, yo, draw lp through) in each of the sts indicated, yo, draw through all lps on hook.

Example of 2-hdc dec

Double crochet decrease (dc dec): (Yo, insert hook, yo, draw lp through, yo, draw through 2 lps on hook) in each of the sts indicated, yo, draw through all lps on hook.

Example of 2-dc dec

Example of 2-tr dec

Treble crochet decrease (tr dec): Holding back last lp of each st, tr in each of the sts indicated, yo, pull through all lps on hook.

US		UK
sl st (slip stitch)	=	sc (single crochet)
sc (single crochet)	=	dc (double crochet)
hdc (half double crochet)	=	htr (half treble crochet)
dc (double crochet)	=	tr (treble crochet)
tr (treble crochet)	=	dtr (double treble crochet)
dtr (double treble crochet)	=	ttr (triple treble crochet)
skip	=	miss

For more complete information, visit

AnniesAttic.com

Buyer's Guide

Caron International Inc.
Customer Service
P.O. Box 222
Washngton, NC 27889
www.caron.com

Coats & Clark
(Red Heart, TLC, J&P Coats,
South Maid, Aunt Lydia's,
Coats Opera, Moda Dea)
Consumer Services
P.O. Box 12229
Greenville, SC 29612-0229
(800) 648-1479
www.coatsandclark.com
www.modadea.com

The DMC Corp.
77 S. Hackensack Ave.

Port Kearny Building 10F
South Kearny, NJ 07032
(973) 589-0606
www.dmc-usa.com

Elmore-Pisgah, Inc.
550 Orchard St.
Old Fort, NC 28762
(800) 633-7829
www.elmore-pisgah.com

Jelly Yarns
362 Second Street Pike/#112
Southampton, PA 18966
(215) 953-1415
www.3dimillus.com
www.jellyyarns.com

Jo-Ann Fabrics & Crafts
Customer Care
2361 Rosecrans Ave.
Suite 360
El Segundo, CA 90245
(800) 525-4951
www.joann.com

Lion Brand Yarn
135 Kero Rd.
Carlstadt, NJ 07072
(800) 258-YARN (9276)
www.lionbrand.com

Spinrite Yarns
(Bernat, Patons, Lily)
320 Livingstone Ave. South
Listowel, ON
Canada

N4W 3H3
(888) 368-8401
www.spinriteyarns.com
www.bernat.com
www.patonsyarns.com
www.sugarncream.com

Tahki-Stacy Charles, Inc.
70-30 80th St. Building 36
Ridgewood, NY 11385
(800) 388-YARN (9276)
www.tahkistacycharles.com

Toner Plastics
699 Silver St.
Agawam, MA 01001
(413) 789-1300
www.tonerplastics.com

Special Thanks

Sandy Abbate
Country Mini Stocking
Vineyard Wine Set

Cynthia Adams
Scrappy Stripes

Carol Alexander
Cotton Candy

Ginny Alvord-Clark
Colorful Carnival
Spring Squares

Barbara Anderson
Charlie Chimp

Dionne Barratt
Sweetheart Coasters

Elaine Bartlett
Dimensional Squares
Kitchen Helpers

Amy Brewer
Say it With Hearts

Shelle Cain
Purple Pizzazz

Cindy Carlson
Denim Blues
Scrapbooking Keeper

Belinda "Bendy" Carter
Beaded Elegance
Doggy Barbells
I Love My Pet Mat & Toys
Stretchy Style
Raspberry Sorbet Belt &
 Blueberry Tassels

Sue Childress
Bath Boutique
Flower Garden Bolero
Snipper Keeper

Kathryn Clark
Star Sparklers

Donna Collinsworth
Baby Chicks
Baby's Bowling Set
Blooming Violets

Dot Drake
Butterflies

Kathrine Eng
30-minute Cloche
Blooms at the Beach
Chocolate, Blueberry &
 Cranberry
Picnic Mats

Darla Fanton
Reversible Tote Bag

Nazanin S. Fard
Bubble Gum Baby
Rosebuds 'n' Beads T-Shirt

Sharon Fotta Anderson
Golf Club Covers

Norma Gale
Square Dance

Kathleen Garen
Color Bands

Gloria Graham
String of Lights

Stacey Graham
Diamond Dog Collar
Tennis Ball Snake

Michele Guyan
Snowman Stocking

Patricia Hall
Floral Jar Covers

Anne Halliday
Flower Power
Tempting Textures
Woven Ribbons

Cindy Harris
Pot o' Gold
Turkey Basket

Rosetta Harshman
Shamrock Pin

Alice Heim
Book Cover

Hazel Henry
Treasured Bouquet

Tammy Hildebrand
Baby Bunnies
Dig-It Flowerpot Cover
Kaleidoscope Colors

Jennine Korejko
Fancy Feet
Simple Stripes

Rosanne Kropp
2-in-1 Games

Mary Layfield
Cool Aquamarine
Turkey Hot Pad

Melissa Leapman
Summer Tote

Sheila Leslie
Bunny Purse
Harvey the Bunny

Beverly Mewhorter
Cat in the Window
Choo-Choo Train Afghan
Fish Bowl Place Mat
Halloween Garland
Harry the Horned Lizard

Jennifer Moir
Double-Decker Card Set

Nancy Nehring
Fairy Fluff

Sue Penrod
Bee Tidy

Carolyn Pfeifer
Repeating Rainbows

Diane Poellot
Just Geese
Striped Ponchette

Louise Puchaty
Easter Celebration

Agnes Russell
Pretty Tissues

Jocelyn Sass
Patriotic Picnic Set

Darla Sims
Hollywood Halter

Ann Smith
Sailing Away

Shirley Souch
Tissue Holder

Martha Brooks Stein
Scraps Extraordinaire

Brenda Stratton
Wildflowers

Kathleen Stuart
Baby Wrist Rattles
Creature Comforts

Debbie Tabor
Buddy the Butterfly

Angela Tate
Spooky Spiders

Judy Teague Treece
Flower Coasters

Leann Walters
Helicopter Booties

Michele Wilcox
Girly-Girl Pillows
Kitty Toys

Angela Winger
Peppermint People

Glenda Winkleman
Hot-Cross Granny

Lori Zeller
Beaded Blue Jeans Bag
Bodacious Beanbag
Crawly Critters
Little Critters